# A Most Masculine State
## Gender, Politics, and Religion in Saudi Arabia

Saudi women are often described as either victims of patriarchal religion and society or successful survivors of discrimination imposed on them by others. Madawi Al-Rasheed goes beyond these images to explore the historical, political, and religious forces that made them enjoy far fewer rights than their counterparts in other parts of the Muslim world. Under the patronage of the state and its religious nationalism, women became hostage to political projects in which they must represent contradictory expectations. As symbols of both piety and modernity, women's emancipation is delayed and thwarted. Drawing on state documents, media sources, and women's voices, Al-Rasheed explores persistent gender inequality in what many Saudis and outsiders consider a unique situation. She examines the intersection between gender, religion, and politics that perpetuates women's exclusion. The author unveils projects initiated by the state, social controversies, religious rulings, and vibrant debates that dominate discussions of the 'woman question'. While women's struggle for greater recognition and equality has already started, the author sees light at the end of the tunnel.

Madawi Al-Rasheed is Professor of Anthropology of Religion at King's College, University of London. She specialises in Saudi history, politics, and society. Her publications include *Contesting the Saudi State* (2007), *Kingdom Without Borders* (2009), and *A History of Saudi Arabia* (2010).

*Cambridge Middle East Studies*

*Editorial Board*

Charles Tripp (general editor)
Julia Clancy-Smith
F. Gregory Gause
Yezid Sayigh
Avi Shlaim
Judith E. Tucker

**Cambridge Middle East Studies** has been established to publish books on the nineteenth- to twenty-first-century Middle East and North Africa. The series offers new and original interpretations of aspects of Middle Eastern societies and their histories. To achieve disciplinary diversity, books are solicited from authors writing in a wide range of fields including history, sociology, anthropology, political science, and political economy. The emphasis is on producing books affording an original approach along theoretical and empirical lines. The series is intended for students and academics, but the more accessible and wide-ranging studies will also appeal to the interested general reader.

A list of books in the series can be found after the index.

# A Most Masculine State

*Gender, Politics, and Religion in Saudi Arabia*

**MADAWI AL-RASHEED**

*King's College, University of London*

**CAMBRIDGE**
UNIVERSITY PRESS

# CAMBRIDGE
## UNIVERSITY PRESS

32 Avenue of the Americas, New York NY 10013-2473, USA

Cambridge University Press is part of the University of Cambridge.

It furthers the University's mission by disseminating knowledge in the pursuit of education, learning, and research at the highest international levels of excellence.

www.cambridge.org
Information on this title: www.cambridge.org/9780521122528

© Madawi Al-Rasheed 2013

First published 2013
Reprinted 2013

*A catalog record for this publication is available from the British Library.*

*Library of Congress Cataloging in Publication data*
Al-Rasheed, Madawi.
A most masculine state : gender, politics, and religion in Saudi Arabia /
Madawi Al-Rasheed.
    p.   cm. – (Cambridge Middle East studies ; 43)
Includes bibliographical references and index.
ISBN 978-0-521-76104-8 (hbk.) – ISBN 978-0-521-12252-8 (pbk.)
1. Women – Saudi Arabia – Social conditions.   2. Muslim women – Saudi Arabia
– Social conditions.   3. Feminism – Saudi Arabia.   4. Feminism – Religious aspects –
Islam.   5. Women and religion – Saudi Arabia.   6. Sex role – Saudi Arabia.
7. Women's rights – Saudi Arabia.   I. Title.
HQ1730.A64   2013
305.4209538–dc23        2012028649

ISBN  978-0-521-76104-8  Hardback
ISBN  978-0-521-12252-8  Paperback

*To Zyad and Loulwa*

The essential ambiguity of the state derives in part from the fact that in its very structure, with the opposition between financial ministries and spending ministries, between its paternalist, familialist, protective right hand, and its socially oriented left hand, it reproduces the archetypal division between male and female, with women being linked to the left hand as its administrators and as the main recipients of benefits and services.

Pierre Bourdieu, *Masculine Domination*

# Contents

# Acknowledgments

I am greatly indebted to the Leverhulme Trust for a two-year Research Fellowship that allowed me to research and write this book. The support of my department at King's College London, in particular Paul Janz, has been great.

Many Saudi men and women were supportive of this project. I benefited from discussions and correspondence with Ahmad al-Wasil, Badriya al-Bishr, Fawziya Abu Khalid, and Umayma al-Khamis. Their insight, critical voices, and writing illuminated many of the discussions in this book. Others kept me informed about rapid changes and alerted me to new sources and developments in Saudi Arabia. Their regular emails and YouTube video clips narrowed distances and bridged the gap. Mishael sent me official documents, letters, and sensitive stories that allowed me a glimpse of the restrictions imposed on women in Saudi Arabia. Muhammad's regular emails, photos, and YouTube clips were a flood of enthusiasm and perseverance. Bloggers drew my attention to their regular commentaries. To all those, I express my appreciation and gratitude.

My colleague Marat Shterin has been a source of tremendous support and encouragement. He had to bear the burden of running seminars and teaching classes during my two-year fellowship. Our discussions about state and religion were of great value. He offered insights on religion and gender drawn from his expertise in Christianity, Judaism, and new religious movements in the West. My colleagues at the Middle East Study Group offered great feedback and constructive criticism on seminar papers and oral presentations of the material in this book. Special thanks are due to Professor Sami Zubaida, Nelida Fuccaro, and Nadja al-Ali.

I am also grateful to Deniz Kandiyoti for her valuable comments and Arshin Adib-Moghaddam for insights on a paper presented at a British Academy event.

At Cambridge University Press, Marigold Acland has been a source of encouragement and support. I have worked with her for more than a decade; her enthusiasm and professionalism are always exemplary. Mary Starkey was more than a copy editor. Her meticulous attention to detail and style, in addition to her comparative perspective that occasionally alerts me to insights from South Africa, are always appreciated.

Finally, my sister Loulwa was a source of great support and intellectual stimulation. She kept me informed about publications in France and read chapters of the manuscript. Her zero tolerance for 'obscurantism' added a touch of rationality in a world whose inner logic may have escaped many observers. My daughter, also called Loulwa, offered a comparative perspective, drawing on her interest in English literature, feminism, and history. She patiently listened to stories and anecdotes with an appreciated calm and serenity. My son, Zyad, commented on my ideas in his usual argumentative style. His occasional dismissal of *ad hominuim* and *ad feminum* remarks inserted the wit of a young personality in endless days of working and reworking manuscripts. My husband offered most valuable distractions at times when writing a book often turns into a full-time obsession. Without their help and encouragement, this book would not have seen the light.

# Introduction

## The 'Woman Question' in Saudi Arabia

Saudi women often conjure up contradictory images. They are either excluded, heavily veiled victims of their own religion and society, or wealthy, glamorous, cosmopolitan entrepreneurs benefiting from inherited wealth and state education. Notwithstanding these sensational stereotypes, the 2010 Global Gender Gap Report demonstrates that Saudi women lag behind in economic participation and political empowerment, although in health and educational attainment they may achieve better scores. The country has a very high gender gap index, ranked at 129 out of 134.[1] Saudi women remain excluded from full participation in society, despite a recent increase in employment. In 2008, the unemployment rate for women was high, reaching 24.9%.[2] Their employment opportunities increased during a four-year period, but women remain underrepresented in the economy in general. Their economic marginalisation is combined with strict rules that affect their lives as women. Their movement, educational choices, employment, and even health are subject to decisions made by their male guardians. In the West, the ban on women driving attracts attention and comment, but the deep-rooted exclusion of women and their subordination at the legal, social, political, and economic levels remains perhaps unmatched in the Muslim world.

Throughout the second half of the twentieth century, an early generation of educated Saudi women highlighted their plight and scrutinised

[1] Ricardo Hausmann, Laura Tyson, and Saadia Zahidi, *The Global Gender Gap Report*, Geneva: World Economic Forum, 2010.
[2] Patrice Flynn, 'The Saudi Labour Force: A Comprehensive Statistical Portrait', *Middle East Institute*, 65, 4 (2011), pp. 575–86.

their own subordination through a plethora of literary texts, fiction, poetry, and editorial essays. It must be noted that girls' mass education started as late as 1960, thus delaying the development of awareness and articulation of the 'woman question', itself a reflection of Western socialist feminist thinking on gender inequality in capitalist society.[3] A handful of early female literary figures benefiting from education in neighbouring Arab countries spoke as women, but their voices failed to reach a mass audience. Many women published their poetry, novels, and essays in Cairo and Beirut. When they wrote in the local press, many used pennames. But they were the nucleus of a small emerging intellectual community. Their awareness of their subordination and reflections on their own marginalisation failed to reach the rest of the female population. The voices of this first generation of educated women remained marginal. In the 1970s, Saudi society began to enjoy the many opportunities, services, and benefits of the new oil wealth without concerning itself with serious questions relating to political and civil rights and gender equality. The ban on independent associations, mobilisation, and weak organisational potential, still observed today, prevented women from developing into a pressure group to push for greater equality and an end to exclusion at a time when Saudi Arabia was just beginning to enjoy the benefits of sudden wealth. We may find answers to questions regarding why Saudi women were keen to engage with writing at a time when they were completely excluded from the public domain. Bourdieu reminds us that women are drawn into 'the domain of production and circulation of symbolic goods (publishing, journalism, the media, teaching, etc.)'.[4] This helps to explain why Saudi women have been active in teaching and in the production of literary texts at a time when their exclusion from other spheres of economic and political activity was severe.

Today the situation is different. We begin to hear multiple voices attempting to investigate the issue of women's status, and reaching out to society with calls for reflection on women's persistent marginalisation. Women are challenging society through daring voices, critical texts, and real mobilisation. With the expansion of communication technology and satellite television over the last decade, Saudi women are now part of the public sphere, inserting their campaigns and voices into the national

---

[3] The concept of the 'woman question' has its roots in socialist feminism, in which women's domesticity in marriage is considered to be rooted in the economic realm of capitalist production. See 'The Woman Question', transcribed by Sally Ryan for Marxist.org, 2000 at http://www.marxists.org/archive/eleanor-marx/works/womanq.htm.

[4] Pierre Bourdieu, *Masculine Domination*, trans. Richard Nice, Cambridge: Polity Press, 2001, p. 92.

agenda. After decades of ignoring the 'woman question', both state and society recognise a problem, although there is still no consensus with respect to causes and solutions.

*A Most Masculine State* explores the interconnection between gender, politics, and religion that shapes and perpetuates the persistent exclusion of Saudi women. It identifies the historical roots of what might appear to outsiders as an extreme form of gender inequality, marginalisation, and exclusion. This problem remained ignored by historians of the country and social scientists until very recently, when the 'woman question' began to be discussed vigorously both within Saudi society and the international community.

## GENDER, POLITICS, AND RELIGION

In other Arab countries where anti-colonial secular nationalism defined gender relations and the contribution of women to the modernisation of the nation, women found themselves incorporated in national projects and visions that had mixed results in contributing to improving their status and legal rights. As Deniz Kandiyoti reminds us, the liberation of women was used by secular nationalist elites as a symbol of progressive politics. As such, any adequate analysis of the position of women in Muslim societies must be grounded in a detailed examination of the political projects of contemporary states and their historical transformations.[5] Even when states intervene in the private realm through the creation of new institutions and legislations, they often provide limited emancipatory potential. In her opinion, emancipation is dependent on democratic development and the strengthening of civil society. In the majority of post-colonial states in the Muslim world, the nationalist emancipatory project coincided with authoritarian rule and quasi-civil society organisations. The question of women and their emancipation persisted as an urgent project in the absence of serious change in women's status. From Egypt to Iran and Turkey, Kandiyoti questions the rhetoric of secular nationalist elites who made the question of women central to constructing modern nations. When women are elevated to a special status, they become 'privileged bearers of national authenticity'.[6]

---

5 Deniz Kandiyoti (ed.), *Women, Islam and the State*, London: Macmillan, 1991.
6 Deniz Kandiyoti, 'The Politics of Gender and the Conundrums of Citizenship', in Suad Joseph and Susan Slyomovics (eds.), *Women and Power in the Middle East*, Philadelphia: University of Pennsylvania Press, 2001, pp. 52–8, at p. 52.

Furthermore, nationalist struggle and its connection with anti-colonial liberation movements added another dimension in determining the position of women, who were constructed by nationalist elites as a 'gateway' for Western colonialism. Colonial discourse that singled out women as oppressed and in need of liberation was seen as yet another attempt to facilitate colonial penetration and subjugation. As a response, nationalist elites equally endeavoured to highlight the urgency of liberating women, and made it an important precondition for national renaissance. Yet, in this appropriation, women were endowed with the added burden of preserving national identity, tradition, and culture. Arab nationalist discourse in countries such as Egypt and Iraq among other places developed a paternalistic protectionist approach to gender reform.[7] Education and participation in the workforce were considered essential for nationalist revival. According to Suad Joseph, national leaders from Atatürk to Nasser used women to imagine their communities as modern. As such, women became emblems of modernity.[8] But authoritarianism remained anchored in the patriarchal sensibilities of constituencies as rulers cooperated with these constituencies to confirm the subjugation of women rather than challenge it. The state reinforced the control of sub-national communities such as tribes, ethnic groups, and sects over women.[9]

In some instances, but not always, the state endeavoured to break local loyalties around tribe, ethnic group, and religious circles, and transfer this loyalty to a central agency, namely the state itself. The regulation of women's private and public lives became important in this transformation. While the state may seem to liberate women from private patriarchy, it may also cooperate with certain conservative constituencies in order to perpetuate this control. The patriarchy of family and community can sometimes be reproduced in the public sphere. The role of the state in this evolution is well theorised in radical, Marxist, and liberal feminist debates. The state may be central in the resolution of certain key conflicts between private patriarchy (e.g. the domination of male relatives within the institution of marriage) and capitalist forces that aspire to free women's labour but at the same time confirm their domesticity. In the context of her analysis of Britain, Sylvia Walby challenges the limitations

---

[7] Mervat Hatem, 'The Pitfalls of the Nationalist Discourse on Citizenship in Egypt', in Joseph and Slyomovics (eds.), *Women and Power*, pp. 185–211; Shereen Ismael, 'Gender and State in Iraq', in Suad Joseph (ed.), *Gender and Citizenship in the Middle East*, Syracuse: Syracuse University Press, 2000, pp. 33–57.

[8] Joseph (ed.), *Gender and Citizenship*, p. 6.

[9] Joseph and Slyomovics (eds.), *Women and Power*, p. 13.

of previous feminist approaches to state and gender, especially Marxist and liberal feminist perspectives. She reminds us that the state is both patriarchal and capitalist. Its intervention does not always generate the same outcomes across time and place. Nevertheless, the state may seek the preservation of patriarchal structures to promote capitalist development as it embarks on the regulation of employment, citizenship laws, fertility, marriage, divorce, adoption, and sexuality. The state may use legislation to free women to enter the labour force, but its intervention does not automatically lead to the elimination of gender inequality. On the transformation of patriarchy from the private to the public domain, Walby argues that 'patriarchy changed in form, incorporating some of the hard won changes into new traps for women. Women are no longer restricted to the domestic hearth, but have the whole society in which to roam and be exploited'.[10]

Away from the specificity of the industrial capitalist world, in newly formed post-colonial states in North Africa, Mounira Charrad's excellent differentiation between three phases in the relationship between national states and communitarian patriarchal structures is illuminating. She identifies a first stage when, after decolonisation, the state emerges in close alliance with tribal kin groups to adopt conservative family law, confirming private patriarchy (Morocco). A second phase follows whereby the state develops in partial alliance with tribal kin groups and stalls between alternatives before finally enacting a conservative family law policy (Algeria). In the third phase, in national state formation, the state evolves in relative autonomy from kin grouping and promulgates a liberal family law, expanding the legal rights of women (Tunisia).[11] As the historical analysis of gender relations within Saudi Arabia in this book will show, the Saudi state remains dependent on kin and tribal solidarities for its consolidation. The difference from the North African cases studied by Charrad is the historical alliance of the Saudi state with a different kind of solidarity – religious nationalism – discussed below. Despite breaking the military and political autonomy of the tribes after its formation, the state endeavoured to keep their tribal ethos, which, among other things, keeps women in a patriarchal relationship under the authority of male relatives. The state forged an ongoing alliance with the Wahhabi tradition and its ideologues, whose support and loyalty are still cherished for the

[10] Sylvia Walby, *Theorizing Patriarchy*, Oxford: Blackwell, 1990, pp. 200–1.
[11] Mounira Charrad, *States and Women's Rights: The Making of Postcolonial Tunisia, Algeria and Morocco*, Berkeley: University of California Press, 2001.

stabilisation of the polity, obedience to monarchy, and the imagining of a Saudi nation. In return, it has not been possible for the state to become an autonomous agent, capable of moving towards any 'liberal' understanding of gender relations. Since the 1960s, the state has oscillated in its gender policies between severe restrictions and partial liberalisation, without being able to initiate progressive gender policies. Liberalisation came with many caveats that above all ensured that when women were freed from private patriarchy, the state would step in to regulate and control the outcome, often in favour of a conservative approach to gender relations.

In Egypt, historical analysis confirms that professional nationalists who worked within the state over more than a century appropriated the notion of family honour and elevated it to create national honour. As such, the state took over the guardianship of family honour from fathers and brothers.[12] Moreover, through extensive welfare women were drawn into the state as recipients of benefits that they had previously received from their kin. The state assumed the role of a control agency, shaping the prospect of women's emancipation and entitlement to benefits. Most post-colonial states in the Arab region championed women's causes, thus generating state feminism, often under the patronage of the wives and daughters of authoritarian leaders. Perhaps Jihan al-Sadat and Suzan Mubarak remain obvious examples. In Kuwait, female relatives of members of the ruling elite patronise women's charities and civil society.[13] Since the 1960s, Saudi princesses have established charitable organisations that deal with education, orphanages, and other welfare services for women. These initiatives are not exceptions, but signs of a general trend in which the 'woman question' is often entangled with wider political issues that dominate the gender politics of nation states in the region.

The anti-colonial nationalism that emerged in countries from Egypt to India was a response to a historical moment of subjugation and loss of sovereignty. As such, there is a vibrant debate among scholars as to its origins and differences from the classical cases in Europe, especially those associated with eighteenth-century state-consolidation

---

[12] Beth Baron, 'Women, Honour and the State: Evidence from Egypt', *Middle Eastern Studies*, 42, 1 (2006), pp. 1–20.

[13] In her study of women's associations in Kuwait, Haya al-Mughni highlights the fact that these associations were an extension of the patronage networks cultivated with the ruling group. See Haya al-Mughni, *Women in Kuwait: The Politics of Gender*, London: Saqi, 2001.

projects. The classical theories of Eric Hobsbawm, Ernest Gellner, and Benedict Anderson agreed on a modernist, instrumentalist, and constructivist approach privileging the role of elites, states, cultures, institutions (education, army), and language, often associated with top-down state initiatives or structural economic transformations triggered by industrial and capitalist development.[14] Others, such as Anthony Smith, privileged cultural factors and the role of pre-modern *ethnie* that is at the core of nationalist projects.[15] Yet these theoretical positions proved partially inadequate as frameworks to account for late anti-colonial nationalism. Here the work of Partha Chatterjee on India and Joseph Massad on Jordan are revealing despite their different interpretations. Nevertheless, both agree on the merit of situating this nationalism within the context of the colonial encounter. According to Chatterjee, Indian nationalism has culture at its heart and is by definition opposed to the colonial state. It combined an inherent contradiction between a Western modernist strand and anti-individualist, traditionalist longing for authenticity and continuity with a classical Indian tradition. Anti-colonial nationalism in India overemphasised a spiritual dimension underpinned by superiority to materialist Western dispositions, yet it aimed to combine material modernity with the glorification of an essentialised cultural tradition. Indian elites imagined their nation as capable of achieving this difficult task and strove to make it a reality. The glorification of Indian peasantry and past tradition was an integral aspect of this anti-colonial nationalism. The glorification of the Indian woman as repository of spirituality, perseverance, domesticity, and authenticity was from the very beginning paramount. The same woman must also embrace modernity, with education being the first avenue for emancipation.[16]

In contrast, Jordanian nationalism, according to Massad, was very much a top-down colonial project rather than an anti-colonial development. As a country, Jordan was a British invention, forged out of Transjordan in the 1920s. First, a state was created with an imported monarch,

---

[14] Eric Hobsbawm and Terence Ranger (eds.), *The Invention of Tradition*, Cambridge: Cambridge University Press, 1992; Ernest Gellner, *Nations and Nationalism*, Oxford: Blackwell, 1993; and Benedict Anderson, *Imagined Communities*, New York: Verso, 2006.

[15] Anthony D. Smith, *Nationalism and Modernism: A Critical Survey of Recent Theories of Nations and Nationalism*, London: Routledge, 1998.

[16] Partha Chatterjee, *Nationalist Thought and the Colonial World: A Derivative Discourse*, Minneapolis: University of Minnesota Press, 1986; Partha Chatterjee, *The Nation and its Fragments: Colonial and Postcolonial Histories*, Princeton: Princeton University Press, 1993.

then a nation had to be invented with the help of two paramount institutions, the army and national law. Forging Jordanian nationalism depended on Bedouin culture, which was celebrated and romanticised in ways reminiscent of the glorification of the Indian peasantry, itself a fragmented and diverse constellation. Women came to the forefront with the invention of modern personal law, in which their status, marriage, divorce, and rights were fixed as if they were extensions of an authentic old Islamic tradition. The glorification of Bedouin culture was meant to homogenise the fragments, and more importantly to transfer loyalty from tribal chiefs and genealogically and primordially based traditional identities to the newly installed monarch and an invented Jordanian nation.[17] The top-down project proceeded; but with time, bottom-up resistance and challenges from the constituencies that it was meant to homogenise and amalgamate as citizens emerged. Written tribal histories, manufactured by tribal intellectuals and produced in 'scientific' historiography and heritage manuals, competed for a place in the national narrative as legitimate claims to assert an autonomous tribal past and its relevance to the contemporary nation. The reinvention of Jordanian tribal genealogies and its fixing in textual sources, Andrew Shryock reminds us, reflects competition between a colonial invented nationalist monarchical narrative that draws on Bedouin heritage and bottom-up imagining of the tribal fragments that constitute the nation.[18]

## AMBIGUITIES OF 'SAUDI' NATIONALISM

Where there were clear nationalist projects connected with state building in the Arab world, we find that the 'woman question' was a persistent preoccupation, the analysis of which was entangled with wider political projects and the invention of new states and anti-colonial struggles. But Saudi Arabia is a country where there was no anti-colonial struggle or secular nationalist movement. As such, it is perhaps controversial to invoke nationalism (in its European or Arab variants) as a framework to understand gender issues. Classical constructivist theories of nationalism in both Europe and the rest of the world fail to account for the imagining of

[17] Joseph Massad, *Colonial Effects: The Making of National Identity in Jordan*, New York: Columbia University Press, 2001.

[18] Andrew Shryock, *Nationalism and the Genealogical Imagination: Oral History and Textual Authority in Tribal Jordan*, Berkeley: University of California Press, 1997.

Saudi Arabia, a country that was not conceived as a result of anti-colonial nationalist discourse (India) or colonial practices on the ground (Jordan) that amount to feeling, believing, and acting like a nation. The project of state building, following the violent conquest of Abd al-Aziz ibn Saud (Ibn Saud) and directly linked to British imperial intervention after the First World War over almost thirty years, resulted in the amalgamation of regions, tribes, ruling elites, and chiefs into a state rather than a nation. In this respect, domination came without hegemony or consensus, but was articulated using the idioms and principles of nationalism, that is, the congruence between national and political boundaries, common culture, and language. Cultural specificity, regional identities, and sectarian and tribal belonging continue as lived realities, competing in the pursuit of narrow interest, and refusing to melt away under authoritarian rule and state constructions of a specific genre of nationalism, better understood as religious nationalism. Unequal distribution of oil wealth, together with weak notions of citizenship, contribute to exclusion and the perpetuation of narrow traditional identities. The country continues to call itself the Kingdom of Saudi Arabia, an appellation that does not invoke a national identity or people but a reference to the Al-Saud family that brought it together in 1932. The contemporary Saudi project of building a nation, however, should not mask early rudimentary unsuccessful and short-lived projects that aspired to unite, narrate, and create an alternative to the fragmented Arabia of the past.

While all regions that became part of Saudi Arabia in 1932 were immersed in local identities, revolving around tribe, family, oasis, or city, an Islamic Arab national identity articulated by local Arab intelligentsia began to develop in the Hijaz early in the twentieth century. The cities of the Hijaz, mainly Mecca, Medina, and Jeddah, were the most ethnically diverse and cosmopolitan regions in Arabia. Nevertheless, the Hijaz produced a trend articulating an Arab Muslim identity developed in the context of Ottoman rule. This trend grew in the heart of well-established ancient links with Muslims from the Arab and non-Arab world.

From the nineteenth century, substantial networks of *ulama* and *madrasas* were established in Mecca. Muslims from all over the Islamic world found in the holy city a refuge, especially at times when nineteenth-century anti-colonial movements, mostly led by *ulama* activists, began to gather momentum. It was in Mecca where they rallied behind their cause and gathered funds, not only from their compatriots but also from other Muslims residing in the Hijaz.

Muslims established endowments, orphanages, charitable foundations, and schools in the holy cities.[19] Amidst this Islamic cosmopolitanism, local Hijazi cosmopolitan elites articulated the nucleus of an Arab
Muslim identity.

It is in the context of the urban Hijazi cosmopolitanism in which
indigenous inhabitants intermingled with other Arabs, Turks, Africans,
Indians, and central and South East Asians that a discourse about an
Arab Muslim identity was developed by elites who resided in the main
cities. Like all those who espoused Arab nationalism in the first quarter
of the twentieth century, the Hijazi intelligentsia consisted of the elite
who benefited from transnational connections with the Arab and Muslim
world, the early introduction of schooling, civil service, and bureaucracy
that grew around the Hashemite Sharifian emirate. The Hijazi elite, under
Sharif Hussein, aspired to free the land of the Arabs from Ottoman rule,
increasingly seen as a foreign Turkish occupation, and crown Hussein as
king of the Arabs. The local Arab intelligentsia of the Hijazi cities took
part in the wider articulation of Arab Hijazi heritage that was spreading
across the northern Arab provinces of the Ottoman Empire, mainly in its
eastern Mediterranean regions.

The establishment of the first Arabic school in the Hijaz in 1905,
the al-Falah school, by the well-known merchant Muhammad Ali Riza
(1889–1969), ironically belonging to an immigrant family from Persia,
must have been a contributing factor. The Hijazi Arab nationalism that
was endorsed by local Hijazis and other Arabs residing in the Hijaz was,
however, different from the secular Arab nationalism of the same or later
historical periods, for example 1950s Nasserism and 1960s Baathism.
From the very beginning, Hijazi Arab nationalism was anchored in Islam,
given the sacred status of the region and role of the Hashemites in its
endorsement and propagation; both led to the 1915 British-supported
Arab revolt against the Ottoman Empire.

Under British-sponsored Saudi attacks on the Hijaz between 1918 and
1925, this intellectual trend developed into a political party that called
for King Hussein to abdicate in favour of his son, Ali. From Jeddah, the
formation of the Hijazi National Party (HNP) was announced by twelve
activists who met in the house of a local notable, Muhammad Nasif, who
later proved to be a Saudi loyalist. The party chose Muhammad Tawil
as leader and Muhammad Tahir al-Dabbagh as secretary. All twelve

---

[19] Muhammad Qasim Zaman, *The Ulama in Contemporary Islam: Custodians of Change*,
Princeton: Princeton University Press, 2007, p. 256.

founding members were well-known urban Jeddah and Meccan personalities. They included Meccan *ulama*, the Jeddah *qaimmaqam* (resident
governor), wealthy merchants, and municipal councillors.[20]

After the abdication of Sharif Hussein, al-Dabbagh, the party's secretary, pledged allegiance to the new Sharif, Ali. In his allegiance speech,
al-Dabbagh stated:

> Upon the request of the *umma*, your father has abdicated in telegram 69, date 4
> Rabi al-Awal 1343AH. The *umma* decided to pledge allegiance to your Majesty
> as a constitutional king on Hijaz only on conditions that you improve the *umma*'s
> material and non material conditions, and you accept a national elected parlia-
> mentary *majlis* whose members are elected from all Hijazi areas. Internal and
> external affairs should be conducted by ministries responsible to the *majlis*.[21]

A caller announced in Mecca after the noon prayer that King Hussein had
abdicated and the *umma* had elected his son Ali as the new king. King
Ali immediately informed Ibn Saud of his new position and called for a
conference to discuss peace between Najd and Hijaz. Ibn Saud rejected
the offer: 'No peace between me and you as long as you inherit the *mulk*
[kingship] from your father in Hijaz. You know that Hijaz is for the
Muslim world. There is no difference or special standing for one *taifa*
[group] over another group'.[22]

In the two pamphlets distributed by the HNP, we have several references to *al-umma al-hijaziyya* (the Hijazi nation), with emphasis on
*al-Muslimin* (Muslims) from Hijaz and adjacent territories, and *al-bilad
al-hijaziyya* (the Hijazi land). The party used such pamphlets to address
Hijazis and others, drawing on a common Muslim national identity. In a
letter sent to Ibn Saud to appease him and halt his attacks on the Hijaz,
the party declared:

> We Arabs are one nation honoured by God with Islam. The Hijazi land is the
> spring of Islamic light and it is the land of all Muslims...The Hijazi people
> met in Jeddah. Its *ayan* [notables] and those of Mecca and Taif from the *ashraf*
> [descendants of the Prophet] and urban Arabs, and other notables declared Ali
> King only in the Hijaz. We appeal to your Arab *shahama* [chivalry] to halt the
> attacks and send dignitaries to negotiate to protect the holy land, people and
> wealth.[23]

---

[20] Abdullah al-Hanafi, *Ifadat al-anaf fi akhbar bilad al-haram (1290–1365 AH)* [News of
the Holy Land], vol. 4, 2005.

[21] al-Hanafi, *Ifadat al-anaf*, pp. 588–9.

[22] al-Hanafi, *Ifadat al-anaf*, p. 590.

[23] al-Hanafi, *Ifadat al-anaf*, p. 598.

HNP combined three identifying elements that marked it as different
n what was common in central Arabia, the heartland of the alternative
__di political project. It endorsed a nationalism that was anchored in
territory (Hijaz), ethnic group (Arab), and religious belonging (Islam).
This emerging nationalism was territorialised, but it confined itself to the
borders of the Hijazi territory regardless of how loosely this was defined
and marked at the time.

After Ibn Saud occupied the Hijaz in 1925, he announced that those
who had abandoned the Hashemites were secure and immune from
attack, while he could not guarantee the safety of those who remained
loyal to the Hijazi ruling clan. The HNP was eventually disbanded, marking the end of a fleeting historical moment.

Hijazi Arab Islamic nationalism was, however, a top-down initiative
that failed to establish roots in the tribal Hijazi hinterland, let alone
in the heartland of Arabia. The HNP's pamphlets and various letters
sent to those who stood to threaten security in the Hijaz, such as Ibn
Saud and Khalid ibn Luay, reflect the vast gap between what the party
proposed, for example constitutional monarchy, Hijazi autonomy, and
Arab Islamic nationalism, and what their opponents and the rest of the
population endorsed. Khalid ibn Luay, the chief of the Khurma, had
challenged Sharif Hussein's authority and defected to Ibn Saud as early
as 1914; he told Muhammad al-Tawil that he intended to purify the Hijaz
from the Sharif's atheism and tyranny.

Hijazi Arab Islamic identity meant little to Ibn Luay, who belonged to
one of the largest tribes of Hijaz and Najd. As this tribe had both Hijazi
and Najdi branches, its chief's main concern was to escape the authority
of Hussein and his tax collectors, while guaranteeing his autonomy and
independence. His personal quarrels with Sharif Hussein and his son
Abdullah in 1917 were his immediate concerns rather than an overarching
identity, anchored among an urban elite.[24]

The two holy cities, Mecca and Medina, had their own distinctive
cosmopolitan religious identities as places of worship, religious learning,
and sanctity, claimed by all Muslims. Their indigenous inhabitants intermingled with immigrants who had settled there after the pilgrimage; many
sought religious education or refuge from their own countries after such
countries had succumbed to colonial rule. From Morocco to Indonesia

---

[24] Joseph Kostiner, *The Making of Saudi Arabia 1916–1936*, Oxford: Oxford University
Press, 1993, pp. 17–18; Joshua Teitelbaum, 'Sharyf Husayn ibn Ali and the Hashemite
Vision of the Post-Ottoman Order: From Chieftaincy to Suzerainty', *Middle Eastern
Studies*, 34, 1 (1998), pp. 103–22; and Joshua Teitelbaum, *The Rise and Fall of the
Hashemite Kingdom of Arabia*, London: C. Hurst & Co., 2001.

and Central Asia, Muslims took up their abode in the holy cities, thus creating cosmopolitan Islamic communities among whom the bond of Islam rather than ethnicity or nationalism prevailed.

Sharifian rule in the Hijaz and its subsequent claims to lead the Arabs against the Ottomans generated a trend that culminated in the HNP, imagining the inhabitants of the region as sharing common bonds with the Arabs of the north. Hijazi Arab Islamic nationalism may have been influenced by the Arab nationalism of the Levant, but it remained anchored in Islamic heritage. In the Hijaz, there emerged a kind of a short-lived Arab Islamic identity in the context of the Arab revolt of 1915, which was mainly a bid to replace Ottoman rule over Arab territories with that of the Sharifs of Mecca. It was an attempt to reclaim an Islamic state–kingdom that would endow the descendants of the Prophet, the Hashemites, with the leadership role that non-Arabs had usurped. The centrality of the religious cities that were the heritage of all Muslims imbued early Hijazi nationalism with an important Islamic dimension from the very beginning.

Unlike other regions that were incorporated in Saudi Arabia, the Hijaz exhibited clear-cut cleavages between the cosmopolitan multi-ethnic population of the cities and that of the countryside. The cleavage between *hadar/badu* (sedentary/nomadic) was more pronounced than in other areas, especially in Najd. The urban people of Jeddah, Mecca, and Medina were diverse ethnically, linguistically, and religiously – many belonged to different Islamic schools of jurisprudence – while the *badu* population was ethnically homogenous (Arab), yet divided along cultural, tribal, and genealogical lines. This cleavage militated against the development of an overarching solidarity between the Hijazi *hadar* and the *badu*, and was later one of the indigenous factors that thwarted the Sharifian project of creating an Islamic–Arab state that aspired to have the Hijaz as its centre while hoping to expand beyond Arabia. The Hijazi hinterland played an important role in the Arab revolt under Sharifian leadership, but later proved to be one of the factors that led to its demise when Hijazi tribal groups switched allegiance as early as 1918 and sided with the rising Al-Saud dynasty against their Hashemite arch-enemies. Immediately after the demise of the Ottoman Empire and the shrinking of its nominal suzerainty over the holy cities, Khalid ibn Luay switched allegiance from the Hashemites to Ibn Saud, and was key in opening the gates of the Hijaz to the latter.

The defeat of the Hashemites and the incorporation of the Hijaz in the Saudi realm in 1925 brought an end to that Islamic Arab nationalist project. Many of the advocates of this newly founded trend either left the Hijaz with the exiled Sharifian rulers or were incorporated within the new Saudi realm. Many had to moderate or even suppress their enthusiasm for the defeated project as a prerequisite for joining the newly emerging Saudi state. The failure of the project at the grassroots level and the change in British imperial designs for the region was attributed to many factors: the political defeat of the patrons of the project (the Hashemites); the strong cleavages between the cosmopolitan Arab elite and the rest of the Hijazi population; the fragmentation of the elite itself; the divided Hijazi mercantile and trade economy; the quest for the security of the annual Muslim pilgrimage; the low level of literacy; the limited communication and printing infrastructures, both important for the creation of national consciousness and solidarity; and the international context of British imperial designs were all factors that contributed to the end of a fleeting historical experiment at a time when neither the structural conditions of the population, the Al-Saud, nor British imperial power would have allowed its growth. As will be shown later in this book, calls for educating women originated in the Hijaz, with those associated with Arab Islamic Hijazi nationalism articulating the need to introduce women's education in formal schools to combine modernity with preserving Islamic authenticity (as in India). This project was defeated by an alternative Saudi religious nationalism with specific narrow Wahhabi undertones, as will be shown in Chapter 1.

The 1932 Saudi state was constructed as a project to restore a unified religious nation, under the banner of Wahhabi Islam.[25] This makes nationalism in its well-studied secular manifestation and colonial and anti-colonial variants a controversial principle to invoke here. But tracing the historical formation of the country and the discourse under which this was carried out leaves scope for investigating a different type of nationalism, specific to Ibn Saud and his *ulama*'s project of imagining Saudi Arabia, better thought of as religious nationalism.

The invented 'Saudi' nation articulated an identity by claiming to apply the *sharia* (Islamic law) in all aspects of life and submitting to a universal Islamic ethos. Wahhabiyya under state patronage was turned into a quasi-nationalist project, the purpose of which was to provide a universal discourse about unity, authenticity, and tradition, deriving its legitimacy from divine sources rather than man-made modern constructions

---

[25] Madawi Al-Rasheed, *A History of Saudi Arabia*, Cambridge: Cambridge University Press, 2002, 2nd edn, 2010.

of national identity. However, as in secular nationalist and anti-colonial nationalist projects, women were singled out as fundamental pillars of this imagined religious community. The focus on the 'woman question' seems to be prevalent in both variants of nationalism, the secular and religious, despite differences in legitimation narratives, aspirations, and solutions. The Saudi case seems to be a hybrid, where the classical categories found in theories of nationalism cannot be easily applied for analytical purposes, yet a homogenising religious variant inserted into the nationalist narrative was possible to forge.

Wahhabiyya is often held responsible for the many restrictions imposed on Saudi women.[26] The exclusion of Saudi women, which delayed their emancipation and activism, is often attributed to Wahhabi teachings, considered to be the most restrictive within the Islamic tradition. Unlike other Muslim countries, Saudi Arabia applies the strictest interpretations of the Wahhabi teachings, which have so far even prevented women from driving. Women in other Muslim countries are taught in mixed schools and universities, and seek jobs in mixed offices, but Saudi women remain segregated in education and the workforce. While other Muslim women are treated as legal persons, Saudi women remain under the guardianship of their male relatives, who control their mobility, marriage, work, and education. Their persistent exclusion and dependency is often attributed to Wahhabi *ulama* and their many *fatwas* on women. In their turn, Wahhabi *ulama* excel in issuing *fatwas* that deal with all aspects of women's lives, from marriage to wearing high heels. In this respect, they are not exceptional among Muslim scholars, who have been issuing such opinions for centuries. Moreover, they may not differ from orthodox religious traditions such as Judaism in which women's lives are subjected to serious restrictions. Wahhabi *ulama*'s rulings on women should be considered as channels for conservative frustration rather than restrictions to be taken literally. Moreover, the patriarchy and misogyny of the religious tradition does not seem unique.

Wahhabiyya alone cannot explain why women's emancipation is delayed in Saudi Arabia. Soraya Altorki argues that 'it has sometimes been asserted, especially in the West, that "Islam is responsible for the marginal status of women in Saudi Arabia". This ahistorical contention, however, flies in the face of the fact that her inferior position results from cultural and social constructions by men and not from formulations in

---

[26] Khaled Abou El-Fadl, *Speaking in God's Name: Islamic Law, Authority and Women*, Oxford: Oneworld, 2001.

sacred texts'.[27] Similarly, Lila Abu-Lughod criticises Western reification of Islam in discussions of gender inequality where a colonial discourse that seeks to 'save' Muslim women persists. In this discourse, Muslim women are often talked about with the objective of 'saving' them from the perils of their religious tradition. This reification of women masks the complexity of historical dynamics.[28] Authors who draw our attention to the historical dynamics rather than an essential vision of Islam do not seek to absolve Islam from any wrongdoing, but they see this religious tradition in the light of its mutations and transformations over historical time and in interaction with other political, economic, and social factors.

In this book, I argue that it is not Wahhabiyya as an ahistorical coherent corpus of religious knowledge that is responsible for the persistent exclusion of Saudi women. Rather, it is Wahhabiyya as religious nationalism under the auspices of the state that may explain why women have lagged behind in this part of the Muslim world and why gender equality was never a project promoted by either political leadership or the Wahhabi *ulama*. Here, religious nationalism is defined as a form of politicised collective representation, embedded in institutions, the purpose of which is to create a godly community.[29] Wahhabi religious nationalism offers a space where religion and politics meet to create an alternative to the secular model of the nation state. With the consolidation of the contemporary Saudi state, Wahhabiyya was turned into religious nationalism, a politicised religious tradition serving as an umbrella to construct a homogeneous nation out of a fragmented, diverse, and plural Arabian society.

Wahhabi religious nationalism is a project that goes beyond simple piety and conformity to Islamic teachings. It has been the main contributor to a persistent tradition whereby women have become symbols of national identity and authenticity. Like secular nationalism, Wahhabi religious nationalism seeks to preserve the family and women's status within this private domain in order to achieve the ultimate restoration of the pious religious community. Women become boundary markers that visibly and structurally distinguish this pious nation from other ungodly

[27] Soraya Altorki, 'The Concept and Practice of Citizenship in Saudi Arabia', in Joseph (ed.), *Gender and Citizenship*, pp. 215–36, at p. 233.

[28] Lila Abu-Lughod, 'Do Muslim Women Really Need Saving? Anthropological Reflections on Cultural Relativism and its Others', *American Anthropologist*, 104, 3 (2002), pp. 783–90.

[29] Roger Friedland, 'Religious Nationalism and the Problem of Collective Representation', *Annual Review of Sociology*, 27 (2001), pp. 125–52.

polities. Hence, the obsession with their bodies, appearance, segregation, purity, and sexuality tend to reflect the process whereby women have become signals marking the boundaries of the nation. This appropriation of women was historically important to the state, the ideologues of religious nationalism, and the rest of the constituency – and, surprisingly, to many women too.

As secular and anti-colonial nationalism did not emerge in Saudi Arabia, religious nationalism was the framework that defined women's role in society. Women were appropriated to become an integral part of national development and identity. In this respect, nationalism, whether secular or religious, had similar outcomes, mainly projecting gender relations as a function of greater political projects. Secular nationalism may have improved certain aspects of women's lives and their legal status, but this remains contested in the literature on countries where it is well entrenched.[30] While secular nationalism aspired in its rhetoric to a modernity in which women are central, religious nationalism constructed women as icons for the authenticity of the nation and its compliance with God's law. In both cases, women are turned into symbols, representing anything but themselves. In this respect, the boundaries between secular and religious nationalism may be blurred, as both appropriate the 'question of women' to create national and collective identities, albeit with different outcomes.

The Saudi state was constructed as a project to purify society and return it to an authentic Islam. In this project, women were from the very beginning a central pillar, a visible sign, and an instrument of this process. Religious nationalism aspired to create 'godly women', whose fate is determined by God's design for this world. When the state introduced girls' education, it pledged that this was not meant to change their situation but to confirm their domesticity under the guidance of religious scholars. Girls were therefore introduced to an ideological education co-opted by the state and religious ideologues in order to return women to the tradition of the *sahabiyat*, the early female companions of the Prophet, rather than to challenge their subordination and seek modern solutions to their exclusion.[31] Wahhabiyya alone is not the only variable

[30] Margot Badran, *Feminists, Islam and the Nation: Gender and the Making of Modern Egypt*, Princeton: Princeton University Press, 1995.

[31] Saudi Arabia may not appear unique, as other groups who build their legitimacy on religious nationalism may endeavour to educate women, but this education is meant to restrict their empowerment. For comparison with ultra-orthodox Jewish women, see Tamar El Or, *Educated but Ignorant: Ultraorthodox Jewish Women and their World*, Boulder: Lynne Reinner, 1994.

that can explain gender inequality, but its transformation from a religious revival movement to a state project aiming at consolidating a political realm should be investigated to understand the extreme marginalisation of Saudi women.

We have established that religious nationalism, like other nationalist collective projects, seeks to control women in the pursuit of grand political designs and communal identities; yet Saudi Arabia has the added burden of tribalism conceived as a mode of social organisation, and not conducive to gender equality. But to claim that tribalism and social conservatism are independent variables responsible for the subordination of women misses an important dimension. Tribalism survives and flourishes within state structures across the Arab region. Such social and cultural explanations fail to capture the complexity of tribalism in its historical manifestation and under the auspices of the contemporary state as it interacts with other structural factors. There is no doubt that Saudi society today retains aspects of tribalism, for example tribal endogamy and patriarchy, both of which restrict women's choices and place them under the authority of an overarching male guardian. But this tribalism is not unique to Saudi Arabia. In other countries where tribalism survives as a social and cultural fact, we find that women have been able to overcome its limitations, engage in mobilisation, press for their rights, and gain advancement. Tribalism has not stopped Kuwaiti women from securing political participation and citizenship after a long struggle.[32] Similarly, in tribal Oman, women assume public roles at a high level in state institutions, for example as ambassadors and deputy ministers, despite persistent gender inequality in legislation pertaining to marriage and divorce.[33] Both Kuwait and Oman have well-known tribal groups incorporated in the state. Is Saudi tribalism, then, more restrictive and so different from that in other Gulf countries? Several Saudi tribal groups have branches in Kuwait and Saudi Arabia, not to mention other Gulf countries. Surely they share similar tribal and patriarchal inclinations. The only difference seems to be related to the incorporation of tribal groups in states with different trajectories and no claims to restoring nations to authentic Islam under the banner of a religious nationalist movement. This makes arguments about restrictive tribal codes less convincing as a single variable behind the persistent exclusion of Saudi women.

---

[32] Haya al-Mughni and Mary Ann Tetreault, 'Citizenship, Gender, and the Politics of Quasi States', in Joseph (ed.), *Gender and Citizenship*, pp. 237–60.

[33] For gender inequality in Oman, see Khalid al-Azeri, *Social and Gender Inequality in Oman*, London: Routledge, forthcoming.

We must search elsewhere for sound explanations that move beyond essential cultural or religious arguments. It seems that the only difference between Saudi Arabia and other Arab countries stems from the fact that these countries do not construct their legitimacy on the basis of religious nationalism like Saudi Arabia, and as such it has been easier to move towards greater flexibility on gender questions. In neighbouring Gulf states, we find that women were not subjected to the restrictive requirements of religious national politics as much as their Saudi counterparts. As such, they were not locked in the requirements of preserving a pious community.[34] They have achieved relatively better citizenship rights, economic participation, and empowerment than Saudi women.

If Wahhabism as religious knowledge and tribalism as social organisation are not sufficient variables to explain the persistent exclusion of Saudi women, where else should we look for convincing explanations to account for the severe gender inequality in the country? This book considers the role of a state founded on religious nationalism as an important variable that has so far provided a framework in which the exclusion of women came to signify the uniqueness of the Saudi political project. It is the interaction between the state, religious nationalism, and social and cultural forms of patriarchy that seems to have locked Saudi women in a situation considered by many to be unique in its extreme forms of exclusion. In this respect, this book is inspired by the pioneering work of several scholars who identify the state as a critical actor. In her seminal edited volume on gender and citizenship, Suad Joseph asserts that 'no actor is more critical to the gendering of citizenship than the state. As such women have been caught between the conflicting demands of nation-building and state-building projects'.[35]

The Saudi state claims to be an Islamic state different from other postcolonial Arab states in the way it upholds the piety of the nation, which became increasingly defined in terms of excluding women, minimising their appearance in the public sphere, and restricting their citizenship rights and participation. While Islam features in the constitutions of many Arab states, it has not assumed the role of a religious nationalist project the way it has in Saudi Arabia. The piety of the Saudi state is measured

---

[34] On Kuwait, see al-Mughni, *Women in Kuwait*; on the United Arab Emirates, see Jane Bristol-Rhys, *Emirati Women: Generations of Change*, London: Hurst & Co., 2010; on Oman, see Mandana Limbert, *In the Time of Oil: Piety, Memory and Social Life in an Omani Town*, Stanford: Stanford University Press, 2010; on the Gulf in general, see Alanoud Alsharekh (ed.), *The Gulf Family: Kinship, Politics, and Modernity*, London: Saqi, 2007.

[35] Joseph (ed.), *Gender and Citizenship*, p. 7.

by its compliance with the strictest Islamic interpretations and *fatwa*s. If women are invited to participate in society, they are confined to roles that serve the nation's image as Muslim and pious. Their participation as teachers, administrators, and, more recently, appointed members of the Consultative Council is placed within *thawabit shariyya*, the established parameters of *sharia*, defined and fixed by the ideologues of religious nationalism, who are represented by the government-appointed Higher Council of Ulama.

Within the parameters of religious nationalism, women become recipients of wide-ranging welfare services from health to education. Such services are often tailored to confirm their position as subordinate members of society whose main and ultimate role is to demonstrate the piety of the state and its leading role in maintaining an authentic nation, faithful to the teachings of pristine Islam. So women are educated to become good mothers who contribute to producing the obedient, homogeneous, and pious nation. The state has thus privileged the role of the Wahhabi *ulama* in defining what is permissible in gender relatio.s, while it may overlook them in other areas of political and economic life. Since its creation, the state has granted the *ulama* the ultimate role of arbitrating women's position in society, a situation that is not common in other Arab or Muslim countries.

But only if we are prepared to trace the historical context in which restrictive *fatwa*s on women are produced can we understand that the state remains more powerful than its own religious scholars and is capable of overcoming their opposition to certain changes in gender relations. Hence, the state remains the ultimate arbiter, capable of either overlooking certain *fatwa*s and opinions or promoting them for purely political reasons. This became clear in the 1960s when the state intervened to introduce girls' education amidst resistance from religious scholars in order to promote itself as a modernising agent in Saudi society. The situation was reversed in the 1980s when the state worked together with the *ulama* to impose greater restrictions on women for the purpose of enforcing increased Islamisation to boost its religious credentials. It restricted scholarships for women to study abroad and enforced greater surveillance of women in the public sphere, to the extent that many lost the limited opportunities granted to them in the previous decade.

In the post-9/11 period, we find the state willing to reverse decades of restrictions and promote itself as a champion of women's emancipation – though within limits and according to the aforementioned *thawabit shariyya*. King Abdullah's rule is seen as a time when state feminism began to define women's prospects in the country. He is described as a supporter of women's emancipation and rights. The state is, therefore, capable of overlooking certain religious opinions, with a view to encouraging greater visibility for women. It can easily silence objections from religious scholars over its new policies. The post-9/11 period put pressure on the state to seek a more inclusive policy towards women. Its international reputation as the least favourable to women's emancipation became too embarrassing for the Saudi regime, which is constantly seeking legitimacy abroad. As a result, Saudi women were turned into icons, exchanged in a complex game between the state and its religious nationalism on the one hand, and the state and the international community on the other, without this being resolved in permanent gains for women. An international context hostile to Saudi restrictions on women that erupted with Saudi involvement in nourishing radical religious trends prompted the state to respond by highlighting a gender policy favourable to women's participation. This international pressure pushed the Saudi state to consider increasing women's visibility, economic opportunities, and contribution to public debates. Moreover, women's mobilisation in the real and virtual worlds led to greater visibility and expressions of discontent with existing restrictions. In 2011, at the height of the Arab Spring, which led to the overthrow of several Arab authoritarian regimes, the Saudi king announced that women would be given seats on the Consultative Council and could participate in future municipal elections. The day the king announced the news, 25 September, is seen as a historic date for women's emancipation in Saudi Arabia. Women expressed their joy over the decision and hailed the king as a reformer. This poses the question of why authoritarian states champion women's causes and adopt feminist policies. In the Saudi case, the quest for a new international legitimacy, new local patronage networks among women, and a serious desire to channel the increasing mobilisation of Saudi women into state-approved projects pushed the leadership to promote women's emancipation and empowerment at a time when the whole population remained unrepresented in an elected national assembly. Moreover, in its attempt to erode the authority of the religious authorities the state was determined to restrict their control over women's issues gradually.

Authoritarian states need women as allies against men who challenge the state and criticise its general exclusion of the population from the decision-making process. Other historical examples of authoritarian states championing women's causes confirm that such initiatives do not often lead to real advancement or equality, nor do they undermine authoritarianism itself.[36] The recent Saudi state interest in women's advancement does not challenge authoritarian rule per se. On the contrary, it casts a soft veil over one of the most authoritarian states in the Arab region and weakens the many Islamist voices that have become loud in criticising the state.

This oscillating history of state gender policies informs our understanding of the persistence of women's exclusion and their occasional and sporadic appearance in the Saudi public sphere. Saudi women have not been able to enjoy many rights taken for granted by other women in the Muslim world. From education and work to the right to drive a car and travel alone, Saudi women remain hostage to the project of a masculine authoritarian state negotiating its survival and legitimacy on the basis of remaining faithful to the tenets of religious nationalism and the *ulama* ideologues who support it. Today, the state's quest for new local allies and international legitimacy pushes it to become a 'feminist' state in opposition to its historical character as a most masculine state. Moreover, as the state is challenged by Islamist dissent, it finds in women natural allies against the radicalisation of men.

THE OIL FACTOR

With increasing oil revenues, the state was able to build new legitimacy deriving from welfare services delivered to the population, but its oscillating quest for religious legitimacy and modernity remains unabated. In fact, oil wealth is a mixed blessing.[37] It allows the state to introduce mass education that benefits women, but it fails to increase their participation in the labour force. Like the state, the oil industry remains masculine. In such an industry, there are no serious wide-ranging opportunities for women's economic participation. As a result, the first generation of educated Saudi women took employment in the education sector as teachers and administrators rather than in the growing oil industry. Later, they increasingly found a niche in writing and journalism, to be followed by careers in medical services, first as auxiliaries and later as doctors. With economic liberalisation since the late 1990s, the Saudi business and financial community celebrated female entrepreneurs, not only locally but also internationally. Businesswomen became regular participants in economic

---

[36] See, for example, Melinda Adams, '"National Machineries" and Authoritarian Politics', *International Feminist Journal of Politics*, 9, 2 (2007), pp. 176–97.
[37] Michael Ross, 'Oil, Islam and Women', *American Political Science Review*, 102, 1 (2008), pp. 107–23.

forums held in Jeddah. This latest phase coincided with the country's increased economic openness, privatisation, and liberalisation of the economy. It also coincided with growing internal Saudi Islamist dissent against the government, the development of reformist democratic trends, and terrorism.

Moreover, oil wealth allowed Saudi men to have monthly wages as employees in the state sector for the first time. With the exclusion of women from the labour force, men were confirmed in their role as the sole breadwinners and their wives as recipients of financial support from both the state and their male guardians. Men with surplus wealth were able to employ foreign domestic servants to replace Saudi women in the domestic sphere. As a result of successive oil booms, women then had a double exclusion: one from the general economy and one from the domestic sphere. Oil wealth allowed many women freedom from domestic services and the traditional roles still performed by women across the globe, but it also deprived Saudi women of control over their own lives. This situation was hardly conducive to women's emancipation or gender equality. Women lost their traditional control over the domestic roles they had historically performed, while they partially penetrated the general economy in deliberately designated sectors, the purpose of which was to care for society and reproduce the future generation of obedient and pious citizens. Today women's participation in the labour force does not exceed twelve per cent.[38] Oil wealth turned women into commodities exchanged by men who can afford them.

Oil has contributed to maintaining women's general exclusion until the present day, and has influenced the way the gender gap is formulated and discussed in the Saudi context. Women are often constructed as protected, provided for, and confined members of society. Their consumption patterns and the amount of money they spend on consumer goods such as cosmetics and clothes make international news.[39] Their education does little to deconstruct this image. In fact, it confirms them in the position of educated and idle women. Ironically, it is not uncommon for both men and women to cherish the way Saudi women are honoured as a result of trading their rights for affluence and protection. Many Saudi women see themselves as protected 'jewels' freed from the burden of sharing household expenses.

[38] John Sfakianakis, *Employment Quandary: Saudi Arabia Economics*, Riyadh: Banque Saudi Fransi, 16 February 2011 (electronic publication).

[39] In November 2011, Al-Arabiyya reported that Saudi women spend SR 4 billion on cosmetics. See http://www.alarabiya.net/articles/2011/11/23/178704.html.

Gender inequality would have followed a different trajectory had women been drawn into the labour force. The state and society, however, preferred to employ foreign workers rather than local women. It is certain that lack of skills and illiteracy delayed women's entry into the labour market. Their work is still regarded as a luxury to be enjoyed but not a necessity, despite the fact that today many women do contribute their wages to support their families. Saudi society retains the rhetoric that women's wages are for their own consumption, but the reality of many contemporary women attests to a different situation. Stories about fathers delaying the marriages of their working daughters in order to appropriate their salaries are abundant in the Saudi press. This has prompted the *ulama* to issue *fatwa*s against such fathers, as will be shown later in this book. Single women and divorcees search for jobs not to spend wages on luxury goods but to support families when both the state welfare services and their own men fail to provide for them. The plight of women and children abandoned by men makes headlines in the Saudi press. Without serious employment opportunities, such women remain on the margins of society, living on charity and welfare.

Oil wealth also provided the necessary financial means to enforce sex segregation in schools and the workplace, thus confirming the state's compliance with the requirements of religious nationalism. It allowed the state not only to exclude women from the workforce but also to maintain strict sex segregation and provide separate educational institutions. In countries where this was an unaffordable financial burden, states allowed girls and boys to be educated in the same institutions at least at elementary level or at higher educational institutions. Without oil, the Saudi state would not have been able to create parallel institutions and impose on its private and public sectors the segregation witnessed in the country. The same wealth also allowed investment in new technology to enforce this separation. So male lecturers communicate with female students by phone and video conferencing, without coming face to face with them. In the 1980s, oil wealth also allowed the state to employ foreign Ph.D. supervisors and pay for their travel to Saudi Arabia in order to supervise female Saudi students who were not allowed to travel abroad to enrol in foreign universities. Distance learning became an alternative to allowing Saudi women to leave the country without a male guardian. The same oil wealth also allowed the state to expand its religious police to monitor the public sphere and ensure that women and men remain compliant with the requirements of religious nationalism. Women's veiling and invisibility could only be enforced with heavy investment in surveillance, thus maintaining the image of Saudi Arabia as a pious nation and the state as the legitimate Islamic polity.

## WOMEN BETWEEN STATE AND OPPOSITION

As women were transformed into symbols of the piety of state and nation, they also became central to opposition discourse that challenged state vision. As the state singled out women as a field on which to exhibit its Islamic credentials, their education, work, and personal role in society turned into contested domains, with multiple actors pushing their agendas through an appropriation of women as objects rather than as subjects with their own voices. Islamist opposition to the state is often voiced via accusations of the corruption of women. From opposition to girls' education in the 1960s, Juhaiman's revolt in Mecca in 1979, and Jihadi violence in 2003, we come across actors who single out women as an axis along which to challenge the state. Throughout researching this book, I came across men's voices debating women as symbols representing their own political, religious, and social visions. From the successive kings who ruled over Saudi Arabia to Jihadis challenging their authority, multiple political actors continue to appropriate women in this way.[40] I was fascinated by how women are so important to both state grand political designs and opposition movements. Drawing women into the grand politics of the country was always an intriguing exploration of social dynamics and political aspirations. This took place at a time when women themselves were still not in a position to articulate their own views on issues relevant to them. Until recently, it seems that only men were able to represent women. Many actors promoted a masculine discourse about women in which the feminine voice was either totally absent or subdued. This was true of both the state and society.

After an international crisis related to terrorism on 9/11, Saudi women became inseparable from discourses about Islamic fanaticism. After all, some of them were the mothers of the fifteen hijackers who attacked the Twin Towers in New York and precipitated a decade of constant conflict under the rubric of the War on Terror. Western journalists flooded to Saudi cities to investigate the roots of terrorism, its ideology, and the society that served as its incubator. Western non-governmental organisations designed research projects to enlist Saudi women in the War

---

[40] Madawi Al-Rasheed, *Contesting the Saudi State: Islamic Voices from a New Generation*, Cambridge: Cambridge University Press, 2007.

on Terror.[41] As mothers, they were endowed with the responsibility of educating children in moderate Islam, recognising early warning signals of radicalisation, and protecting the rest of society from terror. Women became gateways to controlling the zeal of young radical men. It is at this juncture that the state decided to include women in, for example the National Dialogue Forums in order to contain the crisis of terrorism and extract loyalty to the state from women.

For the first time, global media and Western women's groups came face to face with Saudi women, whom they had always seen as oppressed, marginalised, and excluded. Their entry was obviously mediated by the state, which was desperate to shake its negative image following 9/11. Although Saudi Arabia had not been colonised, this made no difference to the flourishing Western discourse on Saudi women as oppressed by their own religion and society. As such, they were in need of being 'saved'. The state adopted an open-door policy which resulted in globalising 'the question of Saudi women'. In an attempt to defend itself against terrorism accusations, the state endeavoured to show a soft side by increasing the visibility of women. At this juncture, the 'victimhood narrative' about Saudi women persisted, but occasionally it was impregnated with stories about confident, professional, educated women, who have partially escaped this victimhood and demonstrated that they can be agencies of enlightenment, modernity, and progress. Stories about successful businesswomen appeared in the local and international press to confirm the exceptionalism of individual women amidst a persistent alleged 'woman problem'.[42] Religious conservatism was blamed for the delayed progress of women, while the Saudi leadership was hailed as a progressive force gradually eliminating obstacles on the road to full emancipation and gender equality.

## THE STATE AS PROVIDER AND ARBITER

*A Most Masculine State* captures how the state remains an important agent in determining and shaping the position of Saudi women. It must be mentioned that a state-centric approach to the 'woman question' should not undermine two important reservations. First, the Saudi state, like

---

[41] For example, Women Without Borders, an Austrian women's rights organisation, took an interest in Saudi women as part of its programme to combat terrorism. See Edith Schlaffer, Ulrich Kropiunigg, and Fawziah al-Bakr, *Bridging the Gap – But How? Young Voices From Saudi Arabia*, Vienna: Women Without Borders, 2010.

[42] See Andrew Lee Butters, 'Saudi Women's Quiet Revolution: More Rights and Greater Freedom. But too Slowly for Some', *Time*, October 2009.

other states, should not be seen as a single entity with a clear, unified vision. On the contrary, it consists of multiple actors and institutions that may have contradictory interests, projects, and impacts on the 'woman question'. I have discussed these elsewhere,[43] but it is worth reiterating here that, on gender issues, there are multiple official voices and state institutions that articulate irreconcilable visions on gender, for example the religious institutions, economic forums, labour and social affairs ministries, the media, and other state agencies that operate in ways that may hinder a common gender policy and consensus over urgent reforms. Yet this multiplicity and inconsistency may offer an overture for women, encouraging a greater role in the economic, political, and economic sphere – for example initiatives that benefit elite women and business classes or traditional religious groups within the religious and educational institutions of the state. This becomes clear as I trace past and contemporary debates and obstacles to emancipation under the auspices of various princes, officials, and institutions. Second, a state-centric approach should not negate women as agents who may endorse state projects, resist patriarchy at the personal and political levels, adopt hyper-feminist agendas, or retreat into ultra-conservatism, defending the system that excludes and marginalises them. The chapters in this book demonstrate that the Saudi state does not simply 'act' while women 'react'. Saudi women are an emerging divergent constituency, an agency with their own interests, voices, and projects, so clearly documented in the chapters on women's literature and activism. If women appear to accept state empowerment initiatives or endorse religious interpretations that continue to exclude them from the public sphere, they are simply engaging with strategies the purpose of which is to bargain with an entrenched classical patriarchy that is in deep crisis, as described by Deniz Kandiyoti.[44] While patriarchy has been theorised in many ways within radical, Marxist, and liberal feminism, Sylvia Walby considers the concept indispensable for an analysis of gender inequality. At an abstract level, patriarchy is a system of social relations, embodied in six structures at the practical level: a mode of production, work, patriarchal relations in the state, male violence, patriarchal relations in sexuality, and patriarchal relations in cultural institutions.[45]

---

43 Madawi Al-Rasheed, 'Circles of Power: Royals and Society in Saudi Arabia', in Paul Aarts and Gerd Nonneman (eds.), *Saudi Arabia in the Balance: Political Economy, Society, Foreign Affairs*, London: Hurst & Co., 2005.
44 Deniz Kandiyoti, 'Bargaining with Patriarchy', *Gender and Society*, 2, 3 (1988), pp. 274–90, at p. 282.
45 Walby, *Theorizing Patriarchy*, pp. 19–20.

Saudi Arabia is part of the 'patriarchal belt' that has been a character-istic of the region. As such, Kandiyoti argues that when this patriarchy enters a crisis, women continue to use all the pressure they can muster to make men live up to their obligations. The crisis is related to the impact of new market forces, capital penetration, or processes of chronic immiseration. She adds that women's 'passive resistance takes the form of claiming their half of this particular patriarchal bargain-protection in exchange for submissiveness and propriety'.[46] Like other women, Saudis engage in both resisting patriarchy and bargaining with it, whether they are liberal, Islamist, or simply un-politicised.

I argue that neither Islam nor tribalism alone is sufficient to account for the persistent exclusion of and discrimination against women. In gen-eral, articulate Saudi women avoid openly invoking the state's major part in enforcing and perpetuating their own exclusion and extreme margin-alisation. This does not mean that Saudi women are unable to identify the real causes behind their existing problem; it is a strategy to avoid confrontation with the state at a time when they have not achieved soci-ety's consensus over the need to shake gender relations and move towards greater equality. Authoritarian rule in Saudi Arabia, lack of civil society, and women's inability to emerge as an autonomous pressure group have pushed women to search for alternative and less risky arenas to challenge their own subordination. In general, it has become common for women in authoritarian states to appeal to the same agency that deprives them of their rights and confines them to second-class citizenship. In her compar-ative study of Egypt and the United Arab Emirates, Frances Hasso asserts that women more than men need authoritarian states, not least for their ability to police men and extract resources from them within a corporatist family framework that requires men to provide for wives, children, and parents.[47] My reading of Saudi women's multiple voices reveals that they too expect the state to play the role of provider and arbiter in gender matters.

Like Faisal before him, King Abdullah is seen by many Saudi women as a champion of women's emancipation.[48] His orchestrated speeches about women invoke a patriarchal position as he refers to women as his

---

[46] Kandiyoti, 'Bargaining with Patriarchy', p. 283.

[47] Frances Hasso, *Consuming Desires: Family Crisis and the State in the Middle East*, Stanford: Stanford University Press, 2011.

[48] Biographers of Faisal stress his contribution to the modernisation of Saudi Arabia and his leading role in girls' education: see Joseph Kechichian, *Faisal: Saudi Arabia's King for All Seasons*, Gainesville: University of Florida Press, 2008.

'mothers, daughters and wives'. For the first time in history, photos of the king and the Crown prince surrounded by women circulated in the Saudi press; this was interpreted as a sign of the current leadership's support for women. In images and speeches, women are talked about as weak subjects who need to be looked after, provided for, and protected. The modernity of the state comes with paternalistic welfare and provisions, combining a difficult and contradictory commitment to provide for women without seriously empowering them. Women look for the state to provide education, employment, and health care. Recently women have mobilised as groups, seeking employment. Teachers regularly assemble in front of the Ministry of Education and demand that officials honour the king's pledges to provide jobs for women. They vent their anger against minor civil servants, who are held responsible for delaying the implementation of promises made by the king. Women also demand that the state become an active agent in mediating family disputes and marital problems. While they approach the massive state bureaucracy dealing with social and welfare services for a wide range of benefits, they often seek direct help from princes within the state. It has become common for heavily veiled women to queue outside governors' offices on specially designated days to ask for financial help from individual princes. They hand letters demanding financial aid to divorce a husband or bring an absentee husband to honour his commitment and provide for abandoned children. Women also call upon the state to act in their favour and protect them from the aggression of men. The state remains a provider for women, an important resource to compensate for the loss of support from their family. Saudi women willingly seek state patronage in order to compensate for men failing to live up to their expectations. This offers ample opportunities for the state to hijack the 'woman question' to enforce its own patriarchy.

Moreover, women see the state as an arbiter that can resolve gender inequality in their favour. From the women's perspective, the king must act as an arbiter between religion and society on the one hand and their own interests as women on the other. But this has become increasingly difficult as women adopt different expectations from the state. Islamist women appeal to the king to gain more rights while remaining faithful to the Islamic tradition, while liberal women look to the state to curb exclusionary religious opinions and implement international treaties on gender equality. So it may appear surprising that some women request greater surveillance of the public sphere and an elimination of 'corruption' and 'Westernisation' in order to protect their interests as women. They call upon the king to increase the number of religious police and to employ women in this force to safeguard against the country drifting into social chaos and moral degeneration. They demand that the state enforce the ban on mixing between the sexes, as many women would not like to work in mixed surroundings. Rather than increasing women's employment, mixing between the sexes in the workplace is seen by some women as yet another obstacle to finding jobs. Many housewives prefer that their husbands do not encounter other women in the workplace. Some women see mixing between the sexes as a threat to their own interests. Guarding their marriages against the hazards of men being exposed to other women remains high on the agenda of some women. A Saudi housewife explained to me that her marriage would not survive if her husband worked with other women in the office. She was simply expressing her worries as a woman, concerned with the security of her marriage and family. Similarly, many women expect the state to resist calls for lifting the ban on driving because this would free men from the responsibility of sharing the burden of running family affairs. Women also call upon the state to control the media, in their opinion a source of corruption. They object to the opening of Saudi media to global and commercial influences that sexualises women and fetishises their beauty. Many women consider this *infitah* (openness) as representing a direct threat to the security of their marriages and family lives. But there are other women who offer a different perspective on their own position and what they expect the state to do for them.

Liberal women push for greater flexibility that would enable them to enjoy wider employment opportunities, even if this means relaxing the prohibition on mixing between the sexes and lifting the ban on driving. They explain the low economic participation of women as a function of their inability to enjoy freedom of movement, of which driving is only one aspect. They demand greater freedom of movement and less dependence on either their male relatives or foreign drivers for transport. The low salaries for jobs such as teaching makes working outside the home a less attractive option if women have to pay a substantial proportion of their monthly salary to foreign drivers. They prefer to stay at home. These contradictory aspirations reflect the diversity of Saudi women, who seek the state as arbiter of gender questions. The state is called upon either to resist increased liberalisation or to speed up the process by which women can begin to enjoy greater participation in society. The division between Islamist and liberal women does not necessarily mean that the first seek tradition while the latter aspire towards more freedoms. Both women are engaged with strategies to negotiate a better deal for themselves. Both engage with discourses in order to secure a place within the national narrative. As Hafez reminds us, 'women are not passive terrain on which secularising states and religious groups vie to gain control. Instead women often engage with these multiple discourses in ways that may also translate into activism and not necessarily into passivity and oppression'.[49] While diversity is inevitable, it has delayed reaching a consensus with regard to gender inequality. Women and society remain divided on the extent of change and its many directions.

In state discourse, divisive gender issues are considered too problematic to lead to satisfactory arbitration. According to many men and women, the state must carefully introduce gradual reforms in order to remain faithful to the foundation narrative of the state and its religious credentials. So, in debating whether Saudi women should be allowed to drive, the king and other princes may voice their support, but they hesitate to pass a decree that lifts the ban on driving, as this may antagonise conservative religious scholars whose defence of the realm is needed at times of political crisis. Revolutionary change in gender relations is depicted as a threat to the social and political stability of the kingdom, a stability that rests on a bargain between the princes and the religious scholars. The first have the upper hand in running the political and economic affairs of the country while the latter are in charge of the social stability of the nation, its commitment to Islamic teachings, and, above all, its identity. This bargain has meant that gender issues are often left to religious scholars and society, without the state intervening to resolve contradictions and divisions. In this bargain, women's rights are negotiated between the princes and the scholars with the women concerned not being able to reach a consensus over change. Gender relations are the most obvious arena where religion and politics cooperate and may occasionally collude.

But the state must not be seen as a neutral arbiter. It has its own agenda when it comes to gender matters. The state is capable of altering its policies, and may reverse certain religious rulings pertaining to women as it strives to meet different conflicting demands. The state as a powerful agent in society is forced to make concessions and embark on projects, the purpose of which is to confirm its centrality in modernisation. While it remains faithful to religious nationalism, the Saudi state is increasingly eager to appear modern. Its quest for modernity pushes it to adopt policies often unacceptable to the ideologues of religious nationalism or to women who still honour their rulings as a framework determining their role in society. Consequently, the modernity of the state must be moderated to uphold old commitments, namely preserving the piety of the nation. Increasing higher education and employment opportunities, and allowing greater media visibility for women in the post-9/11 period, allow the state to appear as an arbiter that follows a difficult course in a society that remains divided on gender issues. In this context, the king is constructed as a reformer who cannot rush his subjects into accepting greater emancipation for women.

With more than five decades of state education, Saudi women have already begun registering their voices in the local media as columnists and as novelists with their own aspirations. Women's words expressed in short essays and literature become an arena where their aspirations and sometimes contradictory visions can be traced. In this book, I explore women's words as articulations of aspirations not necessarily all aiming at greater emancipation and empowerment. While a growing number of Saudi women desire greater gender equality and roles in the public sphere, many others resist such a drastic change. In the absence of civil society organisation and mobilisation among women, women's literature is a window of opportunity to capture women's projects. Many of the Saudi women I interviewed pointed me towards this literature, which while fictional helps position women as critical voices. They have argued that through literature they can send messages that remain censored in real-life situations. The fictional nature of literature provides a shield against harassment, imprisonment, and punishment. One Saudi novelist told me that she can discuss daring topics in her novels without being harassed, as there is no law in the country against fiction, while real mobilisation and organisation around women's rights bring about greater risks. Had she been active in political or social mobilisation, she would certainly end up in prison, she said. This literature is important as a social statement and a critical discourse that challenge many taken-for-granted stereotypical images of Saudi women. Many novelists deconstruct these images and offer a profound critique of society, culture, and religion. Novelists mix reality and fiction in order to challenge gender inequality.

But Saudi women remain divided on the degree of emancipation they require the state to facilitate. Some women invoke contemporary international discourse on gender equality and aspire towards the elimination of all forms of gender discrimination, while others seek the Islamic tradition as their reference point when they write on women's issues. Whether liberal or Islamist, Saudi women are modern in the sense that they identify women as a subject rather than an object to be handled by men. Their modernity is expressed in engaging with the 'woman question', an arena that had previously been a non-issue. They seek confirmation of their role as citizens with rights, seen by many as being hijacked by others. The only difference between so-called liberal and Islamist women is in their identification of the roots of the problem, namely the culprits in their marginalisation, and the solutions they propose to resolve it. Liberal women complain about strict Wahhabi rulings while Islamist women blame tribalism, which corrupts an allegedly pure Islam sympathetic to women's emancipation. It is common among liberal women to criticise *fatwas* and religious scholars when they issue them to maintain the exclusion of women. Islamist women are more inclined to blame society's backwardness, which allegedly corrupts a proper understanding and application of Islam. Yet it is possible to come across a third group of women writers who defend Wahhabi *fatwas* on, for example, the guardianship system, sex segregation, and the ban on driving. However, they all look for the state to resolve their inequality in a society that has so far denied them basic rights. The state as provider and arbitrator is cherished, and it continues to be expected to resolve complex issues contributing to the persistent gender inequality considered to be one of the most severe in the Muslim world.

## ACADEMIC WORK ON SAUDI WOMEN

A persistent problem facing researchers is the limited historical knowledge about and current research on Saudi women. Most of the academic literature on the country has focused on history, politics, oil, security, and Islamism. Compared to other Muslim women, who have been the subject of much serious academic research in history and the social sciences, Saudi women's gender issues remain the least studied. A previous generation of male scholars researching Saudi issues benefited from access to other men, and would have found it difficult to reach women in a sex-segregated society for the purpose of research. However, since the 1980s, a handful of Saudi, Arab, and Western scholars have published a number of outstanding contributions.

Soraya Altorki must be considered the first Saudi anthropologist to have written a full monograph on elite Hijazi women.[50] That was

---

[50] Soraya Altorki, *Women in Saudi Arabia: Ideology and Behavior among the Elite*, New York: Columbia University Press, 1986.

followed by exploration of women and development in Unayza in central
Arabia.[51] More recently, she mapped the historical, social, and economic
transformation of Jeddah, one of the most heterogeneous cities in the
country.[52] Her research was the starting point that encouraged scholars
to explore gender issues in the country. Libyan scholar Sadeka Arebi published a pioneering anthropological monograph on Saudi women writers.
Her access to Saudi Arabia was limited, but she succeeded in analysing the
literary production of the first generation of Saudi women writers.[53] Several chapters in this book follow her pioneering work and trace the most
recent literary orientation of a young generation of Saudi women writers.
Eleanor Doumato investigated the historical exclusion of women from
sacred precincts under the influence of Wahhabism.[54] She highlighted
how the exclusion of women is a form of monarchical legitimacy used by
the state to enforce its piety.[55] She also explored the long-standing polarity
in Saudi society between women as breadwinners and as domestic icons.[56]
*A Most Masculine State* draws on her earlier pioneering work on power
and gender and moves on to the recent changing relationship between
women and state. More recently, Mai Yamani investigated aspects of
women's lives and identities, focusing mainly on Hijazi women.[57] Benefiting from greater accessibility to the country after 9/11, Amelie Le Renard
explored young women's strategies and sociability in the urban centres
of Riyadh.[58] There are also several unpublished Ph.D. dissertations on
Saudi women, written mostly by Saudi women students.[59] In addition,
international reports on women and policy-oriented research focus on

---

[51] Soraya Altorki and Donald Cole, *Arabian Oasis City: The Transformation of Unayzah*,
Austin: University of Texas Press, 1989.
[52] Soraya Altorki and Abu Bakr Bagader, *Jeddah: um al-rakha wa al-shida* [Jeddah: A City
of Affluence and Hardship], Cairo: Dar al-Shorouq, 2006.
[53] Sadeka Arebi, *Women and Words in Saudi Arabia: The Politics of Literary Discourse*,
New York: Columbia University Press, 1994.
[54] Eleanor Abdella Doumato, *Getting God's Ear: Women, Islam and Healing in Saudi
Arabia and the Gulf*, New York: Columbia University Press, 2000.
[55] Eleanor Abdella Doumato, 'Gender, Monarchy and National Identity in Saudi Arabia',
*British Journal of Middle Eastern Studies*, 19, 1 (1992), pp. 31–47.
[56] Eleanor Abdella Doumato, 'Women in Saudi Arabia: Between Breadwinner and
Domestic Icon?', in Joseph and Slyomovics (eds.), *Women and Power*, pp. 166–75.
[57] Mai Yamani, *Changed Identities: The Challenge of New Identities in Saudi Arabia*,
London: Royal Institute of International Affairs, 2000, and 'Saudi Youth: The Illusion
of Transnational Freedom', *Contemporary Arab Affairs*, 3, 1 (2010), pp. 7–20.
[58] Amelie Le Renard, *Femmes et espaces publics en Arabia Saoudite*, Paris: Dalloz, 2011.
[59] For a comprehensive list of Saudi Ph.D. dissertations, see Kingdom of Saudi Arabia,
Ministry of Higher Education Saudi Arabian Cultural Mission to the USA, *Directory of
Doctoral Dissertations of Saudi Graduates from US Universities, 1964–2005*, 2006.

education and women in professional roles as teachers, doctors, and businesswomen.[60] Human rights organisations such as Human Rights Watch and Amnesty International regularly report on Saudi women's exclusion, in addition to highlighting the plight of immigrant women domestic workers in the country.

Despite this growing literature, the Saudi 'woman question'[61] has not attracted sufficient academic attention due to difficulty accessing the country, which is only gradually being opened up for academic research. Gender remains an unexplored terrain that could benefit from further investigation. With the exception of Doumato's short article on women and legitimacy, previous research on Saudi women did not directly deal with the role of the state and religious nationalism as frameworks for exploring the persistent gender discrimination in Saudi Arabia. It is hoped that this book will fill a gap in understanding the intimate relationship between gender, politics, religion, and the state. Weaving a gender narrative with politics and religion provides a framework for future research on specific aspects of women's lives.

METHODOLOGY

The methodology adopted in this book is grounded in tracing the historical trajectory of the state, its gender initiatives, and the responses of both men and women to urgent questions about women and their place in society. Official statements, women's literary discourses, religious treatises, and men's opinions on women and gender relations provide ample

---

[60] On education, see Roula Baki, 'Gender-Segregated Education in Saudi Arabia: Its Impact on Social Norms and the Saudi Labour Market', *Education Policy Analysis Archives*, 12, 28 (2004) (electronic journal). On Saudi women doctors, see Dalal al-Tamimi, 'Saudi Women in Academic Medicine: Are They Succeeding?', Department of Pathology, College of Medicine, King Faisal University, 2004 (electronic publication). On women and the media, see Naomi Sakr, 'Women and Media in Saudi Arabia: Rhetoric, Reductionism and Realities', *British Journal of Middle Eastern Studies*, 35, 1 (2008), pp. 385–404. Women entrepreneurs are discussed in Dorothy Minkus-McKenna, 'Women Entrepreneurs in Riyadh, Saudi Arabia', UMUC Working Papers Series, no. 2009-002, University of Maryland University College. On general Saudi women's rights, see Eleanor Abdella Doumato, 'Saudi Arabia', in Sameera Nazir and Leigh Tomppert (eds.), *Women's Rights in the Middle East and North Africa: Citizenship and Justice*, Freedom House, New York: Rowman & Littlefield, 2005, pp. 257–74. For a general perspective on women in Saudi Arabia, see Mona Almunajjed, *Women in Saudi Arabia Today*, New York: Palgrave, 1997. On polygamy and law, see Maha Yamani, *Polygamy and Law in Contemporary Saudi Arabia*, Reading: Ithaca Press, 2008.

[61] See Ryan, 'The Woman Question'.

sources to be read as a window through which debating gender can be documented and analysed.

I rely heavily on women's literature as a way to capture Saudi women's voices in the absence of real and visible mobilisation or developed civil society. Until recently, Saudi women expressed their aspirations in writing to communicate their dreams and needs, especially when they were denied visibility in the public sphere as agents and prevented from organising themselves in independent civil society organisations. A number of interviews with Saudi women writers and professionals supplement the textual sources. This has become easier with the increasing opportunities for travel and communication. I have met Saudi women at book fairs in Beirut and conferences around the world where opportunities for interviews became possible. I spent hours communicating with women students, activists, bloggers, and novelists. The growing number of Saudi women studying in Britain made it easier to establish contacts and pursue women's aspirations. Many Saudi women students visited me at King's College, London, and shared their thoughts with me. Many students were themselves preparing Ph.D. dissertations on women in various regions in Saudi Arabia.

New communication technology such as email, Skype, Facebook, and Twitter facilitated long encounters and exchanges in which women's voices found their way to the pages of this book.[62] Some interviews are acknowledged in the notes, but other voices remain anonymous. Furthermore, I have followed a plethora of Saudi women in blogs and Internet campaign pages. These new spaces became increasingly important with the Arab Spring of 2011, in which mass protest movements swept the Arab world and led to the overthrow of several Arab presidents. The revolt was driven by profound economic and political grievances against authoritarian and corrupt regimes. Saudi women found inspiration in this Arab revolt and contributed their own thoughts about their status in a country that remains the least open to women. I followed their electronic campaigns to drive, participate in elections, and to press for the release of their male relatives held without trial by Saudi security services for long periods. I received emails and petitions from women activists eager for their voices to reach a wider audience. I also became the recipient of long letters, attached to emails that women sent me to expose their plight.

---

[62] The study of women Internet users has just begun to attract academic attention. On Saudi women, see Touria Khannous, 'Virtual Gender: Moroccan and Saudi Women's Cyberspace', *HAWWA*, 8 (2011), pp. 358–87.

One woman familiarised me with her tragic story as a successful businesswoman, caught between various state security agencies, which led to her demise as a woman and an entrepreneur. Many women contacted me with a view to seeking asylum in other countries. From wives of important royalty to ordinary young women, I tried to help without getting too involved in the courses of action they sought to pursue. On many occasions, we exchanged information in the cafes of London, where I listened to an outpouring of grievances and injustices. For reasons of confidentiality, I will never be in a position to publicise these cases, although they remain important narratives informing my analysis in this book. Of course, I have not drawn on all the stories that I came to know of over many months. Some of these stories are too sensitive to publish; others cannot be verified. I selected a sample of these data while remaining faithful to an ethical approach in which storytellers cannot be identified. I also participated in media programmes with Saudi women in which we debated reforms and highlighted the restrictions on women in general. I corresponded with many others during which they informed me of their aspirations. Without asking, many Saudi women activists put me on their mailing lists, bringing a wealth of information that cannot all be incorporated in this study. I tried to balance my textual sources with insights I personally received from women of various orientations. It has become common to refer to women as divided between those who seek liberal reform and those who cling to an Islamist agenda. I have used these labels but with caution.

In my conversations and analysis of women's texts, I found that labels such as liberal and Islamist do not reflect common grievances shared by all women. They all demand greater recognition, services, legal change, and opportunities, but they may differ in their identification of the causes of their subordination and the solutions they seek. They all experience the limitations of their Saudi context. They all demand that state and society recognise them as individuals excluded from decision making and wide economic opportunities. I found class divisions more relevant to understanding women than simple ideological schisms. Wealthy Westernised elite women enjoy far more freedoms than young marginalised divorcees and mothers, many abandoned by absentee husbands. Equally, so-called Islamist women are often privileged, especially the small minority that is connected through kinship to important religious figures in the country. In general, I found that all categories of women have reached that critical stage whereby a feminist consciousness is slowly but steadily developing, regardless of their ideological orientation or class position. While this

consciousness has not yet been contained in women's civil society organisations, it has in effect bypassed this stage by seeking the Internet and
new communication technology to form pressure groups campaigning for
specific rights. Saudi women are now vocal, articulating their grievances
in ways that their mothers were not in a position to pursue. They are also
active in publicising their plight, reaching out to local and international
media, and pushing for change. This book engages with women's texts
and voices in ways that highlight this new development that has taken
place over a very short period of time.

THE BOOK

Having identified the Saudi state as an important player in gender relations, this book proceeds towards an understanding of state policies and
women's responses. It relies on a plethora of official discourses and documents and women's articulation of their vision. The historical legacy
of Wahhabism as religious nationalism determining the incorporation
of women in the grand political project is discussed in the first chapter
to set the historical context in which women were singled out as symbols that could make or break the pious nation. This historical legacy
continues to determine gender policies and hinder greater flexibility on
gender questions. Religious nationalism aspired to homogenise society
through applying strict rules ensuring that women remain invisible. Their
invisibility was important to draw the line between the pious nation and
others. The Saudi state project depended on the exemplary behaviour
of certain women, who made the project a viable unifying force in a
fragmented country. From the eighteenth century onward, Wahhabi religious nationalism aspired to create an ideology of order in which women
became boundary markers representing the authenticity of the nation. But
this ideology needed institutions in which it could be embedded. Hence,
Chapter 2 examines the first initiative to educate girls in a society where
formal education had been absent or rudimentary. The controversies surrounding this new initiative in the divided 1960s society were fierce, with
the state arbitrating between those who supported mass schooling for
girls and those who resisted it. In the 1960s, the state remained faithful
to religious nationalism, but it also wanted to enforce its modernity at a
time when Arab post-colonial states took it upon themselves to modernise society and increase women's education. The progressive role of the
state as a benevolent educator is still invoked today as an indication of
its centrality as arbiter and provider. The state entrusted the education of

girls to religious scholars, a concessionary move that enabled it to overcome opposition at the time. The state assured its religious scholars that education was not meant to challenge traditional gender expectations but to confirm women in their role as good mothers who could educate their children in piety and respect for Islamic tradition. Supporters of girls' education argued that it is in the interest of Saudi men to have educated wives in order to limit the increasing possibility of men seeking educated partners from elsewhere in the Arab world. The increasing education of men leads them to prefer well-educated women at the expense of Saudi women, according to campaigners in favour of girls' education. Therefore, the national interest of men and the preservation of the religious purity of Saudi Arabia undermined the emancipatory power of education.

Education generated many paradoxes and controversies and much opposition, but it remained central to the state's narrative about its modernity. Without serious expansion of employment for women, the early generation of educated women realised that education was no guarantee of greater inclusion. The image of an idle, educated woman, immersed in consumption and freed from the burdens of domesticity brought about by the first oil boom of the 1970s, contributed to delaying women assuming greater roles in society. But this education created the nucleus that would several decades later emerge to articulate its own vision and aspirations.

With education, many Saudi women felt empowered. But in the 1980s, the state reversed its early enthusiasm for women's emancipation and returned to honouring strict religious interpretations. Chapter 3 explores the many religious opinions that aspired to return women to confinement and restrict their movement, marriage choices, education abroad, and employment. The state crushed the Mecca Mosque uprising of 1979 but endorsed the demands of the rebels, mostly centred on the excessive openness of Saudi society and its alleged corruption by Western influences. Excessive and restrictive religious opinions provided the *ulama* with opportunities to voice their increasing frustration and marginalisation in determining state policy. Women became the arena of conflict, and multiple actors fought battles to control their choices. From marriage and dress to fitness and travel, women found that no aspect of their private and public lives remained outside the expertise of religious scholars and the enforcement agencies of the state. The *ulama* appealed to the state to enforce their opinions, and the state honoured their wishes. It prohibited women from travelling without chaperones, seeking marriage with outsiders, and being promoted to public office. The 1980s became a setback that many women lamented. It showed how the gender gap in

Saudi Arabia is subject to fluctuation as a result of state interventions, mostly in the service of grand political projects.

State restrictions on women began to be loosened with the increasing pressure put on the state after 9/11. The state wanted to draw in women to support it against the rising tide of religious radicalisation. Women became the soft face with which the state launched its charm offensive against critical international condemnation of Saudi society and religion. The masculine state needed women to dispel negative images of the country associated with Jihadi terrorism abroad and inside the country. 'Women of the state' became important as defenders of the realm and proof of its modernity against stereotypical images circulating in the international media about Saudi women. Women were expected to demystify Saudi society by projecting a modern and enlightened face. Saudi media excelled in highlighting the gender gap and praising exceptional women achievers while also highlighting the plight of female victims of society and its strict religious codes and social norms. It was a state decision to grant women greater visibility and expand their employment and education opportunities. Chapter 4 documents state gender initiatives that coincided with an international terrorism crisis. The cosmopolitan woman became a desired feature of Saudi society, celebrated by the state, official media, and women themselves.

Having benefited from state education, women began to contribute their own voices through fiction. Chapter 5 explores the new generation of women *muthaqafat*, intellectual novelists waging 'war' against their own society and its many restrictions. Unlike their mothers, this generation is more confrontational in demanding a serious change in their position as women. Literature became a safe haven to explore extreme restrictions, marginalisation, and subordination. With great restrictions on women's civil society, Saudi women's voices migrated to fictive spaces in order to register their aspirations. Through a sociological reading of selected novels, and interviews with a number of novelists, the chapter explores how Saudi women's modernity is demonstrated in highlighting themes that deconstruct local tradition and document contradictions and bewilderment. Their novels capture the struggle between men and women and among women themselves. In this literature, the state remains immune, with only sporadic allusions to its role in perpetuating marginalisation, a reflection of the authoritarian nature of a state that does not tolerate direct criticism. Novels became charters inviting society to reconsider the persistent restrictions imposed on women, who are still held back from making a great contribution to society.

The literary productions of an even younger generation of novelists are explored in Chapter 6. The new women celebrity novelists became icons of cosmopolitanism, undermining images of Saudi women as confined and marginalised members of society. Their adventures, desires, and bodies are central themes in this new literature. These novelists aim to unveil women and their desires. Explicit sexual desires and acts, flirtation, and even homosexuality are discussed under the guise of fictional dramas. The collusion between religious nationalism and cosmopolitan modernity is dramatised to dismiss the image of Saudi society as a pious, homogeneous nation. This daring literature unsurprisingly became controversial, and many critics condemned it as sensational and confrontational, tarnishing the reputation of the nation and its pride. A sense of liberation is emphasized in these novels, but they seem to reflect Saudi women's immersion in a neoliberal economy of desires, consumption, and adventure. The increasing immersion of the country in consumption patterns fosters a new sense of a fetishised sexuality that is documented in many novels, written by cosmopolitan women. While there is a serious quest for emancipation in these novels, there is equally a tendency to assert a fantasy, anchored in the reality of a consumerist society, drawn into economic liberalisation. We must resist considering this new genre of Saudi women's literature as 'heroic resistance'. These novels appeared at an important historical moment characterised by a restructuring of Saudi society and its increasing incorporation in a global world economy, in which women become cosmopolitan icons, a barometer for society's modernity and hybridity. The Saudi state took the lead in this restructuring, and women followed with their own words.

The same mass education and economic liberalisation that allowed this cosmopolitanism to emerge also led to the appearance of a counter-trend among women, namely the new religious women. Their vision is discussed in Chapter 7. Unlike a previous generation of pious women, the new preachers and religiously committed women propose widespread state intervention to limit the alleged deterioration of Saudi society into more Westernisation and consumerism. They express themselves in regular columns in newspapers and on the Internet to push for a different interpretation of the threats that undermine their security as women. The *multazimat*, religiously committed women, are an urban phenomenon in which women struggle to limit the impact of the structural economic and social changes experienced over the last decades. They assert the superiority of the Islamic tradition and its historical cosmopolitanism, universalism, and tolerance. They remain powerful voices appealing to history, tradition, and religion to restore the authenticity of the country and its religious identity. Like liberal women they call upon the state to intervene in their favour. It must be stressed here that division between liberal and Islamist women is not unique to Saudi Arabia, but is also common in other countries from Morocco and Egypt to Turkey and Iran.

To write about gender in my own country may appear to be an attempt to join a plethora of polarised opinions and commentaries that dominate discourses about Saudi women. Writing this book, it seemed that I had two choices: either to confirm women's victimhood or to challenge what is often regarded as stereotypical images of submissive Saudi women. My intention is neither to lament the victimhood of Saudi women nor to celebrate their exceptional achievements. Now that we have so many Saudi feminine voices, texts, and sources, writing this book became an urgent project to capture this diversity and explore how women themselves articulate their dreams and visions while not ignoring the political context in which they live. Women's voices are the beginning of a process whereby women constitute themselves as individuals, the right path on the road to claiming denied rights.

I

# From Religious Revival to Religious Nationalism

> The Wahhabi movement was a classic example of going to see what people were doing and telling them to stop it.
>
> Michael Cook[1]

The contemporary status of women in Saudi Arabia is shaped by the historical legacy of Wahhabiyya and its transformation into a religious nationalist movement under the banner of the Saudi state. This transformation had an important impact on gender after the movement became not only state religion but also state nationalism. Under the auspices of the state, Wahhabiyya transformed personal piety into a public project, the objective of which was to create a moral community under the authority of a political centre. The personal and the public combined to foster the piety of the state. The state was able to manipulate public Islam, enforced by Wahhabi teachings and scholars, to create a legitimacy and a rationale for the foundation of a pious nation. But historically, the contemporary state oscillated between demonstrating piety and Islamic authenticity on the one hand and modernity, reform, and progress on the other. With the changing and evolving political agenda of the state, we find that the religious element, mainly the Wahhabi historical legacy, was co-opted by a state acting in response to evolving political contexts and agendas of changing historical periods.

[1] Michael Cook, *Commanding Right and Forbidding Wrong in Islamic Thought*, Cambridge: Cambridge University Press, 2000, p. 166.

When Wahhabiyya emerged in the eighteenth century, it was a religious revivalist movement sharing in character and orientation many similarities with its contemporaries in the Muslim world.[2] As such, its teachings centred on the cleansing of faith from impurities and a return to authentic Islam. Central to this project was the status and rights of women, their piety and ritual practices. While men's religious practices and piety were crucial for the revival of true Islam, women were nevertheless seen as important pillars for the return to an authentic religious tradition among a stable, settled community.

This chapter explores the relationship between religious revival and the formation of the early Saudi state in the eighteenth century. Central to this relationship were the gender perceptions of urban religious scholars, who aspired towards universalising them and imposing them on the whole of Arabia with the assistance of a political leadership. The transformation of Wahhabiyya from religious revival to religious nationalism in the twentieth century is examined to understand the relationship between gender, religion, and politics in contemporary Saudi Arabia. The modern state of 1932 institutionalised perceptions of gender that sprang up among a narrow religious community in southern Najd. In the absence of a Saudi anti-colonial or secular nationalist movement, Wahhabiyya moved from revival to become a national religious movement, by virtue of its universalistic and homogenising rhetoric. This rhetoric aspired to obliterate local tradition in favour of an overarching universal Muslim ideal. In the twentieth century, Wahhabiyya developed into religious nationalism in which the exclusion of women was a visible sign, marking the boundaries of the pious nation and defining its unity in the absence of Saudi or anti-colonial nationalism.

THE HISTORICAL LEGACY: RELIGIOUS REVIVAL AND GENDER

Wahhabi revival in general, and its position on gender relations and the rights of women in particular, has split the academic community between those who see in its teachings a real potential for the emancipation of Arabian women from the restrictions of tribal society and those who regard its teachings as laying the foundation for later discrimination and disempowerment. Based on the interpretation of Muhammad ibn Abd al-Wahhab's body of writings, Natana Delong-Bas belongs to the first

---

[2] For eighteenth-century Islamic revivalism, see Bruce Lawrence, *Shattering the Myth: Islam Beyond Violence*, Princeton: Princeton University Press, 1998.

camp as she asserts that 'Ibn Abd al-Wahhab's construction of gender was not one that displayed misogyny or sought to render women as second class or invisible citizens. Ibn Abd al-Wahhab's interactions with women reflected concern for social justice. He saw them as human beings capable of serving as positive, active agents in both the private and public realms'.[3] Arguing from a religious studies perspective, her reading of Ibn Abd al-Wahhab's main religious treatises leads her to conclude that he was an emancipator of women in a society that suffered from misogyny and serious discrimination against women. His regulation of marriage, divorce, and inheritance could only be seen within his general intention to reform Arabian religious practices, emancipate women, and protect them against degrading cultural practices. Muhammad ibn Abd al-Wahhab's firm views on punishing transgression such as fornication are seen as inserting a legal framework for the protection of women under *sharia*. Misogyny, according to this reading of the Wahhabi original sources, is attributed to patriarchy and local custom rather than Wahhabi teachings.[4] This conclusion is today the foundation of Islamist feminism in contemporary Saudi Arabia, a theme that I will discuss later in this book. In this reading of the historical legacy of Wahhabiyya, Ibn Abd al-Wahhab placed greater power in the hands of women than was typically the case for other jurists.[5] The founder of Wahhabiyya becomes an advocate of 'the empowerment of women through support of awareness and enforcement of their rights'.[6]

These conclusions must be interpreted in the context of 9/11 and the attempt of some academics to absolve Wahhabi teachings from responsibility for many issues relating to gender discrimination and radicalism. While Delong Bas has adopted a positive reading of Wahhabi texts, the Egyptian theologian Khaled Abou El-Fadl offered a counterview grounded in legalistic terms that attributes the decline in the status of Muslim women to Wahhabi interpretations, the triumph of authoritarian discourse, and the decline of the juristic tradition.[7] By analysing Wahhabi *responsa* on women, Abou El-Fadl documents how the interpretive authoritarianism that underlines Saudi religious opinions has

---

3 Natana Delong-Bas, *Wahhabi Islam: From Revival and Reform to Global Jihad*, London: I. B. Tauris, 2004, p. 124.
4 Delong-Bas, *Wahhabi Islam*, p. 125.
5 Delong Bas, *Wahhabi Islam*, p. 125.
6 Delong Bas, *Wahhabi Islam*, p. 125.
7 Khaled Abou El-Fadl, *Speaking in God's Name: Islamic Law, Authority and Women*, Oxford: Oneworld, 2001, pp. 170–208.

become dominant, thus leading to *fatwa*s on the prohibition of wearing high heels, visiting graves, travelling without a guardian, clapping the hands, and the seduction of women's voices.[8]

While Wahhabiyya continues to split religious studies specialists, the historian Eleanor Doumato, adopting an anthropological interpretive perspective, highlights the negative experience of women under Wahhabi teachings. She argues that 'in asserting their own brand of orthodoxy, the Wahhabis denigrated techniques of personal and spiritual empowerment in contradiction to orthodox standards that were available to women and condemned communal rituals that appealed to women's needs'.[9] She argues that the expansion of Wahhabi teachings led to the erosion of social and religious spheres in which women were prominent, most notably in healing rituals. The Wahhabi *ulama* replaced women as healers when they endowed the religious word with the power of healing, thus contributing to the shrinking of women's religious ritual space across the Arabian Peninsula. Further than that, the Wahhabi religious scholars instigated an atmosphere of suspicion and hostility towards women who sought an alternative ritual space to help with issues related to fertility, love, and marriage. The strict condemnation of women's witchcraft, sorcery, and exorcism rituals, allegedly so common in Arabia at the time, created the foundation for marginalising women even in areas where they had for centuries maintained a certain power and monopoly. Religious men, who claimed authority on the basis of their knowledge of the religious tradition, eventually replaced women even in those social spheres where they had previously enjoyed considerable influence.

It is not the intention here to resolve the contradictory readings of the Wahhabi legacy, but to examine the relationship between religious revival and the project of state formation, first in the eighteenth century and later in the twentieth, while highlighting the centrality of gender constructions in both periods. There is no doubt that the early eighteenth-century Wahhabi religious revival was entangled from the very beginning with the project of enforcing Islamic law, a substantial part of which involved its application to issues relevant to women. More importantly, Wahhabiyya was from the very beginning a project entangled with enforcing the doctrine of commanding right and forbidding wrong. It is this doctrine and its transformation under the auspices of the state that is most important for

[8] Abou El-Fadl, *Speaking in God's Name*, p. 177.
[9] Eleanor Abdella Doumato, *Getting God's Ear: Women, Islam and Healing in Saudi Arabia and the Gulf*, New York: Columbia University Press, 2000, p. 40.

understanding the historical subordination of women and their persistent exclusion from the public sphere in Saudi Arabia. The early experience of Muhammad ibn Abd al-Wahhab, first in al-Uyayna and later in Deriyya, illustrates the centrality of women in his religious revival project.

The Saudi Wahhabi state of the eighteenth century was born out of an act against a woman who committed adultery and received the corresponding Islamic punishment: death by public stoning. Various chronicles tracing the religious career of Muhammad ibn Abd al-Wahhab celebrate several acts that distinguished him from his contemporaries among the *ulama*. He is known to have punished men who did not attend the communal Friday prayers, visited tombs of holy men, asked for their intercession, and revered charlatans posing as pious saints. He cut down holy trees and destroyed shrines revered by the population of Arabia. He set himself the task of applying the *sharia* in matters related to inheritance, *zakat* (alms-tax), marriage, and commercial transactions. He sought to purify the land from signs of blasphemy and debauchery. Local chiefs and rulers tolerated him as long as he did not encroach on their political authority. None saw him as a serious threat until he committed an act that led to his expulsion from a small town in central Arabia.

The stoning of a *zaniya* (an adulteress) in al-Uyayna was the ultimate act intended to purify the community and eradicate fornication. We are told the story and circumstances of the shaykh's expulsion from al-Uyayna:

The shaykh remained in al-Uyayna commanding good and prohibiting evil. He taught people religion and purified their faith from innovations. He administered punishment and asked the ruler to enforce *hudud* [legal rulings]. An adulteress came to him and admitted her sin. She repeated her confessions four times. He asked whether she was in control of her mental abilities. She told him that she was not mentally deranged. He gave her several days to reconsider her confession. She remained defiant. The shaykh gave orders to stone her in public, fully clothed. The ruler of Uyayna, together with a crowd of Muslim men, went out to stone her. When she died, the shaykh ordered that her body be washed and prepared for burial. He asked Muslims to pray at her funeral... People of bad faith were horrified, and started alerting the ruler of Hasa, Sulayman al-Muhammad of the Bani Khalid tribe, to the danger the shaykh represented. He exerted pressure on the chief of Uyayna to expel the shaykh. The shaykh left for Deriyya, where he was received by Abdullah al-Suwaylim and his brother Ahmad, both were receptive to his call.[10]

---

[10] Hussein ibn Ghannam, *Tarikh Najd* [History of Najd], Cairo: Dar al-Shurouq, 1994, p. 86.

It seems that while Ibn Abd al-Wahhab was able to preach *tawhid* (the oneness of God) and destroy physical signs of blasphemy without provoking a harsh reaction, the sedentary Arabian population was agitated by the act of public stoning inflicted on a defiant woman. Perhaps the practice of adultery was so widespread that many, both women and men, feared the punishment. Expulsion deprived the Wahhabi preacher of a home and a network of followers. Ibn Abd al-Wahhab became stateless – to use contemporary parlance, a wandering pariah, *persona non grata*, vulnerable to abuse, theft, and murder. He must have realised after his expulsion that he could not continue to command right and prohibit wrong without a political authority to protect him. Expulsion was often imposed on those who breached the community's moral code or committed an abhorrent crime that endangered the whole group and subjected it to shame, retaliation, and revenge. Muhammad ibn Abd al-Wahhab was expelled because he stoned a stubborn and defiant woman who admitted her sin but failed to repent. In this particular case, he does not seem to have guaranteed the authorisation of the local ruler. His expulsion followed a personal initiative, policing the settlement and enforcing law without the consent of the political authority of the town. He was acting according to the principle of forbidding wrong but without political sanction.

After his expulsion, Ibn Abd al-Wahhab travelled in search of a political authority, in the process transforming his early individualistic approach to *dawa* (call) and preaching into a state project. He sought refuge in the neighbouring town of Deriyya, where news of his preaching gained him popularity. His full integration and admission into Deriyya society was dependent on female sympathy and good will. He was expelled from al-Uyayna because of a woman, but was welcomed in another community thanks to the effort of another woman. Although his hosts were all men, the shaykh's message initially reached the women in his host's household. A woman transmitted the news of 'true' Islam to her friend, the wife of the ruler of Deriyya, Muhammad ibn Saud. It is through this female network, the chronicles assert,[11] that Ibn Abd al-Wahhab was introduced to the ruler of Deriyya who took him under his wing.

The foundation of the first Saudi–Wahhabi state was thus laid down thanks to the efforts of women who appreciated his preaching and approached their husbands with a view to extending a welcome to the

[11] Ibn Ghannam, *Tarikh*, p. 86.

shaykh. The women of Deriyya were perhaps pleased with the news of the punishment of adultery, and might have been more than happy to see the *hudud* inflicted on those women who led their husbands astray, deprived them of security in marriage, and undermined their pure genealogy. The details of the shaykh's reception in Deriyya and the subsequent establishment of the state are well known.[12]

What concerns us here is how the chroniclers of the first Saudi–Wahhabi state emphasised the centrality of the two female characters, the al-Uyayna adulteress and the Deriyya pious sympathiser. Even in the present day, the historical narrative of the state reiterates and fixes these contrasting female images in the historical memory of the people. Saudi history books invoke the centrality of rejecting immoral women and celebrating their pious opposites.[13] From classroom teaching material to advanced historical manuscripts, the population is reminded of the two women: one threatened the Islamic state; the other made it possible as a project. The two women are binary opposites, each contributing in her own way to the political project of establishing a pious and authentic Muslim state. Such a state is not only concerned with spreading *tawhid* and fighting blasphemy, but is above all an entity that engages in the construction of gender roles, establishing a clear separation between those women who pose a threat to community harmony and piety and those who contribute to promoting morality and piety. The adulteress and the sympathiser have remained constant and recurrent images in Saudi history until the present day. Both women's transgression from the rules of the moral community and their endorsement of these rules make or break the political community. Fear of women's power is not unique to Wahhabi religious revivalism, as it dominates perceptions of the female subject in almost all religious traditions. But what is perhaps unique about the Saudi context is the fact that this fear has shaped state policy. One important dimension of the Wahhabi religious revival that is relevant to understanding later state policy on gender was the doctrine of *amr bil maruf wa al-nahy an al-munkar* (commanding right and forbidding wrong). While commanding right seems straightforward, the second doctrine, related to forbidding wrong, bears great influence on how women are perceived, articulated, and controlled.

---

[12] Madawi Al-Rasheed, *A History of Saudi Arabia*, Cambridge: Cambridge University Press, 2002, 2nd edn, 2010.

[13] For a discussion of Saudi history textbooks, see Madawi Al-Rasheed, 'Political Legitimacy and the Production of History: The Case of Saudi Arabia', in Lenore Martin (ed.), *New Frontiers in Middle East Security*, New York: St Martin's Press, 1999, pp. 25–46.

The Saudi polity of the eighteenth century reflected the concerns and interests of a sedentary society that was plagued by internal dissent and fragmentation. The polity was perceived as an alternative to the nomadic tribal organisation that encircled it. While much has been written on Ibn Abd al-Wahhab's endorsement of the doctrine of forbidding wrong, the main authority on the subject remains Michael Cook, who doubts whether the doctrine was a prominent theme in Ibn Abd al-Wahhab's early mission.[14] According to Cook, Ibn Abd al-Wahhab's references to the duty do not suggest any particular urgency or centrality in his conception of his mission. In one letter, Ibn Abd al-Wahhab stated that the duty to forbid wrong should be performed 'nicely and in private, and not in such a manner as to give rise to schism in the community'. He added that 'if the offender is a ruler (*amir*), it would seem that he should not be reproved in public at all'.[15] This position seems to be a reflection of the movement's early reluctance to create dissent if the doctrine was to be applied rigorously among a hesitant and apprehensive population, especially after the stoning of the adulteress in al-Uyayna and Ibn Abd al-Wahhab's expulsion afterwards. He may have feared that the doctrine would be applied against his mission and those who supported it, namely the Al-Saud rulers of Deriyya. His early rejection and eventual expulsion following the forbidding of wrong committed by an adulteress may have moderated his early enthusiasm.

It seems that the doctrine of forbidding wrong became central during the nineteenth century at a precarious moment for the Wahhabi revival when the Al-Saud ruler Turki ibn Abdullah (1823–34) emphasised its importance and later Wahhabi scholars provided the religious justification for it, thus turning it into *rukn*, a pillar of Islam. This reflected the weakness of the second Saudi state following the Egyptian invasion in 1818.[16] The weakness was translated into more vigorous attempts to enforce the duty and make it incumbent on every member of the community. This was the beginning of a process that Cook calls 'officialisation' of forbidding wrong whereby the ruler is under an obligation to send officials to faraway communities to ensure that forbidding wrong is respected and supported. This reflected the quest of the weak nineteenth-century state to monitor communities under the guise of religious purity and conformity at a time when no real power was exercised over them.

---

[14] Cook, *Commanding Right*, p. 169.
[15] Cook, *Commanding Right*, p. 170.
[16] Cook, *Commanding Right*, p. 179.

Turki ordered his emissaries to inspect people who gathered together to smoke tobacco and keep count of those who did not turn up for communal prayers, thus penetrating society at a time when he was not in a position to impose his authority or engage in expansionist wars under heavy Ottoman Egyptian surveillance of central Arabia. Consequently, as the restrictions on *jihad* against polytheism were in place after the Egyptian invasion of Arabia in 1818, the nineteenth-century state had to turn its righteousness inward.[17] This was a strategy to gain legitimacy at a time when warfare against religious innovators could not be carried out.

## WOMEN OF OASES, WOMEN OF DESERTS

Wahhabi concern with gender in the eighteenth and nineteenth centuries reflected the needs of the local towns and oases of southern Najd. In these settlements, religious scholars were mainly focused on applying the *sharia* in densely populated small towns.[18] They saw women as a threat to the internal integrity of the moral community. The pious women of such settlements where marriage, divorce, inheritance, and ritual practices were regulated not only provided signs of conformity but also accrued to the *ulama* who administered the *sharia* a regular income. Wahhabi scholars could not tolerate oasis women who stood outside mosques, collecting the saliva of pious men after prayer, which they used to heal the sick, a tradition that was still observed outside the mosques of Riyadh in the early twentieth century. The *ulama* condemned these women and eliminated their participation in the traditional healing rituals of the settlements, which were later appropriated by pious men, thus excluding women and paving the way for the monopoly of men over traditional space that had been associated with women.[19] As such, the *ulama* began to limit women's participation in the social and folk religious spheres in which they had previously enjoyed a kind of influence. Their exclusion from mosques and social religiosity contributed to tightening control over them and marginalising them as actors in a society that restricted their presence in the public sphere in general.

[17] Cook, *Commanding Right*, p. 179.
[18] Awaidah al-Juhany, *Najd before the Salafi Reform Movement: Social, Political and Religious Conditions During the Three Centuries Preceding the Rise of the Saudi State*, Reading: Ithaca Press, 2002.
[19] Doumato, *Getting God's Ear*, p. 153.

This enforced exclusion of oasis women from traditional arenas of public social and religious interaction became generalised to other women, mainly those who belonged to tribal nomadic groups in the desert. Wahhabi denunciation of the unorthodox religious practices and laxity of oasis women finds an echo in their concern with the lack of religiosity among desert women. Tribal tradition among the Bedouin – for example *urfi* marriage, an old, unregistered marital union, exclusion from inheritance, and heterodox religious practices, such as sorcery, spirit possession rituals, magic, and folk practices of supplication in pursuit of healing, fertility, and marriage – were common among Bedouin women. These practices offered social contexts in which women, long excluded from the political community of men and public space, took control.[20] The alleged degeneration of women could be corrected through instruction and 'commanding good and forbidding wrong' practised by the many religious scholars in the oases, but Bedouin women had to be reached by emissaries whose role combined the occasional and seasonal collection of *zakat* (Islamic tax) and religious instruction. This irregular introduction to the teachings of Wahhabiyya could not be formalised and institutionalised until the early years of the twentieth century when Ibn Saud invented the *hujjar* settlements where Bedouin were forced to live in fixed camps to receive preachers, tax collectors, and subsidies from the royal purse. As Wahhabi preachers maintained their control over the religious practices of women in the oases and punished transgressors, they aspired to do the same among women in the desert where tribal organisation was the main cohesive framework of social, political, and economic relations within and between groups. Tribal Bedouin women, as much as their men, had to be urgently brought to the realm of Islam.

The Islamisation of the settlements of central Arabia via controlling their women had to be extended to the tribal hinterland where 'blasphemous' women were depicted as ignorant of their religion and immersed in un-Islamic practices that survived from the age of ignorance (*jahiliyya*). According to Wahhabi doctrine, such women had to be rescued not only from ignorance but also from the control of their own men. While in Najd the cultural boundaries between oases and desert were ill defined,[21] it was in the oases that salvation had to be sought for the simple reason that the *ulama* were residents of these settlements. Tribal custom that dealt with

[20]  Doumato, *Getting God's Ear*, p. 153.
[21]  Madawi Al-Rasheed, *Politics in an Arabian Oasis: The Rashidis of Saudi Arabia*, London: I. B. Tauris, 1991, pp. 125–32.

transgressing women, for example banishment or honour killing, had to be replaced by the application of *hudud*, Islamic prescribed punishment, thus replacing the tribal code with a religious one.

Wahhabi scholars aspired to take away from tribal men the right to deal with female transgression according to their own tribal honour codes and grant this right to a selected community of learned men whose authority derived from their knowledge and application of *sharia*. When Wahhabi *ulama* insisted on the ruling that women's voices were shameful (*awra*), thus reflecting the intermingling of several communities in the small settlements of Najd, this ruling was not an issue in Bedouin camps where lineages travelled and camped together and where strangers outside the lineage would not be seen except on odd occasions. Tribal women who encouraged their men before raids, composing songs and chanting them loudly, and contributed to the nomadic economy of herding, weaving, and trade with settlements, needed to be brought under the authority of the settlement scholars. Bedouin women's voices would have only been heard by their own chiefs, brothers, and extended lineage. Their forays into the space outside their tents to seek pasture, wood, and water had no equivalent among the sedentary women for whom movement outside their walled neighbourhoods within each town and oasis – especially the elite within each settlement – would be regarded as a dangerous appearance in a space controlled by men and where non-kin would intermingle in mosques, markets, and fields. Only women of humble origins and market traders would be seen in the markets of the oases, while none would have considered attending a mosque ceremony or prayer.[22] Oasis women of the learned religious families and the settlements' *amirs* were confined to their large houses, as can be glimpsed from the accounts of Lady Ann Blunt and Gertrude Bell,[23] the two Englishwomen who visited the oasis of Hail in the nineteenth and twentieth centuries respectively. While the two women travellers visited Hail at the height of its eminence, their description of elite women's lives was not uncommon in other oases of central Arabia, for example in Unayza, Burayda, and Riyadh. Elite oasis women took pride in the fact that they made just two journeys outside their abode – one to move to their husband's ancestral house upon

---

[22] Doumato, *Getting God's Ear*; Soraya Altorki and Donald Cole, *Arabian Oasis City: The Transformation of Unayzah*, Austin: University of Texas Press, 1989.

[23] Lady Ann Blunt, *A Pilgrimage to Nejd, the Cradle of the Arab Race: A Visit to the Court of the Arab Emir and 'our Persian Campaign'*, 2 vols, London: John Murray, 1881, repr. 1968; Gertrude Bell, 'A Journey in North Arabia', *Geographical Journal*, 44 (1914), pp. 76–7.

marriage and one to the grave. Their black cloaks (*abayas*) had to be long enough to erase their footprints on the sand, thus leaving no trace whatsoever of their ventures into public space. Where tribal women enjoyed greater freedom of movement within their group, their settled counterparts, especially those belonging to the upper classes of society, were not to be seen moving between houses unless fully covered and sometimes in the darkness of night. The confinement of elite women was an exception, as commoners and slave women continued to appear in markets and fields. The images that Gertrude Bell took in Hail in 1914 included pictures of veiled women promenading in the public market of the town. This was restricted to women traders, non-tribal women, and slaves. They all were totally covered in black *abayas*. Images of Bedouin women that Bell took during her journeys in Arabia in 1914 reflected greater flexibility, as the Bedouin women who posed in front of her camera sometimes had their faces exposed.[24]

Confinement to the house and within the boundaries of the space reserved for kinsmen, which became a requirement for urban women under Wahhabi rule, had no meaning or precedent among nomadic tribal communities. Many choirs in which Bedouin women performed could only perform outdoors. Herding, milking, and cooking are not activities that can be conducted in closed spaces. In addition to its impracticality, confinement was unnecessary, as such women remained within larger units governed by kinship and local honour codes. More importantly, tribal men and elderly women monitored their women's behaviour. Men were responsible for punishing those who violated their women's honour through raid, plunder, capture, or theft. Recent accounts of Bedouin women's lives confirm these cultural practices that pertain to honour, chastity, and tribal codes relating to sexuality, marriage, and fertility.[25]

The most dangerous situation that faced both nomadic and agricultural tribal women and their urban counterparts was the perishing of their men after raids or hazardous travel. Until the 1930s, raids were common between tribal groups, and between them and oasis dwellers, who were themselves a mixed tribal and non-tribal population, but the violation of women on such occasions was extremely rare in a society where the consequences were so grave. Revenge that was perpetuated for generations

[24] Madawi Al-Rasheed, *Hail: Gertrude Bell's Images of an Arabian Oasis*, 2006, available at http://www.madawialrasheed.org/index.php/site/C7/.

[25] Lila Abu-Lughod, *Veiled Sentiments: Honour and Poetry in a Bedouin Society*, Berkeley: University of California Press, 1988.

between raiding parties acted as a deterrent against the rape, kidnapping, or violation of free women.[26] While raiding parties felt free to cut down palm trees, steal camels, destroy agricultural fields, and damage wells and watering canals,[27] they hesitated before they inflicted any harm on women, even after defeating their menfolk. Abiding by this practice in the warfare of Arabia was cherished and respected, as no group wanted a violation of its women which would eventually lead to perpetual cycles of revenge.

Protecting the free women of a defeated group was expected from the victors, as it demonstrated manly qualities and honour. The worst that could happen to free women was the violation of their honour. Widowed women of defeated men occasionally found themselves incorporated in the victorious party's circles of women and wives. Many women suffered as a result of this eventuality after their men were killed in battle. This practice has survived in Saudi Arabia, and was elevated to a 'state strategy' enforced by the founder of the current state, Ibn Saud, who included among his wives many tribal and non-tribal daughters of his defeated enemies.[28] After the defeat of Faisal al-Duwaish, the rebellious Ikhwan Mutayr leader in 1927, Ibn Saud took his widow as a wife.[29] Such practices reflected a clear and obvious inclination to use marriage and women to integrate an imagined nation with the state, which was at the time represented in the persona of the king and his sons.

It is inaccurate to conclude that by virtue of their economic mode of production nomadic tribal women enjoyed a status more elevated than their counterparts in the oases of Najd. Freedom of movement for the former was possible not because these women were granted rights but because they travelled and lived with people of their own lineage in which relations were built on kinship, trust, and solidarity. Women were denied inheritance rights in communities where the common capital, mainly herds or agricultural land, could not be divided upon the death of a father, as this would threaten the survival of the whole group. Female marriages were dictated by the tradition of tribal endogamy in which women had

[26] On Arabian warfare, see Michael Meeker, *Literature and Violence in North Arabia*, Cambridge: Cambridge University Press, 1979.

[27] Othman ibn Bishr, *Unwan al-majd fi tarikh najd* [Glory in the history of Najd], 2 vols, Mecca: n.p., 1930; Ibn Ghannam, *Tarikh*.

[28] Al-Rasheed, *A History*, pp. 72–80.

[29] Joseph Kostiner, *The Making of Saudi Arabia 1916–1936*, Oxford: Oxford University Press, 1993; H. R. P. Dickson, *The Arab of the Desert: A Glimpse into Bedouin Life in Kuwait and Saudi Arabia*, London: George Allen & Unwin, 1951.

little choice or say in the matter.[30] This was the norm among tribal women and those who settled in oases. In addition to the Islamic *nikah* marriage, unregistered *urfi* marriages were common. Such marriages never died out and continue to be practised even after the establishment of the state and the availability of religious courts that register marriages in contemporary urban and rural Saudi Arabia.[31]

In contrast to women of the tribal periphery, oasis women lived in settlements whose populations consisted of diverse groups belonging to tribal, non-tribal populations, sojourners, and travellers. Early descriptions and maps of central Arabia's oases indicate that extended families and large lineages lived in walled neighbourhoods within each oasis.[32] The only space that was open to all was the local *amir*'s residence, the market, and the main Friday mosque, although some lineages had their own small mosques within their walled neighbourhoods, and some oases had several local lineage and family chiefs without one overarching leadership. Central Arabian oasis dwellers found in the Wahhabi body of literature on segregation and exclusion a solution to the proximity of communities in limited urban space and the intermingling of strangers in walled towns. The Wahhabi movement reflected the fears and agony of men in the oases where population density and diversity created conditions that required greater control of women. It is the fears of those oasis men that became generalised first among the nomadic tribal population of Najd and later among other inhabitants of other regions outside central Arabia, for example in Hasa, Asir, and the Hijaz.

Nomadic tribesmen initially could not conceive of giving up the duty of protecting their own women to strangers or, later, a state committee that commands right and forbids wrong. They themselves had a loose connection with regulated piety and ritual practices, or monitored personal conduct. They had little experience of the institutions of Islam, the mosque, the court, and the study circle. Most nomadic groups did not have a religious figure who would apply the *sharia* and engage in dispute settlement. If a man sought an Islamic legal opinion, he would have to travel to the nearest oasis where there was most likely to be a religious scholar or judge, a journey that a mere few made on special

[30] Germaine Tillion, *The Republic of Cousins: Women's Oppression in Mediterranean Society*, London: Saqi, 1983.
[31] Maha Yamani, *Polygamy and Law in Contemporary Saudi Arabia*, Reading: Ithaca Press, 2008, p. 101.
[32] William Facey, *Saudi Arabia by the First Photographers*, London: Stacey International, 1996.

occasions.[33] They would most probably have travelled to their tribal chief to resolve disputes. Men remained in charge of a private patriarchy springing from a collective duty shared by members of the kin group. Rudimentary knowledge of religious affairs coexisted with beliefs in spirits, folk magic, and minimal religious rituals. A simple monotheistic inclination persisted among nomadic groups until the twentieth century.

The duty to command right and forbid wrong and its later institutionalisation in the towns ensured that the private patriarchy exercised by ordinary men became a religiously sanctioned state duty, thus introducing a new dimension in the subordination of women: institutionalised public patriarchy. The two patriarchies worked together, one enforcing the other at different historical moments until the contemporary period, when the state aspired to replace private patriarchy altogether and emerge as the sole arbiter of women's status, rights, and responsibilities.

The state and the Wahhabi movement gained control of the private patriarchy practised in both the desert and the oasis, first through the many *ulama* and later with the help of what is often referred to as the religious police, thus creating in the process the institutions for state public patriarchy. From 1932 onward, the *ulama* and the state police force worked together. Religion and power became inseparable, thus turning the Wahhabi historical legacy into a state project. In the process, control of men over women became state and national policy.

The Wahhabi project aspired to create an Islamic order that sprang from the conditions of Najdi settlements. These conditions were different from those among nomadic tribal populations or among non-elite women who participated in the economy of the community through agricultural work and commerce. Among Bedouin, there was no need for a committee to guard against moral transgression or a police force to assist in maintaining an Islamic moral order. The tribal honour code and fear of consequences were enough to deter potential transgressors.

While desert Arabian women may have enjoyed greater freedom of movement than their urban counterparts, it is certain that they too were subjected to the same restrictions of patriarchal society. Even women who actively participated in the economy of trade, herding, farming, or

---

[33] On tribal religion in Arabia, see Alois Musil, *Manners and Customs of the Rwala Bedouins*, New York: American Geographical Society, 1927. On the twentieth century, see William Lancaster, *The Rwala Bedouin Today*, Cambridge: Cambridge University Press, 1981.

fishing were not exempt from subordination.[34] Although the necessities of economic participation required greater flexibility in restrictions on their movement, women remained subject to the will of men. Only elite women may have exercised some kind of authority over men, yet they experienced greater restrictions – in, for example, marriage choices. Elite women were married off within a strict endogamous system, and only occasionally offered to men of a similar status outside their lineages. This was often a function of political alliances rather than the individual choices of women.

The urban Wahhabi revivalist movement offered a standardisation and institutionalisation of patriarchal practices through resorting to a higher religious authority, supported by the state. The movement universalised the restrictions on women that were born out of the needs of Najdi settlements. It endeavoured to create a universal moral order in which gender relations are uniform, thus paving the way for the project of homogenising society. It focused on the family and its religious and moral propriety, in addition to unifying religious ritual and law, both of which promised to create the underlying conditions for the consolidation of an imagined religious nation in which control over women is central.

## A RETURN TO COMMANDING RIGHT AND FORBIDDING WRONG

The establishment of the contemporary Saudi state three decades after the conquest of Riyadh in 1902 prompted the Saudi leadership to strengthen its commitment to forbidding wrong as a mechanism of homogenising religious practices and moral codes. The doctrine of forbidding wrong became prominent because it was the mechanism that ensured the emergence of a unified high culture based not on common history, language, or ethnicity but on common religious practice, rituals, and law. It seems that the power of the state rather than the scattered references to the doctrine in Ibn Abd al-Wahhab's treatises created a Saudi model in which society should be forbidden from doing wrong publicly while the rulers should be advised in private by secret advice (*nasiha*). The doctrine of forbidding wrong was incorporated in what Michael Cook calls a 'Hanbalite state' that grew among a Hanbalite majority in central Arabia.[35]

---

[34] On women in traditional Gulf societies, see Baqir al-Najjar, *al-Mara fi al-khalij al-arabi wa tahawulat al-hadatha al-asira* [Women in the Gulf and difficult challenges of modernity], Casablanca: al-Markaz al-Thaqafi al-Arabi, 2000, pp. 15–28.

[35] Cook, *Commanding Right*, p. 188.

Cook asserts that the curtailment of *jihad* against polytheism after 1932 meant that the righteousness of the state needed to be turned inward in a manner similar to the nineteenth century. So forbidding wrong became inversely proportionate to the power of the state to launch war against infidels, innovators, and those who threaten its public piety. It is the quest for legitimacy that made the state endorse a vigorous approach to forbidding wrong, which has influenced and shaped the perception of women in the public sphere until the present day. As the state finalised its military expansionist *jihad* campaign, it directed its attention to proving its piety within the realm. However, the concern was not simply with piety. Rather, the state was mainly concerned with creating a common homogeneous constituency where regional, tribal, and other differences would eventually disappear, paving the way for a more efficient, central-ised state to rule over a homogeneous nation. At times of uncertainty and weakening of central authority, controlling the public sphere through the doctrine of commanding right and forbidding wrong became even more urgent. It was urgent in the nineteenth century, but intensified after various regions came under the authority of the Saudi state.

From the 1920s, the state's *ulama* began a vociferous campaign to Islamise not only the region's inhabitants but also Muslim pilgrims, the only foreigners who visited Arabia at the time. It seems that an official committee for commanding right and forbidding wrong was established in Mecca as early as 1928 after it was suggested by the king's Egyptian adviser, Hafiz Wahba. Wahba advised Ibn Saud to create a bureaucratic body of this nature to control the excesses and religious zeal of the invad-ing Saudi army, known as the Ikhwan, which began to harass the pilgrims and punish practices they deemed inappropriate in the newly emerging Islamic state. In 1928, Ibn Saud could not afford the loss of income from Muslim pilgrims who were increasingly being pursued by the Ikhwan in Mecca for their heterodox rituals. He acted on Wahba's advice and established the first nucleus of a bureaucratic body that became known as the Committee for the Promotion of Commanding Right and Forbidding Wrong.[36] While a loose body of vigilantes had already been present both in Riyadh and among the conquered tribal and sedentary population, the Hijazi committee was the first step towards the institutionalisation of the doctrine of commanding right and forbidding wrong. It was also a step towards restricting the influence of Hijazi *ulama* who at the time were more diverse and vibrant than their Najdi counterparts. The Najdi

---

[36] Cook, *Commanding Right*, p. 188.

scholars who took charge of the committee turned it into a bureaucratic institution whose surveillance of the public sphere became notorious in Saudi Arabia. Michael Cook concludes that the state's adoption of the doctrine of forbidding wrong led to its transformation from an apolitical and individual doctrine of forbidding wrong into a bureaucratic function, discharged by a set of committees under the supervision of a general director with ministerial rank.[37]

While the 1928 Hijazi committee was first concerned with restraining the Ikhwan in their dealings with pilgrims, its sphere of activity incorporated a wider range of responsibilities and surveillance. One important responsibility was the exclusion of other religious sources of authority in the Hijaz. The committee focused on a whole range of visible practices deemed un-Islamic. Among other things, it endeavoured to banish women from the public sphere – not only in Mecca but also elsewhere, under the pretext of *sad al-tharai*, a pre-emptive principle prohibiting acts that potentially lead to moral chaos and sin. While the immediate concern of the state in the late 1920s was to avoid jeopardising state income from the pilgrimage, the religious identity of the new political realm had to be established to distinguish it from the alleged laxity of the previous Hashemite polity and its overlords in Istanbul. Muslim pilgrims visiting Mecca under the new Saudi regime must see the political change reflected in the public sphere; Mecca had to be purified from laxity, a clear sign of the Islamic credentials and legitimacy of the new era. Meccan and Muslim women pilgrims had enjoyed relative freedoms under the ancien régime of the Hashemites, but from this time on restricting women from venturing into the public domain became the marker of a new Saudi political legitimacy.[38]

From these early days of consolidation, the Saudi state used women to establish its Islamic credentials, especially against those who might have offered an alternative Islamic piety. While religious revival fixed the status of women and aspired to homogenise them, the state made use of women in more practical and utilitarian ways, as the stories of the king and his conquests in the following section will illustrate.

RELIGIOUS NATIONALISM AND GENDER

In around 1902, Abd al-Aziz ibn Saud returned to Riyadh from exile in Kuwait to restore the vanished Saudi state. According to the national

---

[37] Cook, *Commanding Right*, p. 192.
[38] On the Hijazi context prior to the Saudi state, see Mai Yamani, *Cradle of Islam: The Hijaz and the Quest for an Arabian Identity*, London: I. B. Tauris, 2004.

narrative, he assembled a force of about fifty able men and headed towards his ancestors' capital, now under the authority of a new ruler, Abd al-Aziz ibn Rashid of Hail, and his representative, Ajlan ibn Muhammad, who resided in the Masmak palace with his wives. The recapture of the city proved to be difficult, and the raiding party decided to hide until night fell. The story goes that Ibn Saud divided his men into three groups, one of which managed to occupy a small house adjacent to the governor's palace. According to a famous Saudi historian, the story unfolds as follows:

Ibn Saud and his men arrived at night at the gates of Riyadh. They secretly entered the house of the local governor, Ajlan, who ruled on behalf of the Rashidi emirate of Hail. They immediately found the governor's wife, who informed the raiding-party that the governor was in Qasr al-Masmak with his garrison. Ibn Saud and his men waited until the morning in the governor's private quarters. When the governor emerged after dawn prayers, he was attacked by Ibn Saud's men. News of this heroic act spread across Riyadh. The inhabitants rushed to greet their legitimate ruler and swear allegiance to him. This is how Ibn Saud was successful in the battle of Riyadh, his first attempt to unify the country.[39]

Ajlan's wife was either terrified or sympathetic to the cause of Ibn Saud. Regardless of her state of mind at that important historical moment, she must have been an invaluable informer. Ibn Saud and his men waited all night, and when Ajlan returned to the Masmak palace, he was attacked and killed by Ibn Saud's cousin, Abdullah ibn Juluwi. Ibn Saud was then declared ruler of Riyadh.

The centrality of this personality in the foundation myth of Saudi Arabia attests to the importance of constructing gender as an integral part of the political unification of Saudi Arabia, a process that started with Ibn Saud's successful return to Riyadh, thanks to the role played by a woman. The capture of Riyadh does not fit within a heroic narrative, as there were no swords or large-scale bloodshed, the main ingredients of Arabian raids at the time. The story builds on events marked by surprise attack and the manipulation of female fears. According to oral versions of the story, Ajlan's wife was restrained with a rope all night lest she escape and spoil the surprise element of the attack. Other versions claim that she

[39] Abdullah al-Othaymin, *Tarikh al-mamlaka al-arabiyya al-saudiyya* [History of Saudi Arabia], Riyadh: Maktabat al-Malik Fahd al-Wataniyya, 1995, vol. II, pp. 52–3. For an examination of the poetics and politics of the story of the capture of Riyadh, see Madawi Al-Rasheed, 'The Capture of Riyadh Revisited: Shaping Historical Imagination in Saudi Arabia', in M. Al-Rasheed and R. Vitalis (eds.), *Counter Narratives: History, Contemporary Society and Politics in Saudi Arabia and Yemen*, New York: Palgrave, 2004, pp. 183–200.

voluntarily provided information on the whereabouts of her husband, who was probably spending the night with a co-wife. Because of her jealousy, which was situated in the context of a polygamous marriage, she willingly informed the raiders about her husband's location and expected time of return. It is probably impossible to ascertain the exact details of what took place between Ibn Saud and Ajlan's wife. But it is certain that this brief encounter under the dark sky of Riyadh in 1902 remains alive in the historical imagination of the state. No historical account or lesson is complete without reference to Ajlan's wife, whose contribution to the conquest of Riyadh, and later Arabia, was paramount.[40]

How do we interpret and understand Ajlan's wife? Is she a collaborator, a terrified victim, a bitter and jealous co-wife, or a courageous woman? We can objectively argue, however, that her role as a woman was so important that she remained a crucial personality, who contributed to the success of the capture of Riyadh, regardless of duress, courage, fear, or jealousy. The so-called battle of Riyadh was dependent on a woman and the information she provided. Unexpectedly, Ajlan's wife occupied – and continues to occupy – a central position in the foundation and legitimacy narrative of a very masculine state.

If the collaboration of the female subject was crucial for the foundation myth of the state, we find that the founder continued to invoke women as important for state consolidation. In Ibn Saud's many encounters with foreign writers and in his private daily *majlis* (council) where the king's confidants gathered, one common subject seemed to be recurrent: the king talked about women as sources of pleasure, comfort, and sexual indulgence. Women who were talked about in this manner were concubines or of humble origin. Obviously, such discussions were mainly for entertainment; they have never found their way to the Saudi national narrative, but remain confined to the old Orientalist monographs of the early twentieth century. In such monographs, glimpses of the king's evening talk among his loyal and trusted companions occasionally appear in the narrative, adding a sensational dimension to the life of the man who unified Arabia.

However, the official national narrative about the foundation of Saudi Arabia features – and indeed celebrates – other types of women. These are members of the royal household, who serve as exemplary figures, supporting the monarch, encouraging him, and in their own way providing knowledge deemed important for the state. Ibn Saud's sister Nura

---

[40] Al-Rasheed, 'The Capture of Riyadh Revisited'.

(1875–1950) is such a figure. Her name is fixed in the historical imagination as the king's *nakhwa* (war cry), *Akhu Nura!* (the brother of Nura). He invoked her name at times of stress, anger, and war to give him the courage and resolution expected in such situations. Her name was meant to inspire the king, as he derived pride from this fraternal association with her. In a society where female names are not mentioned in public, it was common to invoke the names of important female relatives to inspire men to defend their honour, especially at times when such behaviour is expected, for example in battle or confrontation with other men.[41]

During childhood, Ibn Saud's sister was a delightful and spirited playmate, and in later life she became a source of support and courage, especially after the family's exile in Kuwait following defeat in 1891. We are told that she played an important role in pushing her brother to embark on the long journey to re-establish their family's rule over Arabia. Later, after Riyadh fell into his hands, Nura remained supportive, managing the royal household and dealing with mundane matters that would have distracted the king from his more urgent business. No day passed without the king visiting her in her private quarters, where he exchanged news with her and sought advice and assurance.

More importantly, Nura agreed to be married off to a rival Saudi prince, Saud al-Kabir (Saud ibn Abd al-Aziz ibn Saud ibn Faysal ibn Turki), an arch-enemy who in the early 1910s had taken refuge with his mother's tribe, the Ajman, to challenge the king's right to the throne. Nura offered herself up to effect a lasting reconciliation between the competing men of her family, whose rivalry was threatening the survival of the nascent Saudi state. After the king brought the rebellious Ajman under his control and pacified his rival relative, Nura continued to cement the relationship between the contenders and the wide tribal milieu in which their competition was fermenting. Placing Nura in the intimate confines of Saud al-Kabir's household was a political strategy that the princess willingly accepted for the sake of the stability of her brother's domain. She used contacts with the Ajman tribe through her husband's affines to contribute to the pacification of this rebellious tribe and their chiefs. She served as a messenger between the king and the women of the tribe, especially the mother of their chief, Dhaydan ibn Hithlayn.

---

[41] A glimpse of the relationship between the king and his sister is found in several Arabic and English sources. See Dalal al-Harbi, *Nisa shahirat min hajd* [Famous Najdi women], Riyadh: Darat al-Malik Abd al-Aziz, 1999, pp. 148–55.

While Nura operated comfortably in the world of competing chiefs and their women, some of whom needed support and paternalistic attention from the king, we are told that she was also comfortable with some aspects of modernity into which Saudi Arabia was slowly being drawn. Hers was the face that greeted the wives of travellers and writers who visited Riyadh with their husbands in the 1920s. On several occasions, she hosted foreign women and introduced them to the intimate secrets of the royal female household, revealing a composed posture and an engaging personality. Violet Dickson was one such woman, who admired the princess when she encountered her in Riyadh in the 1920s.[42]

Nura's celebrated 'modernity' is demonstrated in her willingness to have the first telephone line in Riyadh, connecting her house with the king's palace. An early hotline of communication between a brother and a sister, joined by blood, common vision, and mutual support, added to this woman's responsiveness to and engagement with modernity. From her new marital abode, she kept in touch with the monarch and provided him with inside information about a whole range of urgent issues in addition to continuous support and encouragement.

Nura's death in 1950 came as a shock for the king who mourned a loyal and supportive sister. News of her death prompted him to cancel a previously organised banquet marking the fiftieth anniversary of his reign in Riyadh. Foreign guests and invited local notables were told that the king was in no mood to celebrate. An important state event thus passed without pomp or joy. Saudi Arabia had to wait another fifty years before the state organised the centennial celebration in 1999. But the memory of Nura lingers until the present day. King Abdullah named the first women's university after her, Princess Nura bint Abdulrahman University in Riyadh, in 2008.

Comfortable with both traditionalism and modernity, Nura is a celebrated woman whose legacy underpins the Saudi incorporation of gender in the state. Her story illustrates the shift towards state consolidation in which women were beginning to surface as important contributors. She offers a constructed role model that confirms the state's vision of women. Women are an auxiliary force that is cherished in times of exile, displacement, rivalry, and political strategies. They are symbols that need to be endowed with multiple meanings. Piety, wisdom, sacrifice, trust, and intimacy all define the moral universe in which women are expected

---

[42] See H. R. P. Dickson, *Kuwait and her Neighbours*, London: George Allen & Unwin, 1986, p. 259.

to operate. Nura is a role model, not only for other Saudi princesses but for the whole nation.

## THE CONTEMPORARY STATE AND RELIGIOUS NATIONALISM

The foundation of the Saudi state of 1932 was not a function of anti-colonial struggle or secular nationalism. Nor was the state an embodiment of a unifying national culture, shared history, printing, or other factors that are often attributed to the emergence of nationalism in both Europe and the third world post-colonial states.[43] Although important internal factors contributed to the process of state formation, the state was born following the struggle between two foreign powers, the Ottomans and the British, on the eve of the First World War. The political and cultural fragmentation of Arabia, coupled with illiteracy, militated against the emergence of a 'national culture'. A polity was formed prior to the emergence of a national discourse, whose seeds were often associated with a national intelligentsia in other parts of the Arab world and state institutions such as the judiciary and the military.[44]

Neither the sedentary population of the cities and oases nor the nomadic tribal groups that were incorporated in the Saudi state had a sense of a developed national identity to be mobilised in the quest for a state. Some regions did have distinct cultural traits – mostly related to their religious significance, ecology, economic mode of production, and social organisation. Such regions were known by their names. The Hijaz, Asir, Najd, and al-Hasa were regional autonomous units, ruled by local chiefs in cities and oases, while maintaining tenuous relations with either the Ottomans (prior to 1918) or the British imperial power on the Gulf coast. With the exception of the Hijaz, discussed in the introduction, no region produced an intellectual elite who articulated a national identity for their own region, let alone the whole of Arabia.

On the eve of the formation of the contemporary Saudi state, and with the exception of the Hijaz, where an Islamic Arab nationalism had a short-lived experience, its regions lacked a national intelligentsia or movement imagining a national unity within each region or across regions.

---

43 These factors are listed in the main texts on the rise of nationalism. See Benedict Anderson, *Imagined Communities*, New York: Verso, 2006; and Ernest Gellner, *Nations and Nationalism*, Oxford: Blackwell, 1993.

44 For comparison, see Joseph Massad, *Colonial Effects: The Making of National Identity in Jordan*, New York: Columbia University Press, 2001.

Neither Arabia nor its fragments had cross-regional institutions, military force, or any other organisation that transcended local identities and regional belonging. The fragments had two important interconnecting forces: trade[45] and Islam. Trade linked various parts of Arabia along trade routes, while Islam provided an umbrella world view that manifested itself in belief and practices, the most important of which was the pilgrimage to Mecca. But none of these forces was able to create regional integration or interdependence, let alone national culture, national intelligentsia, or institutions. *Ulama* networks linking central Arabia and the regions were developed, but they remained dependent on personal connections, kinship, and small study circles, based primarily on face-to-face interaction, and the exchange of religious treatises, letters, and *responsa*. These networks were not embodied in long-lasting institutions that would survive individuals, religious scholars, and learned families.

Internal diversity within the regions of Saudi Arabia – between tribal and non-tribal populations, shaykhly nobility and commoners, and warriors and labourers – created identities that remained anchored in primordial constructions of the self and others. The idea of a shared culture upon which a state could claim sovereignty was not developed or imagined. The fact that Saudi Arabia had not been directly ruled by a foreign power may have delayed the emergence of Saudi nationalism, which might have arisen in opposition to foreign domination or colonialism. Wahhabi opposition to the Ottoman Empire's nominal suzerainty over parts of Arabia, mainly the Hijaz, led to the demise of the movement in 1818. Furthermore, the low level of literacy and education, in addition to the absence of institutions (military, educational, social, and economic) must have been contributing factors that delayed the formation of a national discourse or consciousness across regions. Needless to say, cross-regional legal and military institutions were also absent.

Before 1932, nobody in the interior of Arabia had imagined a Saudi nation or narrated its origins, characteristics, and aspirations. The rest of what became Saudi Arabia was submerged in local identities celebrated in poetry and narratives. Although ethnically all inhabitants – with the exception of small pockets of non-tribal communities and foreign settlers in the Hijaz – claimed Arab descent, confessed to Islam, and spoke a dialect of Arabic, the idea of the nation in pre-modern Arabia had little significance. Cultural and religious diversity rather than uniformity was

---

[45] Al-Rasheed, *Politics in an Arabian Oasis*.

the norm. No group had a project to homogenise culture, define its contours, or articulate its future in the form of a state, thus inhibiting the development of a Saudi nationalism. Homogenising religions was a different matter, as this became the project leading to unifying fragments of an imagined nation.

In the absence of a unifying national narrative and against the background of fragmented primordial identities, after 1932 the Saudi state transformed the eighteenth-century Wahhabi religious revival into religious nationalism. The transformation succeeded in allowing a central power to rule over territories that had very few common cultural traits and lacked a historical memory of being part of a single polity. The Saudi state of 1932 was imposed on regions that had no heritage as one nation governed by one state. A political community had to be created after the fact to justify the emerging state. To unify a dispersed and culturally diverse population that had maintained its autonomy vis-à-vis foreign powers, the Saudi state relied on transforming Wahhabi Islam into religious nationalism. Wahhabi religious nationalism aspired to provide a common overarching Islamic identity in the absence of a common culture and the prevalence of deep-rooted local urban and tribal identities. The new movement looked back to the example of the Prophet, who managed to unify tribes and regions under the banner of Islam to create a state. This became the model to be adopted in Saudi Arabia. After 1932, Wahhabiyya preached unity on an Islamic rather than a national or cultural foundation. It aspired to homogenise religion against cultural diversity and fragmentation. By promoting the ethos of a Muslim nation, it provided the justification for the emerging state.

Under Wahhabi religious nationalism, the project of the 1932 state became entangled with specific constructions of political community. The community was homogenised not only in its apparent religious praxis and compliance with religious law but also in the uniformity of its values, appearance, and lifestyle. Two important developments were crucial for the project: the creation of cross-tribal military–religious force under the name of the Ikhwan and the sedentarisation projects targeting the nomadic Bedouin tribes to shift them to sedentary agricultural work. While these projects did not bring the fragments together, they were mechanisms allowing central authority to incorporate one element after another in its unification project. The project linked each fragment to the state without allowing them to mix under its banner. It was only in the later phase of increased urbanisation – the oil economy and rural–urban migration from the 1950s onward discussed in the following chapter – that the fragments came face to face with each other. In the second half of the twentieth century, the emerging state bureaucracy, including the army, oil industry, education, media, and civil service, allowed the fragments to mix and interact, after they were subjected to the discourse of being one pious nation. Up to that moment, the discourse was an imaginary propaganda under the banner of religious scholars who aspired to purify faith and in the process bring the fragments together in common law, ritual practice, and religious orientation.

In the first half of the twentieth century, homogenising religion was the first mechanism through which the nation was to be constructed. If conquest was the way to establish power, religious nationalism was the means to create a nation out of the fragments. Becoming an Islamic nation was from the very beginning a project of imagining the different fragments as one single pious entity. With the development of the state and its religious and educational institutions, a much later project associated with the influx of oil wealth, membership in the political community was entangled with becoming Muslim as defined by Wahhabi religious nationalism.

The history of the political events that culminated in the foundation of the Saudi state in 1932 privileged men as political actors. In archival sources, local chronicles, and travel literature the focus was always on the role of important men, a category that included Ibn Saud, his sons, *ulama*, early Arab aides, functionaries, tribal chiefs, colonial officers, military advisers, and foreign intermediaries. Conquest that led to political centralisation, and eventually the rise of the modern state, was obviously a masculine affair, the work of men who combined chivalry, diplomacy, and piety to bring about a historic break from the age of blasphemy, religious fragmentation, and cultural diversity. As Wahhabi religious nationalism sought to create a moral community, women were invested with special significance in the project of nation building, despite the fact that they were denied a space in the public sphere. Imagining the newly emerging Islamic/Wahhabi nation depended on articulating gender roles suitable for the purity of the new emerging political and religious community.

The centrality of the Wahhabi national narrative meant that Saudi Arabia never developed an indigenous, secular anti-colonial nationalist movement similar to those in other Arab countries. The country was immersed in local political struggles between emirates whose legitimacy rested on a combination of tribal traditional authority, ability to generate meagre surplus, control of trade routes, protection of the pilgrimage, and patron–client relationships with the superpower of the time. The expansion of each emirate was dependent on its military might rather than its ability to produce a unifying discourse that went beyond the limited confines of the local power base and its narrow primordial or regional identity.

The age of local emirates gave way to a single state in 1932, the date when the kingdom of Saudi Arabia came into being as a sovereign state. All local emirates in the Hijaz, Hail, and Asir vanished, and their territories were incorporated into the emerging Saudi realm with Riyadh as its capital. While the Hijaz remained the religious centre, Riyadh was from that time the political power base and the initiator of a homogeneous national religious culture. The so-called wars of unification of the first thirty years of the twentieth century took place under a strong religious umbrella that had all the elements and characteristics of religious nationalism. Wahhabiyya, the religion of a small minority in central and southern Najd, evolved into a religious nationalist movement under which the process of unification was justified. The Wahhabi movement was keen from that moment to cast itself as the true Islam and shed its previous image as a narrow movement of the Najdi religious scholars of central Arabia. At this historical moment, the movement needed to transform itself from being Wahhabi to being Salafi, the latter anchored in a wider authentic and ancient Islamic tradition that is not specifically central Arabian.[46]

Important Arab religious scholars and activists were instrumental in this transformation. Rashid Rida, a Syrian scholar previously associated with the Salafi modernist trend that had its roots in Egypt under Muhammad Abduh, came to play an important role in carving a place for Wahhabiyya that anchored it in the Salafi tradition, thus appealing to very sceptical Muslims in the 1930 and 1940s.[47] After his disappointment with the demise of the Sharifian Hijazi project, and his subsequent introduction to Wahhabism by the Hijazi Nasif family, he found in this narrow religious movement a Salafi revolution under the umbrella of the state.

The religious nationalism of the Wahhabi movement after 1932 had never attracted supporters from all over Arabia, let alone the Muslim

---

[46] Hamadi Redissi, 'The Refutation of Wahhabism in Arabic Sources, 1745–1932', in Madawi Al-Rasheed (ed.), *Kingdom without Borders: Saudi Arabia's Political, Religious and Media Frontiers*, London: Hurst & Co., 2008, pp. 157–81.

[47] Basheer Nafi, *The Rise and Decline of the Arab Reform Movement*, London: Institute for Contemporary Arab Thought, 2000.

world as a whole; it was a specific religious tradition anchored in a narrow and isolated niche in central Arabia. From this limited base, it mobilised various tribes and non-tribal groups, eventually enlisting them in wars that lasted more than thirty years, to impose a religio-political realm on the disparate parts of Arabia. At the same time, it needed to enlist famous Arab religious scholars to construct it as a pan-Islamic Salafi movement with an appeal beyond its narrow ethnic and regional origins.

In reality, Wahhabi religious nationalism was a sectarian, exclusive project that drew on religious dogma and interpretations within one Islamic school of jurisprudence: the Hanbali school. It positioned itself against narrow identities of tribe, ethnic group, regional specificity, and linguistic difference. It claimed unity on the basis of Islam, defined in local parochial terms. Wahhabiyya was linked to a specific community of central Arabia, namely the *hadari* (sedentary) population of the oases of Najd and Qasim, where Wahhabi theology and doctrine were developed by specialist religious scholars. Its language was that of purging, purifying, obliterating, and eradicating difference, especially that emanating from faith, tribalism, regionalism, and cultural practices. It endeavoured to circumvent alternative priesthoods, for example those associated with folkloric Islam, Sufism, Shiism, and other holy personalities revered at the local level by the Arabian population. It strove to curb alternative and competing religiosity, folk sacred spaces, and religious figures to ensure monopoly over the interpretation and dissemination of religious knowledge and authority. It fought holy men in Arabia to establish the authority of its own interpreters. It denounced the religions of all others to secure its spread among a hesitant and resistant population. The religious project of elimination was in need of military mobilisation and political leadership.

The project of imagining the religious nation was linked to homogenising religious creed and practice. After conquest, a state was needed to impose specific religious interpretations on the various regions and apply a narrow definition of Islamic law that negated historical diversity and pluralism. Wahhabi religious nationalism propagated its narrow creed and practice as the only road to salvation. Opposition to the project of this aggressive religious nationalism was dubbed blasphemy and an offence against God rather than the nation. Homogenising religion became a priority for the state after conquest. For this purpose, the state endeavoured to enforce uniformity through law and public appearances. Judges from the central Najdi heartland, preachers, vigilantes, and religious educators were the first to be sent out to distant regions. Their presence was an indicator of the subjugation of territories and the Islamisation of space. The state was also able to monitor and control all religious practice that deviated from Wahhabi principles, especially in areas that had important historical and religious significance, for example in the holy cities of Mecca and Medina and the Eastern Province where a substantial Shia community lived. Monitoring public space and religious practices could only be achieved fully in the oil era.

Religious nationalism promoted a narrow definition of belonging to the pious community. Only those who adopted its jurisprudence, religious ritual practice, gender interpretations, and strict creed qualified to belong. This religious nationalism was based on a perpetual cosmic struggle between good and evil, which rejuvenated faith and ensured that practice conformed to the set principles of good religiosity. Above all, the struggle contributed to drawing strict boundaries between those who belonged to the pious nation and those who did not. The latter were branded enemies of Islam. The religious struggle needed the resources of the state and its support, hence the alliance between the religious doctrinaires and the political leadership. The political leadership needed the common identity articulated by the preachers and the legitimacy this bestowed on it. In return, religious doctrinaires received protection and subsidies for their services in the pursuit of defining identity and enforcing loyalty to the state.

The political leadership adopted the discourse of equality, universalism, and the strict definitions of boundaries that Wahhabiyya imposed in the public sphere. The Wahhabi religious scholars propagated the discourse of the equality of believers to mask serious inequalities, exclusion, and even discrimination. The universalism of their Islamic message concealed its exclusive and narrow religious interpretations, which were presented as the only ones valid for the community. The universalism of Wahhabi religious nationalism was imposed as an act of faith and salvation. The movement claimed to represent Islam, but in reality it represented the narrow solidarity of one group of scholars drawn from southern Najd and Qasim who achieved a monopoly of the religious field. They swore allegiance to the Al-Saud leadership in return for domesticating the Arabian population and extracting its submission to the religio-political leadership.

One of the most noted contributions of Wahhabi religious nationalism to the formation of the state was its capacity for military mobilisation. The movement invoked the concept of *jihad* against unbelievers, mostly other Arabian Muslims who refused to submit to the authority of the

Al-Saud. Between 1902 and 1932, under the auspices of the Al-Saud, Sunni Muslims, along with Shia, Sufis, and Ismailis, were subjugated under the pretext of purifying their faith and teaching them true Islam. They were attacked as non-believers in true Islam rather than territories or people who defended their local autonomy against the invading troops. Those who resisted the imposition of Saudi religious nationalism and the political submission it entailed were fought and defeated by specially formed military units by the name of *jund al-tawhid*, the soldiers of monotheism, or *ikhwan man ta' allah*, the brothers of those who obey God, better known in the literature on Saudi Arabia as the Ikhwan. The unification of Arabia under the leadership of the Al-Saud was a political project in religious guise. New territories were incorporated in the Saudi realm, losing all local autonomy and independence. They were turned into provinces ruled through governors and representatives sent from Riyadh. Their rudimentary local educational institutions and judiciary were abolished and replaced by ones that were administered by the central authority and under the guidance of the specialist religious scholars.

Sunni legal schools such as the Hanafis, Shafi'is, and Malikis were all suppressed, while the Hanbali legal tradition, from which Wahhabiyya arose, was promoted. While Wahhabism succeeded in homogenising Sunni Muslims, it failed to achieve its ultimate goal, namely mass conversion from Shiism or Ismailism to Wahhabi Islam. It ensured for several decades, however, that no signs of non-Wahhabi worship and ritual practices appeared in the public sphere. Non-Wahhabi communities have continued to be denounced in regular *fatwa*s and publications. Wahhabi religious nationalism provided a narrow definition of who belongs to the polity and moral community, while at the same time it posited itself as the only possible universal path to salvation.

### THE FUSION OF GENDER, RELIGION, AND POLITICS IN RELIGIOUS NATIONALISM

As the Wahhabi revival movement became religious nationalism under the banner of the contemporary state, it aspired towards transforming Arabian society from tribally, culturally, and regionally fragmented entities into a religiously homogeneous society, thus changing the criteria according to which people belonged to community. This involved a dissemination of the religious propriety of an urban class of religious scholars throughout the whole of Saudi Arabia. This religious nationalism returned to the texts, religious opinions, and *fatwa*s of pre-modern times in order to imbue the new nation with piety, propriety, and conformity. Through their religious texts, the *ulama* reconfigured the newly emerging Saudi Arabia as one pious nation. Their narrative aspired towards fixing the boundaries between good and evil, faith and blasphemy, insiders and outsiders, pious and impious, and moral and immoral subjects. In this project, women became moral symbols. Like all forms of religious nationalism, Wahhabiyya sought to restore the family, not the autonomous individual, as the elemental unit of which the social is composed, hence its constant preoccupation with public modesty, purifying the public sphere, and limiting the potential threat of mingling binary opposites, mainly men and women.

The Wahhabi *ulama* endeavoured to generalise its perceptions and constructions of gender on the nation, constructed as a moral and pious abstraction. Women became a religious and ethical subject rather than a social agency, and were required to be at the service of a masculine religious state. However, the female religious subject was not an individual citizen, but an important pillar of the family under the patriarchal authority of its male members.

The Wahhabi movement was turned into an overarching religious culture that promised to unify not only fragmented people, practices, and appearances, but also legal codes and institutions. In this project, women were central. Their early invisibility in the public sphere distinguished the newly created realm not only from previous polities but from other Arab states, which were beginning to define themselves by drawing on secular nationalism at the beginning of the twentieth century. Wahhabi religious nationalism defined the newly emerging religious nation in opposition to other Arab nations and the world, hence the birth of the so-called and much-celebrated Saudi *khususiyya*: exceptionalism. No other country in the Arab region espoused, propagated, or capitalised on exceptionalism to mark its difference, while the Saudi claims remain a solid disposition manifested at all levels of public discourse.

To produce the homogeneous polity that imagines itself as having a unique common religious culture/sacred space, women were the cornerstone of differentiating the nation from other nations in its environs. Controlling women's religiosity, appearance, movement, education, work, economic activity, property, and the social aspects of their lives – for example, marriage – are the most cherished devotions of Saudi religious nationalism, its priesthood, and the state.

After the consolidation of the state, legislation keeping women in their approved place in the private family sphere was maintained and defended.

Consequently, women were denied individual legal personality, and were placed under the authority of their male guardians and the state, each reinforcing the other's patriarchy. Women became important not only for the physical reproduction of the new pious nation but also as the repository of its morality, ethics, and religious purity. This required that they should then be controlled lest they undermine national piety and morality. Also, their marriages should be regulated according to a strict policy of national endogamy, whereby women's marriages with outsiders, even Arab Muslims, became controversial and in need of special permission from the highest state authority, the Ministry of Interior.

The priesthood of Saudi religious nationalism was preoccupied not only with women's public modesty and morality but also with their private purity, ritual performance, and religious compliance with prescribed teachings and preaching. Since the 1930s, the surveillance of the public sphere – streets, shopping centres, restaurants, hotels, schools, universities, workplaces, conferences, book fairs, car parks, and festivals – has been notorious. Religious education in schools and in media forums has ensured that even the private lives of women – ritual performances, purity, and pollution – attains conformity in the intimate confines of home and family. This surveillance of the public and private spheres sent an important signal to the population, mainly that there was no space that could not be penetrated by the state and its religious vigilantes. All was under the gaze of the state and its priesthood. The household itself was penetrated – first by preaching in the public sphere, for example mosque and school, and later in the media with the television becoming the main tool to influence the private family domain.

Fear of being watched and monitored was therefore a natural outcome, a deterrent against disloyalty, resistance, and transgression. The fusion between religion and politics led to the monitoring of intimacy between men and women – not only in public but also in the private context of family, marriage, and conjugal life. The state surveillance agencies strove towards the separation of men and women in the public sphere, thus keeping gender boundaries clearly defined and controlled. They preferred not to have women going outside private houses; such ventures were a threat to family and nation. The confinement of women became important for controlling marriage choices. It subverted possibilities that threatened not only family purity and tribal endogamy but also national endogamy, especially after the nation became host to a huge expatriate community as a result of the massive oil revenues that are the entitlement of those who belong to the nation. Women's work outside the house not only threatened the reproduction of the future pious generation but also exposed them to a large pool of potential marriage candidates, especially in spaces that are now less segregated, for example the public sphere with its growing shopping centres, parks, and entertainment and recreation facilities. The obsession with women as religious and ethical subjects is a reflection of the increasing need to symbolise the uniqueness of the pious nation and guard against its contamination by non-indigenous elements.

Although the emerging state initially denied women any presence or role in the public sphere, it nevertheless remained gendered – that is, a state whose legitimacy derived from the perpetuation of control over and exclusion of women, who were believed to threaten its integrity and morality. Its national narrative propagated contradictory images of women. It constructed both acceptable and rejected gender roles. In fact, the foundation of the state depended on the perpetuation of a social order in which the pious woman was celebrated while the defiant one was subject to punishment, control, and purgation. Religious nationalism dictated how women should be treated, controlled, and talked about in the public sphere. The norms, rules, and regulations that sprang from the imagination of men in the oases of Najd became mechanisms for controlling all Arabian women, a heterogeneous category that included tribal elite women, slave women, traders, peddlers, healers, peasants, and herders. The religious nation was dependent on submerging all categories of women into an undifferentiated mass, aided by the imposition of a single dress code, legal framework, and religious education.

Religious nationalism needed state institutions in order to meet its aspirations, namely the creation of a homogeneous moral and pious community in which women define the boundaries. The 1928 committee that promoted commanding right and forbidding wrong in the Hijaz was the first institution that aspired to achieve this goal. Furthermore, the network of religious scholars who were dispatched to all regions, oases, and deserts were instrumental in establishing networks that connected the Najdi religious elite with grassroots communities. They facilitated the integration of the periphery with a centre based in Riyadh. They also removed regional religious authorities from their old historical monopoly over their own local communities. The Wahhabi religious networks aspired to make the regional and cultural fragments one religious nation, abiding by their religious doctrine, interpretation, and practices. This aspiration was before the advent of oil, and as such it remained a futuristic project.

For the first half of the twentieth century, the religious nation remained an abstraction. The complete success of the project was dependent on resources, mainly surplus that would be invested in the establishment of institutions and infrastructures that homogenised and connected the fragments. The state had to wait for oil wealth in the second half of the twentieth century in order to effectively bind fragments of the population through educational institutions. Its educational resources, religious institutions, media empire (newspapers, radio, and television), and the infrastructure of roads, airports, and, later on, surveillance cameras and communication tools were mechanisms whose use and application embodied the vision of religious nationalism in which women were central.

Gender relations and the status of women in Saudi Arabia became hostages to the political project of the state and its religious nationalism; the first was by nature a contingent and evolving project, while the second was an unbounded vision, which drew on the divine and aspired to create the Kingdom of God on earth, in which women were the most visible signs. The tension between changing state politics and universal religious nationalism continued to haunt Saudi women in the decades that followed the establishment of the modern state. Wahhabi religious nationalism invented an 'ideology of order'[48] in an attempt to link religion and nation state. In this fusion of religion and nation, women were integrated as fundamental symbols.

[48] Mark Juergensmeyer, *Global Rebellion: Religious Challenges to the Secular State, from Christian Militants to Al Qaeda*, Berkeley: University of California Press, 2008.

2

# Schooling Women

## *The State as Benevolent Educator*

The government of Saudi Arabia has always recognised the importance of providing educational opportunities to girls as well as boys.

Ministry of Education, Saudi Arabia[1]

While Wahhabi religious nationalism insisted on a return to authentic Islamic tradition, the state endeavoured to project itself as an agent of modernisation. Schooling girls in Saudi Arabia became one of the state's most publicised achievements. The education narrative combines important, appealing dimensions. Schooling girls projects the state as a progressive and modern development agency. The narrative asserts that the state was committed to the education of girls amidst fierce social and religious opposition from the ideologues of religious nationalism. To resolve the contradiction, the state introduced education while remaining faithful to religious nationalism. This was achieved when the state put girls' education under the authority of religious scholars. Consequently, education became the most important instrument of religious nationalism, homogenising the nation and guarding its piety. When it introduced the first school, the state claimed that it did not deviate from the principles of religious nationalism, thus reflecting the impossible task of combining modernisation with traditionalism, often expressed in the idiom of 'modernisation within an Islamic framework' or 'modernisation while remaining faithful to the principles of Islam'. The education of girls had to be put under the guidance of the religious scholars in order to remain

[1] Ministry of Education, Saudi Arabia, available at http://www.moe.gov.sa/openshare/englishcon/index.htm.

within the parameters of reproducing the pious nation and confirming women in their traditional roles.

The state's education narrative highlights the role of two kings, Saud (r. 1952–64) and Faisal (r. 1964–75), with the latter assuming all the credit for a revolutionary step in a 'conservative' society. In particular, Faisal's wife, Iffat, is singled out as the mind behind the initiative of extending education to girls. This narrative ignores the calls of writers, columnists, essayists, and literary figures – especially those in the Hijaz, who as early as the 1920s had called for the schooling of girls. The education of girls had not been as alien to society as is often assumed in the process of highlighting the role of the state as educator.

No account of educating girls is complete without demonstrating the opposition of the guardians of the religious tradition, especially in the heartland of Wahhabi territory, Najd, and the triumph of the state over this opposition. The fact that girls' schools were opened in the 1960s amidst 'fierce' resistance demonstrates the supremacy of the political over the religious in matters related to development and progress. Since 9/11, Saudi writers who aspire towards further liberating the social sphere from the control of religious scholars have continued to remind their audiences of the old, well-rehearsed story of opposition to girls' education in order to draw parallels between the past and the present, thus expressing their wish to see the same firm subjugation of the religious exercised by the political leadership in the present.

This chapter identifies the many voices in favour of educating girls that had been in circulation before the first girls' state schools opened in 1960, and captures the debate that accompanied their opening. Opposition to girls' schools is often attributed to Wahhabi conservatism. In reality, the new proposed schools threatened existing educational structures run by local *ulama*, who upheld the principles of religious nationalism. While at one level the school could be an embodiment of this religious nationalism, at another it was seen as the space where their hold over the social sphere could be thwarted, weakened, and eventually lost. Opposition to schools reflected serious concern with 'foreign elements', so alien that they could undermine the purity of tradition and its adoption and reproduction by Saudi girls. Opposition to schools reflected the widening gap between two completely different projects, one aiming to restore the religious nation, the other to create a modern state.

EARLY VOICES CALLING FOR GIRLS' EDUCATION

Before the state took it upon itself to establish schools for girls, several writers, journalists, and poets had called for educating girls. Two Hijazi writers, Muhammad Awad (1906–80)[2] and Ahmad Sibai (1905–84), expressed their views on the subject. In his book *Khawatir musarraha* (Authorised thoughts), published in 1926, Awad wrote a short essay on women's identity and the need to be educated.[3] The essay speaks to women, although only a minority among them would have been able to read it at the time. He invokes both the Arab nation and the Islamic tradition in order to encourage women to take up education seriously. By invoking previous examples of what he calls 'Hijazi women', Awad reminds his audience of the great achievements of historical figures to inspire contemporary women. He urges women to accept the need to learn reading and writing. He wants women to

Think about how the Arab *umma* was formed. Think about how the Hijaz can be strong and elevated. To write what you think is the way to progress. You need to know your religion and your duties towards your husband. You need to know how to bring up your children. You need lessons about how to reform your house and nation. I do not need to remind you to learn sewing and knitting, but knowledge and morality are your priorities. Ask history about women like Khadija, Aisha and Asma, the daughters of Abu Bakr... Ask about Zaba, the Queen of Palmyra, Balqis, the Queen of Yemen... Aren't you impressed that these are the daughters of the Arabian Peninsula, most of them are from the Hijaz.[4]

Awad's message to women invokes clear nationalistic sentiments revolving around three concentric circles: the Islamic community, the Arab nation, and the Hijaz homeland. The emancipation of women would inevitably lead to the revival of past glories. He associates women's education with progress expected in the twentieth century. He asks women to abandon *taqlid* (imitation) and laziness in order to 'break the chains' that control them. He wants women to think, read, and write so that they are prepared for the future. Women, according to Awad, should acquire skills for the benefit of the community. Awad's proposition regarding the introduction of modern education was not well received. He reported that in 1927 a group of scholars wrote to Ibn Saud asking him to punish Awad and send him into exile for his corrupting ideas. Recent critics of Awad see him as having failed to develop, despite his good intentions. He belonged to the first generation of writers who aspired to move the

[2] In one source, Awad's date of birth is 1914. See Shakir al-Nabulsi, *al-Libiraliyya al-saoudiyya bayn al-wahm wa al-haqiqa* [Saudi liberalism between myth and reality], Beirut: al-Mouassasa al-Arabiyya li al-Dirasat wa al-Nashr, 2010, p. 15.

[3] Awad's book *Khawatir musarraha* was published in 1926, but sections that are relevant to women's education were reprinted in the Saudi journal *Huqul*. See Muhammad Awad, 'Kayfa anti' [How you are], *Huqul*, 2007, p. 68.

[4] Awad, 'Kayfa anti', p. 68.

country in the direction of modernity, but he remained unknown. According to Abdullah al-Ghathami, Awad was a historical witness without having an impact on change. This led to the triumph of the conservative elements in Saudi society, as they were not confronted by a strong, challenging intellectual countercurrent.[5]

Ahmad Sibai was another Hijazi writer, who in 1936 wrote in support of women's education. He paints a gloomy picture of the ignorant woman in order to encourage women's education. For him, an ignorant woman is unsuitable for the bringing up of real men. She is more likely to exert unnecessary pressure on her sons, thus creating a man who has nothing to do with masculinity, or indulging every whim of her son to create a spoilt man, or unable to control her son's desires, thus producing a social misfit. He concludes that ignorant women 'produce men that are bad for society. But the blame should be put on those who refuse to educate women. The emancipation of the nation requires good men. But those do not grow by themselves, they need the hands of mothers who are educated'.[6]

In addition, Sibai attacks those who object to girls' education. He laments that they accuse others of Westernisation and neglect of religion. Those opposed to girls' education 'forget that religion calls for knowledge for both Muslim men and women. They also forget those exceptional Muslim women who played an important role in Muslim civilisation. Such women participated in war and the spread of knowledge. People used to travel to see them and learn from them'.[7] Like Awad, Sibai invokes the glorious past in order to support his argument in favour of education. Women should be educated for the sake of men, starting with their sons. During his time, the tradition of educating women in *kuttab*s, religious study circles, run by instructors called *faqiha*s, proved to be inadequate, according to Sibai. These study circles are 'chaotic, unregulated and fertile ground for the transmission of *khurafat*, mythologies... We need new schooling based on reason and logic'.[8]

Both Awad and Sibai were aware of the Hijazi female religious scholars known as *alimat al-haramayn* in Mecca and Medina. These were women who excelled in religious studies including *hadith* and *fiqh*. Some

[5] Abdullah al-Ghathami, *Hikayat al-hadatha fi al-mamalaka al-arabiyya al-saudiyya* [The story of modernity in Saudi Arabia], Casablanca: al-Markaz al-Thaqafi al-Arabi, 2004, p. 63.

[6] Ahmad Sibai, 'Hajatna ila talim al-banat shai yuqiruhu al-mantiq' [We need to educate girls], *Huqul*, 2007, p. 69.

[7] Sibai, 'Hajatna ila talim al-banat', p. 69.

[8] Sibai, 'Hajatna ila talim al-banat', p. 69.

learned women were known by formal titles such as *waitha* (preacher), *alima* (scholar), *faqiha* (specialist in *fiqh*), and *muhaditha* (*hadith* reciter). The lives of these female scholars are documented in several classical chronicles, and continue to provide inspiration in the contemporary context. Their religious knowledge is recalled to demonstrate the need for women's education and participation in society. In a recent study, the lives and achievements of the Tabariyat of Mecca, a group of women scholars who belonged to the Tabari family, are celebrated as historical examples of a vibrant community of female scholars who taught religious studies.[9]

Hijazi writers and journalists were pioneers in calling for girls' education early in the twentieth century. But, in the heart of Najd, there was the lonely voice of Abdullah al-Qasimi (1907–96). Al-Qasimi was brought up in Burayda, a city in the heartland of Wahhabi religious teachings and scholarship, but as he moved to al-Azhar in Egypt for further religious training, he abandoned his previous convictions to become one of the most controversial intellectual figures in Saudi Arabia in the twentieth century. In his early writings, he seems to have called for a rationalisation of religion, but in his later years he was better known for his sharp criticism of religious dogma and Arab culture in general. In his 1981 book *al-Kawn yuhakim al-illah* (The universe judges God), al-Qasimi abandoned all faith in favour of outright atheism.[10] In his other books, he called for a rational enlightenment that would free the Arabs from oppression and mythological thought. His daring criticism of Wahhabi teachings earned him the wrath of his compatriots. He became persona non grata and remained in exile in Egypt until his death. His views on women's education were summed up in an article entitled 'Is She a Human or a Commodity?', published in 1946.[11] It opens with an onslaught on male bias against the emancipation of women. He traces the oppression of women through several civilisations but highlights how Islam was most generous towards women, as its teachings recognised their

[9] Lamiya Shafi'i, *Makanat al-mara al-ilmiyya fi al-saha al-makiyya* [Women's status in the intellectual arena of Mecca], Mecca: Um al-Qura University, n.d.

[10] Abdullah al-Qasimi, *al-Kawn yuhakim al-illah* [The universe judges God], Tunis: n.p., 1981. For a biography of al-Qasimi, see Jurgen Wasella, *Min usuli ila mulhid qisat inshiqaq Abdullah al-Qasimi 1907–1996* [From fundamentalism to atheism: The story of Abdullah al-Qasimi (1907–1986)], trans. Muhammad Kibaybo, Beirut: Dar al-Kunuz al-Adabiyya, 2001.

[11] Abdullah al-Qasimi, 'al-Insan hiya am sil'a' [Is she a human being or a commodity?], *Huqul*, 2007, pp. 70–5; Wasella, *Min usuli*, pp. 76–80.

contribution to their families and society. Al-Qasimi wrote this article while he was still contemplating a religious renaissance and before he completely abandoned faith:

The history of women's oppression is a long history of injustice, selfishness, and ignorance... Man was able to control woman to the extent of killing her. He made her a commodity that he can sell and buy, give as a gift, and enjoy her as he likes. He put a curtain on her so that she is not seen; he forbids her from going out. Islam recognised her value and gave her rights. But excluding women from education has remained. Man does not want her to have a strong weapon that she may use against him. Because knowledge is a weapon... Women must be knowledgeable in all aspects of life. Those who object to her education on the ground that she will mix with men, we say to them that all worship involves mixing between men and women. Take the pilgrimage, the preaching, the prayers, and war. They all involve men and women being together.[12]

Like Awad and Sibai, al-Qasimi reiterates the importance of women's education for men and the nation. He attributes the ignorance of the *umma* to women's lack of knowledge and asserts that a society whose women are educated is often better than one whose men are educated. Society becomes sick if women are ignorant, as myth and tradition become entrenched in the minds of people. Educated women heal the body and soul of the nation. He calls for *tajdid* (renewal) and *aql* (reason) to promote a renaissance that has become urgent for the Arab and Muslim world. Women are expected to play a special role in this renaissance.

Much of the early men's writing on women's education remained dormant in the historical imagination and was buried in an attempt to highlight the pioneering role of the state, depicted as the first to initiate the project and think about it. It is only recently that these writings have been celebrated in local Saudi publications.[13] However, the state was not in a position to respond to these calls until the 1960s, when oil wealth allowed the rhetoric of development to materialise in the opening of the first state-run girls' schools in the country. Between 1932 and 1960, Saudi girls' literacy rate was the lowest in the Arab world. A small minority of girls received rudimentary literacy and arithmetic in the *kuttab*s, the small, informal study circles that emerged around instructors,

---

[12] al-Qasimi, 'al-Insan', p. 70.
[13] The Saudi journal *Huqul* dedicated one special issue to the subject of 'Women in the Culture of the Arabian Peninsula' in which several early articles on women's education were reprinted. See *Huqul*, September 2007. Some articles appeared as newspaper columns while others included lengthy sections of books.

who combined religious education, mainly memorisation of the Quran, with rudimentary literacy.

## FROM *KUTTAB* TO SCHOOL

With the exception of a handful of private schools for boys in the Hijaz, Saudi Arabia had no formal educational institutions. From the 1930s onward, the state started the first initiative to establish formal schools for boys. This was accomplished with the establishment of Idarat al-Maarif al-Ama (the general directorate of education). At the time, there were 700 boys enrolled in twelve private and state schools. By 1951, there were 226 schools with 29,887 boys enrolled.[14] These schools coexisted with the traditional *kuttab*s, the study circles run by religious scholars in mosques or homes.

In the absence of formal state schools, girls had limited educational opportunities. In the Hijaz, there were two schools available: al-Sawlatiyya and al-Hazaziyya. Indian Muslims established endowments and schools in Mecca. Al-Sawlatiyya was one such school, initiated by a wealthy Calcutta woman, Sawlat al-Nisa, in 1875. The school's first principal, Rahmat Allah Kayrawani, is said to have had some involvement in the anti-British Indian mutiny of 1857, after which he migrated to Mecca.[15] Girls were taught to memorise the Quran but without learning how to write. In the Hijaz, elite girls were educated in informal *kuttab*s by female teachers (*faqihas/alimas*) or at home. In such schools, they memorised the Quran while they remained illiterate, and learned needlework and some arithmetic.

Born in Mecca, Sharifa Nur al-Hashemi (d. 2012), the mother of famous poet, essayist, and sociologist Fawziya Abu Khalid, recalls her quest for education at a time when only limited opportunities for educating boys and girls existed in the Hijaz. Sharifa Nur was sent to the *kuttab* circle of a *faqiha* called Shathiliyya. This informal education often stopped at puberty, when girls were expected to remain in seclusion until they married.[16] Sharifa Nur was interested in learning how to write on the wooden board, an act that infuriated her teacher. The other girls

[14] Fuad Hamza, *al-Bilad al-arabiyya al-saudiyya* [Saudi Arabia], Riyadh: Maktabat al-Nasr al-Haditha, 1936, p. 227.
[15] Muhammad Qasim Zaman, *The Ulama in Contemporary Islam: Custodians of Change*, Princeton: Princeton University Press, 2007, p. 256.
[16] Soraya Altorki, *Women in Saudi Arabia: Ideology and Behavior among the Elite*, New York: Columbia University Press, 1986, p. 19.

were summoned to witness the severe punishment to which she was subjected at the age of seven. Her wrist was slashed with a knife, and the
bleeding almost killed her. She still has the scar on her wrist as a testi-
mony of her determination. She never abandoned the desire to read and
write. As her children went to school, she explored their new notebooks
and tried to acquire limited literacy on her own. With eleven children,
it was not possible for her to join the adult literacy classes that were
introduced later on. Adult literacy classes were not initially very popular,
as they clashed with women's many household responsibilities. Furthermore, public opinion was not in favour of adult education. Proverbs
and folk sayings such as *yawm shab waduh al-kuttab* ('when he got old,
they took him to the *kuttab*') reflected society's lack of enthusiasm for
adult literacy classes. Sharifa Nur continued to rely on self-help, using
her children's school textbooks, until she surprised her husband by reading a sign in the street.[17] She later developed her entrepreneurial skills,
starting a small dressmaking business and a training centre for women.
In 2007, she published a short biographical piece in which she traced
her struggles, perseverance, and achievements in a society that restricted
women's activities and learning opportunities.[18]

In Najd, girls did not enjoy even the limited opportunities of the Hijaz.
As late as the 1950s, girls of the Al-Saud households may have had regular
exposure to a school-like education within the compounds in which they
lived. According to Fahda bint Saud, a daughter of King Saud (r. 1952–
64), two Arab teachers were brought to their residential compound to
teach them basic literacy skills. Later, four Palestinian women instructors
followed to teach the girls Arabic, mathematics, English, history, and
geography.[19] While King Saud taught some of his daughters at home,
it is known that Crown prince (later King) Faisal (r. 1964–75) sent his
daughters to Switzerland for education. According to Loulwa al-Faisal,
her father 'was convinced that girls should be educated to contribute to
their nation. He started with his own daughters'.[20]

These limited initiatives were, however, not available to all girls,
including those who belonged to the Al-Saud collateral branches. Most

---

[17] Sharifa Nur al-Hashemi, 'Imraa saudiyya min jil al-umahat al-awail' [A Saudi woman
from the mothers' generation], *Huqul*, 2007, pp. 110–17.

[18] al-Hashemi, 'Imraa saudiyya'.

[19] Abdullah al-Washmi, *Fitnat al-qawl bi talim al-banat fi al-mamlaka al-arabiyya al-
saudiyya* [Discord over girls' education in Saudi Arabia], Casablanca: al-Markaz al-
Thaqafi al-Arabi, 2009, pp. 35 and 159.

[20] al-Washmi, *Fitnat al-qawl bi talim al-banat*, p. 159.

upper-class girls growing up in Riyadh in the 1950s would have had limited education in the household. Families often hired the services of local religious scholars, often blind, to visit their households and instruct women in rudimentary Quranic studies, *hadith* recitation, and limited literacy. The instruction revolved around teaching women enough Quranic verses to perform their prayers, in addition to lessons relating to purity, ablution, and other matters relevant to performing religious rituals and obligations. During the month of Ramadan, the visiting blind shaykh would come to the household every evening in order to lead the extended *tarawih* prayers after breaking the fast. His daily appearance was often combined with supplication and occasionally a time for questions about matters related to fasting and other rituals and religious obligations. Women used the opportunity to ask about missed fasting days, acts that break the fast, and the requirements and rules of *sadaqa* (alms giving). The tradition of the visiting blind scholar continued throughout the 1970s, even after girls' schools became available in the country. The concern with women's piety prompted many families to keep the tradition of the visiting shaykh, who continued to instruct old women and girls, especially those who had missed joining a school because of their advanced age.

In some upper-class families, the instruction gained from the religious scholar was supplemented by hiring the services of Arab women tutors. In the 1950s, teachers came from Syria, Lebanon, and Egypt. They would live in the household and hold private, informal lessons, drawing on imported Arabic texts. Their role often extended beyond giving literacy lessons. Such women were companions who were often seen in upper-class households from the 1950s onward. In addition to teaching Arabic and mathematics, their instruction covered a wide range of areas from designing house furniture to creating new fashionable wardrobes. Fadia Basrawi, whose extraordinary life in the 1950s and 1960s will be discussed later, recalls a visit to the household of Princess Sarah, the wife of the governor of the Eastern Province, Saudi ibn Juluwi, in 1961, where she was received by a Lebanese seamstress.[21] Such women performed multiple tasks, including teaching, dressmaking, companionship, and household management. Drawing on their connections with their country of origin, Arab women mediated the entry of Saudi women into new circles of consumption and taste brought from abroad, in addition to literacy. They

[21] Fadia Basrawi, *Brownies and Kalashnikovs: A Saudi Woman's Memoir of American Arabia and Wartime Beirut*, Reading: South Street Press, 2009, p. 108.

often accompanied elite women during travel to Arab capitals, mainly for medical treatment or shopping. The opportunity for travel remained limited throughout the 1950s and 1960s, even for elite women. Many women did not have passports and saw no urgency in getting them. Only medical reasons prompted some elite women to seek health services abroad.

From the 1950s onward, only a small number of girls were sent abroad to boarding schools for education. They belonged to the first generation of Saudi bureaucrats and merchants, mainly resident in the cities of the Hijaz and in Riyadh. Not many families dared to take this path as the risks and stigma were considered to be too great. Many of the boarding schools in Arab capitals were Christian missionary institutions established in Cairo, Beirut, and elsewhere. While many families sent their sons to such schools, and later on these boys benefited from the first wave of state scholarships, only a small minority of parents would allow their girls to travel abroad for education. The daughters of the first generation of Saudis whose jobs required extended periods of residence abroad were the first to benefit from the opportunity to acquire formal education in Arab cities. According to Altorki, the earliest group of girls attending boarding schools came from the elite families.[22] This trend did not start until later in the 1950s.

Another enclave where limited girls' education existed was in the Eastern Province, where Aramco (the Arabian American Oil Company), the U.S. oil company in Saudi Arabia, established its headquarters. American schools for the American and Western expatriate community flourished within the walls of the Aramco compound. But these schools were not so popular among the Saudi employees of the company, who constituted only a very small minority in the 1950s. One girl whose father joined Aramco in the 1940s was Fadia Basrawi (b. 1951). In 1956, her family was one of the first three Saudi families ever to move into the Aramco oil camp at Dhahran.[23] Basrawi joined the American school, where she was introduced among other things to American nursery rhymes, brownies, nativity plays, and the American celebration of the Fourth of July. She vividly describes Christmas in the desert camp:

Every Christmas, this tiny speck of the Arabian desert turned into a hushed, shimmering, magical, winter wonderland. A six-meter high conical-shaped hedge in a roundabout in the middle of Dhahran became a resplendent Christmas tree

---

[22] Altorki, *Women in Saudi Arabia*, p. 19.
[23] Basrawi, *Brownies and Kalashnikovs*, p. 17.

sprayed with generous mists of artificial snow... But there was something not quite right about this paradise.[24]

As a young girl, Basrawi was aware that the Wahhabi *mutawwa* were surveying and controlling the lives of Saudis outside the camp wall. 'Under their vigilant eyes, all Saudis were forced to conduct themselves as the Wahhabi ulema believed daily life to have been conducted in the 7th century AD during the Prophet Mohammad's lifetime'.[25]

Later she was sent to boarding school in Beirut and the American University for higher education. Her experience of the American school at the Aramco camp and later in Beirut could not have been more far removed from her surroundings, where girls were confined to the household. Her autobiography paints a vivid picture of a clash of cultures and traditions that were beginning to take place in Saudi Arabia with the advent of oil. The clash was, however, confined to a walled camp, while the majority of the population remained unaware of the changes that swept the country in later decades. Basrawi fell in love with a Lebanese man while studying at the American University in Beirut. In the early 1970s, she eloped with him to London after her father refused to authorise the marriage. The couple returned to Lebanon where they got married. She still lives abroad.

The majority of Saudi women remained without the prospect of receiving any kind of education, either through a religious scholar or a foreign instructor, let alone in a foreign school. A woman's role in society was to fulfil herself through marriage and children. Yet many women in the pre-oil era made a valuable economic contribution to their households. In the heartland of Arabia, vegetable markets were predominantly run by women in towns like Unayza and Burayda.[26] Many women made important clothing for men, for example embroidered head-covers, which they sold either as pedlars or in markets. Other women traders, known as *dallala*, visited households to sell traditional make-up for women, for example *hina* (hair colour), *sidr* (soapy powder), *dayrama* (traditional lipstick), and *kohl* (powder eye make-up). Other traded items included textiles, threads, needles, dresses, chewing gum, and incense. In Mecca

---

[24] Basrawi, *Brownies and Kalashnikovs*, p. 49.
[25] Basrawi, *Brownies and Kalashnikovs*, p. 49.
[26] On Unayza, see Soraya Altorki and Donald Cole, *Arabian Oasis City: The Transformation of Unayzah*, Austin: University of Texas Press, 1989. On Burayda, see al-Washmi, *Fitnat al-qawl bi talim al-banat*.

and Medina, women traded in the streets, selling food and other items to pilgrims.

The idea of educating girls in formal state schools started circulating in the late 1950s, and culminated in opening the first private girls' school, Dar al-Hanan, in Jeddah in 1957.[27] In Riyadh, the first school, Kuliyat al-Banat, opened in 1960. Under the patronage of Iffat, Faisal's wife, the two schools offered an opportunity for a limited number of girls, but later the establishment was instrumental in familiarising society with formal education beyond religious studies. These early private schools attracted girls from upper-class families, mainly the Al-Saud, their collateral branches, and lineages linked to them by marriage. In addition, the daughters of Arab expatriates and diplomats were the first to be enrolled. They intermingled with their Saudi counterparts, and in the early 1960s outnumbered them.

One such private school was al-Tarbiyya al-Islamiyya in Riyadh, conceived and owned by Sarah, the daughter of King Faisal.[28] The school had three levels: primary, middle, and secondary. Boys and girls were taught together until the age of six, after which they were placed in separate buildings. The curriculum included religious studies, the humanities, home economics, and the sciences. The school also taught English, music, and sport. Girls wore short dresses as uniforms until they moved to middle school at the age of twelve. The short uniform was then replaced by a long blue skirt and white shirt, covered with the *abaya* outside the school doors. The school was well guarded, with a high wall and male porters. The porters guarded the gates and made sure that men, mainly drivers waiting for the girls in the outside yard, would not get in. A waiting driver would inform the porter that he was waiting for a girl, whose name would be called using a microphone. The girl would proceed to the door, completely covered with her *abaya*. Confined behind a high wall, many girls enjoyed formal education in a friendly environment with modern teaching techniques and textbooks imported from other Arab countries. The girls shared the experience of belonging to an emerging elite comprising Saudi and non-Saudi families. Najdi and Hijazi girls intermingled with others from Egypt, Syria, and Lebanon. Foreign girls were the daughters of Arab functionaries who came to Saudi Arabia at a time when local expertise was lacking. Several Saudi girls had foreign Arab mothers who

---

[27] Amani Hamdan, 'Women and Education in Saudi Arabia: Challenges and Achievements', *International Education Journal*, 6, 1 (2005), pp. 42–64, at p. 49.

[28] Description of this private school in the 1960s relies on the author's experience.

helped with homework and attended regular parents' evenings. Other girls had private instructors at home to help with English lessons and other homework.

Girls were grouped according to age sets and placed in separate classes. They were subjected to formal examination and assessment. While innovation was possible in some grades, classes that were assessed by special state examinations, for example the certificates of primary and secondary education, had to adhere to the new national curriculum after the introduction of state schools for girls in the 1960s. Many elite girls flourished and developed into the first cohort of formally and locally educated Saudi women. This early private school, together with a few others scattered in the main Saudi cities, offered great opportunities for a very small minority of privileged girls. Other less fortunate girls had to wait until local primary schools opened their gates in cities and towns.

Under the supervision of an Arab headmistress, Arab women teachers, referred to as *abla*s, were imported from Egypt, Lebanon, and Syria. Unmarried teachers lived on the school premises and were subjected to the same seclusion that Saudi girls experienced outside the school. The teachers created a microcosm of learning far detached from mainstream society, yet not as far as Basrawi's American school at Dhahran's Aramco camp. The school introduced girls to religious education in all its branches, while at the same time English literature and sciences were taught with equal enthusiasm and respect. Private girls' schools continued to be established in Saudi cities even after the state started the first girls' school.

OPPOSITION TO GIRLS' SCHOOLS

Although Saudi Arabia created a Ministry of Education in 1954, headed by Prince Fahad, the ministry was not concerned with the education of girls. Girls' state schools were introduced in 1960, but they remained outside the jurisdiction of the ministry. Girls' education was put under the control of a separate body, supervised by the highest religious authority, Shaykh Muhammad ibn Ibrahim. The General Presidency for Girls' Education supervised the schools, teachers, and the curriculum. Immediately after the opening of girls' schools, only two per cent of girls were enrolled.[29]

[29] Ministry of Education, Saudi Arabia.

Initially girls' schools were not made compulsory, in the face of heated debates about whether girls should be educated outside the home. In the early 1960s, the objections of the religious scholars to girls' education became notorious, marking the first clash between the state as moderniser and religious nationalism. As a development agency, the state saw in institutions such as education an opportunity to act like a modern state. Religious scholars and notables in some towns objected to a new vision that undermined their own control over religious education and literacy. Whatever education had existed before was totally under their supervision. The establishment of formal girls' schools promised to take away their monopoly and introduce new visions that might not remain under their total supervision. The state succumbed to the scholars' pressure when it allowed girls' education to operate under a separate institutional framework, despite being keen to be seen as a champion of development in which women symbolised a shift from tradition and backwardness to modernity. This shift was carefully orchestrated, as it had to be carried out under the slogan of remaining faithful to Islam and tradition. The state clearly declared that 'the purpose of educating a girl is to bring her up in a proper Islamic way so as to perform her duty in life, be an ideal and successful housewife and a good mother, ready to do jobs suitable to her nature such as teaching, nursing and medical treatment'. Preparing girls for jobs suitable for their 'nature' as mothers and wives remained a cherished objective underlying the school curriculum. Only through giving the religious scholars total control over girls' education was the state able to combine development with religious nationalism, in which women and their role as reproducers of the pious nation could be reconciled. As will be seen later in this book, this reconciliation was dictated by the context of the 1960s. The situation would later change, and the state would take the lead in dictating gender policies with limited regard for religious scholars. In the early 1960s, neither King Saud nor King Faisal would have been able to overlook the demands of the Wahhabi establishment to exercise total control and supervision over girls in the country. This was because the state was still fragile, not yet able to challenge the foundation of Wahhabi religious nationalism upon which it rested.

The beginnings of girls' education in Saudi Arabia remain a matter of controversy. In many accounts, the initiative is attributed to King Faisal and Iffat, his progressive wife.[30] More recently, and after the drive

---

[30] Joseph Kechichian, *Faisal: Saudi Arabia's King for All Seasons*, Gainesville: University of Florida Press, 2008, p. 117.

to rehabilitate the deposed King Saud, we come across statements that attribute girls' education to his own vision. It is not without significance that the historiography of the era of the two kings has focused on girls' education to justify a claim to developing the country. The political battle between the Saudi brothers over the throne in the 1960s was later translated into claims and counterclaims that dominate the historiography of women's education. It is extremely interesting to note that while Saud and Faisal are remembered as completely different kings, the education of girls seems to play an important role marking their difference. The lavish lifestyle of Saud and his extravagant household, which was filled with women, is often contrasted with the austere and puritanical lifestyle of Faisal. The former brought in Arab teachers for his many daughters to Nasiriyya where he had his compound, but Faisal sent his to schools in Switzerland. In the 1960s, his daughters Sarah, Latifa, and Loulwa came to play leading roles in education and charity. In 1962, Sarah established the first women's charitable organisation in Riyadh, al-Nahda, providing literacy classes, training, and other services for women.[31]

In 1960, a royal decree attributed to King Saud gave the order to open the first girls' school. The decree stated:

In consultation with religious scholars, orders are given to establish schools to educate girls in religious matters (Quran, Creed, and Fiqh), and other sciences that are accepted in our religious tradition such as house management, bringing up children and disciplining them. We gave orders to set up a committee, *haya*, consisting of ulama of high rank who jealously guard religion, to supervise the matter under the guidance of sheikh Muhammad ibn Ibrahim. Teachers should be selected from the Kingdom and others who are known for good creed and faith.[32]

The historiography that promotes Faisal as the champion of reform has equally focused on his own initiatives and that of his wife Iffat and their daughters in patronising women's education and promoting charitable institutions serving women.[33] The narrative about Faisal as a moderniser remains strong despite recent attempts to ameliorate the image of his predecessor, King Saud. Faisal is seen as a 'nation builder' through his development vision, which was anchored in Islam. His education initiatives are not only central to providing the necessary skills for a growing economy

---

[31] Full details of al-Nahda charity are available at http://www.alnahda-ksa.org/pages/home.html.

[32] Quoted in al-Washmi, *Fitnat al-qawl bi talim al-banat*, p. 172.

[33] Kechichian, *Faisal*, p. 117.

but also for homogenising the nation through a uniform educational curriculum. The introduction of girls' education had to be negotiated with a number of rejectionists who made their voices heard in several towns.

It seems that objections to girls' schools were the strongest in Burayda, a famous town in Qasim and the home of Abdullah al-Qasimi, mentioned earlier. The town is often considered to be one of the areas that staged the fiercest opposition to girls' education in formal schools. Immediately after the royal decree, Burayda was exempted from opening a school after its people objected. It is also in Burayda that the first school was forced to shut down, after a number of the city's scholars and notables called for a boycott.[34] One religious scholar warned the inhabitants of Burayda:

You Muslims, beware of the dangers. Get united to go to the government and scholars to show them the truth and ask them to close these schools that teach modern material. The outside of these schools appears to be good but inside there is corruption and chaos. The schools will end up promoting unveiling and debauchery. If you do not act now before it is too late, you will regret it.[35]

Perhaps the ability of the city's judge, other *ulama*, and notables to organise themselves and travel to Riyadh as a group, first to meet King Saud and later Crown prince Faisal, earned them notoriety as 'rejectionists' of girls' education. The delegates also met up with the grand mufti, Muhammad ibn Ibrahim, with a view to reversing the decision to open a school in their town. According to one account, a popular Burayda judge gathered almost 800 men drawn from the Committee for the Promotion of Commanding Right and Forbidding Wrong and, *mutawwa*, who descended on Riyadh in eighty cars. When they arrived, they pitched huge tents on the outskirts of the capital, as they were not allowed to enter the city. 'It seems that Faisal refused to authorise their entry into the capital for fear that Nasser of Egypt would think that there was a revolution in Saudi Arabia'.[36] This is extremely interesting, as the Burayda march on Riyadh took place at the height of tension between Saudi Arabia and Egypt, only a couple of years before the Yemen war, in which both countries participated, broke out in 1962. Crown prince Faisal allowed the judge and six men to enter the city, but the crowd defied his orders and marched into Riyadh. His reply to their objections was summed up in a statement: 'No one will stop people who come to the school and no one will be called to it if they reject it'. He assured them that no police force would be sent to

[34] al-Washmi, *Fitnat al-qawl bi talim al-banat*, p. 92.
[35] al-Washmi, *Fitnat al-qawl bi talim al-banat*, p. 44.
[36] al-Washmi, *Fitnat al-qawl bi talim al-banat*, p. 41.

coerce people to bring their girls to the school.[37] Like other small towns in Najd, Burayda had its own small study circles for girls, the *kuttab*s that were run by female *mutawwa*. As early as the nineteenth century, women had been selling fruit, vegetables, and items of clothing in the market. Yet the city was able to stage serious opposition that attracted the attention of the nascent Saudi press in the early 1960s and earned the city the title of the most conservative, and later radical, city in the Qasim. Yet not all Burayda people objected to schooling girls; a small minority was in favour.

While Burayda's rejection of schools for girls is often attributed to the conservatism of its people and their adherence to radical Wahhabi teachings, it seems that they were responding to a new education system that promised to make the *ulama* who had for centuries controlled the education of boys and girls in the town redundant. The new schools were destined to rely on foreign Arab teachers rather than *mutawwa*. These teachers were trained in disciplines other than religious studies, thus promising to undermine the old indigenous educational centres and their instructors. The sight of foreign women teachers who would move into the community, spreading new values and styles of living, was unbearable in a town such as Burayda, or any other town in central Arabia. The religion of these 'foreign teachers' was treated with scepticism and even condemned by many Saudi religious scholars who saw it as lacking the purity of their own Wahhabi tradition. In girls' schools, the danger was even greater, as educating girls in such alien environments would remove them completely from the control not only of their parents and families but also of their traditional *mutawwa* instructors. They would begin to learn new sciences and lifestyles, borrowed from their new Arab teachers. Foreign Arab teachers were thus seen as a threat to the purity of the religious nation and its integrity. Their corrupting influence among Saudi girls was feared at a time when an increasing number of Arab immigrants was arriving in the country to take jobs that could not be performed by Saudis who lacked the necessary skills. A couple of decades later, fear of the corrupting influence of foreign Arab teachers on Saudi girls would be replaced by fear of Westernisation and its local agents, namely those Saudi women who borrow ideas and lifestyles from the West.

It is interesting to compare reactions to the prospect of these foreign Arab teachers with those who came to teach at the first men's university that opened in Riyadh in 1957. The university is remembered as 'a tower

---

37 al-Washmi, *Fitnat al-qawl bi talim al-banat*, pp. 42–3.

so high and remote, a school on the edge of town, with foreign teachers who dress in different clothes, their faces look different so do their words and manners'.[38] Because the university was so remote, there was no objection or resistance for almost four decades after its establishment. While the university may have remained aloof and estranged from society like 'a sleeping princess in an enchanted castle',[39] the story of girls' schools was different. The schools received young girls who were responsible for the reproduction of the nation and its tradition. As such, it was considered vital that girls should not be corrupted by foreign teachers, who would not be situated on the edge of town but in the middle. Unlike the university, girls' education reached the heart of the community.

Other towns besides Burayda objected to new schools. On the edge of the desert, the small town of Zulfi staged serious resistance, and it was reported that its inhabitants violently attacked the envoy who was dispatched to the town to rent a building for the new school. According to al-Washmi, however, despite the violent attack in Zulfi, Burayda remains in the historical imagination as the most resistant town. He attributes this to the organisation of their protest and its magnitude, which resulted in delaying the opening of the first girls' school.

Throughout the early 1960s, official Saudi newspapers were saturated with articles calling upon society to accept the new opportunities under the guidance of the king and his religious scholars. Many voices supporting the new education initiatives for girls were those of men, as not many Saudi women were ready to contribute commentaries to the local press at the time. But a few women engaged in the heated debate about girls and education.

The fierce resistance to girls' education in many towns prompted poet and writer Sarah bu Humaid, born in Khobar in 1934 and educated in Beirut, to write in the newspaper *Okaz* urging men not to prohibit their daughters from going to school. In 1962, she urged the government to

... use all means to explain to parents the danger of not sending girls to school. They have to understand that nations cannot be civilised without educating women. It is the responsibility of the educated Burayda people to enlighten parents. Only with education can a woman contribute to her family and nation. Educated girls become good citizens who serve their nation with their work.[40]

---

[38] al-Ghathami, *Hikayat*, p. 71.
[39] al-Ghathami, *Hikayat*, p. 72.
[40] Sarah bu Humaid, 'La tamnau al-ilm an fatayatikum' [Do not deprive your girls of education], *Huqul*, 2007, p. 80.

Another Saudi writer, Samira Khashoggi, director of al-Nahda, wrote about the need to provide education for girls, as they are

...important for the renaissance of the nation. Islam requires women to be educated. We should educate women to make her husband happy, and bring up her children in an appropriate manner. We also need to educate her so that she can worship God. She will become queen in her own kingdom. If we educate her, she will teach her sons proper masculinity (*rujula*). We need to teach women the latest cooking and cleaning styles so that her house becomes heavenly. We need to teach her nursing and medicine to perform first aid. We need to teach her the love of God and nation.[41]

Both bu Humaid and Khashoggi were educated outside Saudi Arabia. They represented the first women's voices to enter the public sphere through the publication of short articles in the local press.

Opposition to girls' schools was overcome, and the first schools opened their doors to a small number of girls after the state negotiated the control of religious scholars over them. Girls of different ages were grouped together without formal assessment and placed in classrooms together. Many parents did not have records of their daughters' dates of birth, and none had identity cards or birth certificates. Registering births was not even sought by parents. The drop-out and truancy rates were high among the girls. This reflected the reluctance of many families to take girls' education seriously. A girl was taken out of school at the first opportunity to marry or if she was needed for housework or to help with family matters. Even when girls stayed in school for several years, literacy levels remained low. Help with homework after school was totally absent, as mothers were illiterate. Arab women teachers had little in common with the girls' social and cultural background. Many of these teachers were seen as alien by the parents and their daughters. There was no continuity between the culture of the school and that of the house.

MIXED BLESSINGS: WOMEN AND THE OIL BOOM OF THE 1970S

One decade of girls' education was too short to change the status of women in Saudi Arabia. In 1970, the literacy rate among men was fifteen per cent and among women two per cent. Only Yemen and Afghanistan

---

[41] Samira Khashoggi, 'al-Mara wa al-talim' [Women and education], *Huqul*, 2007, pp. 81–3, at p. 81. For an exploration of women's activism in the 1960s, see Ahmad al-Wasil, 'Satair wa aqlam sarikha: takwin al-muthaqafa al-saudiyya wa tahawulataha' [Curtains and sharp pens: Saudi women intellectuals and their changes], *Idhafat*, 7 (2009), pp. 82–105.

had rates lower than Saudi Arabia. This is not surprising given that only 412,000 boys and 135,000 girls were enrolled in schools out of a population that did not exceed six million at the time.[42]

Calls for educating women continued, thus reflecting society's resistance and reluctance. Journalist and founder of *Dhahran* newspaper, Abd al-Karim al-Juhaiman (d. 2011), called for greater appreciation for women's education and chastised those who were still reluctant to send their daughters to school. From now on, he warned, it was important to increase enrolment in schools in light of a threatening new danger. The danger, in his opinion, was related to the beginning of a trend in which Saudi men were starting to marry foreign women. Al-Juhaiman observed that many Saudi men who had gone to pursue higher education abroad came back with foreign wives. Two examples are well known. Oil Minister Abdullah al-Tariqi (b. 1925) returned to Saudi Arabia with an American wife after finishing his education in Texas.[43] His successor, Ahmad Zaki Yamani (b. 1933), married an Iraqi from a notable Basra family. Before the mid-1960s, most Saudis did not go farther than Cairo for higher education. But with increased oil revenues, scholarships to study in the United States became common. From 100 students in the 1950s, the numbers increased to almost 10,000 in 1980.[44] The fear that these men would return with foreign wives began to haunt many people in Saudi Arabia.

From the 1960s onward, marriages with foreign Arab women became fashionable among members of the royal family. Several sons of Ibn Saud had among their wives Lebanese, Syrian, Egyptian, and Moroccan women. Talal ibn Abd al-Aziz married into the notable Lebanese Solh family, and Abdullah (king since 2005), married a Levantine woman from the Fustuq family, the mother of his outspoken daughter Adilla. Marrying out became appealing to commoners, although for different reasons. The new oil wealth had suddenly converted Saudi men into valuable assets who appealed to Arab women but angered those who were dedicated to the purity of the nation and its religious tradition. They saw in these marriages a real threat to society and the continuity of its genealogy and tradition. In addition to technocrats, ordinary tribesmen

---

[42] Ministry of Education, Saudi Arabia.

[43] Muhammad al-Saif, *Abdullah al-Tariqi*, Beirut: Riad al-Rayyes Books, 2007; Robert Vitalis, *America's Kingdom: Mythmaking on the Saudi Oil Frontier*, Stanford: Stanford University Press, 2007.

[44] William Rugh, 'Education in Saudi Arabia: Choices and Constraints', *Middle East Policy*, 9, 2 (2002), pp. 40–55, at p. 49.

also married women across the borders, in Jordan, Syria, Yemen, and other Gulf countries.

Al-Juhaiman explains that Saudi men who had acquired education abroad looked for compatible women but, as there was a shortage of such women in the country, they had no choice but to return with foreign wives. Educating Saudi women thus became a necessity dictated by the threat of men undermining the purity of the nation by marrying out. The fear of foreign teachers that haunted the people of Burayda in the early 1960s evolved into a fear of marrying foreign women by the mid-1970s. With greater exposure to other countries through government higher education scholarships, the possibility of marrying out became a reality in Saudi Arabia. Al-Juhaiman saw the solution in increasing the number of educated Saudi women in order to 'militate against Saudi men marrying educated foreign women'. Foreign wives joined foreign teachers as the source of a threat that could be counterbalanced with local education. However, the search for compatible wives may not completely explain the surge in marrying out after the oil boom of the 1970s. Oil wealth brought about a serious increase in the amount of the dowry that men paid to acquire a Saudi wife. Those who could not afford the cost of weddings and gifts to the bride and her family began to be driven out of the local marriage market in search of cheaper Arab options in places such as Yemen, Egypt, Lebanon, and Syria. Marrying out increased among both the elite and the lower classes of the cities, reflecting changes associated with the new oil economy and its impact on social life.

An even greater threat stemmed from sending Saudi girls abroad for education. In al-Juhaiman's opinion, another reason for supporting local education for girls was the limited but visible tendency among elite families to send their daughters to boarding schools where they

... learn different morality and lifestyle. It is better for parents to send their girls to Saudi schools that are under the supervision of our own people and conform to our tradition. This is better for our unity. If the education of girls is not accelerated, we will have women who are either ignorant or educated in alien lands and environments so different from our own tradition.[45]

Al-Juhaiman's article anticipated the new concerns that accompanied the first oil revenues. The industry had a long-lasting impact on gender and perceptions of women. Oil wealth allowed greater exposure to 'foreign' elements in the persona of the teacher, wife, and expatriate worker, all

---

[45] Abd al-Karim al-Juhaiman, 'Nisfuna al-akhar' [Our other half], *Huqul*, 2007, p. 79.

considered a threat to local tradition. Most importantly, an imagined national and religious purity was considered to be under threat from exposure to outside influences. While enabling the nation to achieve its potential in education and development, oil wealth was a mixed blessing, threatening the basic pillar of national purity, namely women. When women adopted new criteria for marriage and wanted to marry out of their tribe or clan, thus exercising choice, the state was alarmed. The story of Princess Mishail, who was caught at the airport eloping with a commoner in 1977, was revealing.

## A DEFIANT GRANDDAUGHTER: LESSONS FOR THE NATION

If Nura, discussed in Chapter 1, represented the ideal gender role that features in Saudi legitimacy narratives, another young Saudi princess was literally sacrificed in a public square after Friday prayers in July 1977 for violating the state and the honour of its masculine persona. Princess Mishail, a young granddaughter of Prince Muhammad, an elderly brother of King Khalid (r. 1975–82), had been married off at an early age to someone who took little interest in her. She was caught at Jeddah airport dressed in men's clothes as she was trying to elope with her lover, the nephew of the Saudi ambassador in Lebanon at the time and a descendant of a family of bureaucrats who served the royal family.

Supported by King Khalid and other senior members of the royal family, her grandfather, Prince Muhammad, ordered her execution, to restore not only his honour but also that of the state and its constructed gender roles. Although the princess had not been caught committing an adulterous act, and certainly there were no four witnesses summoned to court to testify against her, she incurred the ultimate punishment for a *zaniya*, namely stoning to death, which was changed in her case to shooting in a public square. There was no public trial, no court proceedings, and no prosecutors or defendants. The royal family, in particular her grandfather, was the judge, whose ruling was applied to both the princess and her lover. They were executed in Jeddah in front of a gathered Saudi audience.

The princess's relationship with a commoner was not simply a private matter to be dealt with in secrecy but became a public affair for Saudis to watch and draw lessons from. Her public execution carried a strong message to the constituency. It was a warning signal – not only to other Saudi princesses but also to the constituency, both men and women.

Three years later, when Anthony Thomas, a British filmmaker, publicised her story in a film called *Death of a Princess*, which was broadcast on British television, Saudi Arabia broke off diplomatic relations with Britain. The dramatised documentary exposed the dark side of Saudi Arabia to the outside world.[46]

The state legitimacy narrative enforces a clear separation between royalty and commoners (*al-raiya*). The former act; the latter receive orders and obey. Any intimate encounter, for example a love relationship between royalty and commoner, must be subject to the rules of power. Male royalty has a wide pool of women to wed – for example, princesses, tribal nobility, commoners, and even foreign women have been incorporated into the royal household as wives and lovers. But female royalty is restricted in its ability to choose partners. Royal women are given away to other relatives or to a limited circle of colateral branches with whom the Al-Saud had always married. But female exogamous unions remain rare, and the Al-Saud, especially those close to the centre of the decision-making process and power, prefer to remain wife receivers rather than givers. Their women must endure spinsterhood rather than being allowed to marry commoners. In this respect, the family reinforces its role not only as a unifier of Arabia but also as a conqueror of society.

Royal women are to be reserved for the male members of the clan or their equivalent, while the latter are free to diversify and include among their spouses members of different social classes, tribes, and foreigners. A princess eloping with a Saudi commoner erodes the boundaries between ruler and ruled, upsets the political hierarchy, and threatens the very foundation of the state. Eloping with a commoner is a daring act that touches the principles upon which the state was established, namely the separation between power holders and obedient population. Throughout the past decades, the royal family has worked to emerge as a distinct class in Saudi society, assisted by wealth, patterns of consumption, traditional attire, and rituals that are displayed and enacted in public. From weddings to funerals, state banquets, regular open councils, dancing ceremonies and celebrations, and poetry recitations, the rulers inscribe in the imagination of their subjects their difference and superiority. The defiant princess confounded the hierarchy in Saudi Arabia and undermined the separation between royalty and commoner by committing the ultimate

---

[46] For further details on the film's reception, see Thomas White and Gladys Ganley, 'The *Death of a Princess* Controversy', available at http://www.pbs.org.

sin – wishing to marry a subordinate man belonging to a class that serves rather than rules. She violated the ban on intimacy with an 'untouchable', by definition an impure, unknown figure.

The message was meant to reach not only other princesses whose youth and passions could potentially subvert the state-sanctioned political hierarchy, but also all other Saudi women, who receive the same protection that royalty extends to its female members. Through legislation banning unaccompanied women from travelling abroad, enforcing sex segregation, and the prohibition on driving, the state enforced its role as protector of women's honour, which is in the first place the responsibility of their fathers and other male guardians. The state, however, is the agent in society that assumes the role of protector, enforcer, and punisher of transgressors. Much as a careful father watches his young daughters as they venture outside the house, the state employs special agents to play the same protective–controlling role in the public sphere. The religious police watch men and women in public, and monitor their movement, interaction, and behaviour. The execution of the princess was a strong negative symbol, a sign of the authority of the state over the domestic sphere, the triumph of its carefully defined and constructed gender roles, and the elimination of sinful acts that threaten the moral order, regardless of who commits them.

Equally, the public execution of the princess's lover carried a message to Saudi men. It obviously set a precedent for any future violation of the honour of the royal family, symbolised by the molestation of their women. It was a deterrent against overtures, especially intimate ones, between common men and their social and political superiors. Such men are expected to defend the honour of princesses rather than tarnish it with their lust and passion. The family of the executed man collected the body submissively thanking the king for applying God's divine law.

Finally, public execution allows the state to reinforce its commitment to Islamic law, which punishes adulterers with death, and to remind the constituency of this commitment at a time when rapid social change was visible. Equality before Islamic law, in this case, was more important than its application: the public could see that even royal figures are not above the law. Against the background of hierarchy, separation, and distinction, all enforced by royal behaviour and pomp, the state triumphed as an enforcer of a divine law that does not distinguish between ruler and ruled. The execution of the princess reinforced this message in the minds of Saudis. Just as the dramatised public communal prayers and the pilgrimage rituals instil in the nation a sense of momentary equality, the execution of a princess for the sin of adultery created the impression that all are equal in Saudi Arabia. Saudis watching the execution or hearing about it through the private gossip that was rife at the time were expected to applaud justice equally applied. While the princess violated well-established Saudi hierarchies, her execution reinforced the semblance of equality. The number of Saudi princesses who have eloped with Saudi commoners and foreign nationals remains undocumented, but private anecdotal evidence suggests that such acts do occasionally happen. There were no further executions or scandals. Only one princess had to be publicly sacrificed as an example. The fates of others are often buried as family secrets. Regular exposure of such royal secrets would undermine the group's legitimacy and that of the state.

The state can only privilege certain stories about women, and take part in enforcing practices that punish sinners or reward conformists. Female sinners and conformists both find their place in the historical imagination, the ultimate purpose of which is to fix the image of the state as an entity whose morality derives from control of gender roles. From being responsible for introducing girls' education in the 1960s to executing a princess in the late 1970s, the state reinforced its commitment to two sometimes-contradictory projects: modernity through education and commitment to the purity of the religious nation.

The discourse in support of education was hardly about individual women's improvement or emancipation. This applied to both the early 1930 calls and the 1960 commentaries in the Saudi press encouraging society to accept girls' schools. Commentators, both men and women, were keen to educate women for the sake of men and the nation. If women are educated, they become good mothers and wives who produce a future generation of masculine men. Educated women teach their sons real *rujula*, the totality of desired male qualities. The discourse embodied a nostalgia for the Islamic past in which women were prominent as educators in religious matters. Writers considered the recent failure to educate women as an aberration of that past and a break from its cherished ideals. In the call for women's education, the well-being of the nation seems to be a prominent goal that should encourage society to overcome its apprehension and resistance. New arguments in favour of education for girls were put forward in the 1970s. These focused on new developments in society such as the phenomenon of marrying out while studying abroad. Writers argued that the quest for an educated woman as a wife pushed some Saudi men to seek a partner from other countries as Saudi women were still lagging behind. Educating women is a safeguard against this undesired possibility, which promises to threaten the 'purity' of the nation. The integrity and purity of the religious nation necessitate educating women, lest men search for foreign wives.

The euphoria that accompanied the opening of girls' schools did not lead to women being portrayed as developing their economic contribution to society. In fact, arguments in favour of women's education rarely invoked education as a path to economic contribution, employment, or a career. It would take more than a decade to produce women who could replace, even partially, the huge number of Arab teachers. Writers commenting on women's education were still endorsing the view that this education should be geared towards making Saudi women better mothers and wives rather than economically active citizens. However, the need to replace Arab teachers was urgent. This led to establishing the first College of Education in Riyadh in 1970 to produce qualified teachers for intermediate and secondary schools. Similar institutions in Mecca, Jeddah, Dammam, Medina, Abha, and Burayda followed. The stated main objectives of these colleges were to produce qualified teachers, good Muslims, successful housekeepers, and ideal wives.[47] The only economic activity that was expected as an outcome of education was teaching. This remained so for a long time, thus explaining the continuing high concentration of women in educational and teaching jobs.

Employment in the oil industry remained a remote opportunity available only to a very small number of women. The oil sector is a male-dominated industry in which very limited employment opportunities exist for women. Although Aramco brought American women to work in its walled compounds and later employed a very limited number of Saudi women whose parents or husbands were Aramco employees, in general women were excluded from this emerging but dominant economic sector. It has been argued that oil production reduces the number of women in the labour force and favours the persistence of patriarchal structures. Women often tend to have no political influence in societies where oil production is a substantial sector of the economy. With only a few exceptions among oil-producing countries, Saudi Arabia seemed to conform to this pattern in which women's contribution to the economy tended to be limited.[48] Although the state increased educational provisions for women

[47] Ibtisam al-Bassam, 'Institutions of Higher Education for Women in Saudi Arabia', *International Journal of Educational Development*, 4, 3 (1984), pp. 255–8, at p. 256.
[48] Michael Ross argues that oil affects a country's social structures. It reduces economic opportunities for women and their political influence. See Michael Ross, 'Oil, Islam and Women', *American Political Science Review*, 102, 1 (2008), pp. 107–23.

at the level of schools and higher education, there was no urgency to find them jobs when they finished their schooling, apart from working in the educational sector. In the 1970s, neither women nor society demanded greater employment opportunities for women. As long as foreigners could be trusted to do the jobs that became available with the expansion of the state, there was no need to press for women's employment. Women's contribution to the labour force remained one of the lowest in the Arab world. Throughout the 1970s, education was not a straightforward road to a career, given other intervening factors that delayed economic participation such as oil wealth and social expectations. In general, with time, the expansion of women's education led to paradoxes that are still far from being resolved.

## AN EDUCATED BUT IDLE MINORITY

One of the paradoxes of oil and education relates to the fact that without the former, the latter would not have been possible in a country like Saudi Arabia. However, oil wealth has inhibited women's economic participation. First, the oil boom accrued to Saudis new incomes that had never been available before. It allowed an unprecedented expansion in government bureaucracy that offered employment opportunities for the new generation of educated Saudi men. For the first time, regular salaries became available to a growing number of men who in the past would have had only irregular income. In such a new climate, there was no urgent need for women's economic contribution, as the salaried men had at their disposal for the first time a guaranteed and predictable monthly income. Second, oil wealth brought the importation of foreign domestic workers who began to be seen in elite households but were later also adopted by the growing urban middle classes, mainly government employees, technocrats, and merchants.

Among upper-class families, wealth had always allowed women to be relieved from housework – first as a result of the ownership of slaves, freed only in 1962, and later through the employment of Arab and Asian domestic workers. In the 1970s, an unusual situation emerged whereby elite educated but idle women had little participation in the running of their households apart from managing a large number of servants. A good housewife was an educated manager (*mudabira*), a supervisor of children's homework, and a good companion. She was someone her husband could rely on when he had lavish banquets and feasts, demonstrating his newly acquired wealth and prestige. The new wealth allowed upper-class families to replace their slaves with imported servants, first from Arab countries but later from Asia. Yemeni, Sudanese, and Egyptian cooks, coffee makers, and cleaners began to appear in these households in the 1970s. By the end of the decade, even less wealthy families who had never owned slave domestics began to import maids from abroad.

The combination of education, new wealth, and imported domestic labour contributed to the creation of a class of educated but unemployed Saudi women. Freed from the usual household jobs, many women were occupied with the new consumption patterns that began to be noticeable immediately after the oil boom of 1973. Although the large shopping centre was not available then, there emerged new shopping areas away from the traditional small shops in the old centres of cities such as Riyadh and Jeddah. Women ventured into the new shops in Riyadh's al-Wazir Street and al-Thumairi to survey the latest fashions, shoes, and perfumes. Less wealthy women continued to shop in Dira, where traditional garments, incense, cooking utensils, and textiles were sold. Those with less means would go to the flea market in Batha where the second-hand market provided many of the items they needed.

This was the time when many wealthy families abandoned their old, small, mud-brick houses in favour of the newly built villas that emerged in the big cities of Jeddah and Riyadh. Women who were married to men with a regular income, mostly as a result of employment in the expanding government sector, spent time enjoying the new luxuries these salaries provided without having to be economically active themselves. They were able to afford household help and the consumption patterns that became available. No doubt, education brought new awareness and understanding of the world, but this was not automatically translated into a need or desire to become economically active. Women working outside the house, even as teachers or administrators in girls' schools, was not really acceptable to either men or women in the 1970s. This was to change a decade later.

Yet in the 1970s, women were beginning to be seen more in urban spaces. Large numbers of girls in school buses and crowds outside school buildings, in addition to female shoppers, were becoming regular features of urban space, announcing the beginning of a new social phenomenon. Flirting and the harassment of women began in earnest. Previously such behaviour had been most uncommon. But the moment women became highly visible in unfamiliar new streets where there was no community or social network, they were subjected to harassment that made Saudi cities notorious in the Arab world. As women entered this impersonal public space, it became an arena in which to both challenge and confirm tradition. Like the school, urban space, where Saudis and foreigners, men and women, and young and old intermingled, came to embody both the spirit of the religious nation and the forces and styles that from now on threatened it.

If oil freed women from many domestic responsibilities in the private sphere, it made them hostage to abuse in public space. The more women ventured into this new space, the more men harassed them. Men were just beginning to encounter women in large numbers outside the home. Some gathered outside schools waiting for them to come out at lunchtime and catch a glimpse of the new crowds. Others flooded the new shopping spaces that women frequented and squeezed themselves in narrow alleys to touch parts of their bodies, whisper words of endearment, or hand them little pieces of paper with their names and telephone numbers. Those privileged to have cars chased women on the roads. Some women may have enjoyed the new attention, but others felt frightened and intimidated. They preferred to go out accompanied by their husbands and drivers or older women. Men who engaged in this behaviour challenged the very spirit of the religious nation in which women are protected rather than violated and harassed. In later years, women themselves used public space to flirt, date, and exchange relevant information to enable them to reconnect with men they met there. Urban space became an arena for flirtation, challenging many social and religious taboos.

It was not too long after this kind of behaviour became common that the state and its religious guardians embarked on a campaign to reaffirm tradition in the urban spaces. Again, oil wealth allowed greater surveillance of the public sphere through expansion in the employment of *mutawwa*, who roamed the streets chastising men and women and urging them to conform to acceptable styles of dress and behaviour. The *mutawwa* were supported by the police as they roamed the streets in search of immoral behaviour. In the pre-state period, only a limited circle of men controlled women. These were husbands, fathers, brothers, and other male relatives within the family or the extended kin group. However, with the development of state institutions of control and surveillance, the state gave a large number of men the right to control women's behaviour and conduct in the public sphere. Monitoring women's conduct became a collective male responsibility to be upheld by all Saudi men, who were required to correct any violation of the honour of the nation. If men were seen harassing women, they would be chastised, beaten up, and even taken to prison. Women – both Saudi and foreign – whose *abaya*s

revealed their faces and arms were reprimanded with a long stick and told
to be modest. Through its religious vigilantes and police force, the state
took it upon itself to assume a paternal role, guarding women's honour.
If oil wealth allowed the expansion of education for women and delayed
their entry into the labour force, it certainly made possible the imposition
of restrictions on them and the expansion of the circle of men in charge
of guarding their morality and punishing their transgressions.

Perceived as an ultimate good for the nation and its men, the education of women began to have an impact on marriage. While initially
some Saudi men envisioned education as a protection against the danger
of foreign wives, it did not in fact increase women's eligibility for marriage. Education created more questions than answers in a society going
through a transitional period and rapid social change. This is not surprising, as the acquisition of knowledge does not always lead to firm
answers but to a plethora of urgent questions, doubts, and shifting perceptions of reality rather than certainty. Pursuing an education obviously
delayed the age of marriage by several years. When a woman finished
her higher education, she would have already reached an age that was
regarded as too late for marriage. It was very common for a girl to be
taken out of school or college as soon as someone proposed to her. Many
first-generation women who entered the schools never finished their secondary education. Families feared that their daughters would miss out
on marriage altogether if they did not accept their first proposals. It was
unusual in the 1970s for a family to accept delaying marriage until the
girl finished school at the age of eighteen. Moreover, the educated girl
was beginning to be perceived as demanding, independent minded, and
difficult to control. The question of whether a girl should be allowed to
prioritise education over marriage became urgent in the minds of parents.
What does a girl do if her father insists that she should abandon school
in favour of marriage? What responses should she have if her future husband insists on her quitting school or college? Can a woman combine
studying or working with bringing up a family? These were urgent questions that began to circulate in the late 1970s, and we get a glimpse of
them in the next chapter when the responses they received from religious
scholars are examined.[49] Saudis turned to the certainty of the *fatwa* at a
time of uncertain and unpredictable social developments. Many women

---

[49] For an analysis of the transformation of family in Jeddah, see Soraya Altorki and Abu
Bakr Bagader, *Jeddah: um al-rakha wa al-shida* [Jeddah: A city of affluence and hard-
ship], Cairo: Dar al-Shorouq, 2006.

in the 1970s were led to believe that while education was a prestigious asset, it guarantees neither marriage nor career. Nevertheless, introducing girls' education guaranteed the state's role as a benevolent educator that remained faithful to the principles of religious nationalism. By the end of the 1970s, the state had to give the *ulama* more concessions, the most important of which was total control over women's lives. This was an extension of their control over the education system. If education generated controversies, opposition, and paradoxes, the state intervened in the 1980s to assert its commitment to Islam at a time when this was questioned by the rising tide of Islamist dissent. A change in the political agenda began to have a serious impact on women

# 3

## Symbols of Piety

### Fatwas *on Women in the* 1980s

> My wife is an Islamic studies teacher and we have children. She is insisting that I get a maid to help with household chores. I said I will force her to quit her job rather than bring a maid without a mahram. Am I right?
>
> Sheikh Abd al-Aziz Ibn Baz: Force her to quit her job. Don't bring a maid. It is better for her to stay at home with her children.[1]

After the Mecca mosque crisis of 1979, both the state and the religious establishment felt the threat of internal Islamist forces. Juhaiman's seizure of the Mecca mosque was an important signal.[2] His denunciation of the Saudi regime on political and moral grounds drew attention to underlying currents that questioned state development and its rationale. This chapter deals with how the collections of official *fatwa*s on women and the compilation of religious opinions increasingly began to define the permissible and prohibited, particularly with regard to the position of women, their appearance in the public sphere, and marriage. This also became an urgent matter at a time when globalisation threatened the religious nation and undermined its imagined tradition, according to many of those debating the future of the country. The religious establishment and the state worked hand in hand to address the alleged 'moral corruption' of the nation by reclaiming their central role as moral guardians. While Juhaiman held the state and Al-Saud to be directly responsible for corruption, the state gave back the upper hand to the scholars in

---

[1] See http://binbaz.org.sa/mat/1652.
[2] Thomas Hegghammer and Stephane Lacroix, 'Rejectionist Islamism in Saudi Arabia: The Story of Juhayman al-Utaibi Revisited', *International Journal of Middle East Studies*, 39, 1 (2007), pp. 103–22.

terms of decisions on matters related to women, their public presence, and marriage. Traditional and conservative religious opinions were revived, and new interpretations were constructed to create a strict moral order dependent on the conformity of women and their exclusion from the public sphere. As the public sphere started losing its distinctive 'Islamic' appearance, it was important to limit women's presence in a traditionally male-dominated space. The centrality of women for religious nationalism was revived in order to reflect the conformity of the nation to Islamic teachings and the piety of the state at a time when this was being questioned.

## THE 1980S

Born in 1960, Salwa was a bright student belonging to the first generation of women who enrolled in the first state school to open in her town. She finished her high school qualifications and graduated from one of the local universities. She was sent to the United States to pursue a doctorate, and in 1986 she returned to be appointed a lecturer at the same university. She described her experiences and her estrangement from her family and country. She initially thought that her absence in a Western country had altered her perception of her own milieu. She admitted that she must have changed as a result of spending six years abroad, experiencing a different way of life and socialising. However, it did not take her long to realise that her country had changed too. She described the change as a regression that affected her chances as a woman of developing herself amidst newly imposed restrictions and attitudes. Under the shock of the 1979 mosque siege, women in her family adopted a view that this was a punishment for opening up society, allowing development to go too far, and being lax in their religious practices. Those who had not worn the veil diligently adopted it as a religious obligation, and began to lecture others about adhering to it. Women who were illiterate started giving 'sermons' whenever an opportunity presented itself. They constantly repeated Quranic verses and *hadith*s, instructing other women about the danger of laxity in religion and immoral mixing with men. These women had not attended schools, and most of their knowledge in matters related to religion had been acquired through constant watching of Saudi television, especially religious programmes. Also, a new generation of literate women began to appear. As a result of mass education in which several hours were dedicated to religious subjects, young women had become more conversant with matters related to religious education.

They emerged as authority figures on religious subjects in all women's circles. Despite their youth, they were able to establish their religious credentials on the basis of their literacy and ability to confront any situation with religious solutions. Their religious education gave them a new authority over their mothers, especially those who had missed out on the opportunity to acquire formal religious knowledge.

While in the past members of Salwa's family and their neighbours had intermingled during socialising, enjoying music and even dancing and singing, from the 1980s, women and men observed a strict segregation regime. At parties, women and men entered via separate doors and spent evenings socialising with their own group. Although her mother had supported her throughout her education, she now put pressure on Salwa to demonstrate her piety and conformity. Women members of the family were ready to cite religious texts in support of the change, and the increased segregation witnessed in all spheres of social life. Salwa felt that a serious change had taken place in a very short period of time. She attributed this to the shock of the Juhaiman mosque incident. In her view, Saudis had suddenly become desperate to reconsider their 'sins' and do everything according to religious obligations. In her own words, in the 1980s they all behaved as if they were 'born-again Muslims'.

FATWAS ON WOMEN

While this sudden enthusiasm for Islamisation may have been prompted by the immediate crisis of the Mecca mosque siege, religious scholars were quick to respond by increasing their *fatwas* dealing with women's issues. Women were singled out as deserving greater control because they alone could ensure the piety of the nation and its protection from the increasing Westernisation. As wives and mothers, they were responsible for keeping the boundaries between a unique Saudi nation and those accused of corrupting it and diluting its character.

A royal decree in 1971 established the Higher Council of Ulama as a permanent council, whose objective was to issue *fatwas* on matters of creed, worship, and transactions.[3] This council became an embodiment of religious nationalism, serving as a guardian of the piety of the nation. Its membership reflected the monopoly of Najdi scholars over others. From

---

[3] For further details on the establishment of the council, see Nabil Mouline, *Les Clercs de l'islam: autoritéreligieuse et pouvoir politique en Arabie Saoudite, XVIII–XXI siècles*, Paris: Presses Universitaires de France, Proche Orient, 2011.

its creation, seventy-three per cent of its members were drawn from the central region of Saudi Arabia.[4] Its *fatwa*s needed majority approval from members of the council, which was headed by appointed grand muftis. The influence of Grand Mufti Abd al-Aziz Ibn Baz (d. 1999), together with other important Qasimi scholars in the 1980s, was paramount. While the council's role was to issue religious opinions on all matters relevant to public life, *fatwa*s on women became a substantial preoccupation for many of its *ulama* and for the council as a state institution. Their opinions were first published in both huge anthologies and small pamphlets, but now, in the age of the Internet after 2000, old *fatwa*s are preserved on web pages. The *fatwa*s issued by the council relied on two sources: the Quran and the sayings of the Prophet. Occasionally other evidence from the tradition of the early companions of the Prophet and other *ulama* of the past are cited in support of opinions. The body of *fatwa*s examined here derives from one anthology, a massive volume that includes hundreds of *fatwa*s on all aspects of life. These *fatwa*s are signed either by the Higher Council of Ulama or by individual members.

God spoke on women's issues and dedicated one whole chapter in the Quran, Sura al-Nisa, to the feminine persona. The Prophet's *hadith* (sayings and deeds) serve as supplementary guidelines for the articulation of gender in Muslim society. Later jurists excelled in providing extensive and comprehensive rulings pertaining to women. From inheritance and marriage contracts to physical purity and attire, a Muslim encounters a plethora of diverse opinions, reflecting the historical moments in which these opinions are formulated, social development, or the personal inclinations of male jurists. Subsequent elaborations and rulings of Muslim jurists defined the prohibited and permissible, which are in theory the prerogative of the state to enforce. The Islamic legitimacy of the state is measured according to its compliance with or deviation from the prescribed and accepted ruling in a particular social context. While most states of the Muslim world adopted new legislation in most aspects of life, personal and family law remain faithful to *sharia*.

From the 1980s onward, Saudi religious scholars developed extensive rulings dealing with women's issues, which fill several volumes of *fiqh* (jurisprudence). The contents and sheer amount of their *fatwa*s reflect a fetishism amounting to an obsession with all matters feminine. The shock of the 1979 mosque rebellion and the underlying current within Saudi Arabia pointed to 'corruption' as a major axis for criticism. While the

4 Mouline, *Les Clercs de l'islam*, p. 234.

alleged corruption of the regime had an important political dimension, the state and its *ulama* focused only on moral issues in which women were central. In addition to opinions pertaining to personal and family life, hardly any aspect of the female body and behaviour is left without being regulated by a *fatwa*. Saudi *ulama* produced more than 30,000 *fatwa*s on women.[5] These *fatwa*s responded to urgent social issues and new patterns of behaviour and consumption, but their rationale was to restore the legitimacy of the realm in the face of rising criticism.

In one of the most comprehensive contemporary Saudi *fatwa* anthologies, issued by the Higher Council of Ulama, one whole chapter is dedicated to women, amounting to more than 140 pages. If the section dealing with marriage is counted, we find more than 300 pages listing rulings that deal with women's issues.[6] The opinions of the main religious figures, personalities such as Abd al-Aziz Ibn Baz and Muhammad al-Uthaymin, were prominent. In addition to the large anthologies, individual *fatwa*s were published in short pamphlets and circulated within Saudi Arabia. Most importantly, the *fatwa*s were the foundation of the religious curriculum in schools and universities. This ensured that the children and the youth of the nation were socialised into accepting these opinions from an early age.

Whether the sheer volume of rulings on women is a response to a rising demand for religious opinions at a time of drastic and rapid social change, such as has been the case since the 1980s, or whether it is simply a demonstration of the *ulama*'s narrow range of expertise – or perhaps obsession – seems irrelevant. It is important to note that scholars who are employed by the state, and often work in its many religious institutions, issue these *fatwa*s. Their fetishism can only be interpreted as a reflection of their marginalisation in political and economic matters, which left them in control of only one remaining field, the social arena, and in particular issues relevant to women. As the state gradually came to be seen as losing its Islamic identity, the *ulama* embarked on a project whereby the visible signs of adherence to Islam needed to be promoted and privileged in order to inscribe in the imagination the centrality of

---

[5] Anwar Abdullah, *Khasais wa sifat al-mujtama al-wahhabi al-saudi* [Characteristics of Saudi Wahhabi society], Paris: al-Sharq, 2005.

[6] I rely on the most authoritative collection of official *fatwa*s issued by the Higher Council of Ulama. Many *fatwa*s are signed by Ibn Baz and al-Uthaymin, but others are issued and signed by the Higher Council of Ulama. See Khalid al-Jurayssi, *Fatawi ulama al-balad al-haram* [*Fatwa*s of the *Ulama* of the Land of the Two Holy Mosques), Riyadh: Maktabat al-Malik Fahd al-Wataniyya, 2007, hereafter *Fatawi*.

the pious nation. From 1980 onward, the pious nation was dependent on the visible signs of piety, which women in particular were doomed to represent. Their invisibility in the public sphere was, ironically, a visible token of state piety and the nation's commitment to Islam. But other factors contributed to the surge in *fatwas* on women. The increase in the number of educated women seeking jobs and public roles, in addition to their visibility in the public sphere – especially the newly created urban shopping centres and modernised local markets – brought about new circumstances that required religious intervention to limit the prospect of situations developing in an uncontrolled way. As many women began to be employed as teachers and nurses, their movement had to be regulated, in addition to maintaining their segregation from men at universities, the workplace, and elsewhere. In the 1980s, the 'new businesswomen' began to appear as the owners of small businesses, mainly catering for women. From fashionable boutiques to women's sports centres and beauty parlours, women were beginning to take part in new economic opportunities created around the consumption of new lifestyles. As the trappings of modernity began to creep into Saudi cities, a new social and economic order needed to be regulated. The *fatwa* was a readily provided answer to many questions arising out of new situations.

Issues relevant to women were resolved by resorting to *fatwas*. But what is a *fatwa*? A *fatwa* is a *hukm*, a ruling in response to a question. It is the mufti's or other *ulama*'s answer to a query, either real or hypothetical. The one qualified to issue the ruling should exhibit piety (*wara*) and religiosity (*diyana*), and be known to have resisted the intervention of Iblis (Satan).[7] Can a *fatwa* change with time and place? This is a controversial question that is dealt with in the anthologies of Saudi scholars. The majority reject the view that *fatwas* are contextual – that is, bound by time and place. They distinguish between fixed rulings that are eternal, and outside the changing social and historical moments, and those that serve the requirements of *maslaha* (the public good) – that is, specific to a particular context. The first is certainly fixed; the second is potentially changeable.

A full examination of the corpus of *fatwas* on women in the 1980s reflects opinions that enhance the exclusion of women from the public sphere, the prohibition on women occupying leading public roles, the control of their bodies, and their secondary status in the public realm in general. Marriage and polygamy were promoted as religious

---

[7] *Fatawi*, pp. 37–8.

obligations. Furthermore, state scholarships for women to seek higher education abroad were restricted. The *ulama* requested a *mahram*, a male guardian, to represent women and accompany them when travelling, thus creating insurmountable obstacles. At the same time, any activity that enhances women's piety and morality was encouraged. While the state can only celebrate the contribution of specific women to its foundation and legitimacy (Chapter 1), the *ulama* provided detailed religiously sanctioned opinions that fix women in a particular framework, the purpose of which is to guard the symbolism of gender politics in the kingdom. This became especially urgent in the 1980s as a reaction to possible threats from radical Islamists and the changing social sphere.

WOMEN IN PUBLIC OFFICE

In the 1980s, Saudi *ulama* categorically rejected female eligibility for the offices of political (*imara*) and religious (*imama*) leadership and justice (*adala*).[8] Unaffected by contemporary theological debates among Muslim scholars elsewhere, they retained a strict interpretation of Prophetic sayings, always finding in them proof of women's unsuitability for such high positions. Women are described as weak creatures, subject to natural cycles that reduce their ability to act, assess, and evaluate situations requiring courage, speed, and other cherished masculine qualities. Scholars resort to natural qualities (*tabi'a*) and biological facts on the basis of which they construct an image of women as weak, hesitant, emotional, and lacking full control over their bodies and minds. Their emotional tendencies, which arise from certain bodily dispositions, disqualify them as full members of society – and certainly exclude them from the administration of justice.

Saudi *ulama* argue that the leadership of the Muslim community involves certain requirements. A leader is required to inspect his subjects, mixing with them, leading them militarily in war, negotiating treaties with other states, and travelling to distant locations, all of which do not 'correspond to women's nature'. So the *fatwa* concludes that there is consensus among Muslim scholars that women should not occupy such a demanding position. Equally, the administration of justice is not suitable for women, since they have diminished mental capabilities and excessive emotionality. For this reason, they should not become judges. Their exclusion from political and judicial roles does not, however, negate

---

[8]  *Fatawi*, pp. 1949–54.

the fact that they can be knowledgeable in the sciences of religion. Pious and knowledgeable women were consulted in the past, but they never sought leadership.[9] This opinion opens a space for women in gaining religious education and all matters relevant to the main Islamic sources, but clearly excludes them from aspiring towards leadership positions.

The idea of women's diminished mental capacity is elaborated in many *fatwa*s. The general opinion states that Islam elevated woman to a high position, as it made it compulsory for men to support her financially, protect her, and treat her with respect. Islam gave her half the inheritance of a man, as she is not obliged to support a family. As Saudi Arabia began to be exposed to new discourses about women's rights, the *ulama* adopted a defensive position to highlight that Islam remains a religion that gave women important rights. They insisted that it is the men's responsibility to provide financial support for their families, despite the fact that many women sought jobs as teachers. Getting a job was dependent on the consent of a woman's guardian. Islam's designation of women as half witnesses in court is attributed to women's forgetfulness and occasional fatigue as a result of their bodily functions related to menstruation, pregnancy, and childbirth. But in matters that are strictly related to other women, a woman can count as a full witness, for example in asserting a claim about nursing children (breastfeeding).[10]

In the public sphere, if women attend a sermon or a lecture, they should be seated in the back rows because *sadara* (priority in seating arrangements, for example front rows), even in a segregated area, is frowned upon for women. God and his Prophet appreciate women in *muakhira* (the back row) rather than *sadara* (the front row).[11] A good Muslim woman is one who willingly and eagerly occupies the last of the last rows. Her subordinate legal, religious, and social status must be anchored in physical space. Occupying the last row, behind the men, not only guards the latter from her potential danger but also confirms her subordination.

Many of the Saudi *fatwa*s on women and leadership echo pervasive past and contemporary religious opinions in the Muslim world. However, the importance of such opinions in a country that is founded on religious nationalism is perhaps unique. In Saudi Arabia, women define the religious and moral character of the nation but cannot lead it. The

---

[9] *Fatawi*, pp. 1952–3.
[10] *Fatawi*, p. 951.
[11] *Fatawi*, p. 1948.

detailed descriptions of women's weaknesses that permeate these religious opinions reflect a concern with the strength of the nation, seen as a masculine entity led by men. Women play an important auxiliary role within their families but cannot be trusted with leading the nation. The masculinity of the state and the nation needs to be upheld by relying on Quranic and *hadith* sources, thus anchoring the nation's destiny in the sacred tradition.

These *fatwas* circulated at an important historical moment when women's education opened up new opportunities for literacy and economic participation. These opportunities were absent in the past when women were confined to the household and preoccupied with traditional roles. The changes that swept Saudi Arabia required fixed boundaries that women could not cross.

## WOMEN'S BODIES, BODIES OF THE NATION

Weak and subject to cyclical variation in mood and judgement, the female body is seen as a source of *fitna* (chaos) among the believing nation. The total veiling of the body, including the face, is regarded as a requirement in the public sphere, excluding the context of prayer and pilgrimage. Sex segregation should always be respected, even in hospitals, where it is preferable for patients to be treated by professionals of the same sex. Scholars have urged the state to establish all-female hospitals, banks, and businesses to create segregated ghettos marking compliance with their interpretation of Islam.

When in public, women should never wear white clothes if such attire is the prerogative of the men of the country, lest they be seen as imitating them and confusing gender; hence the persistence of the black *abaya*, which is not only a cultural code of dress but has also attained a religious significance. Notwithstanding the fact that nothing in Islamic sources specifies the colour of women's clothes, Saudi scholars have elevated black to the rank of a religious obligation.[12] The colours black and white in the public sphere have become national symbols, similar to the country's flag; both imply religious inscriptions, signs of the piety of the state and nation. If women were to opt out of dressing in black, they would not only violate a religious ruling but also threaten the state and its symbols, very much like altering the national flag or anthem, which are never modified except at times of political change. Women in black distinguish

[12] *Fatawi*, pp. 1811–35.

Saudis from non-Saudis. They are visible signs of being part of the nation, defining membership by means of clothes at a time when many foreign women arrived in the country.

The contamination of the nation by the cross, a symbol for the influx of Western and Far Eastern expatriate labour, is articulated in the *fatwa* on textiles that have a cross motif. Can women wear dresses made up of textiles with a motif that resembles a cross? Al-Uthaymin issued a religious opinion stating that it is not permissible to use textile material with crosses. Unless this can be erased, the garment should be destroyed.[13] The sensitivity of al-Uthaymin to textiles with crosses reflects the apprehension of many scholars who were beginning to witness the increasing import of a wide range of goods and the arrival of foreign labour, both representing a visible challenge to the purity of the nation and its identity. If the nation is to remain loyal to Islam amidst the influx of foreigners' attire and their ways of life, then the nation's appearance should equally reflect its distinct identity. Outlawing the cross ensures that contamination is contained at least in the appearance of its people. The official *ulama*'s obsession with the cross, even as a decorative motif on an imported garment, later became a symbol for radical Jihadi violence that aspired to eliminate the many 'crosses in the Arabian Peninsula'.

In the 1980s, distinguishing Saudi women from *nisa al-gharb* (Western women) became extremely important. Drawing the boundaries between pious Saudi women and corrupt Western women was articulated around rejecting the latter's lifestyles and consumption patterns, by then both readily available inside Saudi Arabia. Thanks to the influx of expatriate labour, which included the wives of expatriates and single women who worked in hospitals as doctors and nurses, contact between foreign elements and the indigenous population became an everyday possibility. The volume of *fatwas* that aspired to create moral and physical boundaries reflected a concern with contamination, borrowing values, and adopting new alien patterns relating to beauty and lifestyles.

Along with the use of dress as the marker of national identity, colouring the hair became forbidden for women. According to a *fatwa* on dyeing women's hair, 'pious women should not succumb to Western fashion. Western women colour their hair in yellow, red, and blue to attract attention to themselves and lead men astray. Our women have imitated them and sometimes our men have requested their women to colour their hair. They can only use *hina* to darken grey hair but they should

---

[13] *Fatawi*, p. 1906.

not imitate Western women'.[14] Avoiding the imitation of *kafirat* (infidel women) should go as far as avoiding hairdressers, wearing wigs, and even parting hair on the side of the head. Avoiding visits to hairdressers coincided with a time when many salons started opening their doors in the main Saudi cities. Some of these salons were owned by Saudi women who employed an increasing number of foreign Arab and Asian stylists. Saudi women's hair and its styling began to be problematised. Relying on the authentic tradition of Muslim women from the times of the Prophet onwards, a contemporary woman's hair should be parted in the middle and partitioned in three sections. The side parting is not only associated with contemporary infidel women but was also a practice among women during the *jahiliyya* (age of ignorance). As such, it should be avoided by pious women.

These prohibitions are extended to cover almost all aspects of the body and its appearance in a desperate attempt to curtail the influence of new consumption, lifestyles, and appearances, all believed to have been brought to the country by foreigners. Wearing high heels, perfuming the body, eliminating excessive facial hair, and tattooing the skin for decoration or marking a tribal identity are all prohibited. The body is the medium for expressing only an Islamic identity, defined according to specific guidelines from the *ulama*. The quest for maintaining this identity is translated into compilations of *fatwa*s on almost all aspects of the body. The Saudi *ulama* provided opinions on all matters relevant to the female body. The main concern was with guarding Saudi women from contamination by infidel women and their ways of life. The more Saudi women came into close contact with foreign women, the more urgent the *fatwa*s became. They were seen as the only shield against the adoption of new lifestyles, even if these were hidden under the veil.

Fear of the female body is expressed in several *fatwa*s on purity and pollution, under the general subject of female blood (*dima al-nisa*).[15] In particular, female blood carries a disproportionate potential for polluting not only men but also public places of worship. While women are allowed to attend a mosque, seated in a separate area, they are to be excluded during menstruation, childbirth, and other occasions of bleeding. Saudi *ulama* reiterated well-established religious opinions, but the urgency and sheer number of these *fatwa*s reflected the increasing opportunities for women to appear in public. Their inner purity was reasserted as *fatwa*s

[14] *Fatawi*, p. 1910.
[15] *Fatawi*, p. 1906.

circulated to deal with situations of ambiguity and increasing erosion of what was regarded as an authentic tradition.

The Saudi *ulama* follow the strictest interpretations on all matters feminine. The legitimacy narrative of the state requires the construction of gender relations in the most conservative manner. The quest to exhibit the Islamic identity of the nation rather than tribalism, or conservatism, lies at the heart of the persistence of such interpretations. In fact, this is a reflection of political developments, requiring the *ulama* to adhere to the most restrictive interpretations.

Banning new women's lifestyles and consumption patterns at the level of the *fatwa* did not deter the importation of new trends into the Saudi public sphere, including the hairdressers and the informal sports centres where women exercised and enjoyed massages and beauty treatments. No government department is currently capable of issuing licences for commercial women's sports clubs, but many sprang up informally and functioned under the guise of 'beauty salons' where women enjoyed gym and exercise classes.[16] The more these unlicensed venues appeared in the urban centres of the main cities, the more *fatwa*s were needed. Many *ulama* regarded these new urban spaces as islands of immorality where women intermingled behind closed doors. The *ulama* imagined a corrupt world in all women's boutiques and sports centres where women's behaviour could not be controlled. Changing rooms where women tried the latest imported fashions were prohibited, as they became suspicious spaces. A woman taking her clothes off to try a dress in a shop was previously unheard of. Although only women were admitted into these shops, the newly created boutiques were imagined as a source of corruption in the eyes of many men in Saudi Arabia. They not only feared men's infiltration of shops through back doors but also intimacy between women. A *fatwa* was issued banning women from taking their clothes off outside their husbands' houses. This is regarded as a violation of the principle of *sitr* (modesty) and may encourage *fahisha* (debauchery). A woman is allowed to change her clothes only in her parental or husband's home.[17]

The sheer number of *fatwa*s condemning these new urban spaces did not deter women from using the services on offer. What actually determined their enthusiasm for these novel venues was the cost. The

---

[16] As late as 2007, government departments were not authorised to issue licences for women's sports facilities. It was reported that unlicensed sports clubs are threatened with closure. See 'Saudis Clamp Down on Women's Gym', available at http://news.bbc.co.uk/1/hi/8020301, 27 April 2007.

[17] *Fatawi*, p. 1954.

modernity of wealthy women was reflected in their regular visits to places where the body could be the centre of attention, receiving treatment and pampering. From a religious perspective, the female body is regulated through adherence to the principles of purity. But the new spaces introduced other criteria according to which the body can be treated and looked after. Those women who could not afford such luxuries found in these *fatwa*s an opportunity for asserting their morality, piety, and boundaries as pious women, although they may have aspired to be in a position to afford these new luxuries. The class divide within Saudi Arabia, which began to be increasingly visible, took a gender-specific turn. Being wealthy meant that the trappings of modernity could become affordable, while women with limited means were excluded by virtue of their socio-economic status. *Fatwa*s on women dealing with minute aspects of their appearance and lifestyle became notorious, as they reflected a moral and pious mechanism to denounce what is not affordable.

## WOMEN, MARRIAGE, DIVORCE, AND THE NATION

Saudi *ulama* encourage *nikah* (Islamic marriage) to fulfil the ultimate purpose of creating families, the backbone of the pious nation. While fixing the centrality of marriage in the lives of young men and women, the *ulama* have endeavoured to undermine parental authority if it delays marriage, which is seen as a deterrent against sin and temptation. The responsibility of encouraging marital unions falls on the parents, mainly the father. He is forbidden to delay the marriage of a daughter, and is under an obligation to facilitate a suitable match. Fathers are prohibited from delaying the marriages of working daughters to appropriate their income. A father can take from a daughter's salary that which she does not need, but under no circumstances can he postpone her marriage with a view to benefiting from her income. If a guardian is suspected of greed, his guardianship over his daughter will be suspended and another male member of the family can marry her off.[18] The novelty of women's income, mostly gained from teaching jobs in the many schools opened in the country, produced a new situation. The *ulama* feared that the salaries of single women could become an obstacle to early marriage. As women's wage labour became common among a new generation of women, mainly school teachers, the consequences of such new income on their marriage chances became problematic. In theory, women's wages belonged to them, but the *ulama* received queries from the public

---

[18] *Fatawi*, p. 1322.

regarding ownership of the salaries women received. Cases of fathers refusing to accept a suitor for a daughter came in the form of questions to the Higher Council of Ulama demanding clarification. In various *fatwas* on marriage, the *ulama* undermined private patriarchy if this stood in the way of marriage.

While benefiting from women's wage labour cannot be an obstacle to marriage, education cannot be a priority at the expense of marriage either. Women themselves are under an obligation to marry. Refusing marriage in order to continue education is outlawed. Women are advised to accept marriage and then reach an agreement with their husbands to continue their education, as long as they are not occupied with family affairs such as nurturing children. Only primary education is seen as necessary, after which women have no need to continue unless they pursue a career that benefits the nation, such as medicine. Education that allows women to read and write, mainly to understand religion, is encouraged, but acquiring other advanced knowledge is a matter of debate, in the opinion of al-Uthaymin.[19] As more and more women aspired to continue their schooling, and even enrol in universities, cases of women refusing early marriage became more common. The *ulama* regarded this as an invalid excuse. At the same time, they moderated women's education ambitions and insisted that the priority for women is to marry rather than stay in education for several years. They saw no harm in negotiating continuous education with a husband as long as this does not distract women from the important task of bringing up a family. Such situations would not have presented themselves in the past, but with increasing educational and employment opportunities for women, Saudi religious scholars had to reassert the priorities for the nation and the marriage of its women. Their many *fatwas* on concrete questions pertaining to delayed marriage, wage labour, and parental authority reflect the changes that swept Saudi Arabia in the 1980s. Their responses aspired to deal with these changes and limit their impact on the centrality of marriage for reproducing the nation.

To encourage marriage, the *ulama* issued *fatwas* regarding the permissibility of seeing the bride's face and hands prior to marriage. They allowed a man to look at a woman's face after engagement provided that the gaze does not involve lust or temptation. After the engagement, a man is given permission to see the woman in a public place, for example if she is walking outside the house. However, a woman should not beautify herself for a man before the marriage contract, as she remains forbidden. This also may lead to deception and exhibiting a beauty that a woman

[19] *Fatawi*, p. 1323.

may not have. Furthermore, men and women should not indulge themselves in long conversations or call each other by phone unless they need
to discuss important practical matters related to their future family. The
conversation should not lead to temptation, even at a distance.[20]

The *ulama* also denounced excessive dowries but refused to fix the
amount paid by the bridegroom, known as *mahr*. They argued that the
rule should be to pay a limited amount of money, which remains the
woman's property. The father may ask for a portion of this money for
himself, but it is better if he does not, as this may deter a man from
proposing to a woman. Equally, the *ulama* regarded spending too much
money and resources on weddings a form of *israf*, excessive spending
that is frowned upon. The motivation is to facilitate marriage and make
it possible even for people with limited means. The poverty of a groom
should not be grounds for refusing to accept him as husband. Ibn Baz
stated that 'when the cost of marriage is low, the chastity of boys and
girls is guaranteed. Grave sins are reduced, and the *umma* is allowed to
grow in number... My advice to all Muslims is to facilitate marriage and
ask for reasonable *sadaq*'.[21] The growth of the religious nation, where
potential sins are eliminated by early and easy marriage, is the ultimate
goal behind the many *fatwa*s on marriage. Many young people who
found the consumption patterns of Saudi society following the oil boom
of the 1970s increasingly difficult to follow appreciated such *fatwa*s.
The cost of marriage increased dramatically, as it became an arena for
social competition and prestige. Young men found it difficult to meet
the expectations, especially the lavish consumption patterns surrounding
marriage and weddings.

After asserting the centrality of marriage, the *ulama* devoted considerable attention to questions regarding the ideal marriage partner for a
Saudi. This became a controversial subject with the increasing urbanisation of society, easy travel, and intermingling between Saudis and foreigners. As more and more Saudis lived in cities where people of different
backgrounds intermingled, the question became an urgent national concern. The ideal marriage partner for a Muslim is subject to many *fatwa*s
giving permission to marry certain categories of people and prohibiting
marriage with others.

In a long *fatwa* on marriage between tribal and non-tribal partners,
the *ulama* debated the principle of *kafa'a bi al-nikah*, compatibility in

[20] *Fatawi*, p. 1356.
[21] *Fatawi*, p. 1361.

marriage.[22] The *fatwa* was a response to a social phenomenon believed to be common in Najd where people insist on marrying within their own tribes or other tribes of equal status. They resist marriages with non-tribal people. A *khatib* (preacher) sends a question to the Higher Council of Ulama asking for answers, as this issue is hotly debated in his mosque. He asks the Council to give a firm *fatwa* based on the Quran and *sunna* in order to resolve the debate. The question is raised with a view to obtaining a *sharia* opinion on marriage between *qabili* (tribal) and *khadhiri* (non-tribal), which he claims is constantly debated among listeners to his sermons. The *khatib* wants to know whether the Najdi preference for marriage is a residue from the *jahiliyya* times when tribal solidarity was prominent, and whether it is sustainable within Islam. The Council clearly states that previous *ulama* disagreed on the meaning of compatibility in marriage but that the correct criteria should be related to piety rather than genealogy. The *fatwa* cites several cases of the pious ancestors, both men and women, who married persons of lower tribal or even non-tribal backgrounds. Cases of elevated Qurashi and Hashemi women who married men of lower status are given to reach a conclusive answer that it is permissible for people of different social and tribal background to marry. According to this *fatwa*, mixed marriages between the *qabili*s and *khadhiri*s are permissible. The Higher Council of Ulama insists on religious compatibility as the defining criterion for the correct marriage.[23] Despite this conclusive *fatwa*, the question of compatibility remained unresolved, as social norms proved to be stronger than religious rulings – even among the *ulama* themselves. Not all *ulama* and judges abided by the ruling. Some judges are known to have dissolved marriages on the basis of the incompatibility of genealogies. In another *fatwa*, al-Uthaymin insists that a tribal woman should not be denied marriage to a non-tribal man. The most important factor in deciding whether to accept a man of a lower status should be the person's piety, morality, and good deeds. He acknowledges social and economic inequality between people, but these should not be considered as determining factors in marriage.[24] Breaking down tribal solidarities in the pursuit of the homogeneous pious

---

[22] Debates about *kafa'a* in marriage are not unique to Saudi Arabia. In Oman, similar controversies are often a reflection of the contradiction between personal status codes and tribal tradition. See Khalid al-Azeri, 'Change and Conflict in Contemporary Omani Society: The Case of Kafa'a in Marriage', *British Journal of Middle Eastern Studies*, 37, 2 (2010), pp. 121–37.

[23] *Fatawi*, pp. 1348–9.

[24] *Fatawi*, p. 1350.

nation can only be achieved through opening the boundaries of marriage and increasing mixing between social groups in Saudi Arabia. Marriages between *qabili*s and *khadhiri*s are given an Islamic justification in order to dissolve boundaries within the nation, especially those anchored in tradition and social norms. Homogenising the nation through mixed marriages between social groups was a priority.

Dissolving marriage boundaries within the nation excludes certain categories of people deemed unsuitable. Prohibited marriage partners include the Shia. Saudi *ulama* outlaw marriage to a Shia, and if such a marriage takes place it should be annulled, lest the person commits great *shirk* (blasphemy).[25] The Saudi *ulama*'s negative views on the Shia are well known, but specific *fatwa*s on mixed marriages began to appear to combat the blurring of boundaries between Sunni and Shia within the pious nation. The religious purity of the Sunnis needed to be guarded against potential contamination by the blasphemy of the Shia, a small minority in the Eastern Province. The Shia are the other within the nation. As such, they are excluded as a potential category that can be incorporated through marriage.

The prohibition applies also to the marriage of a Muslim woman to a *kafir*, a category that includes mainly Jews and Christians in addition to other religious traditions.[26] The Higher Council of Ulama responded to 'rumours' that other Muslim *ulama* have issued *fatwa*s allowing such marriages, especially in countries where they have taken place, for example among diaspora Muslims in Europe. Also, rumours that al-Azhar in Egypt has issued opinions that Jews and Christians are not *kafir*s prompted the Saudi *ulama* to respond. The Council argued that Muslims continue to consider Jews and Christians as *kafir*s with whom marriage is not permissible. Women and their children will convert to these religions upon marriage and lose their identity as Muslims. While the *fatwa* on women marrying outside their religion is prompted by social development among diaspora Muslims, the increasing number of Saudi women travelling abroad must be a factor to be considered when assessing the importance of these religious opinions. As many Saudi women travelled abroad for education, the prospect of marrying in these countries must have presented a real problem for the *ulama*. They insisted that such women could not travel without a male guardian (*mahram*) to obviate such an eventuality.

---

[25] *Fatawi*, p. 1327.
[26] *Fatawi*, p. 1327.

The plethora of *fatwas* on legitimate and illegitimate partners in marriage is crucial for dissolving some internal boundaries and erecting others. The *ulama* consider the nucleus of the nation to be the family and its pious members. They reiterate the role women play in the reproduction of piety and conformity to the standards of a religious nation. Their marriages should thus not only be a priority but should also contribute to homogenising the nation and keeping it uncontaminated by blasphemy.

Reproducing a homogeneous pious nation requires the promotion of polygamy. Since the 1980s, religious scholars have actively promoted polygamy as a religious obligation, and several *ulama* have served as matchmakers. While many Muslim religious scholars have endeavoured to ration polygamy and impose strict conditions for its validity, their Saudi counterparts have spared no effort to propagate it as a national, social, and personal necessity, sanctioned by divine authority. Public calls for the promotion of polygamy, always sponsored by the state, equate women's acceptability with their overall acceptance of Islam. According to a *fatwa*, being the second or third wife of a morally and socially worthy man is far better than remaining a spinster.[27] Saudi *ulama* justify polygamy by resorting to demographic statistics. In their opinion, women outnumber men at any given moment. The frequency of death rates among men is also higher than that among women. They cite examples such as men dying in war while defending the *umma* against its enemies. Also, their travel and work exposes them to death more than women. If polygamy is outlawed, a substantial number of women will remain without partners. This would make these women drift into a life of sin; men might take advantage of the situation and turn women to unlawful situations, such as prostitution. If too many women remain without marriage, there will be an increase in the number of illegitimate births. The *umma* would become corrupt, as diseases such as syphilis would increase in society. Therefore polygamy protects not only women but also the pious nation. Men would also benefit from polygamy, especially at times when the sexual availability of a wife is reduced, for example during fatigue, menstruation, and childbirth. Having an alternative during these times would protect men from seeking illegitimate encounters.[28]

---

[27] Maha Yamani, *Polygamy and law in Contemporary Saudi Arabia*, Reading: Ithaca Press, 2008, p. 72.
[28] *Fatawi*, pp. 1420–1.

One of the most cherished arguments in favour of polygamy relates to increasing the size of the population and strengthening it: the physical reproduction of the *umma* leads to its empowerment. In order to achieve this objective, polygamy becomes a religiously sanctioned solution not only to men's personal desire and an alleged demographic imbalance, but also to the ultimate objective of increasing the population. A barren woman is an obstacle to the achievement of this objective, but polygamy allows men the opportunity to contribute to empowering the *umma* through procreation.[29]

The scholars' promotion of polygamy did not go unheeded. It increased dramatically after the first oil boom of the 1970s, and spread in regions where it had been rare. Men of all social classes and tribal backgrounds competed to engage in polygamous marriages to mark their prestige and newly acquired wealth. At the same time, they could claim to be contributing to the ultimate purpose of empowering the pious nation through the number of children they produced. However, many men have found that their first wives do not approve of polygamy. Whether a man can go ahead and acquire a second wife without the consent of the first became an issue in need of resolution by the religious scholars. A man describes his dilemma to the Higher Council of Ulama. He claims that he wants another wife for the simple reason that one is not enough to satisfy his desires. As he is pious, he prefers not to slip into sin. He intends to keep his first wife, but he would like to take another one. The first wife does not give her consent. What does he do? The Council provided the *fatwa* that he could go ahead with a second, third, or fourth marriage, as this is legitimate from the *sharia* perspective. The first wife has no right to object, as her objection is not grounded in any legitimate religious position.[30] The only condition for the permissibility of polygamy remains *adl* (justice) in the treatment of the wives a man acquires. And the religious opinion states that 'a woman with a half, third, or quarter of a man is better than [with] no man'.[31]

Polygamy should not in any circumstances distract men from performing their religious obligations, the most important of which is the performance of the Friday communal prayers. A polygamous man who acquires a new virgin cannot miss this important religious obligation under the pretext of the many demands on him to distribute his time equally between several wives.[32]

---

[29] *Fatawi*, p. 1421.
[30] *Fatawi*, p. 1423.
[31] *Fatawi*, p. 1424.
[32] *Fatawi*, p. 1427.

In addition to *nikah* and polygamy, Saudi scholars have also theorised and promoted controversial forms of marriage, such as *misyar*. In *misyar* marriage, men are under no obligation to provide homes or subsistence for their wives. *Misyar* is also a mechanism to evade objections from the first wife, as this marriage can remain a secret, at least in its early phase and before the birth of children. Up to three *misyar* wives can be combined with the first wife, without the usual cost of *nikah* being an issue. *Misyar* marriage allows a woman to remain in her family household, especially if she looks after ageing parents or for other reasons. The husband occasionally visits his wife, but without incurring any financial responsibility towards her maintenance. Shaykh Ibn Baz responded to a question about *misyar* marriage by issuing a *fatwa* making it permissible. Like *nikah*, *misyar* marriage should have the permission of the woman's guardian, two witnesses, and the consent of the spouses. If these conditions are met, then such a marriage is lawful. The marriage should not remain a secret affair, although the husband can visit his wife during the day or at night, depending on convenience.

The promotion of *misyar* marriage in Saudi Arabia seems to have coincided with the revival of temporary marriage (*mut'a*) in Iran in the 1980s. Saudi Arabia entered a long competition with Iran over the demarcation of the state's Islamic identity. Saudi scholars were compelled to follow the footsteps of their Shia rivals in rendering certain sexual relations licit. Although *misyar* is different from *mut'a*, it was reinvented as an authentic solution to modernity and its discontents by the Saudi *ulama* who make it their business to find solutions, always anchored in their interpretation of Islamic tradition, to the changing social and economic context. Contemporary problems of late marriage, spinsterhood, and other social changes that swept the country in the latter half of the twentieth century have been tackled by religious scholars in the form of new, sometimes controversial, *fatwas*. Women in polygamous marriages, together with those who contract *misyar*, are symbols of the flexibility of religious opinions within the fold of Islam. Physical reproduction is not simply a private matter, the prerogative of two consenting adults; it is also a religious priority, sanctioned by the religious scholars. The legitimacy of the Islamic state is dependent on as many women as possible accepting traditional and reinvented marriages.

In the context of the fierce competition over Islamic legitimacy between Iran and Saudi Arabia in the 1980s, the Higher Council of Ulama allowed *misyar* but prohibited *mut'a* marriage.[33] The latter is believed to have

---

[33] *Fatawi*, p. 1330.

been allowed during the early Islamic period, but the Prophet prohibited it forever. In the 1980s, *misyar* became an alternative to the Shia *mut'a* marriage. It was seen as a Sunni response to changing social conditions. However, *misyar* marriage remained controversial, not only in the Sunni Islamic world but also within Saudi Arabia. Many Saudi women saw in it a religious solution that serves only men. The debate it generated led to other *ulama* prohibiting it. This did not happen until almost two decades after it was legalised.

As Saudi *ulama* considered marriage a shield against temptation and sin, they were called upon to deal with new situations arising from regular travel abroad to work in government institutions or to study. Both single and married men who embarked on journeys outside the country enquired about temporary marriages they would like to contract, but with the intention of terminating these unions upon their return to Saudi Arabia. The *ulama* objected to marriages contracted with the intention of termination after a fixed period of time. The intent to end a marriage renders it illegitimate. According to Ibn Baz, travel abroad is a great danger, as it exposes the person to blasphemy, alcohol consumption, and fornication. People should avoid such journeys. Marrying abroad is an even greater danger. If a man decides to marry abroad to protect himself from sin with the intention of divorcing after returning home, he is permitted to do so, but he should not make that a condition in the contract. The intention should remain between God and the individual who can terminate a marriage at a later stage.[34] This *fatwa* was interpreted as religiously sanctioned permission to engage in de facto temporary marriage abroad for the protection of men against sin. While the temporary dimension brings images of the Shia *mut'a* marriage, Saudi scholars insisted that it should not have termination as a condition at the beginning of the marriage, as in *mut'a* marriage. The practice was dubbed *zawaj misfar*, 'travel marriage', to draw the boundaries between this practice and *mut'a* marriage, common among the Shia.

Obviously, Islam permits divorce under certain conditions. Saudi *ulama*, like others elsewhere, regarded divorce as a final Islamic solution to marital problems. They adhered to the principle that it is the prerogative of men, and provided detailed *fatwas*, each dealing with the many questions posed by members of society. As marriage is initiated by men, only men are permitted to terminate the union. Justification centres on the opinion that 'men are above women in their *aql* [reason]

---

[34] *Fatawi*, p. 1334.

and vision'.[35] Women could not be granted an absolute right to initiate divorce, as they are emotional. This may cause them to seek divorce in a hurry, as they are prone to lose their tempers more often than men, to the detriment of the stability and continuity of marriage. If a husband's piety and religious observance diminishes, this may allow a woman to initiate divorce in exceptional circumstances. A man's impotence is also grounds for a woman to initiate divorce, if she discovers his condition after marriage. She may also seek divorce if she develops hatred towards him, provided that she returns the dowry he paid. This is labelled *khal*. Before divorce is granted, a husband is under the obligation to demonstrate that he has unsuccessfully attempted three remedies.[36] These are advice (*wadh*), ostracisation (*hajr*), and mild physical punishment (*dharb yasir*), citing the famous Quranic verse (Sura al-Nisa, verse 34).

Saudi religious scholars therefore promoted traditional Islamic marriages and polygamy as well as new forms of unions. Their opinions may not differ from those in other Islamic countries, but the contextualisation of their *fatwa*s on these issues allows us to consider them in the light of the changes that swept Saudi Arabia in the 1980s. The quest to seek Islamic opinions became extremely important in the context of the alleged threats to the morality and piety of the nation. These threats came not only from abroad but also from internal dynamics associated with the country's increased wealth, and the expansion of women's education and employment opportunities. These factors brought new lifestyles and values seen by the *ulama* as undermining the integrity and identity of the nation.

Women's mobility and travel became an important concern, as the *ulama* considered both a threat to traditional gender roles and a source of *fitna* (dissent). They attempted to regulate women's travel for education and work by means of their insistence on the role of the male guardian who would ensure that women abroad continued to conform to the lifestyle prescribed for them at home. Equally, the debate about women driving, which started in the late 1980s, culminated in the famous prohibition *fatwa* in 1991. Both Ibn Baz and al-Uthaymin issued *fatwa*s banning women from driving, following a daring Riyadh driving incident that became a landmark in the recent history of Saudi women's mobilisation. The context of the incident, which took place around the time when Saudi Arabia invited foreign troops to defend the country

[35] *Fatawi*, p. 1430.
[36] *Fatawi*, p. 1429.

against Saddam's invasion of Kuwait, is important in understanding its significance. A group of educated women, mainly university professors and professionals, drove their cars in Riyadh, which led to their arrest and expulsion from their jobs.[37] Resorting to the principle of the prevention of vice, al-Uthaymin declared women's driving an opportunity for great corruption and an invitation for Muslim women to imitate other impious women. His main concern was with 'the pressure that the infidel nations exert on the pious and conservative Saudi society, the last bastion of Islam, to accept driving. Some misguided members of our own society want to imitate other nations because they think that progress requires the loss of our values and religion'.[38] He listed several reasons for the ban, such as the loss of women's modesty, their increased roaming outside the home, rebellion against their families, dissent, freedom to go everywhere for entertainment, great unnecessary expenditure, traffic jams, and an increase in road accidents.[39] Ibn Baz reiterated the *fatwa* on driving as a response to what he regarded as 'the futile press coverage of the debate in al-Jazirah newspaper'.[40] He claimed that the debate had been initiated by those who are ignorant of their religion, and he endeavoured to enlighten people and demonstrate that the ban on driving stems from concerns over the nation's moral integrity. Citing several Quranic verses on modesty and the veil, he reached the conclusion that women should not be allowed to travel alone or with a non-*mahram* driver, and that under no circumstances should they drive cars. These *fatwa*s ended the debate on women driving for a while, but the controversy resurfaced after 9/11, as will be discussed in the next chapter.

CONCLUSION

The surge in *fatwa*s on matters relating to women, marriage, polygamy, and mobility in the 1980s represented a desperate attempt to return to an imagined past and re-fix the boundaries of the pious nation. The opinions and historical religious sources on which these *fatwa*s were based were hardly new in Islamic theology, as they draw on specific strict interpretations of the Islamic texts that are common in other parts of the Arab and Muslim world. The comprehensive nature of these *fatwa*s

[37] Madawi Al-Rasheed, *A History of Saudi Arabia*, Cambridge: Cambridge University Press, 2002, 2nd edn, 2010, p. 162.
[38] *Fatawi*, p. 1942.
[39] *Fatawi*, pp. 1939–42.
[40] http://www.binbaz.org.sa, hukm qiyadat al-mar'a lil-sayara (ruling on women's driving).

as they dealt with almost every aspect of women's lives reflected the magnitude of the new situations that arose in Saudi Arabia as a result of economic and social change. More and more women gained formal education and sought employment. Others came into contact with an increasing number of foreign workers in the household and in the public sphere, including hospitals and schools. The *fatwas* aspired to create a religious discourse that regulates these new situations and opportunities, seen as a threat to the authenticity and specificity of the nation. Saudi Arabia was being exposed to other discourses and practices which the *ulama* denounced as alien, corrupting, and un-Islamic. The reinvention of *fatwas* as a regulating mechanism was a desperate attempt to regain the place of religion in the public domain and restore the boundaries of the nation at a time when both were allegedly being undermined.

The Higher Council of Ulama gave opinions that made new practices either permissible or prohibited. The more new situations arose, the more they improvised religious opinions to ensure society's conformity and assert its identity. The state did little to curb these *fatwas*. Their propagation in newly printed volumes and leaflets, in addition to the media, was tolerated, and even encouraged. Without state finances, such *fatwas* would not have had circulation and popularity. This was a bargain between state and *ulama* which compensated the *ulama* for their removal from the domain of giving religious opinions in matters relating to politics, except when demanded by the state. In return, the state increased their power to regulate the social sphere, in which women were central. The *ulama* provided the aura of Islamic piety that the state needed to boost its Islamic credentials at a time when they were being undermined by both regional and internal political developments.

The Mecca mosque siege in 1979 and the rise of Iran following its Islamic revolution created threatening conditions for Saudi Arabia. The *ulama* were called upon to reassert Saudi Arabia as 'the last bastion of Islam', in the words of Ibn Baz. Restrictions on women were used to assert the Islamic credentials of both state and nation. As the Saudi state grew out of a specific form of religious nationalism, this meant that its legitimacy rested on maintaining the semblance of Islam in all matters of public life. The *ulama* ensured that this semblance is reproduced through successive *fatwas* on women. In general, the 1980s can be considered as a decade of the exclusion and control of women, a reflection of the general trend towards Islamising society and, by implication, the state, that followed the threat of 1979.

With the approval of the state, the Committee for the Promotion of Commanding Right and Forbidding Wrong increased its raids on public spaces and even private homes in search of improper Islamic behaviour. Such raids not only coincided with deliberate attempts to demonstrate piety and conformity, but also reflected the state's concern with its Islamic identity. They did not, however, deter women, who continued to aspire to use the services of the newly opened sports centres, beauty parlours, restaurants, and cafes. These new venues continued to spring up in urban centres, and their numbers increased in the 1990s. Many women continued to be driven by foreign drivers without the presence of a *mahram*. The *fatwas* did succeed in fetishising women to uphold the moral integrity of the nation that rested on their shoulders.

The *ulama*'s *fatwas* on polygamy did encourage the practice, as it was linked not only to the fulfilment of personal desire but also to the ultimate purpose of empowering the nation. This discourse created a universe in which distinctions between a pious nation and others can be articulated at the level of the person, society, and their marriage choices. The *fatwas* fostered a sense that Saudis are moral agents whose everyday lives and practices are regulated, controlled, and conducted according to a set of religious opinions. Men and women became instruments for the promotion of religious nationalism, and each member of society was expected to uphold the morality of the group. This coincided with the state's desire to be seen as Islamic. The state benefited from these *fatwas*, which dealt with the minute aspects of public behaviour and appearance, marriage, and polygamy. While fundamental state interests and policies relating to politics, foreign affairs, the economy, and the military remained outside the reach of the *ulama*, restricting and regulating women's lives turned into an occupation for both the state and its *ulama*. The issuing of *fatwas* on women coincided with the state's desire to restore its Islamic legitimacy at a time when this had come under threat. Restrictions on women and control over their appearance served as important visible signs that reminded Saudis and the outside world of the distinctive Islamic credentials of its people and state.

The historicisation of *fatwas* on women allows a serious examination of the role religion plays in shaping gender roles and the perception of women in a society such as Saudi Arabia. It seems that religion alone cannot explain why women suddenly became subject to greater control and surveillance from the 1980s. Without taking into account the political context that created favourable conditions for the propagation of these *fatwas*, it is difficult to explain why the lives of Saudi women suddenly became the subject of a rather large body of *fatwa*s dealing with the minute details of everyday life. While it is true that Saudi *ulama* adopt the strictest Islamic interpretations, their *fatwa*s reflected wider concerns with the nation, the state, and the reassertion of its tradition at a time when all were believed to be under threat. The reinvention of women as pillars of religious nationalism became an easy solution to a more fundamental problem pertaining to identity and its outside symbols. Women had to bear the burden of being projected as pillars upon which the reassertion of Islamic identity is founded. They became symbols of the piety of both nation and state.

In many Muslim societies, *ulama* and Islamists engaged in similar processes, but they were formulating judgements and producing discourses against an increasing secular realm adopted by their own states. In Saudi Arabia, however, the state and its Islamists worked hand in hand to control women in the pursuit of maintaining legitimacy. The state suppressed the 1979 Mecca mosque rebellion but endorsed the demands of the rebels as it increased its restrictions on women and relied on the *ulama*'s opinions as a framework for regulating women's lives. We shall see in the following chapter that the state agenda in the post-9/11 period changed, and that women were able to benefit from an opening of the public sphere.

# 4

## The Quest for Cosmopolitan Modernity

The glorification of the feminine character implies the humiliation of all
who bear it.

Theodor Adorno[1]

The publication of my photo in the press angered me a lot. I do not know
where they found it. I have been asked for a photo but I refused. I am a
Saudi Najdi *monaqaba* [one who wears niqab] and I do not accept the press
publishing my photos.

Mrs Nura al-Faiz, Deputy Minister of Education[2]

Since 9/11, educated women have been called upon to serve the state's
economic, social, and ideological needs. Educated women give the regime
a soft and sophisticated modern face. While invisible Saudi women had
previously been visible signs of state piety, their recent orchestrated and
well-managed appearance in the public sphere is a reflection of the state's
quest for a cosmopolitan modernity.[3] Under global and local political
pressures, the state is gradually replacing religious scholars in defining
gender roles and the status of women in the country. The state singles

[1] Theodor Adorno, *Minima Moralia: Reflections on a Damaged Life*, London: Verso, 2005,
p. 96.
[2] Interview with Nura al-Faiz, the first Saudi woman to occupy the post of deputy minister.
See Majda Abd al-Aziz, 'Deputy Education Minister: I Will Not Object to Representing
My Country Abroad', *al-Watan*, 23 February 2009. Since this interview, al-Faiz's photos
have been published in newspapers outside Saudi Arabia and circulated on the Internet.
[3] The changes that are so visible in the gender area are not specifically a Saudi phenomenon.
All Gulf states have raised the profile of women since 9/11. Women gained political rights
in Oman, Kuwait, Qatar, Bahrain, and the United Arab Emirates, and have become
publicly active in commerce, education, media, and public forums. For a comparative
perspective, see Sean Foley, *The Gulf Arab States Beyond Oil and Islam*, Boulder: Lynne
Rienner Publishers, 2010, pp. 167–210.

out gender as a criterion for its new modernity, thus inaugurating a new era that requires the celebration of the achievements of Saudi women and their greater participation in the public sphere.

Women are currently invested with new capabilities to demonstrate the new modernity of the state to local and global audiences. The state's sudden shift from emphasis on a traditional piety to a new cosmopolitan modernity allows women greater visibility both locally and internationally. The post-9/11 state seeks to be a global modern entity. This is linked to a state agenda in which women become endowed with new meanings that sustain this new orientation. In order to achieve this objective, the influence of religious scholars is gradually being eroded and slowly undermined as the state allows its media and institutions to attack religious opinions and scholars who volunteer 'radical interpretations' on gender among other things. The state seeks modern religious interpretations to replace previous religious opinions on women. Debating issues relevant to women's role in society and saturating the Saudi public sphere with controversial opinions on women replace the old official consensus on women's issues. The 'radical opinions' on women discussed in the previous chapter are today giving way to dissenting voices amounting in some instances to direct critique of the religious tradition and attacks on its most outspoken guardians. The state endorses only religious scholars who provide the basis for a new 'pious cosmopolitan modernity' – that is, a modernity in line with the new economic and social conditions of Saudi Arabia, yet compatible with the old tradition.

It is no longer possible to uphold the masculine state without impregnating it with a sophisticated female face and voice. The masculine state currently mobilises women, engages in gender reform, introduces new legislation to allow greater economic participation, and silences radical religious scholars whose *fatwa*s do not reflect an understanding of social and economic change. This chapter assesses the pressures on the Saudi state and explains why the modernity of Saudi women is seen as a desperate necessity and an urgent policy to be promoted by princes, professionals, writers, and activists in the post-9/11 period. The chapter captures the current debate on gender in which Saudis are active and traces the masculine state's feminisation of itself.

THE KING'S WOMEN

One noticeable group of women has been given greater visibility in Saudi society in the aftermath of 9/11. Highly educated women who are critical of religious restrictions on their lives have become easily identifiable as a category in Saudi society but without being able to form a formal independent association. They are educated in the sciences and humanities, and many have completed graduate training abroad. They share an urban background and belong to families that have had great involvement in the building of the Saudi state, through serving as bureaucrats or as entrepreneurs who have provided services to the state. These families belong to the sedentary communities of major Saudi cities. A high proportion of this group originates in the Qasim, Hasa, and the Hijaz where merchant families have historically been active.

The Qasim is known for its many religious families and its conservatism, so it seems ironic that many educated women with a Western outlook have also come from this region. This is related to the fact that many families benefited from the early educational institutions and educated their girls. Similarly, Riyadh and its environs have also recently produced women who are members of this emerging educated elite. The Hijaz, in contrast, has had a longer history of women's education and training, and women are now found in professions in both the private and public sectors of the economy.

Today many of these educated elite women belong to different intellectual trends. Some are liberal in their education and outlook. They subscribe to international discourse on gender discrimination and human rights. Their feminism is grounded in a cosmopolitan outlook. They are frequent travellers to neighbouring Gulf countries, other Arab capitals, and the West. In their articulation of gender equality, they invoke United Nations treaties and aspire to see many global recommendations implemented in Saudi Arabia. They do not see any contradiction between the global human rights discourse on gender and moderate Islam. They may be veiled at home in Saudi Arabia, but have no qualms about removing their veils when abroad. For them, the veil is a personal choice rather than a religious obligation that should be enforced by the state and its agencies. They are happy to work in mixed surroundings and travel without a male guardian. They call for lifting all restrictions on women's travel, economic activity, and personal choices. Their cosmopolitanism is combined with a strong sense of their local culture and identity.

Other women belong to modern Islamist trends that celebrate Islamic solutions to the gender issues in Saudi Arabia. They situate emancipation within an Islamic framework, and continue to invoke the Islamic tradition as an ideal source to draw on in order to gain more rights in Saudi society. Their reference point is not the global international discourse on gender equality but an ahistorical Islam where they imagine a glorious past in which women were given exceptional rights before the West adopted these rights for women. Like other Islamic feminists, they see Islam as the framework that should guide their emancipation. They invoke the example of Khadija and Aisha, wives of the Prophet, to defend Islam's emancipatory role, and detest culture and social norms that have obscured the 'true' message of Islam with regard to women's rights and duties. Their enemy is the 'conservative tribe' whose ethical and moral codes enforce the subordination of women. They do not call for equality with men but for complementarity, as they see themselves contributing to society in specific ways that do not negate their identity as women. These women adhere to styles of dress that distinguish them from so-called liberal Saudi women, the cosmopolitan feminists. They wear their veils in a strict manner that reflects serious religious attachment to veiling, and some may wear the *niqab* at international conferences and in mixed surroundings.

Whether liberal or Islamist, today many educated women consider the state as a saviour from strict religious control and a protector against conservative social tradition. The first would like to see the state curbing radical religious opinions, while the second expects the state to limit the influence of cultural and social influences that maintain the subordination of women. Equally, Islamist women demand the intervention of the state to curb the onslaught of Westernisation, which they see as undermining their status as women with special needs and interests. Both liberal and Islamist women look to the state to reverse the previous decades of exclusion and to abandon the *fatwas* that dominated policy and perceptions of the place of women in Saudi society. It appears that all these modern Saudi women expect to rely on an authoritarian state to extract their rights from men, protect them against excessive restrictions, and promote them as the new voices in society.[4] This opinion is widely spread among educated women who occupy professional positions in the fields of university education, journalism, medicine, business, and social work. Most of them have been working for several years but without the publicity and attention of either the leadership or the local and international media.

---

[4] This is not specifically unique to Saudi Arabia. In a recent comparative study of Egypt and the United Arab Emirates, Frances Hasso argues that 'citizen women may need authoritarian states more than we do, not least for their ability to police men and extract resources from them within a corporatist family framework that requires men to provide for wives, children and parents'. See Frances Hasso, *Consuming Desires: Family Crisis and the State in the Middle East*, Stanford: Stanford University Press, 2011, p. 14.

As a cohort, such women began to have more media attention and state recognition than they had ever enjoyed before 9/11. When the state fell under international scrutiny amounting to serious criticism of its social and religious policies following the attacks on New York, this group of women proved to be useful in countering images of Saudi Arabia as a hotbed of radical preachers and terrorists. High-achieving professional women who worked in hospitals as scientists and doctors, together with very successful businesswomen, enjoyed regular exposure to both international and local media, which praised their achievements in a society that imposes so many restrictions on their rights and movement. Stories about women doctors, scientists, novelists, pilots, poets, film producers, artists, entrepreneurs, television presenters, and activists began to appear in the local media with a view to focusing attention on the great achievements of exceptional women.[5] Glimpses of the lives of successful individuals were meant to alter perceptions of the country and its women. The Saudi state wanted to introduce the world to that hidden sphere where no men had previously been able to venture. Grasping the opportunity to open Saudi Arabia up to international media, it made stories about the lives and aspirations of elite and educated Saudi women into regular features.

The stories highlighting the bright side of women's lives were, however, combined with saturation-level alternative stories about women who were raped, abused, and marginalised. The careers of high-profile successful businesswomen, for example Lubna al-Olayan[6] and Nahed Tahir,[7] circulated in conjunction with stories about women subjected to

[5] Saudi local print media, where stories about women circulated almost on a daily basis, include *Okaz*, *al-Madina*, *al-Watan*, *al-Riyadh*, and *al-Jazeera*. International newspapers *al-Sharq al-Awsat* and *al-Hayat* and satellite television station al-Arabiyya were leading news reporting about women to an Arab audience. The Lebanese LBC channel stretched the boundaries even further as it delved into reporting on taboo topics, including sex, homosexuality, and new phenomena such as *immo* girls (girls adopting black Gothic garb) and the *boyat* (girls who dress and behave like boys). Saudi print media that became a regular source on Saudi women in English include *Arab News*, *Saudi Gazette*, and *al-Majalla*.

[6] Lubna al-Olayan is director of the Olayan Group, a private multinational enterprise that has more than fifty companies and affiliated businesses. In 2004, the Arab Bankers Association of North America granted her an achievement award. She was also named the female executive of the year as part of the 2004 Arabian Business Achievement Awards. For further details of the Olayan Group, see http://www.olayan.com/about.aspx.

[7] In 2005, Nahed Tahir was chief executive officer of Gulf One Investment Bank in Bahrain. After completing her undergraduate studies in Jeddah, in 2001 she obtained a doctorate in economics from Lancaster University in Britain. She was recognised by *Forbes* magazine

domestic violence, for example Saudi television presenter Rania al-Baz[8] and a raped girl known as Fatat al-Qatif.[9] The Saudi press searched both for women who were high achievers and for those less fortunate.

After 9/11, the international and local public spheres combined two images of Saudi women. News about awards and recognition given to exceptional high achievers coexisted with stories about women who were victims of domestic violence, poverty, forced marriages, unlawful divorce, and abandonment by male guardians. Educated women talked about the plight of these less fortunate ones and demanded that the state provide protection and care for women who had been subjected to abuse and neglect.

From 2000, the Saudi media employed women in highly visible positions as presenters,[10] and celebrated the achievements of the first female eye surgeon, chief executive, pilot, and deputy minister. Saudi princesses joined the list of achievers and contributors to society. Daughters of previous kings and the current King Adbullah suddenly appeared in international economic and educational forums as patrons of excellence who play leading roles in society. Loulwa al-Faisal,[11] together with the king's

as one of the top 100 most influential women in the world and nicknamed 'desert rose' for launching a $10 billion private equity fund. See http://www.gulf1bank.com/.

[8] Rania al-Baz was a successful presenter on Saudi television. Her husband's jealousy of her successful career pushed him to subject her to severe domestic violence. She underwent several operations to reconstruct her disfigured face. Her case focused attention on the prevalence of domestic violence in the country. Her ordeal was reported in both the local and international media. See *The Guardian*, 5 October 2005. After recovering, she wrote her memoirs: see Rania al-Baz, *al-Mushawaha* [Disfigured], Beirut: Dar Owaydat, 2006. Her book first appeared in French but was later translated into Arabic. For further details on Saudi women working in the media, see Naomi Sakr, 'Women and Media in Saudi Arabia: Rhetoric, Reductionism and Realities', *British Journal of Middle Eastern Studies*, 35, 1 (2008), pp. 385–404.

[9] Fatat al-Qatif was another case that shocked not only Saudis but also the international community: she was gang raped after being abducted from a shopping centre in the Eastern Province. What was even more outrageous was that she was sentenced to 200 lashes by a Saudi judge after her ordeal: see *The Independent*, 29 November 2007. She was Shia, and the case assumed global dimensions and was intertwined with sectarian undertones.

[10] Although Saudi women are now visible in the media, especially the visual media, their promotion has been uneven, as they still lag behind in the promotion of female media professionals to decision-making positions. For further details on the 2004–6 period, see Sakr, 'Women and Media'.

[11] Through her interests in girls' education, Loulwa al-Faisal has become an unofficial Saudi ambassador. She has appeared at the Davos World Economic Forums and attended academic conferences on Saudi women at British and American universities. When Laura Bush visited Saudi Arabia, the princess was interviewed about education and health

daughter Adilla,[12] and Amira, the wife of al-Walid bin Talal, gave regular interviews about their work and aspirations to an audience fascinated by the hidden aspects of lives of Saudi women, especially royalty.[13] For the first time, Saudi audiences can read about the contribution of princesses to the emancipation of women through their charitable and educational work. Many princesses have intervened through charitable organisations to highlight the plight of women, especially those who had been subjected to domestic violence. Furthermore, an increasing number of princesses began to write commentary pieces in the local press in support of serious social change, and called on the leadership to implement it. Most of their commentaries gave opinions on matters relevant to women and gender equality. They specifically addressed injustices, exclusion, and the abuse of women in Saudi society.

The polar images that the Saudi media presented about women were meant to contribute to 'demystifying' and 'normalising' the lives of Saudi women, moving away from the silence that had been maintained in the past over both their success and victimhood. Success stories highlighted role models, while reporting on social ills such as the elopement of young girls, incest, drug and alcohol abuse, depression, unemployment, poverty, honour crimes, and many other issues drew attention to a society that is plagued by serious problems requiring urgent solutions. The subtext of the new attention given to women was often transparent; the press concentrated on attributing many of the social problems faced by women to decades of religious radicalism and a culture of secrecy and misogyny. With official approval and encouragement, the Saudi press wanted to shed the myth about the alleged piety and morality of Saudis and present a 'reality-based' picture of society.

issues that are relevant to Saudi women. A clip of the ABC interview can be seen at http://www.youtube.com/watch?v=nxYSuJzyqow.

[12] Pierre Prier, 'La princesse saoudienne qui defend la cause des femmes', *Le Figaro*, 16 February 2010.

[13] Amira, the fourth wife of Prince al-Walid bin Talal, was interviewed, especially during visits with her husband to France and other destinations. She was filmed in her husband's camp in the desert, where viewers had a glimpse of the life of one of the richest men in the world. Amira called for the lifting of the ban on women driving, and asserted that she will be the first woman to do so. Although these interviews are published in the international press, within hours of their appearance they are usually translated into Arabic and posted on Internet discussion boards. They are usually popular for commentaries and discussion. Commentators are often divided in their evaluation. Some congratulate the princess for enhancing the image of the country abroad, while others condemn her as unrepresentative of Saudi women in general. Clips of interviews on YouTube usually attract hundreds of commentators.

The demystification of Saudi women, especially high achievers, became increasingly important as the state endeavoured to focus attention on gender issues to avoid dealing with more serious demands for political reform.[14] State-controlled media adopted gender as a focus for debate and commentary, thus helping the authorities to divert attention from controversial demands for political participation, respect for human rights, reform of the judiciary, and other pressing political concerns. By the time Abdullah became king in 2005, the public sphere had been prepared to accept social reform, including the plight of Saudi women, as the most necessary and urgent reform. Other reforms, in the fields of politics and governance, had to be delayed and were simply not discussed in public.

By virtue of their education, employment, and close ties with the state, educated women are vocal in their denunciation of strict religious controls. They are outspoken in their criticism of discrimination grounded in religious and social traditions. For them, the marginalisation of Saudi women is a product of decades of radical religious preaching that dominated both the educational institutions and media. While they insist on their respect for Islam and its teachings, they single out radical interpretations by the Wahhabi tradition as a cause of the many restrictions on women, without actually naming it. They call for the adoption of moderate views on gender segregation, driving, employment in non-segregated space, travel, and legal representation. These views are currently disseminated to the Saudi public by the state-owned media. Women who have alternative diagnoses of the 'woman problem' are excluded from official media, but they find ways of reaching their audiences through the many independent religious channels and Internet websites. Those *ulama* and conservative Islamists who oppose the recent changes are also excluded from official channels.

Since 9/11, the voices of women denouncing religious radicalism have reached further as they articulate a vision that coincides with that of the state. So far, such women have been protected, despite their daring positions on issues relevant to women and their occasional appearance in the media and in non-segregated economic forums held inside Saudi Arabia. Local and international media in which they are free to criticise the conservative *ulama* regularly interview them.[15] In almost all their

---

[14] I have dealt with demands for political reforms after 9/11 in Madawi Al-Rasheed, *A History of Saudi Arabia*, Cambridge: Cambridge University Press, 2002, 2nd edn, 2010, pp. 261–3.

[15] CNN, PBS, and Fox News dedicated several programmes to investigating the exclusion of Saudi women. In Asia, *Japan Times* occasionally reported on Saudi businesswomen.

commentaries, they emphasise the drastic change that was noticeable in the aftermath of 9/11. They praise the king for his support and recognition of women's problems. They often comment on this support by listing initiatives taken by the leadership and the many institutions under state control. While many professional women have the support of their families in order to reach their potential in education and work, they need the protection and patronage of the state in the public sphere. They willingly seek state patriarchy as a refuge from what they regard as restrictive religious and social tradition. Any initiative taken by the king or other senior princes to honour these women is often regarded as a major step towards silencing critical religious voices. Many women who were put under state patronage to present a bright image of the country and serve as role models for other women now realise that they are being treated as 'tokens' of the modern reformist agenda of the state. In private and behind the scenes, they express their awareness of the way that they are expected to play the role of strong achievers who demonstrate the modernity of the country through the success of its women. However, they are willing to go along with this agenda, as it is an irresistible opportunity to gain more rights and visibility. Many educated women see the patronage of the state as a necessity.

A small group of women among this educated elite who have become vocal is drawn from commerce. Elected women members of the Jeddah Chamber of Commerce and Industry (JCCI) are emerging as the new face of Saudi entrepreneurial women. The vice chair, Lama Sulyaman, in addition to Aisha Nattu and Fatin Bundagji, were members of the management board in 2010.[16] Their mission is so far centred on lifting restrictions on women's businesses, especially requirements such as the ban on women obtaining commercial licences, having male general managers in all-female businesses, and women travelling without guardians. Another prominent businesswoman is economist Nahed Tahir who, in 2005, became chief executive of Gulf One Investment Bank. While entrepreneurial women seek greater freedoms that allow them to conduct their business affairs without restrictions, they voice their demands within an Islamic framework. The Khadija bint Khuwaylid Business Women's Centre, established in 2004 at the JCCI, derives its name from the Prophet's first wife who was a successful businesswoman. Maha Futaihi, the wife of the minister of labour, is the director of the centre. She regards it as a forum to promote women in business and develop their technical

[16] Jeddah Chamber of Commerce and Industry, http://www.jcci.org.sa/jcci/.

and managerial skills.[17] In 2010, the centre organised a discussion forum on women and national development under the patronage of Princess Adilla, the king's daughter. In many state-sponsored forums on businesswomen, the contribution of Saudi women is anchored in a religious framework and is seen as a continuation of an early tradition of successful trade and entrepreneurial skills. Surveying women's businesses and assessing needs for training and development are part of the programmes that this centre provides.

In the Riyadh Chamber of Commerce, a similar businesswomen's group is also emerging. One outspoken businesswoman, Huda al-Juraisy, commented on the gradual changes under the auspices of the state. To capture the skills of women and their wealth, 'the government must work hard to improve their status and allow greater contribution'.[18]

Many women praise the government for taking an evolutionary approach to gender issues, as they fear a backlash from conservative members of society. Salwa al-Hazza, head of ophthalmology at King Faisal Hospital in Riyadh, named Arab Woman of the Year by the Dubai-based Arab Women Students' Centre, aspires to change Western stereotypical images of Saudi women. Although many women see themselves as victims of discrimination, al-Hazza asserts that Saudi women are strong because they need to overcome many obstacles to succeed. Among these are the need for male permission to start a business, a separate banking system, minimal government assistance, and lack of business experience. On the other hand, Saudi businesswomen seem to have very high educational

---

[17] According to the centre's information source, 'the Al-Sayedah Khadijah Bint Khuwailid Businesswomen Center (AKBK) works in collaboration with the private sector and government officials to lobby for the removal of obstacles facing women, in order to empower them both economically and socially to become active participants in national development. It seeks to reform current legislations and policies to become supportive of women's advancement. In addition, the Center is keen on raising awareness and providing networking and educational opportunities for female entrepreneurs, working women, job seekers, and potential entrepreneurs. The Center was named after Prophet Muhammad's (PBUH) first wife Al-Sayedah Khadijah Bint Khawilid, a successful businesswoman who remains a role model for Muslim women today. Known for her business skills, wisdom, and her values and ethics, she was also able to balance between her family and career. With such a prominent figure as an inspiration, the Center aims to follow in Al-Sayedah Khadijah's footsteps to become a national and international resource for women's advancement in Saudi Arabia'. In 2010, the centre produced a major report on Saudi businesswomen that sums up its vision. See Noura Altourki and Rebekah Braswell, *Businesswomen in Saudi Arabia: Changes, Challenges and Aspirations in a Regional Context*, 2010, available at http://www.akbk.org.sa.

[18] Riyadh Chamber of Commerce and Industry, available at http://www.riyadhchamber. com/indexen.php.

qualifications.[19] Equally, Maha Futaihi praises efforts by the government to increase women's participation in the economy by widening employment opportunities.[20]

Between victimhood and achievement, businesswomen and professionals try to navigate a difficult path, but since 9/11 they have considered the state to be on their side against those who object to women's emancipation in the country. The narrative of the state as saviour tends to be prominent among this group of women. When questioned about government delays in lifting restrictions on women, they are more likely to justify the delay rather than question it. For example, the exclusion of women from municipal elections in 2005 was seen as a justifiable measure given how complicated it would be to set up special women's voting centres across the country. Al-Hazza argued that '[the] election was new to the country . . . and the government will need more time before allowing women to vote'.[21] Similarly, professor of higher education Hind al-Khuthaila wrote that 'the political leadership has its own vision with regard to delaying women's participation'.[22] Another female Islamist activist, Suhayla Zayn al-Abdin, defended the exclusion of women from the 2005 elections on the basis that it was too early for women to enter this field given the novelty of elections in the country.[23] This was the government's justification for excluding women from the elections. Prince Mansur, head of the Ministry of Municipal and Rural Affairs, said that women would be included, at least as voters, in the second round of elections due in 2009, but these elections were postponed to 2011.[24]

While businesswomen aspire to a free entrepreneurial atmosphere that allows more women to achieve greater participation in the private sector, many journalists and writers focus on general discrimination and marginalisation. They have become regular commentators on women's social problems, especially those related to marriage, divorce, and violence. Women activists single out child marriage as a perversion in Saudi

---

[19] On women entrepreneurs in Riyadh, see Dorothy Minkus-McKenna, 'Women Entrepreneurs in Riyadh, Saudi Arabia', UMUC Working Papers Series, no. 2009-002, University of Maryland University College.

[20] 'Saoudiyat ynadidna bi muntada Khadija bint khuwailid' [Saudi women condemn Khadija Bint Khuwailid Centre], *al-Jazeera*, 25 December 2010.

[21] *Japan Times*, 2 August 2005.

[22] Hind al-Khuthaila, 'The Meaning of Saudi Elections', *American Behavioral Scientist*, 49, 4 (2005), pp. 605–9, at p. 609.

[23] In 2005, these views were expressed on Al-Jazeera television in the context of a debate on the exclusion of Saudi women.

[24] *al-Quds al-Arabi*, 25 February 2005.

society.[25] They call upon the state to introduce a minimum marriage age for girls. Writer and journalist Halima Muthafar wrote a scathing attack on such marriages in the local newspaper *al-Watan*. She commented on the case of a thirteen-year-old girl who became a divorcee, after a short marriage to a man in his fifties: 'It is time to initiate a law that criminalises child marriage and punishes parents who arrange such marriages for their daughters. These marriages have given us a reputation as abusers of children'.[26]

Controversial Saudi television presenter Nadine al-Budayr, who had worked for the American-owned al-Hora Arabic television channel in Dubai before moving to Rotana, shocked Saudis after she published an article entitled 'My four husbands and I' in the Egyptian newspaper *al-Masri al-Yawm*.[27] She called for equality and demanded that women should be allowed to have four husbands.[28] In other articles published in the Kuwaiti newspaper *al-Rai*, she endorsed premarital sex, as it is 'a way of creating a durable emotional bond, perhaps stronger than all marriage documents'.[29] In addition to these articles, al-Budayr occasionally publishes comments praising individual members of the royal family.[30] In January 2011, she glorified Abdulaziz, a son of the deceased King Fahd, for his generosity when he sponsored the weddings of several Saudi couples.

Writer and activist Wajiha al-Howeider has become a regular commentator on the exclusion and plight of Saudi women. In 2008, her short YouTube video clip showing her driving inside Saudi Arabia on Women's Day focused attention on the need to lift the ban on women driving. In

[25] Child marriage became a hot issue for Saudi activists who posted a video on YouTube in which they interviewed girls about marriage. The video was produced by an organisation that defends women's rights but is still not formally recognised in the country. See http://www.youtube.com/watch?v=IZzKaATvyJU.

[26] Halima Muthafar, 'Child Marriage Is a Reflection of Perversion', *al-Watan*, 16 February 2010.

[27] Nadine al-Budayr's article is posted on http://www.almasry-alyoum.com/article2.aspx?ArticleID=236320. Other articles can be found on Shafaf al-Sharq al-Awsat (Middle East Transparent), a secular liberal news web page: see http://www.metransparent.net/spip.php?page=auteur&var_lang=ar&id_auteur=231&lang=ar.

[28] *Khabar*, 14 December 2009.

[29] Al-Budayr's two-part article entitled 'Hayati ka aziba' [My life as a single woman] angered many Saudis. In 2010, it was reported that Shaykh Mutrif al-Bishr, a judge in the Qatif court, had demanded that the government withdraw her Saudi citizenship. See *al-Quds al-Arabi*, 6 October 2010.

[30] Nadine al-Budayr, 'An yakun amiran mitaa' [To be a generous prince], available at http://alraimedia.com.

April 2010, she participated in a conference in the Netherlands on Human Rights and New Media where she highlighted the need for banning child marriage and the guardianship requirement. She identified the state as the agency responsible for ameliorating the status of women and institutionalising gender equality.[31] In her short articles published on the web, she discusses the cases of widows, orphans, spinsters, and minor girls who are subjected to restrictions and abuse because they are not allowed to represent themselves in court. While many women journalists specialise in highlighting stories about achievers, al-Howeider is more focused on the plight of ordinary Saudi women. She depicts how male relatives often take advantage of these women under the guise of the guardianship requirement.[32] Among the new generation of Saudi women, al-Howeider is perhaps one of the few women who does not adopt an apologetic view when discussing the role of the state. She clearly attributes many injustices inflicted on women to the complicity between the state and religious scholars. She is also critical in her interpretation of the cultural and social norms of her country. For these reasons, she has not been able to publish commentaries in the mainstream Saudi press. While many Saudis think that Nadine al-Budayr has gone too far to achieve the publicity she craves, al-Howeider is seen by a few as deserving respect and support.

The high visibility of educated women since 9/11 could not have materialised without the state's policy of highlighting the achievements of women and encouraging their greater participation in the public sphere. It was a conscious decision to create more opportunities for women and to be seen as leading social reform. The exposure of Saudi Arabia to outside scrutiny following 9/11 meant that both men and women gained access to outside media. In addition, the consolidation of new newspapers and satellite television, together with the spread of the Internet, meant that Saudi society could no longer remain isolated. The state promoted this new openness and allowed many women to appear in international forums and local venues. It is now normal for Saudi women to work as presenters and panellists in official Saudi local and satellite television channels such as al-Ikhbariyya and al-Arabiyya. By allowing women greater visibility, the state was guaranteed a consensus among them that it alone can save them from decades of marginalisation. It also aspires to be seen thus by international audiences.

---

[31] *al-Quds al-Arabi*, 26 April 2010.
[32] Al-Howeider's articles are posted on minbar al-hiwar wa al-ibda: see http://www.menber-alhewar1.org./index.php.

The discourse that holds radical religious scholars responsible for the exclusion of women suited the state at a time when it was aspiring towards greater control of the religious field for the completely different purpose of fighting terrorism and the appeal of radical religious thinking. As the state is currently embarking on limiting the interference of religious scholars and institutions in public affairs, it has found in elite women a source of support. The interests of this group of women coincide with those of the state at this historical moment. While the state guarantees their recent visibility and recognises their achievements, they have supported and welcomed the new initiatives introduced after 9/11. The visibility of elite women is accompanied by several state initiatives to substantiate the new policy directions aimed at acknowledging the contribution of women, improving their status, and increasing their participation in society and the economy.

## STATE INITIATIVES

One of the first initiatives taken to curb the influence of religious scholars and marginalise them after 9/11 was to remove girls' education from their control.[33] After the opening of girls' schools in the kingdom, the General Presidency for Girls' Education was put in charge of overseeing the curriculum and the provisions for women's education. In 2002, a fire broke out in one of the schools in Mecca in which at least fourteen girls were killed. Reporting on the incident, journalists blamed the religious police for allegedly blocking the escape of girls who were not wearing proper Islamic dress. The government responded by placing the education of girls under the responsibility of the Ministry of Education. The move was seen as an indication of the reformist agenda of the state that had begun to restrict the control of religious authorities over one of the major fields that affected women's lives, namely education. The fire incident took place at the worst time for the country, a year after 9/11 and at the height of international condemnation of Saudi Arabia over its religious radicalism and conservative tradition. Its religious curriculum was being questioned and scrutinised by American and international media. The death of the girls at the school was taken to symbolise the harsh and inhuman conditions for women in a country that had produced fifteen of the terrorists who destroyed the Twin Towers in New York. The

---

[33] For a general assessment of the new Saudi educational reforms, see Michaela Prokop, 'Saudi Arabia: The Politics of Education', *International Affairs*, 79, 1 (2003), pp. 77–89.

government had to react swiftly to disperse the deluge of international condemnation and internal agitation over the loss of innocent lives. The school incident was blamed on the religious police who refused to allow the exit of the girls.[34] The larger question relating to the conditions of the buildings where girls are taught and the unsuitable, unsafe rented schools was practically ignored. Removing the education of girls from the control of religious institutions was seen as a positive move towards marginalising religious institutions that had become too large and influential.

In June 2004, the state dedicated one session of the newly established National Dialogue Forum to discussing women's affairs. Women participated in the meeting, and presented their views on matters related to their current situation and future economic prospects in a country where they form the majority of university graduates but remain marginalised in the labour force. Tension erupted during the meeting between those who support more traditional roles for women and those who aspire towards greater participation and visibility. Some women were accused of promoting a Western agenda, with the purpose of destabilising society and threatening its Islamic piety and authenticity. One religious scholar, Muhammad al-Orayfi, accused women teachers of not wearing the appropriate Islamic dress in schools and reminded the audience of the women's driving demonstration in 1991. He argued that although these women had been suspended from their teaching jobs, they had returned to their positions and were continuing to spread Western ideas among their students. The debate ended without serious consideration of the major challenges of absorbing the increasing number of educated women into the Saudi economy. Some female participants thought that conservatives and traditionalists hijacked the meeting. One participant called upon al-Orayfi not to use the occasion of the National Dialogue Forum to dig up old grievances. Wafa al-Rashid could not control her tears as she addressed the meeting and listed the contributions of women to building the nation. She lamented that some men do not pay attention to women's intellect and continue to judge them by their appearance. This prompted some women participants to send a separate list of recommendations to Crown prince (at the time) Abdullah, who privately met with a small number of female delegates. Publicly debating women's role, in the carefully designed

---

[34] The controversy over whether the religious police were to blame for the deaths continued in Saudi Arabia after the merger of girls' education with the Ministry of Education. Prince Naif, the interior minister, dismissed any allegations that the death of the girls was caused by reluctance to allow them to leave the school. See http://news.bbc.co.uk/1/hi/world/middle_east/1893349.

forum and under the sponsorship and patronage of the state, underlined the latter's narrative about its progressive role in a sea of traditionalism and conservatism. The state's project to marginalise the religious scholars and curb their control of state institutions could not be halted by al-Orayfi's intervention. The ferocity of his attack on women delegates reflected a desperate attempt to regain some of the influence scholars had enjoyed in this area of social life since the foundation of Saudi Arabia. The National Dialogue initiative on women fixed the image of the state as a champion of women's emancipation and confirmed the official narrative about the conservatism of Saudi society. More importantly, it allowed the state to remind the constituency that women's issues, together with a whole range of public affairs, are centrally controlled by a royal family with its own vision for the development of the country. Scholars of religion were beginning to lose their monopoly over the social sphere in Saudi Arabia. Any scholar eager to remain in his position and enjoy the patronage of the state must from now on moderate his critique of the many innovations introduced in the area of gender relations. In fact, the only way for religious scholars to remain relevant is to provide religious interpretations and evidence in support of the state's gender policy on sensitive and important issues.

Expansion of women's higher education was seen as a step towards providing equal opportunities for women, who so far had attended women's branches of Saudi universities. These branches taught a limited range of subjects and excluded women from pursuing careers deemed unsuitable for them. The computer and library facilities for women's campuses were criticised as inferior to those available to men. Women had limited access to libraries on special designated days, which was not sufficient for higher education. In 2008, King Abdullah announced a new initiative to establish a women's university, named after Nura, Ibn Saud's famous sister, mentioned in the first chapter. Based in Riyadh, Princess Nura bint Abd al-Rahman University for Girls has the capacity to educate 40,000 girls in medicine, computers, management, and pharmacology, according to official sources. Under the presidency of Princess al-Jawhara bint Fahad, the university was inaugurated in 2010.[35] It was meant to reflect the leadership decision to bring the education of girls to a level compatible with its new policy of promoting education for women.

In 2009, to increase the visibility of the state's commitment to improving women's status in the country and to demonstrate its concern with

[35] See http://www.reuters.com/article/idUSTRE49S65L20081029.

gender equality, the king announced a series of new appointments. For the first time, a woman was appointed as deputy minister in the Ministry of Education to work under the minister, Prince Faisal ibn Abdullah, the king's son-in-law. The appointment was considered a major step towards recognising the need to engage women in policy matters and delivery of services based on their needs. The new appointment was praised by the king's daughter, Princess Adilla, in the local press. She said, 'I am proud and happy for the appointment of Anud al-Fayez in the Ministry of Education. I hope that other government sectors will soon see women appointed to high positions'.[36] Al-Fayez immediately gave several media interviews while refusing to have her photo published. However, pictures of the new deputy minister circulated on the Internet, which resulted in a plethora of commentaries that either condemned the appointment of a woman or congratulated Saudi women who had waited for a long time to occupy such a high position in a state institution. A woman in a high government post was a divisive move, but its supporters triumphed over those who objected, at least in the public sphere. After this appointment, King Abdullah announced on 25 September 2011 that women will be appointed to the Consultative Council in 2015, and they will participate in future municipal elections as both voters and candidates.

In addition to the expansion of education for women, the Saudi leadership is now more inclined to focus on gender issues in political speeches. After a silence of several decades, high-ranking officials, including the king, princes, and princesses, have recently begun to express opinions regarding women's emancipation, education, and employment. Since 2005, King Abdullah has occasionally received women in a private *majlis* to reinforce the impression that the state is the protector of female rights and interests, as defined by Islam. Women accompanied him during visits abroad in 2005 and 2006. Other ministers and members of the royal family have insisted that women enjoy full rights in the kingdom. Carefully selected highly educated and articulate women have appeared at international economic forums, in diplomatic circles, and at academic conferences, accompanied by officials and important princes. In 2010, a women's delegation accompanied Prince Khalid, the governor of Mecca, on a visit to the French Senate House. Highly successful women were selected to visit France in order to 'cement greater understanding between Saudi and French societies' and above all to shatter the myth about the

---

[36] *al-Riyadh*, 15 February 2009.

backwardness of women in the country.[37] Several speakers, including Princess Loulwa al-Faisal, gave introductory talks highlighting the history of women's education and achievements. The audience was introduced to the names and careers of female scientists, physicists, and researchers. While many women see these initiatives as part of the 'charm offensive' of the state, they willingly participate in these occasions and highlight their achievements.

In addition to education at home, the state reinstated the scholarship programmes that allow women to study abroad. By 2010, twenty-five per cent of scholarships went to women, thus marginalising the many objections to this since the 1980s. The state makes the most of female students on government scholarships who are sent abroad for education. The increasing number of women who receive such scholarships allows the state to use them as a cohort of 'ambassadors' whose mission is to change outside perceptions of Saudi women. In addition to pursuing higher education, many Saudi women students in the United States and Britain are now seen as a bridge between their own society and the West. Many are approached by Western media for commentaries on their own society. High achievers in British and American universities are applauded in the local press. Their efforts to alter the image of Saudi Arabia are often welcomed by the leadership. The Saudi Arabian Women's Association (SAWA), a women's forum launched in 2010 in Britain under the patronage of Princess Fadwa bint Khalid, consists of students studying at British universities and other professionals. Their mission statement clearly states that the association's role is to become a bridge between Saudi women and the British media to present a brighter image of the country and 'dispel vague and unclear images of Saudis in general'.[38] Many observers mistook this new forum for an autonomous women's civil society association campaigning for greater gender equality in Saudi Arabia. However, since its launch in 2010, it has become clear that the association is part of the state's initiative to change public opinion in favour of a better appreciation of its reforms in matters relating to women. Members of this association and other female students become strong defenders of the Saudi leadership as they attend seminars, public lectures, and forums in which matters related to Saudi Arabia are often discussed abroad. Their concern is often to change Western perceptions of the country and demonstrate their achievements.

[37] See *Middle East Online*, http://www.middle-east-online.com/.
[38] *Saudi Gazette*, 7 September 2010.

When pressed by the international media about the subordination of Saudi women, both officials and women students explain that the state is ahead of society in that it endorses female emancipation, which needs to progress slowly, otherwise the process will backfire and cause social chaos, discontent, and open confrontation. Government officials explain the state's position on women's issues as one of support for full female participation, but that this needs to be negotiated with conservative elements in Saudi society. Several princes have argued that women are held hostage by traditional cultural values rooted in tribalism and misinterpretation of Islam. Unless these archaic traditions become weak, the state is not in a position to go against the general understanding of the position of women or their prescribed roles. They often refer to how the state allowed elite women – mainly princesses, entrepreneurs, artists, and academics – greater visibility in well-defined and protected surroundings, for example in chambers of commerce, international economic forums, educational forums, diplomatic circles, and the media. But the state remains unreceptive to demands for the establishment of a ministry for women's affairs.

So far, state initiatives have not included permission for independent non-governmental women's organisations defending women's rights to be established. A virtual Saudi women's rights forum was blocked. Women's human rights are incorporated in the agenda of the newly founded state human rights organisation, which reports directly to the king and minister of the interior. Both the Human Rights Commission (HRC) and the National Society for Human Rights (NSHR) consider cases where women are victims of abuse, neglect, and discrimination. So far, women have been granted a presence in areas that never challenge the authority of the state. The employment of women and their role in the charity sector remain under state control; they are, in fact, sanctioned and promoted by the state as tokens of its progress and reform.

Since 9/11, state initiatives on women have been part of the modernising of authoritarian rule. The state offers a legitimate space for women to mix with men, vote in selected elite forums (chamber of commerce elections – but not in municipal elections until 2015), and be members of the state's own human rights organisations (but it denies them the right to form their own independent human rights forums). Educated women have proved to be crucial for reinvigorating a state desperate to shed a well-established negative image that is no longer confined to Saudi Arabia, but has spread abroad with increasing globalisation and international scrutiny of the gender-based exclusion and discrimination in the country. Equally important is the drive of the state since 9/11 to regain its control over certain social and educational spheres, historically under the control of the religious scholars and the institutions created for them. While the economy, foreign policy, the military, and other key areas in government have been outside the control of the religious scholars for a long time, since 9/11 the state has gradually been eroding their monopoly over social affairs, in which women are central. The series of initiatives discussed above have made it clear to both Saudi society and the international community that the king and the royal family are back in control of the country in all its sectors. At another level, the state is increasingly allowing gender to become a central concern debated in the public sphere. This is extremely important at a time when the state has endeavoured to silence any debate about political reform. Debating gender has become a substitute for general political activism.

## DEBATING GENDER IN THE PUBLIC SPHERE

The increased visibility of Saudi women in the post-9/11 period is a product of interrelated domestic and global factors. The state introduced a series of initiatives whose purpose was to modernise authoritarian rule at a time when change was increasingly demanded by sections of Saudi society. Changes in the area of gender and women's roles became extremely important as symbols of the new modernity of the Saudi state. The state, through its media empire, had to convince both the international community and its agitated local constituency that a new era was inaugurated with the accession of Abdullah to the throne in 2005. However, changes in gender policy had already started immediately after 9/11 when Saudi Arabia came under increasing international pressure. The state had to reverse its restrictive post-1979 policies on gender in which it had endorsed social and religious conservatism. Faced with the crisis of global and local terrorism, increased local demands for political change and reform, and greater scrutiny by the international community, the state had no choice but to adopt the rhetoric of social reform and substantiate it with specific gender-related initiatives aimed at demonstrating its commitment to the emancipation of women. The cosmopolitan women described above became the new face of Saudi Arabia after the public sphere was saturated with images of bearded Saudi Jihadis, polishing their rifles in hiding-places in Afghanistan, Iraq, and Saudi Arabia, quoting verses from the Quran and *hadith* calling upon Muslims to perform *jihad,* and celebrating their own contribution to suicide bombs and war against infidels. The soft face of the cosmopolitan, sophisticated, and articulate woman was the best weapon the state could summon in its war not only against terrorism but also against its demonisation in the international community.

Greater foreign media access to Saudi Arabia was allowed following the events of 9/11. This resulted in a wider coverage of Saudi society. While most international media attention was focused on terrorism, and Saudi efforts to curb radical religious opinions and financial support to charities allegedly sponsoring terrorism, many Western journalists also highlighted what they considered to be the 'plight of Saudi women'. American, British, and French media that had begun to broadcast in Arabic, such as al-Hora, the BBC, and France 24, developed a special interest in Saudi women and reported on their situation. Al-Hora employed Nadine al-Budayr, the outspoken Saudi journalist mentioned earlier, to present a special women's programme in which she interviewed Saudi women and highlighted their marginalisation. International human rights organisations produced fuller reports that criticised aspects of gender discrimination and restricted legal rights.[39] Most of the reporting on Saudi women by outsiders accused the radical Wahhabi tradition of maintaining exclusion and discrimination against women. One can say that immediately after 9/11, the marginalisation of Saudi women became a truly global concern. Most outside reporting on women focused on their problems, but from 2005 positive stories about the achievements of Saudi women began to appear in Western media, highlighting the reforms of King Abdullah.[40] The increased interest of the international media and non-governmental organisations in Saudi women cannot be ignored in assessing the recent change in the state's position on gender. The globalisation of the 'Saudi woman question' pushed the Saudi leadership to respond to accusations relating to gender discrimination, thus precipitating heated debates inside the country.

This sudden international media attention was echoed inside Saudi Arabia. Old Saudi newspapers, new print and satellite media ventures operating inside the country and in neighbouring Dubai, and Beirut-based Saudi-sponsored television channels all cooperated to unveil the 'problem' of Saudi women. Men and women were invited to participate

---

[39] See Human Rights Watch, *Perpetual Minors: Human Rights Abuses Stemming From Male Guardianship and Sex Segregation in Saudi Arabia*, New York: Human Rights Watch, 2008; and *Saudi Arabia: Looser Rein, Uncertain Gain*, New York: Human Rights Watch, 2010.

[40] 'Saudi Women's Quiet Revolution', *Time*, 19 September 2009.

in discussion programmes that dealt with a whole range of issues such as unemployment, education, marriage, divorce, violence against women, and youth problems. Such media forums had never been available to women and, after 9/11, a young generation of women activists and writers was given a platform. Previously many Saudi women had written commentaries in local newspapers, but they had never been able to have a presence on television. This sudden and orchestrated publicity led to gender issues assuming great importance in a society that had not been used to airing controversial issues in the public sphere, let alone watching its own women debating highly controversial matters on television. In previous decades, the *ulama* had resolved all debates on women through *fatwa*s, but after 9/11 they were were reduced to just one voice among many others, all competing to define the future of Saudi women and their rights.

Loosening restrictions on the local media, which became free to report on the many social and economic problems, was an important outcome of the 9/11 crisis. In many respects, this coincided with the expansion of Internet services in Saudi Arabia that brought about alternative forums for debate and discussion of all matters related to social, political, and economic problems. The state adopted a new policy that allowed local journalists to voice criticism of social issues attributed to 'misinterpretations' of religion. Writers of all persuasions provided opinions and commentaries on current gender policies, thus shattering the semblance of consensus that had prevailed during the previous decades. The *fatwa*s discussed in the previous chapter became the subject of controversy without these controversies being resolved. While the old *fatwa*s continued to be revered and defended by many Saudis, new revisionist religious interpretations on women's issues began to appear. Both official *ulama* and others not directly employed by the state religious bureaucracy initiated these opinions. However, religion is no longer the main field defining the status and freedoms of Saudi women in the post-9/11 period. The state emerged after the crisis as the sole arbiter of women's rights, freedoms, and participation in society.

A special emphasis in the media on the problems of Saudi women was deemed necessary as an indicator of the changing state policies. This was understood as permission to identify a set of problems and expose their prevalence and impact on women. The 'question of Saudi women' became a regular domestic concern in the pages of the local press, in addition to being a prominent subject in international media. Domestic violence, the unemployment of women, the marriage of minors, mixing between the sexes, the guardianship system, the ban on driving, drug abuse, the elopement of young girls, and representation in the courts were hotly debated both inside Saudi Arabia and abroad. As most of these issues were discussed in the official media, it seems that the state encouraged an exposure of social ills in which women were central as victims. Journalists spared no opportunity to delve into the most sensitive issues, for example incest, rape, and violence against women, all previously taboo topics discussed only in private.

In general, commentators on women's problems were divided on the causes of gender discrimination in Saudi society. Like the international media, some Saudi writers, journalists, and gender activists attributed many of these problems to the restrictions imposed by the religious scholars and their *fatwas*. They spared no opportunity to remind their audiences that the strict Wahhabi interpretations of a previous era were responsible for the delayed emancipation of women and continuous restrictions on their full participation in society. Several liberal Saudi print and visual media outlets became platforms to elaborate this position. The 'problem of women' was seen as a reflection of radical religious opinions that produced terrorism and pushed Saudi society towards intolerance and hatred of the other. According to many liberal writers, the exclusion of women is but one area needing to be addressed. It is compounded by the circulation of radical *fatwas* on almost all aspects of life. Many argued that sex segregation and continued surveillance of the public sphere by the religious authorities created conditions for greater social ills. These writers, among whom were members of the appointed Consultative Council, called for limitations on religious dogma to free the social sphere. Writers argue that this would lead to greater recognition of the role women play in the future of the country.

This recognition is only possible if women are more visible in society. Liberal writers celebrated every initiative taken by the leadership to honour women while they continued to highlight women's achievements in education, innovation, and employment. In addition to reporting on the suffering of Saudi women, Saudi society was suddenly introduced to a cohort of women active in business, medicine, education, sciences, literature, and even aviation. The names and careers of these women became the subject of many newspaper articles and interviews on local and satellite television. There was a deliberate attempt to highlight women's talent and capabilities while at the same time pointing to their daily struggles, the abuse they endured, and their marginalisation. The state recognised talented women, a move that culminated in the leadership taking steps to include women among delegations travelling to other countries under the auspices of the king and other princes. In 2010, surrounded by a crowd of women, the king and Crown prince posed in front of cameras to mark a historical moment, according to the local press. A photo opportunity in which the king was surrounded by a group of women was interpreted as a sign of the new change in state policies towards gender and women's rights.

In their writings, both men and women scrutinised excessive religious restrictions, surveillance, and control which led to direct confrontation with religious scholars and the Committee for the Promotion of Commanding Right and Forbidding Wrong. The committee's regular raids and interventions in spaces where 'immoral behaviour' had allegedly been spotted were now regularly highlighted in the press. Unfair rulings against women's interests in religious courts were equally discussed as indicators of the general disempowerment of women. Saudi liberal writers criticised scholars who signed marriage contracts between minor girls and old men. They called for an end to child marriage and the introduction of a legal age for marriage for both men and women. They criticised judges who divorced women from their husbands on the basis of ambiguous interpretations of compatibility between the spouses. Sentences passed on rapists were condemned as lenient. Writers demanded severe punishment for those violating or abusing women. They called for an end to the ban on women driving as an economic necessity that would benefit the growing number of women teachers. Cases of teachers killed in road accidents as a result of careless foreign drivers became notorious. The message was clear. Social pages of the Saudi press, in addition to television discussion programmes, became arenas to call for a recognition that Saudi women face marginalisation and discrimination. Saudi liberals aspired to break not only the silence over gender problems but also the monopoly of religion in determining the permissible and prohibited. They looked to the state to deliver a new era whereby the social sphere would be freed from radical religious opinions. Media forums discussing gender equality became a substitute for formal women's organisations dealing with women's rights. In the absence of such organisations, traditional and new media replaced formal and classical channels for mobilisation.

This new discourse on gender was neither new nor unanimous. It had its roots among a small circle of Saudi writers, novelists, and journalists as far back as the 1960s. What was new in the post-9/11 period was its flourishing in official media outlets and the extent of the freedom it was given to circulate in the public sphere. This could not have happened without clear state endorsement of its messages. While the state's main immediate concern was to fight terrorism and limit the propagation of radical Jihadi opinions, Saudi liberals used the opportunity to link terrorism with other social issues, one of which was gender discrimination. In order to fight terrorism, less restrictive gender policies were needed. Greater visibility of women was encouraged as a counterbalance to the general state of intolerance and radicalisation believed to be prevalent in Saudi society. Fighting terrorism necessitated fighting radical religious opinions in general, especially those pertaining to sex segregation and discrimination against women. Great social liberalisation would inevitably lead to the triumph of moderate opinions and social positions, all necessary to undermine radicalisation and the appeal of Jihadi ideology and violence. The subtle linkages that many Saudi liberals hoped to make were not well received in many religious circles.

Islamist activists who remained within the fold of the religious tradition began to introduce a discourse that holds social and cultural dimensions, known as *araf ijtimaiyya*, responsible for the exclusion of women and their plight in Saudi society. Unlike liberal writers, they located the roots of gender discrimination in society rather than religion. Without openly criticising the religious establishment, many religious scholars and Islamist activists endeavoured to enlighten their audiences about the need to separate social norms from religion. In this way, they avoided a critical reading of the many *fatwa*s on women or a direct confrontation with highly revered religious scholars. Many Islamist activists, both male and female, argued that a previous generation of *ulama* had incorporated the social and patriarchal sensitivities of Saudi society into their religious opinions on important gender issues. They simply confirmed exclusionary social habits without being able to draw the line between culture and religion. This trend became popular among many writers and religious scholars who absolved Islam from being responsible for discrimination against women. They attributed current discrimination to society's tribal heritage and conservatism. Famous scholars such as Salman al-Awdah adopted this position, thus avoiding a direct clash with the interpretations of a previous generation of *ulama* who are still respected in Saudi Arabia. He appeared weekly on MBC television in a special programme called *Hajar al-zawiya* (The corner) in which he highlighted the need to understand how restrictions on women are a reflection of Saudi social conservatism rather than simply Islam. Other religious scholars offered a new opportunity to revisit old *fatwa*s and opinions, since these had been based on confusing social conservatism with religion.

Famous contemporary religious scholars began to consider the ban on women driving as a reflection of social norms rather than a clear religious prohibition. While these *ulama* hesitate to call directly for an immediate suspension of the ban, they have highlighted the need to educate society to separate social norms from religious law. They implicitly support the current ban on the basis that Saudi society is not ready for such a revolutionary move. Only after men have been educated to accept women driving can the ban be lifted. Debate is seen as a positive move in the direction of freeing the religious field from the limitations of culture and social norms. Two important principles should not be conflated, as they may not be the same. One is *ayb* (shame) and the other is *haram* (religiously prohibited). According to some religious scholars many in Saudi society, including the *ulama*, have not made this distinction, which resulted in confusion and increased restrictions on the role of women in society. What is socially unacceptable has become a religious prohibition. The ban on women driving is a good example of the confusion. Famous scholars voiced opinions that Saudi women will be allowed to drive in the future but that this depends on creating a favourable educational context that facilitates acceptance of the idea. A cultural shift is needed before society rushes into something that is more likely to lead to dissent if important preparatory educational work is not provided in advance.

Since 9/11, religious scholars have entered into an equally fierce debate among themselves as they take different positions on women. After the long-standing consensus regarding the prohibition on mixing between the sexes, the religious community is, for the first time, divided over this issue. While all religious scholars forbid *khilwa*, the presence of unrelated men and women in any confined space, they deliver different opinions on *ikhtilat*, mixing in the public sphere such as at work, debate forums, shopping centres, and higher education. Some scholars argue that *ihktilat* is not an Islamic principle but rather a modern invention. Scholars are beginning to distinguish between predetermined and accidental *ikhtilat*. The first is not encouraged, while the second is permissible. The state allowed limited *ikhtilat* in specific contexts, for example in press conferences where women journalists are allowed to be seated with men, or in highly prestigious economic forums and newly established scientific universities, such as King Abdullah University of Science and Technology (KAUST). These initiatives brought about the beginning of friction between religious scholars on the meaning of *ikhtilat*. In contrast with the 2004 National Dialogue meeting, in 2008, and in the context of the seventh National Dialogue Forum held in Burayda with the theme Work and Employment Opportunities, the employment of women in mixed areas was discussed. Shaykh Abdul Muhsin al-Obaikan opened the sessions by insisting that there is nothing in *sharia* that forbids women from working in mixed environments as long as they conform to Islamic dress codes. He argued that mixing between the sexes at work is not a prohibited *khilwa*. This opinion was shared by others attending the forum, including Basma al-Omayer, director of a centre within the JCCI, who argued that article 106 of a labour law that prohibits *ikhtilat* had been abolished as a result of a royal decree. She anticipated seeing more mixing at the workplace in Jeddah, a city known for openness and cosmopolitanism. Between 2004 and 2008, and as a result of increased state initiatives on gender issues, a change was clearly visible. The previous conservative stance of religious scholars on women's employment was suppressed in favour of discussing the conditions under which women can be allowed to increase their participation in the economy. Women's employment is now taken for granted, but whether they should be allowed to work with men remains controversial.

The state watched the debate on *ikhtilat* without taking sides unless religious scholars directly criticised specific initiatives with clear state approval. After the inauguration of the co-educational KAUST, dubbed the new House of Wisdom, in 2009, Shaykh Saad al-Shithri, a member of the Higher Council of Ulama, voiced his rejection of *ikhtilat* in the new university. In a discussion on the recently established independent Islamist television channel al-Majd, the shaykh was asked by a caller to provide a religious opinion on mixing between men and women at the new university. He argued that the leadership might not be aware of the potential mixing, and that as a religious scholar he is under obligation to draw attention to the dangers of such a policy in the land of the two Holy Mosques. He also questioned whether the new university curriculum had been designed with a view to conform to Islam and its teachings. The university project was devised under the guidance of the Saudi oil company Aramco with no consultation with the religious establishment. While the shaykh absolved the king from any wrongdoing, he attributed the unlawful mixing to the work of administrators and called for the establishment of a *sharia* committee to examine the curriculum of the new university lest it contain unacceptable teaching material. He argued that 'mixing between the sexes in the land of the two Holy Mosques is unacceptable'.[41] While old higher educational institutions were designed with respect for the opinions of the religious scholars, the new university is seen as a project outside their control. As a science establishment, the

---

[41] *Arab News*, 5 October 2009.

university was developed by an oil company, seen as more suitable for such a grand project. Aramco was the first to employ women in the Eastern Province where it developed the oil industry. Its patronage of the new university shocked many religious scholars who are now beginning to feel that the new project is another step towards depriving them of their control over society through education.

Shaykh al-Shithri was not the only one who condemned *ikhtilat* in the new university. A famous shaykh, Abd al-Rahman al-Barrak, issued an opinion in which he argued that those who encourage *ikhtilat* are *murtad* (apostates) who should be killed if they do not change their opinion. He encouraged scholars not to become the 'keys to evil' who promote *ikhtilat* and make it acceptable by issuing misguided religious opinions. Those people want Saudi Arabia to follow the evil of other Muslim countries where cinemas and dance halls are abundant. Al-Barrak called for those scholars who accept *ikhtilat* to be expelled from their jobs. Another religious scholar, Yusif al-Ahmad, went as far as to argue that *ikhtilat* was an absolute prohibition even in the Mecca mosque. He called for redesigning the mosque in such a way as to create a separate section for women. This was interpreted as a call to demolish the mosque and rebuild it with a view to make stricter sex segregation possible. Other shaykhs condemned *ihktilat* after amateur video clips of a mixed student party at the inauguration ceremony of KAUST circulated on the Internet. Although the majority of staff and students are not Saudis, many scholars regarded this as offensive, as it promised a troubling future under the auspices of the current king.

The fiercest criticism of *ikhtilat* was voiced against Prince Faisal, the king's son-in-law and minister of education, and his deputy, Nura al-Faiz, who was dispatched to visit a school for boys. Shaykh Nasir al-Omar was horrified that a prince, ignorant of religious studies, would assume the role of mufti and claim that he did not breach any religious principle when he encouraged mixing in special educational forums. The prince, according to al-Omar, had violated the initial pact between the founder of Wahabiyya, Muhammad ibn Abd al-Wahhab, and the Al-Saud. He also violated the principles of the oath of allegiance (*baya*) to King Abdullah, to whom it was rendered on condition that he upholds the principles of Islam. In a lecture, al-Omar warned that the prince is

... [treating] our women like concubines to be enjoyed by all. The prince claims that parents approve of *ikhtilat* and therefore he will not do anything about it. Many parents approve of their sons going to *jihad* in Afghanistan and Iraq but the government put them in prison. Our prisons are full of them. Why doesn't the state allow them to go if they have parental approval? The prince's argument is void. How can he assemble boys and girls in halls together? This is what disturbs peace. This is what undermines the state. This is what makes people angry, and at this time of upheavals in the Arab world he should not provoke people. This minister and his team meet and mix with our girls. Our girls and boys are not a horde of mares, a group of concubines for him to enjoy. He teaches our children to disobey God. His *munkar* [sins] are now public and we advise him in public. Unfortunately a *wazir* [minister], this time from the royal family, is doing this. We take refuge in God and ask him to do justice. He wants to corrupt our girls. He is not a person of knowledge. His mistakes are public. Our ancestors were worried about *ikhtilat* when it started fifty years ago. Shaykh Muhammad ibn Ibrahim was in charge so mixing did not happen. The rhetoric of *islah* [reform] is like that of the Pharaoh, who wants people to see what he sees. He tells us that we are backward and the world has moved. Why don't you make our schools new and modern? Is this the reform that we should take from the West? He took from the West the worst aspects and left the good aspects. We want action against this chaos. This man unveiled the secrets of the king's household. People are talking about it on the internet. The Custodian of the Two Holy Mosques must act now. The *ulama* too must act on this. Have pity on our girls. Parents should act, as we will not know what happens in the future.[42]

Female Islamists joined the *ulama* who rejected mixing in condemning *ikhtilat*. Nura al-Saad, an academic specialising in religious studies, whose position will be fully explored in Chapter 7, wrote a letter condemning workplaces that allow mixing between the sexes. She responded to Lama Sulayman, deputy chair of the JCCI, who declared that women's employment would be restricted without mixing. Al-Saad considered this opinion a call for Westernisation and the loss of morality:

For fifty years, women have been employed without mixing in this country. This is the corner[stone] of our tradition. Our first aim is to obey God and give our society good deeds. We never felt any difficulty in doing our jobs without mixing. Those who call for mixing want to import foreign women to take our jobs. Now they are calling for *ikhtilat*. The next thing they will call for is legalising *khilwa*. They are guided by United Nation ideas about ending gender discrimination not by the Quran. We, the women of Saudi Arabia, have not complained about segregation between the sexes. Only those Westernised women and half men who want to enjoy working and looking at women are making noise about it. We reject *ikhtilat* because it restricts us and limits our freedom at work and education.[43]

Many female Islamists fear that *ikhtilat* in universities and at work would deter women whose families are not in favour of mixing from taking up

---

[42] Nasir al-Omar, oral sermon.
[43] *Harf*, http://www.harfnews.org.

the new job opportunities. While *ikhtilat* would provide new opportunities in education and employment, from the female Islamist perspective
it threatens to create new conditions for exclusion. When Princess Adilla
patronised a forum organised by the Khadija bint Khuwaylid Centre
to promote women's participation in national development, thirty-six
female academics working in religious universities as lecturers in *sharia*
and Islamic education issued a statement against the forum which is seen
as a step towards normalising *ikhtilat* and ending gender discrimination
as stated in the UN documents; both are 'against our Islamic tradition
and *sharia*... the state must intervene and prohibit such forums that do
not represent us and our aspirations as Muslim women. The state must
protect our religion and secure the future of the new generation according
to Islamic tradition'.[44]

A week later, 700 female Islamists signed and circulated a petition
condemning the centre's concern with *ikhtilat*, without expressing the
wide interests of Saudi women. The petition claimed that the centre and
its director do not represent Saudi women:

We expected the centre to deal with the moral and economic problems of women
but we were disappointed that the centre did not offer any practical solutions.
Those who run the centre are obsessed with allowing more *ikhtilat* which embarrass many women and deprive them of real employment opportunities. Women
in contemporary societies suffer from sexual harassment as a result of *ikhtilat*.
Furthermore, the centre degrades motherhood and bringing up children. They
use the term *rabat biyut* [housewives] in a derogatory way to tarnish and belittle
women. In the forum there were dubious activities, women were unveiled and
had their legs exposed. There was also music, not to mention the participation of
foreign agents such as the wife of the American ambassador and others.[45]

The liberal Saudi press launched a serious attack on al-Shithri and other
radical scholars who were perceived as challenging the decision of the
king and undermining his new policy to promote women's education.
More than fifty opinion pieces were published in the local press and
on liberal Internet websites condemning the shaykh and others who objected. The fiercest condemnations were published in the liberal newspaper *al-Watan*. As al-Shithri was a member of the Higher Council of
Ulama, he was singled out as someone who challenges state policy from
within and disobeys the will of *wali al-amr* (the ruler), thus invoking
association with Jihadi terrorists. Al-Shithri was sacked within several

[44] 'Saoudiyat yunadidna', *al-Jazeera*, 25 December 2010.
[45] 'Saoudiyat yunadidna', *al-Jazeera*, 25 December 2010.

days of appearing on television in 2010. Counter-arguments supportive of the shaykh were simply ignored by the king.

In such a climate of heated debate, many official *ulama* remained silent on the *ikhtilat* endorsed in the new university, while others defended state policy. In 2010, Issa al-Gaith, a judge in Riyadh, wrote an article condemning 'those sheikhs who issue radical opinions on *ikhtilat*'. He argued that 'we should protect our national interest without causing confusion and dissent. Above all religious scholars should not cause chaos and undermine the leadership. Our country and leadership respect the *sharia* and we should not adopt radical views in applying it'.[46] These comments from a high-ranking judge in support of government policy were a reflection of the change that has swept Saudi Arabia since 9/11.

The most supportive opinion in defence of state policy on *ikhtilat* was issued by Shaykh Ahmad al-Ghamdi, director of the Mecca branch of the Committee for the Promotion of Commanding Right and Forbidding Wrong. Al-Ghamdi declared that *ikhtilat* is not prohibited in Islam and is not grounded in *sharia*. He praised the new mixed university as a gigantic step towards achieving knowledge, and accused those who criticised it of hypocrisy and ignorance in religious matters. He argued that the households of those who prohibit it are full of foreign maids who intermingle with the male family members. *Ikhtilat* is normal in the lives of Muslims in general and Saudis in particular. He went as far as to say that the term *ikhtilat* is a novelty in Islam and could not be justified, as men and women had mixed in public places in the ancient Islamic past. He also argued that men and women performed visits to Mecca and engaged in the ritual of *tawaf*, circumambulation of the Ka'ba, together.[47] The opinions of someone in charge of purifying Islamic space from unlawful *ikhtilat* were a reflection of the new government policy.

The liberal press promoted al-Ghamdi's opinions, and interviewed him several times to counter al-Shithri's prohibition on *ikhtilat*. Both *al-Watan* and al-Arabiyya satellite television channel dedicated space and time to promote al-Ghamdi's moderate opinion. While al-Shithri lost his job as a member of the Higher Council of Ulama, al-Ghamdi remained as head of the Committee in Mecca, thus reflecting the state's preference for promoting *ulama* and religious civil servants who support its general agenda. On 11 March 2011, al-Ghamdi was finally removed from his post under mounting pressure by the neo-Wahhabi *ulama*, who mounted a fierce

[46] *Harf*, http://www.harfnews.org.
[47] See http://www.alarabiya.net/articles/2009/12/93988.html.

and aggressive attack on not only al-Ghamdi but ministers of education, information, and the head of the royal court. The new rejectionist religious scholars are believed to operate under the patronage of the Ministry of Interior and its Committee for the Promotion of Commanding Right and Forbidding Wrong.

Religious scholars are today free to voice opinions against the previous consensus on the prohibition of *ikhtilat*, and many support state initiatives by delivering the right *fatwas*. Those who offer moderate opinions legitimising limited aspects of gender mixing under the auspices of the state and in the public sphere are celebrated in the official press. In contrast, those scholars who continue to categorically condemn *ikhtilat* issue their *fatwas* on their own websites or participate in the many new private religious television channels, as they would be denied a platform in state-owned media. This was exactly Nasir al-Omar's strategy. Official *ulama* such as al-Shithri who publicly challenge state policies on gender mixing are no longer tolerated. They risk being dismissed from their jobs, and their opinions are discussed and rejected in the official press.

The debate on *ikhtilat* in educational institutions is accompanied by an even more heated controversy regarding the employment of Saudi women in contexts that involve mixing between the sexes in public places or in jobs seen as degrading. With the rising rates of female unemployment, the Ministry of Labour under Minister Ghazi al-Gosaybi (d. 2010) proposed that shops selling lingerie items should replace their salesmen with women. The proposal drew on religious arguments in favour of allowing women a private space when they shop for such items instead of having to deal with salesmen. The proposal was not enforced, as opposition was so fierce. Only in 2012 did the feminisation of lingerie shops become law, and many women started replacing foreign men in these shops.

Another proposal to employ women as cashiers in shopping centres was circulated in 2010. It seems to have been implemented in some limited parts of the private sector. This was part of the Ministry of Labour's initiative to expand employment opportunities for women. When several supermarket chains in Jeddah employed a small number of women as cashiers, there were many objections to the move and calls for a boycott of the supermarkets. State agencies did nothing to remove the cashiers from their jobs in this private sector, thus indicating approval of these new employment opportunities. But in November 2010, Riasa al-Ama lil Buhuth wa al-Ifta (the directorate for research and *fatwa*), part of the Higher Council of Ulama, issued a *fatwa* against the employment of women as cashiers. Signed by the grand mufti, Abd al-Aziz al-Sheikh, and six other members, the *fatwa* prohibited Muslim women from working as cashiers who would have to mix with their male managers and customers.[48] Other Saudis who objected to this kind of employment did so on religious and nationalistic grounds. Jobs involving the employment of women in open shops where they would come into contact with strangers were regarded as unlawful *ikhtilat*. In addition, these jobs were seen as menial and unworthy of Saudi women. Commentaries on the proposals emphasised how degrading it would be for Saudi women to work as cashiers, defined as *mihan wathia*, degrading jobs, and thus a mixture of religious and nationalistic discourse circulated to undermine the proposal prior to the official *fatwa*. This discourse draws on images of Saudi women enjoying a high status as guardians of the tradition whose place is in the confines of the family home, where their attention should be dedicated to raising children and strengthening their piety.[49] A Saudi woman working as a cashier would create chaos (*fitna*), as this would confuse the boundaries between elevated and respected Muslim women and others, mainly foreign workers employed in shopping centres. Those against the proposal claimed that such jobs would be the beginning of the disintegration of Saudi society and its increasing Westernisation. They feared that Saudi Arabia would become like other Muslim countries, eventually precipitating a loss of exclusiveness as an Islamic society. Employers would select women on the basis of their smiling faces and physical beauty to attract customers, according to critics. Initially employers would respect the veil, but later would probably insist on its removal. According to opponents, this is the way Westernisation creeps into Saudi society, following the principle of *tadarruj*, or gradual evolution.

Those expressing opinions in support of the employment of women as cashiers congratulated the Panda supermarket chain for its daring

[48] The *fatwa* highlighted the *fitna* that results from women mixing with men in shopping centres, as they would require training to operate cash machines. This training, coupled with the prospect of women touching men's hands as they handle change, was prohibited. For the text of the *fatwa* (number 24937), see http://www.alifta.net/Default. aspx#. Other affiliated websites, for example, Islamway, publicised the *fatwa* and recorded various sermons in support of its ruling. One religious scholar, Shaykh Faisal al-Shadi, commented on the *fatwa*'s strength. He attacked those liberals who give the example of female street vendors found in Saudi Arabia and argued that women vendors are single traders who work on their own and there are often *qawaid*, old women, unlike the young cashiers. To listen to his comments, see http://www.islamway.com/?iw_s= Lesson&iw_a=view&lesson_id=103897&scholar_id=368.

[49] Muhammad al-Ghabashi, 'al-Aham fi fatwa tahrim amal al-kashirat' [Most important in *fatwa* regarding women cashiers], available at http://www.lahaonline.com/articles/ view/37080.htm.

move and urged Saudis not to listen to those calling for a boycott. They supported their argument by drawing on the high unemployment figures among Saudi women and the rising level of poverty among a substantial number of women. They cited the number of women beggars roaming the streets and concluded that it is better for women to earn a living. A job that pays SR1,500–3,000 is an opportunity for an unskilled woman to gain an income. One author invoked early Islamic history, mainly the age of the Prophet, to argue that women's involvement in economic transactions is as old as Islam itself. He gave the example of the Prophet's wife Zaynab bint Jahsh who was a woman experienced in selling and buying.[50]

While the debate was raging in the press and on the Internet, the state did not take any measure to reverse this development, thus indicating to the constituency that it does not object to women taking such new jobs. As the *fatwa* had the signature of several members of the official *ulama*, it would have been impossible to sack all of them as al-Shithri's dismissal indicated. In fact, these new employment opportunities correspond to the objectives of the 2005–9 development plan in which the government promised to create more employment for women not only in the traditional sectors of education and health but also in telecommunication, management, and tourism. Special charitable training programmes were set up to help divorcees and widows gain an income through the sale of household items and food. The plan urged the private sector to employ more women. Official *ulama* asserted their autonomy in the case of the cashiers, but the employment of women in new contexts continued. The *fatwa* did not seem to change the course of events or reverse the permission given to employ women in supermarkets, at least in Jeddah, thus indicating yet again the triumph of the state's political agenda over that of the religious establishment. Faced with a deluge of articles in the press condemning the *fatwa* against women as cashiers, the grand mufti declared in Mecca that the *fatwa* was non-binding to all. He called upon journalists to respect the *fatwa* and its initiators.

The Saudi press started reporting on what is regarded as a new development: the phenomenon of Saudi women working as migrant labourers. These include a small number of teachers and nurses who recently sought employment in Kuwait and Qatar. The phenomenon was condemned on Internet sites, and was seen as a reflection of the shortcomings of the state, which had failed in its welfare projects and consequently pushed women

---

[50] Hasan bin Salim, 'al-Mara al-cashir' [The cashier woman], *al-Hayat*, 2 November 2010.

to migrate in search of jobs. When news about Saudi women working
as maids in Qatar broke out in the foreign press, there was even greater
outrage. Saudi officials denied knowledge of such cases. It is difficult to
verify these stories in the absence of official statistics inside Saudi Arabia
or in neighbouring Gulf states. The story about Saudi maids in Qatar
was reported in the *Los Angeles Times* and other Internet sources.[51] The
Ministry of Labour remained silent on Saudi maids abroad. The employment of Saudi women as maids inside the country remains even more
controversial. According to a study, 'it is now considered a shame and a
disgrace for Saudi women to undertake domestic work'.[52]

Among the plethora of controversies on gender issues, the ban on
women driving remains the most heated. While this debate was silenced
immediately after the demonstration in Riyadh in 1991, it is resurfacing
with the intention of facilitating a partial or total lifting of the ban. In the
past, religious opinions and *fatwa*s were used as a justification for the ban,
but today more nuanced arguments in favour of women driving invoke
economic necessity. The plight of women teachers and their dependence
on foreign drivers, in addition to the cost of employing such drivers, have
become recurrent themes invoked by those in favour of women driving.
Stories about women victims of road accidents caused by reckless foreign
drivers are highlighted with a view to draw attention to the loss of life
as a result of the ban. The press reported an extraordinary story of four
teachers who married their driver in order to guarantee transport to work.
Those in favour of lifting the ban invoke the contradiction in a society
where *ikhtilat* is still unacceptable but the presence of women in cars
driven by foreign drivers is allowed. There is a conscious effort to report
stories of women who have been driving not only cars but also trucks in
rural areas. Interviews with these women familiarise city dwellers with
the normality of driving among the rural population where women may
not have the luxury of drivers.

Muhammad al-Zulfa, a member of the Consultative Council, appeared
on television debates with conservative religious scholars to defend his
position on lifting the ban on driving. He defended a council report based

---

[51] 'Qatar Public Outrage Rises with Demand for Saudi Maids', *Los Angeles Times*,
12 August 2009, and 'Women Upset as Saudis Start Work as Maids', *The Peninsula*, 4 August 2009, available at http://www.menafn.com/qn_news_story_s.asp?StoryId=
1093262965.

[52] Salwa al-Khatib, 'The Oil Boom and its Impact on Women and Families in Saudi Arabia',
in Alanoud al-Sharekh (ed.), *The Gulf Family: Kinship Policies and Modernity*, London:
Saqi, 2007, pp. 83–108, at p. 101.

on a study of the possibility of allowing women to drive. Amira, the wife of al-Walid bin Talal, gave interviews in which she expressed her support for lifting the ban. When al-Walid bin Talal celebrated the achievement of the first Saudi woman to qualify as a pilot, Captain Hanadi, who was sponsored by him to learn to fly aeroplanes in Jordan, the press lamented the fact that Hanadi could not be trusted to drive a car but was capable of flying an aeroplane. The foreign minister, Prince Saud al-Faisal, has assured Western audiences that Saudi women will drive in the near future, when the right conditions present themselves, but argued that preparing Saudi society may take time and patience. Other members of the royal family perpetuate this argument.

The controversy on driving can degenerate into absurd suggestions such as the need for establishing special women's lanes on roads and women-only car-repair centres to deal with emergency breakdowns, in addition to providing special training for traffic police to deal with women. Some writers argue that during the times of the Prophet, women were allowed to ride camels and donkeys for transport. As cars are safer, there is no reason to maintain the ban on women's movement. Driving has become a symbol of men's loss of control over women who will become less dependent on men for leaving their homes and may not ask for their permission. Although currently those women who have drivers enjoy the freedom to leave their homes, driving will allow women even greater circulation. Reports about young girls missing school and instructing their drivers to take them to shopping centres and cafes where they spend hours chatting and smoking the hubble-bubble started appearing in the Saudi press. Some argue that if girls are allowed to drive, truancy and other social ills will eventually increase.

In 2010, the ban on driving was caricatured on the Saudi comedy programme *Tash ma Tash* in a special episode during Ramadan ridiculing Saudi families who prefer employing foreign rather than Saudi drivers. The episode shows the head of the family instructing the driver, a Saudi posing as a foreigner, to take several women of the household to different places in town and fetch others from their relatives' homes. The Saudi driver appears confused and distracted while trying to play the role of an Asian driver. As most families prefer to employ a foreigner rather than a Saudi driver, the programme ends with the sacking of the driver after his Saudi identity is revealed, thus highlighting how society resists Saudisation, especially in the employment of maids and drivers. The message of such comedy is clear: to fight unemployment, foreign labour needs to be replaced by Saudis, and women should be allowed to drive. Both serious commentaries and comedies have contributed to highlighting the urgent need to allow women to drive.

The press began to identify a new problem, namely the 'chaos of *fatwa*', thus referring to the multiple and contradictory opinions of Saudi *ulama* on all matters, including *ikhtilat*, driving, education, and employment, which caused a stir after the al-Shithri affair. The king issued a royal decree prohibiting *fatwa*s that are volunteered by religious scholars.[53] The decree clearly states that only the Higher Council of Ulama and those designated by the Council are allowed to issue *fatwa*s. This informed many self-appointed *ulama* that the government will deal swiftly with the proliferation of *fatwa*s on television and the Internet. Within weeks of the royal decree, independent television channel al-Usra, which hosts regular *fatwa* programmes, was shut down, in addition to the censoring of several websites specialising in issuing *fatwa*s. Famous shaykhs removed the *fatwa* sections of their websites to avoid a complete shutdown. However, the royal decree may be difficult to implement. Many shaykhs have study circles in which they are regularly asked for religious opinions. While the state may be able to censor religious opinions on the web, it is practically impossible to control *fatwa*s issued orally in the contexts of study circles and preaching. Moreover, *fatwa* programmes on satellite channels, some of which are privately owned by Saudis and other Gulf entrepreneurs and are based outside Saudi Arabia, may be difficult to shut down. In the age of globalisation and increased communication technology, controlling *fatwa*s may not be so easily achieved.

While allowing liberal and Islamist critiques of the traditional religious field, and silencing dissident religious voices on the new state gender policy, the leadership remains cautious. It avoids a serious break of relations with the guardians of religious tradition or a direct confrontation with its many pillars. It allows limited *ikhtilat* but continues to uphold the ban on driving. Its primary schools remain segregated, but recently it issued new guidelines for private schools to allow prepubescent boys to be instructed by women teachers. In the social sphere, there is an obvious lack of coordination or vision regarding gender policies. The state has responded to international and local pressures by adopting ad hoc measures that attract media attention and praise in the West and among the liberal circles inside the country. It is clear that there is no consensus on gender reform within the country. The state cannot always rely on supporting *fatwa*s, as the cashier episode indicated, but it can go ahead with

53  See www.majalla.com/en/cover_story/article110707.ece?comments.

new measures by simply turning a blind eye and ignoring even official *fatwa*s on the subject. Big projects such as the new co-educational university (KAUST), the new Princess Nura bint Abd al-Rahman University for Girls, or the appointment of a woman as deputy minister of education are turned into public relations exercises that guarantee the state a high profile as a champion of social reform. The reform so far has stretched the boundaries of debate and controversy in the country, but it has not moved fast on important aspects of gender equality and emancipation.

The state watches the current debates on gender issues with a view to eliminate any dissident opinions that challenge its policies. While the king and other senior princes may stretch the boundaries and approve certain changes in the status of women, their education, and employment, they remain unwilling to confront and directly challenge their loyal constituencies. Cosmetic changes such as those described in this chapter are used to test the ground, but women remain subject to both the patriarchal control of their menfolk and to the control of the state. The state has no interest in an emancipatory project that would undermine the loyalty of its male subjects who cherish their control over their own women. So far, they have shared this control with the state, reinforcing each other as guardians of women, but in general men are not willing to give up the right altogether or allow the state the full privilege. Through its legislation and surveillance, the state allowed not only male relatives but all Saudi men to practise a collective duty, namely, controlling women in the public sphere. Since 9/11, this shared duty between men and the state is undergoing changes that may not be resolved in favour of the emancipation of women. It is more likely that renegotiating the relationship between men and the state could lead to some breakthroughs for women, but this is subject to the political agenda of the state at a given moment.

The state has succeeded in putting gender issues on the agenda of most Saudis, thus diverting attention from calls for serious political reform. Since the accession of King Abdullah in 2005, religious scholars, Islamists, and liberal writers have been debating the political future of the country. Petitions calling for political reform stopped in 2005, after which sporadic letters asking for reform appeared on Internet discussion boards without serious and noticeable responses from either society or the leadership.[54] Instead, women and gender issues have replaced political reform as the main focus of attention on both sides of the divide, the

---

[54] This has changed since the Arab Spring in 2011, as the conclusion to this book will show.

Islamist and the liberal. This seems to satisfy the leadership, which faced mounting pressure for political reform immediately after 9/11 but failed to signal any interest in developing the political system and moving it in the direction of greater political participation.

## CONCLUSION

This chapter has highlighted common interest between the state and a group of educated elite women who have cooperated and promoted the state as a reformist agency in society. It also identified multiple discourses on women, the most prominent of which is that of the state and the liberal and moderate Islamist constituency that dominated Saudi media following 9/11. All aspire to establish the leading role of the king and other princes in the emancipation of women. The chapter also pointed to the current debate within Islamic circles on recent changes introduced by the state. It seems that discourses that challenge the new vision are sidelined and marginalised, a complete reversal of the 1980s when the *ulama* and their *fatwas* determined state policy on many issues discussed here. Today, what appear to be radical *ulama* opinions are simply cathartic strategies venting frustration, but they should not be considered as determining gender policy.

It is clear that Saudis are now given more freedom to criticise radical religious opinions and call for moderate interpretations on matters relevant to women's lives. They are not, however, free to articulate similar criticism of high-ranking officials or to debate the king's vision in the pages of the official press. Those religious scholars who offer moderate opinions are rewarded, while those who object to state gender policies are ostracised and even sacked. As the religious nationalism that had defined the role of Saudi women in society came under attack, the state began to search for an alternative legitimacy narrative in which the emancipation of Saudi women is central. The king's appointee, the deputy minister of education, Nura al-Faiz, asserted her Najdi identity, as demonstrated in an interview she gave immediately after her appointment, cited at the beginning of this chapter. However, fixed and preconceived women's identities are being challenged on the ground, in particular on the pages of Saudi women's fiction. Perhaps this is why al-Faiz needs to assert an aspect of herself that is currently being diluted by state policies and serious social and political pressures. Religious nationalism highlighted purity and tradition while maintaining imaginary boundaries around the nation. Nura al-Faiz's objections to her photos being published in the press immediately after her appointment invoke resistance to this publicity on the grounds of her Saudi Najdi identity, the same identity that religious nationalism defended under the veneer of Islamic universalism and solidarity. While she claims that she is *munaqaba*, photos of her with her face uncovered circulated on the Internet in the months following her appointment. But she initially wanted to assert her local identity at a time when the state was searching for the cosmopolitan woman. The publicity that her appointment received locally and internationally may have made her assertions of identity redundant. Today, a local Najdi–Wahhabi identity grounded in the previous religious nationalism is currently being challenged. Instead, the quest for a cosmopolitan alternative has already started.

Under the pressure of terrorism, the state shifted the focus to cosmopolitanism in which tolerance, pluralism, and diversity are today celebrated at the level of official discourse without real evidence of meaningful change. This cosmopolitanism happens to coincide with the agendas of an emerging affluent and educated Saudi middle constituency who by virtue of education, resources, and opportunities find the old restrictions on personal freedoms, consumption patterns, and economic opportunities unbearable. Women among this group happen to want to escape these restrictions and maximise their chances. The state taking the leading role in opening many new spheres for women is a reflection of its current quest for a visible cosmopolitan modernity which women appearing in the public sphere can project. But it is also a reflection of some women wanting to empower themselves through freedom from old obstacles that hinder their gradual immersion in a new context, characterised by increasing opportunities that remain restricted and heavily regulated by the state. In taming, albeit without abandoning, the previous religious nationalism, and managing its claims to the authenticity and uniqueness of Saudi Arabia, the state tries to fix women as pillars of a new cosmopolitan condition, diverse but rooted in moderate Saudi Islamic credentials in which previously taken-for-granted Wahhabi radicalism is subdued. Women who work and contribute to society are active in formulating the new image of Saudi Arabia as a sophisticated, cosmopolitan space. The quest of the state for the 'modern' cosmopolitan woman, the professional teacher, lawyer, doctor, pharmacist, novelist, pilot, film producer, photographer, artist, and entrepreneur who contributes to society through education and employment, has given rise to the many changes and debates outlined in this chapter. The emergence of this woman can only be achieved under state patriarchy, which has been accepted and sought by elite cosmopolitan women. The 'modern' woman needs to be freed from the control of radical religious tradition and conservative family values and placed under the patronage of the state. The achievements of individual women become the achievements of nation and state. At the beginning of the twenty-first century, Saudi Arabia can only be modern through the cosmopolitanism of its women. As will be seen in the next chapter, new Saudi women's fiction captures the shift towards this modernity.

# 5

# Women in Search of Themselves

Her soul remained hanging in a place that rejects her bright colours. She is tormented by rejection and internal wars the objective of which is to draw the boundaries and close the windows.

Umayma al-Khamis[1]

The literary productions of the first generation of Saudi women essayists, columnists, poets, and novelists are explored in Sadeka Arebi's anthropological monograph *Women and Words*.[2] The fact that Saudi Arabia produced so many women writers in the second half of the twentieth century may have surprised many observers but can be attributed to a number of factors. First, the expansion in girls' education in the humanities and

---

[1] Umayma al-Khamis, *al-Bahriyat* [Women from foreign shores], 1st edn, Damascus: al-Mada, 2006, pp. 66–7.

[2] Sadeka's Arebi's excellent book on women essayists, poets, and novelists captures the richness of women's literature that began to appear in the second half of the twentieth century. Most of the literary work she consulted was produced by women who were born between 1940 (e.g. Fatina Shakr) and 1960 (e.g. Najwa Hashim). In addition to these two, Arebi focused on the work of Fawziyya Abu Khalid, Ruqayya al-Shabib, Raja Alim, Sharifa al-Shamlan, Khayriyya al-Saqqaf, Juhayr al-Musaid, and Suhayla Zayn al-Abdin. Many women of this generation studied abroad in neighbouring Arab capitals. The political context of their work and their commentaries on political issues concerning the whole of the Arab world is contrasted with the narrow focus of the writers in this chapter, thus reflecting the political changes that have swept Saudi Arabia. Arebi's work remains the only authoritative anthropological reading of the first generation of Saudi women's literary productions. Since the publication of her book in 1994, a new generation of Saudi women writers has emerged, and this chapter is an attempt to situate their work in the changes that swept Saudi Arabia since 1990s. See Sadeka Arebi, *Women and Words in Saudi Arabia: The Politics of Literary Discourse*, New York: Columbia University Press, 1994.

175

social sciences, religious studies, and history since the 1960s is an important contributing factor. In 2009, forty-one per cent of all students at the
twenty-four public universities enrolled in arts and humanities subjects.[3]
Second, limitations on women's employment in the wider economy may
have been a contributing factor, pushing an increasing number of women
towards writing. Third, the marginality of Saudi women in the public
sphere with the consolidation of the state project in the second half of the
twentieth century against their historical centrality in social, religious,
and political contexts may have led women towards equally marginal
activities such as literature in a society where fiction, in particular the
novel, has been condemned as an alien, decadent, and suspicious mode
of expression imported from the West. While educated men occupied
key positions in the technologised state apparatus as bureaucrats and
technocrats, that is, 'scientific experts' needed for the process of state-
initiated development projects, for a long time women remained on the
margin, seeking recognition and a voice in writing. Those who write novels are seen as practising an unworthy and dangerous hobby rather than
a profession. And fourth, there is nothing in the Saudi legal restrictions
that is specifically against writing fiction, thus allowing both women and
men a space where they can explore taboo ideas without incurring the
wrath of those in power or their legal practitioners. A woman novelist is
considered less threatening than an activist who mobilises a community
of women. In the words of a Saudi novelist, the novel 'has become
a loophole, it expresses what we dare not say and want to break the
taboo'.[4]

In addition to the above factors, more importantly, the inability of
Saudi women to organise themselves in a feminist movement, establish
their own pressure group, or mobilise as women has pushed them towards
finding expression in fiction. Fiction has become a strategic move to
cope with the authoritarianism and domination that prohibit independent
civil society organisations, promote conservatism, apply strict religious
teachings, and enforce constant surveillance of women in public places.
Confronting the many taboos in Saudi society, such as sex and religion,
in fiction may be easier than addressing such issues in non-fictional styles.
For women, the novel is less confrontational, as an author can always

---

[3] John Sfakianakis, *Employment Quandary: Saudi Arabia Economics*, Riyadh: Banque
Saudi Fransi, 16 February 2011 (electronic publication).

[4] M. Oudina, 'The New Saudi Novel Defies Taboo', Ennahar Online, available at http:
//www.ennaharonline.com/en/culture/4013.html?print.

hide behind an imaginary world, created out of fragments of reality, personalities, and historical moments. Saudi women novelists can also claim that their novels are simply fiction rather than autobiography to escape condemnation for daring language and scenes, both of which have become regular features of the new literature.

Women poets, columnists, and novelists have overcome the limitations of politics, society, and religion by entering the public sphere through their words rather than physical presence or organisations (including state-approved charitable foundations). While the majority of these women published their anthologies and novels in other Arab capitals, several became regular writers in the women's pages of the Saudi press. A few initially wrote under men's names or pen-names, but by the late 1960s, several women had started using their own names. Arebi's cohort of pioneer literary figures were born between 1940 and 1960. After the early writings of the 1960s–70s, Saudi novelists entered a phase of stagnation in the 1980s, a time when the political and the religious cooperated to suppress any creative literary expression, mobilisation, or alternative perceptions of reality. As explained earlier in this book, for a decade following the 1979 mosque incident, conformity and conservatism reigned in the country, supported by the desire of the leadership to demonstrate its piety and Islamic authenticity. Between 1980 and 1990, only eighteen novels were published by women, a small number compared with the explosion in publications since the 1990s.[5]

A new generation of younger women who were born between 1960 and 1970 came to maturity in the 1990s when they appeared in the public sphere in various professions. By 2000, this generation had begun to publish abundant literature that reflected maturity and engagement with feminist themes. While political restrictions on mobilisation and organisation are still in place, and social liberalisation is starting to move at an unprecedented pace (as explained in the last chapter), women writers increasingly take refuge in writing fiction, in which they are beginning to express a feminist consciousness. Women may have been denied a voice and place in the public sphere, but their literature attests to the quest for their right to exist as autonomous individuals. Up to 2008, Saudi women novelists had published 143 novels, 97 of which have appeared since 2000.[6] The sheer volume of their literary productions reflects a serious

---

[5] Samaher al-Dhamin, *Nisa bila umahat* [Women without mothers], Beirut: al-Intishar al-Arabi, 2010, p. 373.
[6] al-Dhamin, *Nisa bila umahat*, pp. 373–8.

change as far as women and society are concerned. Their novels are a real challenge to a society and polity that was founded on narrow perceptions of their role in the nation. By 2000, many women occupied important positions in various sectors of the economy, including business, teaching, and medicine. What concerns us here are those women who entered the public sphere as a result of their literature.[7]

Out of this deluge of fiction, three novelists and their work are discussed in this chapter. The novels of Umayma al-Khamis, Badriyya al-Bishr, and Layla al-Jahni are explored with a view to capturing the changes that have swept Saudi Arabia in recent decades. Their novels explore new realities that were just beginning to impact on the lives of the early generation discussed in Arebi's book. These new novelists are counted among the contemporary *muthaqafat* (intellectuals) who represent the second generation of Saudi women writers to have emerged in the second half of the twentieth century. These novelists are younger than those studied by Arebi in the early 1990s. If Arebi's first novelists, writers, and poets were concerned 'with "double struggle", an effort to free themselves from both local and global discourses of power',[8] a new awareness of their plight as women is expressed in the writings of the second-generation novelists. The first generation of women writers 'have chosen to wage peace rather than war, a process that is by far more demanding of self restraint, of wisdom, and of self discipline'.[9] This choice may still not be apparent among the cohort of writers discussed here and in the next chapter. Many of the new novelists have chosen to wage war against the restrictive norms of society and religion.

The second-generation novelists engage in a harsh critique of their society and its tradition. They also dissolve the category 'Saudi women' and search for bridges at the level of experience with other non-Saudi women. Women are no longer a homogeneous, undifferentiated mass, but a fragmented category in which each element experiences society and

---

[7] Suad al-Mana, 'The Arabian Peninsula and the Gulf', in Radwa Ashour, Ferial Ghazoul, and Hasna Reda-Mekadashi (eds.), *Arab Women Writers 1873–1999*, Cairo: American University Press, 2008, pp. 254–75. Al-Mana is rather harsh in her assessment of recent women novelists. She claims that 'some women writers published works in the 1990s that were neither serious nor authentic' (p. 275). While this may apply to many recent women's novels, it is important to interrogate their work to discover the alleged lack of authenticity.

[8] Arebi, *Women and Words*, p. 298.

[9] Arebi, *Women and Words*, p. 298.

its tradition in different ways. From the authoritarian old mother/mother-in-law, who in many ways assumes masculine qualities,[10] to the playful teenager, adulterer, professional, and sexy wife, contemporary novelists delve into the diversity of the female experience in Saudi society. They move away from simplistic binary opposites such as male/female, subordinate/emancipated, free/oppressed to a more nuanced awareness of the complexity and diversity of the lives of Saudi women. Their novels start with a strong emphasis on the diversity of the local, which a previous generation glossed as Arab or Islamic. In the new novels, the local is no longer Arab/Islamic but fragmented into multiple layers of Najdi, Hijazi, Arab, Asian, and Western, thus reflecting the emerging cosmopolitanism of Saudi society, its contentious relations with foreign elements, especially women, the persistence of patriarchal structures and racism, the collision between Saudi religious tradition and those of the other, and the bridges that women build with non-Saudi women and men. In such novels, the feminine persona is explored in multiple contexts relating to age, career, tribe, education, desire, and social class.

UMAYMA AL-KHAMIS: DECONSTRUCTING THE LOCAL

Nothing illustrates the new cosmopolitan modernity of Saudi Arabia more vividly than Umayma al-Khamis's contemporary fiction.The foreign wife that an early generation of Saudi writers such as Abd al-Karim al-Juhaiman feared in the 1950s and the foreign Arab woman teacher that the Burayda *ulama* deplored in the 1960s (see Chapter 2) have become central figures in the novels of Umayma al-Khamis. If Saudi religious nationalism aspired to maintain purity, rootedness, and tradition, as opposed to social diversity, pluralism, and hybridity, in fiction the country is cosmopolitan and hybrid where boundaries are fluid and shifting against the background of serious efforts to keep them fixed.

The daughter of Abdullah al-Khamis, poet and founder of the daily newspaper *al-Jazeera*, and a Palestinian mother, Umayma was born in 1966. In her own account, she grew up surrounded by books, reflecting her parents' interest in literature and current affairs. She combined her interest in literature with bringing up a family and a job as director of

---

[10] Samaher al-Dhamin explores the theme of the oppressive woman (mother/mother-in-law) in the novels of Umayma al-Khamis, Badriyya al-Bishr, and Layla al-Jahni. See al-Dhamin, *Nisa bila umahat*, pp. 267–95.

educational media. She resigned from her job in 2010 to become a full-time writer.[11] While some of her early fiction was initially published in Saudi Arabia, thanks to familial connections with the world of publishing, two later novels, *al-Bahriyat* (Women from foreign shores) and *al-Warifa* (Lush tree) were both published in Damascus.[12] Al-Khamis comments that 'literature should not have a blunt and obvious message, lest it loses its creativity. The reader is now clever and often gets bored very quickly when he is confronted with a moralising message'.[13] Her fiction draws on real characters that she encounters in everyday life. She tries to anchor her characters in people around her. As women, 'we don't have a wide range of experiences outside our immediate environment. So my novels capture the lives of some people I came to know'.[14] Her novels are concerned with women, whom she loves. She protects them from the others, men, who enter their life and consequently turn it into a difficult journey.[15]

*Al-Bahriyat* is a historical novel that follows the life of Bahija, a Levantine Arab woman, imported at the age of thirteen by the king as a concubine. The king does not want her, as she is pale after leaving her mother. He offers her to his minister, who in turn gives her to his son.[16] She becomes the second wife of a Najdi, Saleh, and, as her name implies, she brings happiness and vitality to her new home. A woman whose identity is a product of harbours is implanted in the desert with its own austerity, aridity, morality, and restrictions. A white face surrounded by a black veil covering her brown hair, from the moment she enters the southern Riyadh mud-brick house, Bahija is the other in her physical beauty and social manners. Her integration into Saleh's pious extended household is a bumpy journey in which difference is rejected and a consolidated effort is exerted to dissolve it. From her mother-in-law, Umm Saleh, to other aunts and female relatives, Bahija encounters the desert with its strict social norms, religious codes, unappealing simple food, and dry atmosphere of women's gatherings. Her Levantine upbringing dictates how she deals with the desert social, moral, and religious

---

[11] Interview with the author, London/Riyadh, 21 November 2010.

[12] Ahmad al-Wasil, 'Satair wa aqlam sarikha: takwin al-muthaqafa al-saudiyya wa tahawulataha' [Curtains and sharp pens: Saudi women intellectuals and their changes], *Idhafat*, 7 (2009), p. 96.

[13] Interview with the author, London/Riyadh, 21 November 2010.

[14] Interview with the author, London/Riyadh, 21 November 2010.

[15] Abdullah al-Ghathami, *al-Mara wa al-lugha* [Women and language], 4th edn, Beirut: al-Markaz al-Thaqafi al-Arabi, 2008, pp. 230–1.

[16] Slavery was not abolished in Saudi Arabia until 1962.

codes. She constantly tries to 'moderate', 'entertain', and 'break' the dry, hot, and stagnant air among the women.[17] She eventually becomes Saleh's favourite wife at the expense of Mudhi, his first spouse, who begins to worry about her allocated 'night' being overlooked as Saleh drifts towards the Levantine beauty. But pious, polygamous Saleh fears God and the punishment that awaits unjust men. Unable to resist Bahija's charm, he occasionally delays his return to his private rooms so that Mudhi will fall asleep and miss her designated 'night' with him. When he does find himself in Mudhi's bed, he turns into a 'wooden board' until she gives up on him, turns her back, and falls asleep.

Despite being the favourite wife, Bahija is a lonely woman who takes refuge in the company of the Moroccan maid, imported with other women who are distributed among her husband's many household units. The flowers that she plants, in defiance of the desert climate and the shortage of water, give her pleasure. Bahija, in al-Khamis's novel, 'will suffer within the family as an alien before she could secure her place. Bahija is always struggling over her alienation and double exile'.[18] Instead of being called Umm Muhammad after the birth of her first son, Bahija retains her first name, Shamiyya – the Levantine. Being subjected incessantly to orders to wear the black veil and perform her prayers regularly with other women, her life turns into a series of obedience, rebellion, and compromises. She feels the pressure of the desert on the foreign women who need to be uprooted from their past, memory, and tradition and on whose bodies a new local text is inscribed. Her thorough and repetitive ablutions before prayers become purification rituals to rid her of her foreign pollution. Her mother-in-law, Umm Saleh, the guardian of the Najdi religious and genealogical purity in the private household, cannot control her revulsion as she shouts, 'Get down and pray lest God punishes us all because of you. Evil will prevail. I don't know where they got these *kafirs* from. God curse you, you Satan's Shamiyya'.[19]

Umm Saleh is a woman who has known a previous era when she had to compete with concubines – from the Persian Ajayib to the Abyssinian Christian Maryama, a gift from the king to her husband to cure his fatigue, as brunettes are known to have that healing power over men – for her husband's affection and love. Umm Saleh has developed a coarseness that is associated with old age and matriarchal power that she now

---

[17] Arebi, *Women and Words*, p. 9.
[18] al-Khamis, *al-Bahriyat*, p. 36.
[19] al-Khamis, *al-Bahriyat*, p. 37.

exercises over the younger women in the household.[20] Umm Saleh's struggles with the king's gifts to her husband establish links between women's suffering, political power, and affluence. An oppressed woman deprived of free will, the concubine becomes an object to demonstrate the generosity of the powerful among his subjects. She arrives in a household where other women have to struggle to assert their worth among men who aspire to obtain and own as many slave and free women as they can afford, all to satisfy sexual desires. The free Umm Saleh, together with her competitors, the slave women, emerge in the novel as characters bogged down in *istilab*,[21] a condition whereby free will is stolen from women. The condition of female subordination creates favourable grounds for the emergence of the oppressive old woman who diligently enforces religious practices among other women, negates their femininity, and sabotages their free will – thus turning herself into a masculine persona.

Umm Saleh hides her sorrows and jealousies behind a veneer of piety, propriety, and indifference – her new weapons, which have replaced perfume and Indian silk. She is the Big Mother, who abandons aspects of her femininity to gain the privileges of men and their masculine authority. She makes sure that no man in her household spends much time with women, which could make him *khikri*, effeminate, or *abu al-harim*, the 'father of women', whose extended conversations with women diminish his masculinity and turn him into a *thur*, stupid bull or docile lamb. When teased about how she ended up sharing Abu Saleh with other concubines and women, Umm Saleh calls upon God to thank him: 'May God make me only share him with women rather than death, illness or travel'.[22]

Among the concubines offered by the king and the princes as gifts to her husband, there were two types: the beautiful ones destined for his pleasure in bed and the black ones destined for domestic work. Her role as the senior wife would occasionally involve preparing one of the slave girls to spend a night with Abu Saleh, washing and perfuming her. After the death of her husband, Umm Saleh turns her attention to her sons' wives, daughters, the spinsters in the family, and domestic servants. She devotes a lot of attention to the alien Bahija who needs to be moulded to fit into this amalgam of private Najdi lives.

Bahija hides her amulets, dubbed *kharabit al-shawam* (Levantine trivia), and abandons her supplication to the Prophet in compliance with

---

[20] For more details on the character of Umm Saleh in this novel, see al-Dhamin, *Nisa bila umahat*, pp. 269–75.

[21] al-Dhamin, *Nisa bila umahat*, p. 267.

[22] al-Khamis, *al-Bahriyat*, p. 49.

local religious tradition. Instead, five daily prayers, and silent funerals, followed by three days of mourning, are the limits of Bahija's new religious life in the southern Riyadh mud-brick house, under the control of her mother-in-law.

At the age of sixteen, the traumas of giving birth in the alien desert are punctuated by folkloric *nafas* rituals, involving the consumption of desert herbs and huge amounts of meat, flour, and butter, all away from the gaze of other envious women. The post-partum forty days of seclusion are spent lounging around with her two big toes tied together so that the inner organs go back to their original shape and size, to ensure Saleh's ultimate pleasure. Husbands are known to express dissatisfaction after their wives give birth, then choosing other young, tight women.

Bahija produces several sons, with only one inheriting her Mediterranean looks, the round, white face and the rosy cheeks. Musaid, the hybrid son, struggles to change his complexion to pass as a pure Saudi. Sitting for long hours in the sun only makes him ill and alerts the others to his tormented inner self, a self that cannot easily be anchored in the cherished pure genealogy of the Najdi family. His insistence on speaking with a heavy, coarse Bedouin accent only accentuates his alien and mixed parentage. As a young child, Bahija's son struggles, with boys bullying him and calling him names such as the 'tomato' or the 'Shawerma vendor'.[23]

A combination of estrangement from her milieu, unwillingness to be fully integrated, and the resistance of the Najdi family to incorporate a stranger leads Bahija to gravitate towards a friendship with Ingrid, the first German woman to be seen in the heart of Najd, another *kafir*, the wife of an engineer brought in by the Ministry of Transport to deal with dams and rainwater in Wadi Hanifa. From Ingrid, she learns new biscuit and cake recipes and receives affection. A circle of foreign women that includes, in addition to Bahija and Ingrid, the Abyssinian Christian maid, Maryama, who hides her cross between her breasts, develops bonds of understanding and sympathy emerging from solidarity made stronger as a result of food exchange. They comfort each other, and in particular, Ingrid the infidel bestows understanding and sympathy against the boundaries of difference. One day, she tells stressed and tearful Bahija, 'You and I are similar'.[24]

The circle of friendship is widened when Rihab, a Palestinian teacher who comes to Riyadh with her father acting as guardian, joins Bahija's

---

[23] al-Khamis, *al-Bahriyat*, p. 32.
[24] al-Khamis, *al-Bahriyat*, p. 73.

intimate group. A product of the Palestinian crisis, Rihab has been imported to work at a school where foreign Arab teachers dominate the profession. In her class, girls between the ages of seven and seventeen are grouped together. She organises them in rows, with the young in the front. In her spare time, she teaches the daughters of Saleh's household who are forbidden to attend the newly established schools. Rihab awaits her dream man, a Palestinian who migrated after promising to return and marry her but fails to honour his promise. Consumerism in the 1970s and the emergence of new shopping neighbourhoods begin to increase Rihab's insecurity in Riyadh.

[The market becomes] a dangerous place for women who were used to familiar roads and faces. Now the roads are wide, lit with big eyes, full of foreigners and workers. Women are harassed and squeezed. Men wink at them. Everybody remembers a woman kidnapped by a taxi driver, who took her to the desert. Those Arab women who venture into the markets without covering their faces are harassed. Male vendors shout to attract their attention: 'Beauty for those who seek beauty'. When women approach them to inspect their merchandise, men lift their white *thawb*s and flash their private parts... women retreat crying and ashamed... Women are always wrong in the market.[25]

As Rihab gets older, she gives up on marrying her Palestinian first love and accepts the proposal of Omar, the Hadrami driver in charge of transporting her to her various lessons. An ambitious and hard-working young man, he develops his skills and ends up as a successful businessman, benefiting from the many opportunities of oil-rich Saudi Arabia. He develops into a gentleman who takes her on holiday abroad.

Suad, another Arab expatriate, joins the chorus of women in al-Khamis's novel. The scene moves to the modern compound where the extended family begins to live after the oil boom of the 1970s. Suad's world is divided between her drunken husband, Saad, her new affair with Mitab, and popular Arabic songs of the Egyptian musicians Abd al-Halim Hafiz and Umm Khulthum. She adopts the new fashion of thin, transparent *abaya*s that became popular in the 1970s despite the objections of other women and men. As a daring woman, Suad is the modern character who begins to threaten tradition, morality, and purity. Her arrival coincides with the Riyadh feast, where the dinner table offers 'the drinks of Qamar al-Din, Irk Sus, Jilab and Tamr Hindi. Every civilisation begins to push its plate onto the *Iftar* table of Ramadan. The Levantine Fatush, East Asian Samosa, Egyptian soup and macaroni, Indian biryani... all

---

[25]  al-Khamis, *al-Bahriyat*, pp. 144–5.

come to the golden cities that emerged suddenly and decorated the face of the desert'.[26]

The women from foreign shores, the *bahriyat*, bring colour to the lives of the desert men, including Saleh, Bahija's husband, who would show his appreciation by flirting with her, repeating the Najdi saying, 'You have aged, my dear, and it is time for me to find a young wife'.[27] Defying the code of modesty, Bahija would reply in a loud voice, heard by all, 'And you my old man, your stuff has expired. It is good only for urinating'.[28]

Saleh dies, and soon afterwards, Bahija starts a battle with cancer in the Mayo Clinic in Minneapolis. After sessions of chemotherapy, she dies a year later, surrounded by her sons. She had filled the garden with her perfume but was left outside, permanently excluded, until her body refused to continue playing the absurd game of seeking acceptance in her adopted home. Despite her efforts, the sands of the desert never relented, and she never felt she had come home. Like most people who live on the edge, she spoke with two accents, neither authentic. She dreamt of returning to her Bahri town where a cool breeze that would not hurt her nostrils blows and where green fields are soft.

Umayma al-Khamis creates binary opposites: the *bahriyat* versus the *sahrawiyat* (the coastal women and their desert counterparts). Initially the distance seems wide and the gap unbridgeable. But she immediately dissolves the boundaries as she searches for the roots of the tragedy of women across cultures on Saudi soil. By dissolving these boundaries, al-Khamis tries to negate the uniqueness of Saudi women and their special place, while also attacking the discourse that celebrates the purity and authenticity of the Najdi region. In Saleh's household, many nationalities and even religions coexist. Everyday life is a complex mosaic of traditions, habits, and modes of interaction. While there is a central authority trying hard to impose its vision and way of life on this mosaic, the fragments shine through, asserting their individual autonomy and agency. Foreign women struggle to maintain their identity. Sometimes they succumb to pressure and conform, but even so, they always remain on the margin, outside local society and culture. Polygamy, its coexistence with the tradition of cohabiting with concubines, and the varied ethnic origins of wives in the early 1960s create multiple levels of conflict, jealousy, envy, and surrender on the part of women. The concubine is a gift given by

---

[26] al-Khamis, *al-Bahriyat*, p. 223.
[27] al-Khamis, *al-Bahriyat*, p. 224.
[28] al-Khamis, *al-Bahriyat*, p. 224.

the king to a member of his entourage, a reward or healing source for a man's weakened desires. The political becomes entangled with the private lives of men and women, thus rendering owning slave women a perpetual tool to enforce the superiority of men over women, the political over the private, and desire over austerity. In her turn, the foreign young wife who is incorporated in the compound is the object of men's choices in the teeth of the objections of other local women. The latter become entrusted with moulding and domesticating the newcomers with the objective of inflicting on them a historical amnesia in which their past is eradicated. But the exercise remains futile because no matter how hard a foreign woman tries to fit in, she will remain the despised other. Only death can free her from being at the intersection of two worlds, *bahriyat* and *sahrawiyat*.

Against the discourse of common heritage, religion, and tradition, the hybridity of Saudi Arabia's heartland, Najd, is the central focus of *al-Bahriyat*, which can be read as a sociological statement and an analysis of social change. Al-Khamis tackles 'the tyranny of history and the dominance of geography'.[29] Her fictional focus cannot be isolated from the reality of Saudi Arabia. She acknowledges that she does not like to have a strong ideological message in fiction for fear of losing the literary beauty of the text, but she does not deny that her fiction engages with the reality of the country. From the 1960s to the novel's date of publication in 2006, al-Khamis challenges common wisdom about the country's homogeneity and pure descent. Her novel is a journey to find the woman inside many women whose origins, backgrounds, and environment have all shaped their experience and personality. Although her heroines are Palestinian and Levantine migrant women in Najd, their everyday encounters with Najdi women and men, as well as with several domestic workers from Africa and Asia, create a prism through which al-Khamis assesses her own society and the place of women in it. She tries to find the woman in that blurred space between the local and the global, namely the space of interaction between Saudis and non-Saudis in the heartland of Arabia.

THE NEW, BEWILDERED COSMOPOLITAN WOMAN

The centrality of interactive hybrid space for women's identity that is dominant in al-Khamis's *al-Bahriyat* is skilfully repeated in *al-Warifa*.[30]

---

[29] Umayma al-Khamis, interview in *al-Sharq al-Awsat*, 6 November 2008.
[30] Umayma al-Khamis, *al-Warifa* [Lush tree], Damascus: al-Mada, 2008, hereafter *al-Warifa*.

The two settings in *al-Warifa* are the new hospital, with its multiple nationalities, and the Najdi household in Alysha, one of Riyadh's neigh-bourhoods where old families lived. Some families trace 'their ancestors to the descendants of Muhammad ibn Abd al-Wahhab',[31] thus anchoring fiction in the reality of old piety. Alysha saw the first modern government hospital.

The heroine, al-Jawhara, is a divorced Najdi doctor who crosses many boundaries both at home and abroad. She enters the public sphere first as a medical student and later as a qualified doctor. At work, she weaves a web of friendships with the New Zealand nurse, Adriane, and Dr Kari-man Bukhari, a Hijazi whose ancestors came from Bukhara. She is forced to seek new friendships, as her traditional household is no longer what it used to be, a small microcosm of tightly knit relatives. She navigates differences and commonality in this mosaic world of Saudi public hos-pitals. As a Saudi woman doctor, al-Jawhara is part of this mosaic, but every day she retreats to Alysha where a different world exists. Here the alleged Najdi 'authenticity' and 'purity' reside; home is thus contrasted with work where diversity is predominant. But if Saudi Arabia is the local context, it is very much diverse. One element of this diversity is the presence of Hijazi workers who have themselves come from outside the Hijaz. The complexity of the intermingling of races, languages, com-plexions, and manners is what makes Saudi Arabia today, and nothing represents it better than the modern hospital. The language of the novel, in which local idioms and phrases intermingle with fragments of English, reflects this diversity. The hospital becomes an arena for asserting local authenticity, challenging norms, and thwarting tradition. From holding on to the *niqab* to secretly smoking cigarettes, female doctors and nurses define their new roles and assert their autonomy. Their audience con-sists of male doctors and administrators, some of whom cannot handle the sight of women doctors hurrying to surgery and consultations. They 'either flirt or turn their faces in the opposite direction. Others hold onto their private parts'.[32]

The global world of the hospital also has a trace of the diversity of the local. Hijazis are referred to as *tarsh al-bahr*, a pejorative Najdi term used to refer to the cosmopolitan population of the Hijaz. Al-Khamis describes how this diversity has come to be a characteristic of the Hijaz and has generated reactions from Najd: 'In general the majority of the people in

---

[31] al-Khamis, *al-Warifa*, p. 39.
[32] al-Khamis, *al-Warifa*, p. 105.

the desert region of Najd would build high walls to exclude them from their social milieu. They secretly call them *"tarsh al-bahr"* [rejects of the sea]'.[33]

The difference between Najd and Hijaz is extended to their women. Those whose ancestors came from Central Asia prior to their migration to Hijaz 'are shy with very white skin and soft complexions. Their voices are low. They would resist any intrusion very politely. They achieve high marks in mathematics and engineering'.[34]

But Kariman does not conform to the stereotype of the docile Bukhari Hijazi woman. She speaks loudly and exhibits an independent personality. She and another student of medicine by the name of Madawi form a 'source of light' and assertiveness among medical students. Kariman marries an Afghani doctor, and returns to the hospital completely changed by the experience. Her youth and vitality 'enter the room where corpses are mummified'.[35] Is their marriage a function of 'chemistry' or the law of the marriage market, asks al-Jawhara. She is saddened by the sight of her friend, whose mood becomes sombre after marriage. But why should al-Jawhara be sad? 'Are not they both *tarsh al-bahr*?' She is reminded of their foreignness. Al-Khamis reports prejudice without a moralising tone, giving strength and force to her message.

Kariman is contrasted with al-Jawhara, who stumbles and hesitates with her veil wrapped around her in the hospital corridors. Al-Jawhara is restrained and contained within the webs of her tradition. She cannot attend 'a medical conference on her own but she wants to be part of a folk dance society'.[36] She desires to appear on television with Kariman to discuss medical issues, but she cannot bring that shame to the men in her family, as she would have to lift her face veil. How could she when her mother would not show her face to her son-in-law but would cover herself with her prayer shawl in his presence? A Hijazi doctor reminds al-Jawhara:

You *shrouq* [a pejorative Hijazi word for Najdis] ask people to do what they cannot tolerate. There is no meaning in women covering their faces. In *niqab* you women look like ghosts. The *ulama* differed on this. God wants to make it easy for his servants. Your manners are harsh. In hospital they shout at me, 'Oi, brother!' The young do not show respect for the elderly. In Hijaz we call older brothers *abeh* and older sisters *abla*.[37]

---

[33] al-Khamis, *al-Warifa*, p. 25.
[34] al-Khamis, *al-Warifa*, p. 25.
[35] al-Khamis, *al-Warifa*, p. 37.
[36] al-Khamis, *al-Warifa*, p. 33.
[37] al-Khamis, *al-Warifa*, p. 114.

Hijazi hybrids are not the only other against whom Najdis measure their authenticity. There is also the more complex case of Sara, a Najdi who was brought up in the Eastern Province but returns to marry a relative in Riyadh. She guards her identity 'as a Najdi brought up and spoilt on the eastern coast with weekly visits to an Aramco camp and occasionally to Kuwait'.[38] Her pure birth is contaminated by the hybridity of her early upbringing away from the homeland. 'The marriage market requires that . . . when the product is rotten, it is incumbent on the buyer to return it and retrieve his money'.[39] Her marriage ends in divorce.

Differences in geographies are compounded by differences in time. Hijri time (the Islamic lunar calendar) is unpredictable, moving between seasons and dancing between the stars, but the Gregorian calendar is fixed, punctual, and respects appointments. The time is symptomatic of society and its differences. Al-Jawhara moves between spaces and times, trying to cope with her status as a thirty-year-old divorcee. She resists becoming a second wife, and refuses suitors suggested by relatives and other doctors. She attends the religious study circle to listen to the *daiya* (preacher) lecturing on the ten ways to conquer a husband's heart. Then she moves to intermingle with American and English nurses, walking with their heads up in the air. She has an encounter with an 'Arabi' Bedouin doctor that shows up the hypocrisy masked by his short *thawb* and long beard, symbols of Salafi piety.

Her opportunity to leave the desert comes with a scholarship to Canada, but this starts a search for a *misfar* marriage, in which a man is needed for two years to accompany her as a *mahram* (guardian). In Toronto, the *niqab* vanishes, and Lieberman, a European Jewish doctor, appears on the scene. The forbidden attraction between the Riyadh doctor and the Jew is bizarre: in Toronto, a Jew and a Muslim struggle with their loneliness and alienation from their surroundings on Christmas Eve. Lieberman muses, 'This world is strange. I am a European Jew sitting with a Riyadh doctor in Toronto. It seems that the new world requires us to stop drawing borders and checkpoints. We can enjoy what our planet gives us; land, sky and trees'.[40] Al-Jawhara, metaphorically referred to as a lush tree, soon finds roots everywhere. But soon it is time to return to her original roots, perfumed by the smell of spices to conceal the new changes in the soil. Upon her return to Riyadh, she finds that women can now become heads of units at the hospital. The central question,

---

[38] al-Khamis, *al-Warifa*, p. 62.
[39] al-Khamis, *al-Warifa*, p. 79.
[40] al-Khamis, *al-Warifa*, p. 253.

however, remains unanswered – how, like so many other able women, she failed to be attractive to her husband.

After showing the heroine dying of cancer in *al-Bahriyat*, al-Khamis returns to the deadly disease, which kills a minor but interesting figure in *al-Warifa*. Bablo, al-Jawhara's father's Christian Filipino driver, accompanies him to the mosques, struggling to hide the smell of his smoking habit. His boss showers him with insults while he remains oblivious and mostly silent, but he observes that 'men don't see women, women don't see me. They are not crazy, they are not happy'.[41] Used to the verdant forests of the Philippines, where trees grow in all directions, Bablo cuts the lush Sidr tree that moderates the ugly high wall, the fence that separates the house from other houses and firmly encircles it. Bablo, who has failed to understand the laws of the desert, eventually develops advanced cancer. Al-Jawhara struggles to get him treated at the hospital. She uses *wasta* (nepotism) to get him chemotherapy. Then he is sent back to the Philippines, where he dies. Al-Khamis seeks to show that the fate of those who cross continents and fail to forge roots in their new surroundings is death.

Writing is for al-Khamis an attempt to 'deal with women's absence and their empty seats in society. Writing is women's first liberation from the tyranny of history and dominance of geography'.[42] While her literature has not been infused with either a strong liberation message or a confirmation of tradition, al-Khamis highlights the diversity of contemporary Saudi society through a careful reading of its public and private spheres. Her objective is not to evaluate Saudi society but to show it as it was/is. She believes that novelists 'show but don't tell'.[43] In her opinion, there has been noticeable change since 2005. Women are more visible. Their situation cannot go back to the way it used to be because they are now aware of their rights. She remains optimistic that the glass ceiling is getting higher. 'There are many voices and women are getting involved in various activities'.[44]

Al-Khamis dissolves the boundaries between the local and the global as they become enmeshed in a complex web of relationships that official Saudi discourse had in the past obliterated, concealed, and camouflaged. She asserts that she is not conscious of deliberately dissolving

[41]  al-Khamis, *al-Warifa*, p. 136.
[42]  Umayma al-Khamis, interview in *al-Sharq al-Awsat*, 6 November 2008.
[43]  Interview with the author, London/Riyadh, 21 November 2010.
[44]  Interview with the author, London/Riyadh, 21 November 2010.

boundaries; only a clever critic spots the process, she says.[45] Her latest novels, published in 2006 and 2007, reflect dramatic changes in Saudi society that laid the groundwork for the complexities she charts. The official religious narratives about the uniqueness of Saudi society and its piety, purity, and exclusiveness came under pressure to the extent that these things no longer exist, not only in fiction but also in reality. The centrality of the foreign woman who is never accepted by local society persists in *al-Bahriyat*, while the modern woman doctor portrayed in *al-Warifa* is central to understanding the experiences of many women in contemporary Saudi Arabia. The doctor emerges from a household that is no longer the tightly knit extended family that it used to be. She is forced to seek new friendships in the public sphere, but she is not socially or psychologically prepared for this new life. Her inexperience makes her relationships with men and women at work troublesome. In the previous era, women had only socialised with their relatives, but today urban Saudi women go out to work with strangers, and this requires adjustments, reflected in the initial clumsiness of al-Jawhara. Travel abroad poses its own challenges, and the journey to train in a foreign hospital is not only a period of scientific study but also a chance to grow both socially and personally. The meaning of friendships between men and women becomes the new terrain, where previous experiences do not help as they are non-existent. Life abroad consists of trial and error, hesitation, confusions, and conclusions.

Al-Khamis revisits history and the place of women in it. She is particularly sensitive to boundaries that separate Saudis from others, women from men, old women from young women, and free women from concubines. Her own hybridity as a product of a Saudi father and a Palestinian mother makes her sensitive to living in between cultures. She depicts such boundaries as porous and rigid at the same time. Al-Khamis is thought of as someone who depicts Saudi society in a clear and honest way, but, like other novelists, she faces the challenges of the persistence of forbidden territories where writers, especially women, are not meant to venture. These forbidden territories can paralyse the ability of novelists to scrutinise aspects of society. Al-Khamis has ventured into the heart of the forbidden without seeking unnecessary sensationalism, an attraction that other Saudi women writers – especially the young generation, to be discussed in the next chapter – have found difficult to resist. Her new

[45] Interview with the author, London/Riyadh, 21 November 2010.

non-fiction book, entitled *Madhi, mufrad, muthakar*[46] (Past, singular, masculine), was published in 2011, and attempts to shed light on her experience of the Saudi education system as both pupil and teacher.

## BADRIYYA AL-BISHR: FEMALE VIOLENCE AGAINST THE FEMININE

Known for her sharp criticism of religious restrictions on women, the sociologist Badriyya al-Bishr is a writer who embarks on confrontational journeys with society and its many radical voices through both fiction and regular columns in the pan-Arab Saudi press.[47] In one of her non-fiction newspaper columns, al-Bishr sarcastically proposes that Saudi women grow beards and take male hormone injections in order to be recognised in society as autonomous contributors to national development. This was in response to Islamist criticism of a government-sponsored forum on women's employment and participation in the economy. She criticises the Islamists and the religious establishment for objecting to *ikhtilat*, which is pervasive but unrecognised in Saudi society: a woman shopper mixes with men in markets and shops, but when she sells products (a reference to the debate on female cashiers), she is regarded by radical religious scholars as practising unlawful mixing.[48]

While al-Khamis's focus is on deconstructing the local and highlighting the bewilderment of the new cosmopolitan Saudi woman, Badriyya al-Bishr is concerned with the traumas of the feminine in Saudi society. Her fiction, especially the novel discussed below, captures the dilemma of the educated woman in a society that does not pay any attention to her aspirations. Unlike al-Khamis's doctor who is not yet ready for the pressures and tensions of the new cosmopolitanism that has swept Saudi society (although she returns home from Canada reconciled to her fate), al-Bishr's heroine escapes to Canada in order to fulfil her dream of being herself rather than part of an undifferentiated community of women, pejoratively referred to as *al-harim*. Both novelists, however, capture the choices and constraints that the new educated and cosmopolitan Saudi woman faces in a society that is still suspicious of its achieving and accomplished women.

[46] Umayma al-Khamis, *Madhi, mufrad, muthakar* [Past, singular, masculine], Beirut: Dar al-Intishar, 2011.

[47] Badriyya al-Bishr regularly writes a column in the Saudi pan-Arab daily newspaper *al-Hayat*.

[48] Badriyya al-Bishr, 'Shart tahawul al-nisa ila thukur' [A condition for women to become men], *al-Hayat*, 8 December 2010.

Married to famous Saudi comedian Nasir al-Qusbi who is the main actor in and producer of the Ramadan television comedy series *Tash ma Tash*, al-Bishr is known for her defence of this very successful, daring, and popular programme that in 2010 entered its seventeenth year.[49] Born in Riyadh in 1967, al-Bishr received her schooling in the capital. She obtained a doctorate in sociology from the Lebanese University in Beirut. Her thesis was a comparative study on globalisation in Riyadh and Dubai.[50] After her doctoral research, she returned to Riyadh to teach at King Saud University. She felt that she was *muharaba*, harassed by her colleagues who since the 1980s had begun to restrict women who were non-conformists or critical of radical religion. Because of his role in a daring comedy, religious scholars issued a *fatwa* branding her husband a *kafir* (an unbeliever). She felt she could not 'send her two young boys to a school where the teacher depicts their father as a *kafir*. It was too much for my children. Also I felt that our lives were in danger, so we decided to move to cosmopolitan Dubai where I can start building my self rather than defending it as I used to do in Riyadh'.[51] Al-Bishr describes the joy that her relatives and friends expressed when they heard of her 'migration' to Dubai. Instead of lamenting her departure, many people said *ya hathukum* (how lucky you are). Al-Bishr is a careful and critical observer of her society, religious establishment, and state. While she celebrates the changes that have swept the country since 9/11, she remains careful not to express unrealistic enthusiasm. At the theoretical level, there are many changes, especially in the press and among the youth, but practically there are still restrictive rules and laws that inhibit the emancipation of women. She says that progressive ideas about women's role in society should become 'nationalised', that is, adopted at the highest levels. If 'our roads are congested and cannot accommodate additional women drivers, it must be the responsibility of the political forces to improve them. If our young men are not ready to share the roads with women drivers, who is responsible for educating them and preparing them for such an eventuality? Change should be a state's programme'. In her opinion, there is hope in the diversity of opinions at the social, religious, and governmental

[49] Badriyya al-Bishr, *Maarik Tash ma Tash* [Battles over *Tash ma Tash*], Beirut: al-Markaz al-Thaqafi al-Arabi, 2007.
[50] Badriyya al-Bishr, *Waq' al-awlama fi mujtama al-khalij al-arabi Dubai wa al-Riyadh* [The impact of globalisation in Gulf societies: Riyadh and Dubai], Beirut: Markaz Dirasat al-Wihda al-Arabiyya, 2008.
[51] Interview with the author, Dubai, 5 January 2011.

levels. As long as there is diversity of trends and opinions, women can win their struggle.

Al-Bishr belongs to the new generation of novelists who 'use a new language, simple and direct, in dealing with subjects that were not evoked in the past, like the right of a woman to be in love or to work'.[52] In fiction, al-Bishr does not seek unnecessary sensationalism, but she delves into creating a feminist consciousness, anchored in the female body while constrained by forces in society ranging from religious mores and norms to cultural values.

Al-Bishr articulates how gender subordination is enforced by both men and women who collaborate to create a moral order that excludes and discriminates against women, especially the new generation with its aspirations for self-expression, choice, and freedom. Her main focus is on how female violence against the feminine is equally aggressive. The struggle of the *muthaqafa* is not simply against the will of men but also against illiterate mothers who were themselves subjected to the worst violence encountered by a girl on her wedding night. Her main female character in *Hind wa al-askar* (Hind and the soldiers)[53] is a woman in love with a man and with writing, both denied her in Saudi society. Hind is a daring young Najdi woman seeking not only romance, love, and adventure but also self-expression in writing, all leading her to a double life in which the appearance of conformity and piety is nothing but a facade masking more adventurous nocturnal affairs, organised with other young women, and literary texts in which she seeks to attain individuality as a woman. Her mother, Hayla, is part of a hierarchy of oppressive characters whose main preoccupation is to control young women, discipline them, inflict physical punishment on their bodies, and turn them into docile and obedient girls to be wed according to criteria that take no notice of women's choices and preferences. The only feasible choice for a mother such as Hayla is to internalise the oppression of men against women and pass it on to her daughters. This gives her a status that is dictated by the institution of patriarchy; the mother thus becomes the greatest defender of men's supremacy. Women are accomplices in their own oppression, as this is the only way to gain recognition in society. According to al-Bishr, every woman longs for the birth of her first son who becomes his mother's

[52] Badriyya al-Bishr, interview with Agence France Press, quoted in Sabrina Jawhar, 'The Real Abuse of Saudi Women', ARABIST.COM, 7 March 2010.

[53] Badriyya al-Bishr, *Hind wa al-askar* [Hind and the soldiers], 3rd edn, Beirut: Saqi, 2011 [2006]. More recently, al-Bishr published *al-Urjuha* [The swing], Beirut: Saqi, 2010.

oppressor. Sons control their mothers' lives, steal their inheritance, and conduct surveillance over their behaviour. Al-Bishr says that 'the son steals his mother's self and wealth but she longs for his arrival'.[54]

Mother Hayla, a soldier in a chain of soldiers, a symbol of the motherland, moves from the regular pinching of her daughter's thighs at the most trivial mistake and disobedience to being in total control of her life. The early suffering of the mother, who married a man fifteen years her senior, is critical in the novel. Her husband raped her on their wedding night. She ran away from her marital house twice, only to be returned to him by her family. All this suffering has not, however, engendered sympathy for the plight of women. The violent deflowering of the mother becomes an act of unbearable violence against the female body that can only be endured by patience and God's mercy. Suffering Hayla turns into a monster mother who seeks perpetuation of the violence, exclusion, and subordination that she herself suffered as a young bride. She has internalised society's fear of the female body to the extent of despising any signs of femininity, especially in her daughter. Like the Bedouin mothers described in Abu-Lughod's work,[55] mother Hayla despises 'sexualised femininity', itself a product of changing social and economic relations, and consumption patterns.

She chooses to inflict bruises, by severe pinching, on one of the most feminine parts of the female body, the inner thigh, a regular punishment for daring and disobedient girls. The female body should be covered and concealed lest it explode and ravage the social and moral order, thus bringing shame to the whole clan. In addition to invoking honour and shame, mother Hayla gets her ammunition of control from religious radicalism that provides her with the terminology of discipline and punishment. Burning transgressors in hell and tormenting them in the grave, God inflicts his wrath on unruly girls. Hind is socialised into 'an aggressive God, who is as angry as my mother'. For women, religion is no longer about piety, healing the soul, or seeking comfort in divine grace, but is a form of alienation. It is an additional weapon with which both men and women inhibit women's self-fulfilment, individuality, and freedom of choice. It inhibits women from being themselves. Hind's mother is a classic example of this case of alienation as she adopts religious attire, manners, and terminology to enhance her ability to control other women,

54 Interview with the author, Dubai, 5 January 2011.
55 Lila Abu-Lughod, 'The Romance of Resistance: Tracing Transformations of Power through Bedouin Women', *American Ethnologist*, 17, 1 (1990), pp. 41–55.

especially her young daughter. Her illiteracy compounds the misery of Hind who fails to convince her mother of the virtues of education and writing. Any chance of female solidarity against oppression and subordination is shattered in the power struggle between two different generations, that of mother and daughter, with other soldiers contributing in their own way to inflaming an endless war between men and women and among women themselves.

Hind's father is a weak retired soldier who can only relate to his young daughter in a patronising and paternalistic manner. He is protective, playful, and loving in a patriarchal way. He loves girls only as helpless objects who need to be sheltered and protected. The true soldier in the house remains the mother who is given all the ruthlessness of a real soldier.[56] In addition to the honorary soldier mother and the real soldier father, Hind comes face to face with another soldier in the making: her young brother, Ibrahim. Aware of the gender inequality that surrounds them, Ibrahim exercises his power over his sister who as a young girl is marginalised and ignored. She is punished for not following his orders or succumbing to his will. A third child, Ibrahim does not occupy a central position in his family hierarchy. He is given menial tasks to perform, unlike his eldest brother *al-bikr*, Fahd, in whom the mother invests love and energy. After an illicit sexual encounter with a Bedouin girl, Ibrahim finds refuge in piety. He changes careers and opts for Islamic studies to deal with the aftershock of illicit sex. He becomes a distributor of Jihadi literature, handing pamphlets to his mother and asking her to distribute them in order to support 'our brothers in Afghanistan'.[57] He travels to Afghanistan to practise what he learned about *jihad*, 'the sixth principle of Islam', according to one radical Islamist interpretation. He returns more sombre and withdrawn, then disappears again, thus leaving his mother in a house full of women. The eldest son has already freed himself from his mother's control and left the family home.

In this book, the family is thus the context in which power relations are played out, inequality is perpetuated, and punishment is inflicted on transgressors. A brother becomes aware of his rights over his sister and demands obedience at an early age. The mother punishes the sister with more pinches and bruises if she disobeys him and refuses to play his games. A subordinate sister learns from an early age that she is a marginalised creature who should be married off as quickly as possible

---

[56] al-Bishr, *Hind wa al-askar*, p. 137.
[57] al-Bishr, *Hind wa al-askar*, pp. 187–8.

to avoid scandal and transgression. She is a burden whose birth carries the seeds of crisis for years to come.

Hind embarks on an adolescent affair that is quickly discovered by her mother. Male lovers sometimes adopt feminine attire, and wear the *abaya* to camouflage themselves when visiting their women. Together with her friend Mudhi, Hind shares the secrets of encountering their lovers who enjoy flirtations that fall short of deflowering the girls for fear of the consequences.[58] Mudhi proves to be more daring than other girls. She leaves her lover sleeping in her room while she goes to school, without worrying too much about her mother discovering him. She orders the maid to bring him coffee in her room, using the house's intercom system. She locks her bedroom door on a lover whose access requires his feminisation. The feminisation of the male lover is a precondition that mediates between the permissible and the prohibited. The rule of the game is for such a lover to impersonate a woman when he accidentally encounters a mother on the phone or sneaks into forbidden territory. For a man to be enjoyed as a lover, he is forced to momentarily and occasionally adopt a feminine identity and suppress his cherished masculinity. His voice, dress, and manners have to be altered to pass as a woman in order to escape the control and surveillance of others. A man becomes a woman to enjoy women. The emasculated and effeminate man penetrates the forbidden rooms of the *harim*. Oppression in the family and strict controls create transsexual spaces where identities are exchanged and altered. But Mudhi's lover is discovered by the mother whose shock leads to prolonged illness and paralysis. She is not capable of inflicting punishment on Mudhi who demands death following the discovery of her affair. The mother remains silent in fear of disgrace. She thanks God that none of Mudhi's brothers discovered the scandal, which would have resulted in the loss of two children: Mudhi and at least one of her brothers who would feel obliged to wash away the *ar* (dishonour) by killing Mudhi. The mother refuses to talk, a form of passive violence exerted on Mudhi following the discovery of her affair. Mudhi becomes a dead flower at the feet of her crying mother. While Hayla practises real violence against her daughter, the passivity of Mudhi's mother is equally aggressive. *Hind wa al-askar* delves into the multiple levels of violence against women by women.

It is not clear whether Hind is less or more fortunate than Mudhi. Mother Hayla discovers the details of Hind's affair and embarks on a

---

[58] al-Bishr, *Hind wa al-askar*, p. 104.

systematic campaign of torture against her transgressing, immoral daughter. Hind's lover belongs to an unacceptable family, 'with whom we do not have a history of marriage exchanges',[59] announces her mother. After several abusive encounters with Hind, Hayla forces her daughter to marry Mansour, her maternal uncle's son and a new graduate of the military academy, in order to avoid scandal. Having no choice in the matter, Hind marries Mansour, yet another in the hierarchy of soldiers who seek women's obedience. The marriage quickly turns into a war between a man who refuses to see his wife as an individual person and a woman whose quest for asserting her individuality is beyond limits. Mansour sees Hind as belonging to an undifferentiated mass of women whose characteristics are already established and known to him. He says to her, 'You the *harim*, women, should be preoccupied with bringing up children and nothing else'.[60] Mansour is unable to see his wife as a unique person with her own desires, aspirations, and fantasies. He cannot understand why she does not enjoy the world of the *harim* in which women produce and bring up children. Women get to like their home, the prison that is considered their protection:

Men understand that houses are created for women. Their iron bars are their borders. With time, women begin to like their prisons which they consider to be the only safe haven. Outside it, there are beasts and wolves who attack them. For these reasons women get old at an early age, they get depressed, get ill, the illness of children and the loss of husbands.[61]

Faced with an uninteresting and bigoted husband, Hind takes refuge in writing, which has a bewitching impact on her, absorbing troubled thoughts in her head. Writing becomes an act of rebellion to counteract her impotence against Mansour. She has never screamed in his face.[62] She entertains the thought of pulling the trigger of his gun to kill him, but admits to herself that she is weak and cannot face blood, even that of her tormentor. Mansour objects to Hind's name appearing next to her articles in the press. Among soldiers, he becomes known as 'Hind's husband'. Hind won the battle for writing with her illiterate mother, but the situation is different with Mansour who can read what she writes. His objections intensify, and she reverts to writing under a pen-name. While Mansour believes that women are for pleasure only, his interest in Hind

[59] al-Bishr, *Hind wa al-askar*, p. 136.
[60] al-Bishr, *Hind wa al-askar*, p. 138.
[61] al-Bishr, *Hind wa al-askar*, p. 139.
[62] al-Bishr, *Hind wa al-askar*, p. 141.

disappears when she becomes his legitimate wife. His real passions are for women who are not *halal*, the forbidden ones whom he seeks outside marriage.

Finally, Hind gives birth to a girl, an act that prompts her husband to divorce her. She returns to her parental home with her despised daughter, Mai. Now free of the constraints of marriage, Hind searches for the limited choices that a divorced woman with a daughter may have. Work in hospitals offers a unique and exceptional opportunity for *ikhtilat* (mixing between the sexes). She starts a new life as a social worker with the hope of asserting her worth and contributing to bringing up Mai. Hind continues to face the intrusive looks and surveillance of other women who practise *talaslus*, indiscreetly following and surveying each other.

Throughout the book, Hind struggles to assert her right to express herself in writing, the only medium in which she can be an individual contributing to the public sphere through regular articles in the press. She faces objections not only from her husband and other men in the family, who consider a woman's name appearing in the public sphere as *awra* (prohibited) for it exposes the private woman and dishonours her male relatives, but also from her mother who assumes the role of an honorary male. The husband of a writer is an exposed man, a *munkashif*, who rejects the idea of writing as a matter of principle regardless of its content. Hind's brother is equally exposed and scandalised as his friends start referring to him as 'the man whose sister writes in newspapers'. Both husband and brother adopt 'survival' strategies to keep themselves untarnished by Hind's provocative act of writing. They both rely on statements such as 'mere similarities in names', or 'the name is unrelated to the family' to salvage their honour whenever they are asked whether Hind is a member of their family.

When all strategies anchored in cultural norms and values to stop a woman expressing her individuality in writing are exhausted, religion becomes the last resort to inhibit her self-realisation and expression. Men invoke the *sharia* to prohibit a whole range of activities such as schooling, work, and writing. *Sharia*-based arguments are centred on *ta'a* (obedience), prescribed by God as a right given to men. Women are instructed to obey their husbands and seek permission for almost all activities that go beyond their traditional roles of motherhood and domestic responsibilities. Women's access to education and work is subject to men's permission. Hind succumbs to pressure and reaches a compromise. She continues to write under a pen-name. Her joy as she comes face to face with her readers' positive and encouraging remarks on her writing is mixed with a deep sense of alienation and negation of the self, as Hind the person is forced to coexist with the persona created by her pen-name. The duality becomes unbearable. Hind seeks personal recognition and immortality through her writings, which liberate her from being enmeshed in a web of relatives, names, and clans. Her quest for recognition on the basis of achieved rather than ascribed qualities is a reflection of a deeper quest to break with tradition and seek modernity. This quest takes her as far as claiming that 'rebellion requires an act of death' amidst the multiple soldiers who thwart her dreams and bury them alive. Tradition involves clinging to that 'Najdi' identity of which she is constantly reminded by her friend Shatha who offers her coffee with dates, an old Najdi tradition, combined with cigarettes, at work. Al-Bishr's Najdi roots prompt her to dismiss the submissive image that flourishes in popular culture about Saudi women. In the context of discussing her work, she argues that Najdi women are stubborn, strong, and rebellious. 'I have never encountered a Najdi woman who was weak and submissive. Only when Najdi women are hungry, they turn into submissive creatures. Their submission is acquired more recently'.[63]

Hind's friend Shatha recounts the story of her father, a thwarted revolutionary who spent time in prison, followed by exile and return to the country. Hind becomes attracted to Shatha's brother Walid who declares that 'he likes the company of a beautiful woman who is also clever and intellectual'.[64] A trip to the desert frees them from the oppression of the city and its many eyes: 'The desert opens its heart to its children who run away from the oppression of the city'.[65] It is in the desert that love and passion are consummated when Walid opens his large cloak and lets Hind enter his inner self. Al-Bishr explains her fascination with the desert, which becomes a place for love and a symbol of freedom from the oppression of the city. This view is contrasted with al-Khamis's depiction of the desert as arid, harsh, and uncompromising. In al-Bishr's view, 'the city is a state project to control and discipline. It is a failed Arab project'.[66] She is 'fascinated by women who are free in the desert, especially those who drive their trucks. When I see them, they say this is our *dira*, our homeland. Here we are free. The city is harsh; mothers are harsh and so is *al-watan*, the homeland'.[67]

[63] Interview with the author, Dubai, 5 January 2011.
[64] al-Bishr, *Hind wa al-askar*, p. 133.
[65] al-Bishr, *Hind wa al-askar*, p. 201.
[66] Interview with the author, Dubai, 5 January 2011.
[67] Interview with the author, Dubai, 5 January 2011.

Hind returns home to face her mother who wants her to agree to another arranged marriage, thinking that Hind has no choices given her divorce. Hind resists and arranges to leave the country clandestinely for Toronto. Escape becomes the only solution. While at the airport waiting for her flight, and killing time by reading the newspaper, Hind notices the face of her brother Ibrahim on the front page. He is one of the Jihadis implicated in a Riyadh suicide bombing. Torn between returning to her miserable mother and seeking an escape from her tormentors, Hind chooses the latter. She cries for her mother, herself, and her brother, all of whom have failed to find real love. All characters are embedded in a web of perpetual violence that leads to death and destruction. Jihadi violence is but one aspect of masculine violence, which is aggravated by forms of feminine aggression, deployed by mothers against their children. Hind escapes by leaving the country, an act that symbolises women's inability to change the situation, leaving many of them desperate enough to flee from multiple layers of violence against women and by women. Women writers have no choice but to leave. This is exactly what Badriyya al-Bishr has chosen to do. She has lived in Dubai with her husband since 2006.

While al-Khamis's doctor returns to the country reconciled with the limitations of her life after a bewildering time spent training in Canada and experimenting with love and individuality, the escape of al-Bishr's heroine to the same country reflects the desperate situation of cosmopolitan women who choose to abandon home and country in favour of finding the feminine self and freeing it from oppression. The West as an escape destination starts to become a recurrent theme in Saudi women's novels, as we shall see in the next chapter. The restrictions of a Najdi family can only be endured if diluted with the hope of leaving it for an open space where one is not identified by name, clan, or family. Al-Bishr appreciates the West not 'simply as a space but as a symbol of civilisation and freedom. In the West, freedom for slaves started, freedom for women started, human rights started'.[68] The act of travelling is a liberating act in her view. 'To leave the place is to acquire freedom, to assert the self'.[69] Al-Bishr chose Dubai as her new home because 'it is cosmopolitan'. 'For an educated woman writer, there is no creativity without cosmopolitanism, without normal relations between men and women. Dubai provides me with that'.[70] Women are afflicted with fatigue if they

---

[68] Interview with the author, Dubai, 5 January 2011.
[69] Interview with the author, Dubai, 5 January 2011.
[70] Interview with the author, Dubai, 5 January 2011.

continue to defend their existence as she did in Saudi Arabia. Now in Dubai, she can dedicate all her energies to building herself as a woman with a feminist consciousness. Despite low levels of readership in Saudi Arabia and the Arab world in general, al-Bishr is optimistic that literature has the capacity to change people's attitudes towards women. The young generation, which is increasingly connected as a result of the media, new communication technology, and travel for study and tourism, is more disposed to engage with literature exposing Saudi society and highlighting its shortcomings. In her opinion, the change so far is theoretical, as no one yet dares to alter their behaviour dramatically. But there are signs that young women do not accept what is imposed on them, and some young mothers allow their daughters freedoms that were not available to them. While the press and the state boast about exceptional women, al-Bishr argues that women are still considered as 'decor'. While the state highlights the achievements of individual women, these remain the products of the investment of their families and their personal efforts. The country is still far from nourishing the talents of its women through education and employment. This is exactly like the project of King Abdullah, which has not been taken on board by the many government institutions. Successful women are products of individual projects, supported by families.

In a country that does not allow civil society to flourish, and stifles real organisation and mobilisation, al-Bishr explains that novelists, writers, and journalists become popular celebrities. Writing novels and in the press is currently the only available alternative to civil society organisations. She notes that there is great demand for novels, and that this explains why so many political scientists, critics, and reformers have started writing fiction. The real reason behind the boom in the novel market is the absence of restrictive laws and rules in Saudi Arabia on fiction, whereas there are clear legal prohibitions on demonstrations, organisations, and civil society: a novelist is not required to apply for a licence. The absence of legal restrictions on writing fiction means that more and more intellectuals choose to express themselves in novels. While many novelists, including for example Turki al-Hamad, Raja al-Sani, Samar al-Moqrin, and Badriyya al-Bishr, are condemned for their daring 'immoral fiction' and many have been the subject of *takfir fatwas*, none has been detained like political and social activists who have directly called for serious political reform.[71] The state has turned a blind eye and has never

---

[71] On the reform movement in Saudi Arabia since 2000, see Madawi Al-Rasheed, *A History of Saudi Arabia*, Cambridge: Cambridge University Press, 2002, 2nd edn, 2010, pp. 261–74.

responded to calls for the prosecution of 'blasphemous' novelists and writers. In fact, the state has protected novelists such as Turki al-Hamad when a *fatwa* depicting him as an apostate was issued in the 1990s for a statement in one of his novels likening God to Satan. This protection was apparent when he boasted that King Abdullah gave him his pen, a symbolic gesture demonstrating his loyalty to the king and the king's approval of his work. A trained sociologist and lecturer in one of Dubai's colleges, al-Bishr has finally found the cosmopolitan space that allows her to develop her potential away from the state of permanent defensiveness that exhausts and drains the energies of many women writers in Saudi Arabia. To escape the fatigue of being a *muthaqafa* seeking wide horizons and self-realisation, leaving the country is one painful but necessary option in a society that thrives on illusions.[72]

LAYLA AL-JAHNI: THE CONTINUITY OF THE AGE OF IGNORANCE

Born in Tabuk in 1969, psychologist and educator Layla al-Jahni exposes racism in a region of Saudi Arabia known for the unique diversity of its population. Like other major cities of the Hijaz, Medina assumes special significance in the Islamic imagination as exemplary of pre-nation-state Islamic cosmopolitanism. Medina, the destination of the Prophet after rejection in Mecca, is where he built the first mosque. It became the meeting space for his early converts, a population that included a mixture of Meccan notables, commoners, and freed slaves. The intermingling of the Meccan exiles with the welcoming local Medinian *Ansar* remains a golden age, to be contrasted with the Meccan *jahiliyya* (age of ignorance) in the Muslim imagination. The Medina epoch is believed to have started a new way of thinking about identity and belonging among the new Muslims. A pious egalitarian fraternity is imagined to have been established by the Prophet in Medina. The narrative about such a fraternity persists in the latent Muslim imagination, as it is regarded as the first experiment in breaking *jahili* social rules, which centred on pride in noble origin, strict marriage customs among *asil* (the aristocratic tribes), and other chauvinistic inclinations of a society that considered a person's worth as a function of his genealogy.

Many Muslims still think of Medina as the hub in which emigrés and inhabitants intermingled, shared scarce resources, and even intermarried. The historical diversity of the city's population endured, with immigrants from all over the Muslim world becoming permanent settlers. In the

---

[72] Interview with the author, Dubai, 5 January 2011.

oil era, Medina, like other main cities in Saudi Arabia, hosted a growing population of expatriate labourers and professionals. Layla al-Jahni takes her reader on a journey of racism, chauvinism, racial discrimination, and prejudice associated with black people in contemporary Saudi Arabia in general, and Medina in particular. In her novel *Jahiliyya* (Ignorance),[73] she challenges racism and exposes its prevalence in Medina through the story of Lin, who falls in love with Malik, a descendant of a slave. In 2009, the novel was selected as one of the five best love stories in contemporary Arabic literature.[74] The chapters of the novel bear the ancient names of the months used in *jahili* Arabian society. Although the novel engages with the present, its historical background is the months that preceded the 2003 American invasion of Iraq.

The survival of the mores and norms of pre-Islamic *jahiliyya* in present-day Medina, despite centuries of Islamic preaching against racism and in favour of religious brotherhood, is explored in the way a young girl is denied the opportunity to practise what her society and religion preach, namely Islamic fraternity and equality. In addition to racism, its inhab-itants do not respect its sanctity. From practising pigeon hunting – for-bidden in this city – to the prevalence of child prostitution, Medina does not seem to have abandoned its *jahili* past. High-rise hotels become meet-ing points for illicit sex and debauchery. The lifestyles of its inhabitants reflect the illusions of a cosmopolitan world, entrenched in consumption and racism.

Beautiful and soft, thirty-year-old Lin wants to marry Malik, but, in the name of paternalistic protection, her father hesitates to give his permission for fear of 'what people are going to say'. He finally refuses to allow Lin the freedom of marrying the man of her choice, telling her, 'People will not see anything but his black colour. They will punish you. I don't want you to suffer'.[75]

Malik's awareness of the limitations of his colour comes at an early age when he is discouraged by his schoolmaster from continuing his education and seeking a place at university. There is no point in exhaust-ing himself with studying, as education is of no use to a black man, his schoolmaster advises him. After all, Malik is just a *takruni*, a des-cendant of black slaves among a pluralistic community that includes, in addition to indigenous Arabs, immigrants and settlers from all over the

---

[73] Layla al-Jahni, *Jahiliyya* [Ignorance], 1st edn, Beirut: Dar al-Adab, 2007.
[74] Ahdaf Soueif, 'Great Arab Love Stories', *The Guardian*, 17 January 2009.
[75] al-Jahni, *Jahiliyya*, p. 51.

Muslim world. In this multi-ethnic Medinan society of today, each group is known by a pejorative name. Najdis call Hijazis *tarsh al-bahr*, Hijazis call Najdis *sarbi*, everybody calls blacks *takrunis* or *abid* (slaves). Newly settled migrant workers have distinct stereotypical communal, national, and shared characteristics: blacks are thick, Egyptians are dishonest, and Lebanese are pimps.[76] Love between Malik and Lin is an act of purification from *jahili* racism. Malik is suspected of having different emotions beneath his dark skin. He is occasionally asked how it feels to be black, thus negating any shared humanity that he may have with others.

The racism of Saudi society and its hypersensitivity to skin colour is fully exposed when women are at stake. An Arabian *jahili* principle dictating that free Arab women cannot be wed to black men persists in contemporary Medina among both men and women who reject the humanity of the other and deny him their daughters. A black man is closer to an animal (*haywan*) in the hierarchy of groups. The taboo is exaggerated as Lin grows into an educated girl with all the characteristics desired in a woman. With the exception of her love for Malik and desire to be his wife, Lin is the ideal loved and protected daughter. Her father's patriarchal love engenders fear about her future in the case of his premature death. A woman always needs a man – an older brother, an uncle, or a close relative – to protect her; but Lin has only a younger brother and an uncle who is an irresponsible young man. The father fails to see Lin as an autonomous individual with abilities that allow her to look after herself.

The situation with her mother is totally different. From a young age, Lin has been reminded that her sex renders her worthless. She is a secondary alternative that must be endured until God responds to the mother's prayers and honours her with a son. The mother tries all strategies to have the desired son. From medicine to amulets, she exhausts all possibilities and is rendered miserable. Her daughter asks God to give her what she desires to make her happy. Young Hisham is born, to the delight of the mother, who until his birth has been tormented by the thought of never being called Umm Hisham. She cherishes her bulging stomach and becomes attached to him while he is still in the womb. She bestows unlimited love and care on the boy who immediately occupies a central place in her heart and house. The mother is happy now that her 'sacred male is born'.[77] Lin is disgusted to see her mother cherishing her baby boy

---

[76] al-Jahni, *Jahiliyya*, p. 108.
[77] al-Jahni, *Jahiliyya*, p. 114.

and continuing to indulge him as an adult despite his failure to achieve anything. Her disgust is concealed under a heavy silence.

While Lin finds solace and escape in reading, writing, and exploring the Internet, Hisham is busy in the sacred sanctity of Medina chasing prostitutes whom he brings home without any consideration for his parents and sister. He degenerates to the extent of picking a child prostitute and bringing her home. His sister comments on his moral degeneration but without him heeding her remarks.

Having lived a life of debauchery, Hisham grows into a failure without education or employment. He searches for entertainment, excitement, and the satisfaction of his sexual desires. He shows no interest in a raging war across the border or anything other than his own desires. His obsession with playing the masculine role leads him to a fixation with his sister's behaviour. He suspects that she is leading an immoral life, and accuses her of being in love with a black man. Together with a friend with whom he shares male solidarity, Hisham embarks on a campaign of surveillance until he catches a glimpse of Lin and Malik together. Lin is aware of the likely consequences, and anticipates death at her brother's hands, not realising what a coward he is.[78]

The situation finally comes to a head when Malik is subjected to heavy beatings at the hands of Hisham, and eventually dies in hospital. Hisham does not, however, touch his sister, who enters an endless world of dreams and fantasy, returning to *jahili* literature and stories. Her life is punctuated by prayers to save the life of her chosen man, to whom she is allowed occasional visits while he lies dying and in a coma. But her mother remains adamant that her unwanted girl has exceeded the limits. She curses the day she saw her face and pleads with the father to punish her.[79] Lin is tormented by years of neglect, marginality, and indifference to her achievements, but her mother cannot break her will and prevent her from remaining by the bedside of her dying Malik.

Lin, young and soft as her name indicates, loses the battle against her father, mother, and brother, all of whom have contributed to her marginality as a woman in the family. Her work in the social security centre exposes her to other girls whose guardians deny them marriage to men they love because they are of a different category, unacceptable to family and society. As she recounts her dilemmas, she remembers a father who is reprimanded by the shaykh for giving his daughter to a black man,

---

[78] al-Jahni, *Jahiliyya*, p. 54.
[79] al-Jahni, *Jahiliyya*, p. 74.

a mere slave. The shaykh refuses to go ahead with the contract, and the marriage is cancelled, even after the girl's guardian gives his permission. A representative of a religion founded on brotherhood and equality among the believers becomes an enforcer of the worst form of racism, based on the colour of the skin. While this racism permeates the lives of people from a young age, it is most obviously apparent in the context of women's marriage.

From the narrow context of the nuclear family, al-Jahni exposes society and its racism. This microcosm reproduces the most exclusionary and discriminatory practices, values, and norms that are often outside its boundaries. Through the act of exposure, love is seen as the only mechanism able to break barriers between those within society and people who had long been subjected to the worst forms of social discrimination on the basis of their skin colour. White and veiled, al-Juhani appeals to the Islamic tradition through classical biographies and narratives about the past, invoking *jahili* discourse that she interweaves with Islamic norms embodied in classical biographies and narratives. Like many women in Saudi Arabia, she sees the current social norms as a distortion of the noble egalitarian Islamic tradition with its emphasis on the equality of all believers.

## WOMEN NOVELISTS AND THE IMMUNITY OF THE POLITICAL

Saudi women's fiction discussed in this chapter does not directly criticise the political framework that perpetuates their subordination and hijacks their *that* (self), as they never stop reminding their audiences. Their literary productions have references to political contexts, such as wars and upheavals (al-Jahni) and powerful kings (al-Khamis), but remain silent on contemporary political practices that impinge on the many themes discussed. Obviously, the novelist is not required to delve into the political, as this may diminish the literary value of her work. Our sample of novelists do not take resistance as their main raison d'être for fear of being marginalised, censored, or punished. Subtle messages to the political do occasionally appear in novels, but these remain mere allusions for fear of censorship and prosecution. Yet these novelists are committed to the emancipation of women and developing a feminist consciousness, both very political commitments. So far, obstacles to such development have been considered religious and social/cultural. There is no obvious condemnation of how a feminist consciousness and empowerment are subject to the interaction of four main factors – political will, religious interpretations, patriarchal social values, and the new market economy of oil and business – each reinforcing the other in a cycle leading to exclusion, discrimination, and marginality. More recently, and as shown in the last chapter, political pressure on the leadership, together with market forces, has prompted the state to empower a selected section of the female population.

In such novels, there is no exploration of how the political cooperates with the religious and the social to perpetuate the subordination of women or how the subordination of women is perpetuated by the oil economy and consumption patterns of late modernity. In fact, during interviews, some women novelists praise the political for suppressing the excessive restrictions of the religious and the social. For example, Umayma al-Khamis acknowledges that there is more free space now to write and criticise practices that contribute to the exclusion of women. 'There is a will among the political leadership to allow this criticism to go ahead and become prevalent in the press', according to al-Khamis.[80] Badriyya al-Bishr praises the many initiatives to empower women that the king has adopted since 2005. She is, however, sceptical about the outcomes. She considers the king's reforms as mere personal initiatives that so far have failed to be 'embedded' in real government institutions. At the level of practice, change is very slow because it has not been grounded in real institutional visions and practices.[81] Like many Saudis, women novelists would like to see themselves represented in an elected forum and enjoying political rights. In 2005, they demanded participation in municipal elections as candidates and voters. They were denied both. In 2011, Hatun al-Fasi led an Internet campaign to promote women's rights in the political arena. Many women resent the prohibition on organising themselves and establishing their own independent civil society forums.

It seems that many novelists hesitate to engage in wider interests beyond the limited feminine subject, situated in most cases within the domestic arena, with occasional references to the workplace and the public sphere. They draw on their experience of the domestic unit, with an awareness that structures of domination reside both inside and outside it, for example in state institutions, religious education and surveillance, and patriarchal social practices and norms.[82] Wider issues of political,

---

[80] Interview with the author, London/Riyadh, 21 November 2010.

[81] Interview with the author, Dubai, 5 January 2011.

[82] Pierre Bourdieu, *Masculine Domination*, trans. Richard Nice, Cambridge: Polity Press, 2001, p. 116.

economic, and social concern that touch the lives of both men and women are alluded to in their literature. In general, with a few exceptions, for example the academic Hatun al-Fasi, the essayist Wajiha al-Howeider, and the novelist Badriyya al-Bishr, most women novelists address, in both fiction and non-fiction, issues that touch only women, their education, employment, marriage, children, and other subjects deemed 'feminine'. In other forums, women have been involved in general campaigns as signatories to political petitions calling for political participation, for example the 2004–5 wave of petitions associated with calls for constitutional monarchy.[83] But the majority of *muthaqafat* in Saudi society accept the limited role that the state allows them, mainly as 'women talking about women'. They have accepted a state discourse that discusses them as a separate category in Saudi society and delivers services to them as women.[84] They become experts on women's issues, with no prospect of a wider engagement with political, economic, and social issues that touch the whole population. This is not only confined to literature but is also apparent in the writings of female journalists. Female Saudi columnists write first about their own 'feminine' concerns and second about wider issues, international affairs, or local non-feminine topics. Their writings are often presented in 'women's pages' of the local press where social, educational, and other matters related to women are discussed. Women in print and visual media are invited to talk and write about women, a practice that has become common in recent years. At state institutional levels, the 'female advisors on women's issues' have become a desirable item of 'decor'. From the deputy director of education to female observers on the Consultative Council, women are called upon to speak only on women's issues. Even the most outspoken women in the cohort of *muthaqafat* hesitate to address issues that do not relate directly to women. The female experts on women have become part of the modernity of the state in which expertise, scientific studies, and the voices of women all combine to boost state legitimacy at a critical moment in its quest for new recognition.

The state's battle with religious extremism and terrorism seems to be a narrow agenda in which women, as well as male intellectuals, have been enlisted. While fighting the state's war, women provide legitimate

[83] This episode in contemporary Saudi history is discussed in Al-Rasheed, *A History*, 2nd edn, pp. 261–74.
[84] For further details on this important development, see Amelie Le Renard, '"Only for Women": Women, State, and Reform in Saudi Arabia', *Middle East Journal*, 62, 4 (2008), pp. 610–29.

links and connections between their own exclusion and marginalisation and the prevalent religious radicalism, both seen as producing the kind of violence that Saudi society has witnessed since 2003. In this respect, women novelists and literary figures do not create their own agendas but are co-opted into political projects that are set up by more powerful agents in society, from individual kings and princes to media institutions, education, and dialogue forums. They hope that their enlistment will eventually lead to women gaining more rights and enjoying fewer restrictions in their own social, personal, and professional lives. In return, women expect the state to rein in the men who control their lives, exacting concessions from them in terms of women's rights, and enforcing rights that protect women from the abuse of men. Freedom to marry without parental consent, travel without guardians, work without permission from family, and legal representation are the wish list that most women novelists expect the state to grant them. However, their hesitation to engage with the political in both literature and non-fiction limits their prospects. The development of an autonomous feminist political consciousness that engages with the wider oppression and exclusion of both men and women is perhaps not yet apparent in Saudi Arabia.

In addition to their abdication from the formal political field, the oil factor and its impact on women's lives is also missing as a dimension in the *muthaqafat*'s discourse. There are occasional references to the 1970s *tafra* (oil boom) and its impact on the lives of women. From the whisky-drinking man who lives in newly built compounds in the new neighbourhoods of Riyadh, to the womaniser who is now able to multiply the number of women in his possession, Saudi novelists try to capture that historical moment of economic affluence and its impact on their lives. The foreign maid who replaced the slave woman of an earlier time is present in the novel but remains in her place. With the exception of al-Khamis's treatment of this important dimension in women's lives, most Saudi novelists remain aloof from the oppression of this category of women in Saudi society. However, unlike Abdulrahman Munif, contemporary *muthaqafat* have not dedicated enough consideration to the oil wealth that altered their lives and directly contributed to their recent exclusion and discrimination. Oil wealth had a profound impact on their lives and on gender relations. From the welfare state to domestic labour, oil opened new opportunities and closed others. While it has not been a total 'curse', it has certainly not been a straightforward enabling factor. Themes relating to consumption, travel abroad, and old and new domestic service are represented in novels, but there is no serious engagement with oil and the new market consumption economy, control, and distribution of resources as prominent themes in women's literature. Women novelists are not under any obligation to address these important dimensions in their literature, but their concern with developing a feminist consciousness, itself a political project, may not be possible without a serious consideration of the limitations and potential of a masculine oil industry.

While the immunity of the political remains a strong orientation in this new literature, it is important to draw attention to its prevalence and popularity among Saudi, Arab, and Western critics and readers. The novelists discussed here are highly educated graduates in the humanities, social sciences, and medicine. Most novelists of the generation considered here combine their literature with family life, and teaching jobs in schools, universities, and colleges. They are privileged women who belong to the emerging intellectual, technocratic, and bureaucratic elite of the country. Both they and their families are products of an expanding government bureaucracy that created employment opportunities in education, media, and other new spheres. Sometimes Saudi women novelists have greater opportunities to meet their audiences and colleagues, especially men, in Beirut, Dubai, London, and Washington rather than in Riyadh. They have received recognition, publicity, and prizes at home and abroad. One of al-Khamis's novels was listed for the Arabic Booker Prize, while al-Juhani has received four awards. For a long time, a previous generation of novelists entered the public sphere through their words only. Today the new generation has many more opportunities to be physically there too. Their voices in literature expand the limited confines of family, tribe, religion, region, and even country for educated women. These women try to assert their autonomy, express their choices, and criticise the religious and social restrictions imposed on them while nevertheless remaining loyal to the state that enforces these restrictions. These contradictions, so apparent in their project, may not be easily reconciled. They depict women in complex relations within the family, in marriage, and at work while challenging fundamental aspects of Saudi society – for example, its alleged purity, uniformity, piety, conformity, racism, xenophobia, and patriarchy. They are truly hybrid in their personal narratives: some are of mixed parentage, others have experienced several worlds inside Saudi Arabia and beyond. An even younger generation is now beginning to define the meaning of being a cosmopolitan woman in Saudi society, the subject of the next chapter.

# 6

## Celebrity Women Novelists and the Cosmopolitan Fantasy

> In the consumer package, there is one object finer, more precious and more dazzling than the other – and even more laden with connotations than the automobile, in spite of the fact that that encapsulates them all. The object is the body.
>
> Jean Baudrillard[1]

> He took his clothes off and kept his long stretched yellowish underpants. He didn't offer me a glass of water or a rose. I didn't see chocolates or fruit. I didn't hear a word or a whisper. He didn't caress me as I imagined. He just sat on top of me like a camel afflicted with leprosy.
>
> Warda Abd al-Malik[2]

The quest for the cosmopolitan woman that both the state and some sections of Saudi society strove to locate and highlight after 9/11 has found its expression in the fiction of an even younger generation of Saudi women novelists. Like the novelists discussed in the last chapter, these young women are urban, educated, sophisticated, and conversant in many languages. They belong to the emerging middle class that has benefited from oil wealth, education, and, since the late 1990s, the free market economy that opened up not only business and investment opportunities but also the media in its old and new forms. Unlike the novelists discussed in the last chapter, the new novelists are extremely young – for example, Raja al-Sani was twenty-four years old when she published her

---

[1] Jean Baudrillard, *The Consumer Society: Myths and Structures*, London: Sage, 1998, p. 129.
[2] Warda Abd al-Malik, *al-Awba* [The return], Beirut: Saqi, 2006, p. 19.

first novel, *Girls of Riyadh*, in 2004.³ Others may be slightly older, but they are still only in their early thirties. The heroines of this younger generation are immersed in a cosmopolitan fantasy, portrayed as cappuccino drinkers, shisha smokers, and globetrotters. They move between home, college, private business, and shopping centre like aspirant, privileged youth anywhere today. While al-Khamis's heroines move between the modern house in Riyadh and the village or farm, the new generation of novelists know only the local modern high-rise shopping centre, the cafe culture, and their equivalents in famous world capitals. Above all, they are 'connected' through their family networks, exploration of the virtual world of the Internet, and regular travel abroad. Their language is a mixture of Arabic and English, with the idioms and abbreviations of email messages, Yahoo groups, Facebook, and Twitter creeping into their everyday language. Heroines are lovers who travel to London and Sharm al-Shaykh to experience freedoms denied at home, such as spending a night with a dream lover, simply sipping a glass of wine in a bar, or sharing time with the opposite sex in restaurants, cafes, and parks. From the new wide avenues of Riyadh to the streets of London, New York, and San Francisco, they skilfully navigate places and cultures. They travel for education, work experience, freedom, and holidays. The novelists and their heroines are products of the neo-liberal capitalist economy that creates 'avenues, means, and commodities of gratification, material and symbolic, often related in one way or another to sexuality'.⁴

At home, heroines shop in glass-and-steel malls, carry Louis Vuitton bags, and blog in Arabic and English. Some transgress so much that they find themselves in the hands of the Committee for the Promotion of Commanding Right and Forbidding Wrong. Others are engaged in playful, carefully concealed acts of courtship and flirtation that do not lead to such dramatic ends. The struggle of these heroines is a battle between them and society, with its many agents of control. In these novels, mothers, fathers, brothers, and husbands work hand in hand with the *mutawwa* to enforce surveillance over young women.

Some women novelists document the lives of 'halfies', hybrid Saudis, some born abroad and brought back to live in Saudi Arabia. While their

---

³ Immediately after the publication of *Girls of Riyadh*, a novel entitled *Shabab al-Riyadh* (The boys of Riyadh) appeared in Beirut. There is no date of publication. See Tariq al-Utaibi, *Shabab al-Riyadh*, Beirut: Dar al-Shafaq, n.d. The novel seems to have attracted no attention.

⁴ Sami Zubaida, *Beyond Islam: A New Understanding of the Middle East*, London: I. B. Tauris, 2011, p. 8.

fathers are Saudis, their mothers may be Arab, American, or any other nationality. They are in between cultures, geographies, and languages. Their numbers increased dramatically with the advent of higher education scholarships that sent thousands of young Saudi men abroad to seek education. Many came back with foreign wives or had several children born in the United States, Britain, Egypt, and other scholarship destinations. While many novelists are themselves 'hybrids', in genealogical, educational, and cultural ways, their heroines stretch hybridity even further. What unites the novelists with their heroines is that both are young urban women who have emerged as a result of the increasing immersion of Saudi Arabia since the 1990s in late capitalism, frequent travel, globalisation, consumer culture, privatisation, and the neo-liberal market economy. In this context, the old Wahhabi religious nationalism finds itself struggling to keep such 'immoral' influences away from the nation while it is itself immersed in the same forces of the new economy. But it too globalised its message, capitalising on new communication technologies from YouTube, Twitter, and Facebook. The battle between the old-fashioned religious nationalism and the icons of the new modernity is, however, difficult to win. The old *fatwa*s survive to condemn excessive consumption, Western influences, and other undesirable ways of behaving and thinking. The youth of the country ignore them, and women challenge them – if not in real-life situations then in novels.

Heroines are depicted as depoliticised and with no interest in the big picture in which women are enmeshed in a web encompassing society, politics, economics, and religion. They seek personal freedoms rather than social rights for themselves as a group. They launch into attacks on the rigid morality imposed in public places and aspire to free themselves from its prohibitions. Unlike a previous generation of Saudi women novelists, these young novelists delve into the lives of cosmopolitan bourgeois women who, since 9/11, have been celebrated not only by the state but also by the international media and literary critics. Such novelists are taken to represent the new voices of Saudi women, despite the fact that many Saudi women do not share their lifestyle, language, international education, consumption patterns, wealth, and privileges. But this successful minority of women novelists and celebrity writers are the new face of Saudi Arabia. The novelists aspire towards *tamayyuz* (distinction) at a time when consumption patterns threaten to homogenise through the acquisition of material goods, aspirations, and behavioural patterns. While many new Saudi women can acquire the new lifestyle and purchase its gadgets, not all can achieve the celebrity status of the new novelists.

Together with outspoken princesses and other female professionals, they are promoted by local constituencies and international audiences and observers aspire to see, promote, and advertise.

International attention dedicated to such new novelists captures an age-old fascination with Muslim women in general and Saudi women in particular. While in the West there is some previous familiarity with the fiction of Arab women novelists, there is no precedent for the new interest in the Saudi women novelists who have emerged in the post-9/11 period, although Saudi women have been writing both novels and non-fiction since the 1950s. Despite previous timid attempts to translate Saudi women's short stories into English,[5] nothing matched the excitement and publicity that surrounded the translation of Raja al-Sani's *Girls of Riyadh* in 2007. The historical context of this new interest in Saudi women's fiction is extremely important for understanding not only their fiction but also the local and international context in which Saudi women are perceived, promoted, pitied, and supported.

Since 9/11, many Saudi women novelists, especially Raja al-Sani, have become 'Muslim celebrities', with special emphasis on their identity as Muslim. Interest in their work goes beyond the literary quality of their novels to touch the deeper political and social contexts that have generated such disproportionate attention being dedicated to a new phenomenon. In the words of al-Sani's translator, Marilyn Booth:

> The contemporary Saudi novel, especially with a female authorial signature fixed to it, is a case in point. Publishers are keen to get their hands on Saudi writing: if there is a single society that contemporary US readers see as encapsulating the mystery of the 'Islamic Orient', it is Saudi Arabia. Within that mystery, the mystery of mysteries remains the Arab Muslim woman, often homogenized and made to stand in for an entire society and history.[6]

The mysteries are believed to have been at least partially exposed in fiction.

When writing fiction, young Saudi women novelists with an eye on international celebrity status embark on a journey of self-orientalising. In

---

[5] An English translation of Saudi women's short stories appeared for the first time in 1998. See Abu Bakr Bagader, Ava Heinrichsdorff, and Deborah Akers (eds.), *Voices of Change: Short Stories by Saudi Women Writers*, Boulder and London: Lynne Rienner Publishers, 1998.

[6] Marilyn Booth, '"The Muslim Woman" as Celebrity Author and the Politics of Translating Arabic: *Girls of Riyadh* Goes on the Road', *Journal of Middle East Women's Studies*, 6, 3 (2010), pp. 149–82, at p. 160.

Booth's opinion, 'it's the harem (in Hollywood) all over again'.[7] Yet the difference between the old well-documented Oriental gaze and the current one stems from the fact that Saudi women have themselves become authors of their own orientalist texts. Moreover, if the old-style 'orientalism' described by Edward Said and others[8] was driven by relations of power, the current self-orientalising Saudi literature is driven solely by commercial, sensational considerations. Young Saudi women write their own orientalist texts in response to market forces in a neo-colonial setting, namely the current Saudi context with its new scrutiny by global media, economic privatisation, and the commercialisation of literature and intellectual production. Young novelists aspire to become celebrities rather than simply literary figures.

Saudi women – rather than foreign male 'orientalist' authors – produce images of idle Saudi women who are desperate for excitement, seduction, love, and adventure in a society that allegedly denies them all these pleasures. Other Arab women novelists have already engaged in this genre of writing, producing work in response to market forces, consumption patterns, and the expectations of an international reading audience. Those whose books have become available in the international marketplace have orientalised Saudi women, who appear as the other, against which an Arab novelist can distinguish herself for a Western audience. In the Lebanese author Hanan al-Shaykh's novels, the Lebanese heroine who finds herself in the desert kingdom escapes from the hell of primitiveness and liberates her soul by moving to Western capitals.[9] In the post-9/11 period, however, it is not only foreign authors who depict Saudi women in orientalist terms. Saudi women themselves are the authors of their own orientalist fiction. As expected, the centrality of sexual desire, romantic love, society's denial, and personal suffering tend to be common, well-rehearsed themes, which have increased in demand as a result of commercialisation and consumption associated with late modernity. As mentioned before, the entry of Saudi women into the late consumer capitalist economy privileges desire and encourages the diversity of the ways in which it can be fulfilled.

---

[7] Marilyn Booth, 'Translator v. Author (2007): Girls of Riyadh go to New York', *Translation Studies*, 1, 2 (2008), pp. 197–211, at p. 199.

[8] Rana Kabbani, *Imperial Fictions: Europe's Myth of Orient*, London: Pandora, 1986.

[9] Joseph Massad's excellent interpretation of the problem of desire and sexuality in literature captures this point when he discusses the work of Hanan al-Shaykh. See Joseph Massad, *Desiring Arabs*, Chicago: University of Chicago Press, 2007, p. 347.

The evaluation of the new Saudi women's literature is dominated by the Oriental gaze that is still fascinated by the hidden lives of veiled Muslim women – their love, passion, and straight and queer sexuality – a gaze that yields fame, celebrity status, and money through publication. The young, female celebrity novelist, veiled or not, is educated, articulate, and attractive. She combines her light, colourful designer veil with the latest Western fashion, from jeans to handbags. Her 'Islamic' femininity is defined in terms of her complete immersion in Western consumerist behaviour in which only a colourful silky veil visually marks any difference. Consumption is not simply about material goods, but involves the consumption of meaning, values, and aspirations associated with late modernity.

The novelist appears at international book fairs, gives interviews to the international press, and defends her fiction in several languages. In fact, she is the translator of her own fiction.[10] While only a few Saudi novelists have regularly appeared in literary forums in the West, many find refuge in neighbouring Gulf countries, where vibrant and more open forums and media are available to women. In 2010, Saudi poet Hissa Hilal participated in *The Million Poet*, a television show, and won third prize for her colloquial poem in which she denounced religious radicalism and restrictions on women. She became a celebrity poet with the help of Gulf media and international attention. Many women novelists still publish their novels outside Saudi Arabia where well-known Arab publishers have identified a market for their so-called daring fiction. So far in this new genre of fiction, two novelists have chosen to publish under pen-names, reflecting a persistent fear of the consequences of producing explicit sexual stories involving adultery and homosexuality. They have thus escaped the celebrity status that awaits those writing under their real names.

The publication of several women's novels since 2000 has coincided with the outbreak of Jihadi violence in the country. Between 2003 and 2008, Saudi Arabia experienced a fierce struggle between militant Jihadis and the security forces. Images of the carnage in major Saudi cities intermingled with regular Jihadi video clips on the Internet. The world came face to face with Saudi men's indiscriminate violence, inflicted on both Muslims and non-Muslims. International media introduced their audiences to individual Saudi militants and their statements. More nuanced websites emerged to specialise in introducing the body of Jihadi literature to interested parties in the West such as policymakers, counterterrorism

---

[10] Booth, 'Translator v. Author'.

agencies, journalists, think tanks, and many others.[11] They captured new realities in Saudi society that the state has struggled to keep hidden from the international community. In such a tense context, the new young celebrity woman novelist is a complete contrast to the bearded young Jihadi brandishing his machine gun and flaunting his suicide belt while uttering Quranic verses, vowing to annihilate the infidels, promising to eradicate the oppression that has befallen the *umma*, and reading his own obituary in which he anticipates an encounter with the promised virgins. In contrast, the new young Saudi woman novelist is focused on this world: her body, desires, career aspirations, and personal advancement. Her personal narrative does not include any long-awaited virgin. The premarital sex and adultery that her heroines engage in are there to shock, normalise, and dramatise. These heroines are living bundles of passions and desires, whose satisfaction is described in great detail in this fiction. Novelists hide behind their heroines to describe not only Saudi society but also their secret sexual encounters and fantasies in a world restrained by many controlling agencies and rendered a restricting and dangerous microcosm for urban young female adventurers.

Women novelists embrace a cosmopolitan fantasy created by market forces – the media and advertising – on the one hand and real political, global, and social pressures on the other, which have made their appearance a much-awaited revelation. Novels in this genre shed the dark, stereotypical images of Saudi Arabia's radical young men and their mentors, and the violence that they are capable of inflicting on both women and the global community. Instead, they depict a much more attractive alternative. Like the successful Saudi businesswoman, entrepreneur, and scientist, these novelists 'normalise' and 'humanise' Saudi society – and in particular its women – by confirming their membership in the neo-liberal globalised commercial and business world elite. The country can then be known not only for its violent men but for its young, educated female authors who write texts such as *The Girls of Riyadh*, *Women of Vice*, *The Return*, and *The Others*, all of which delve into prohibited territories kept away from the public gaze.[12]

---

[11] For examples, see *Jihadica* at http://www.jihadica.com/ and *Jihadology* at http://jihadology.net/.

[12] In this chapter, only these four novels are discussed, as they particularly represent the theme of the chapter. Other Saudi novelists have dealt with similar or related themes, but for reasons of space this chapter cannot claim to cover all novels published since 2000. A good review of Saudi women's novels up to 1999 can be found in Suad al-Mana's chapter on contemporary women's literature in the Arabian Peninsula. See Suad al-Mana, 'The

On the surface, the articulate young cosmopolitan novelist may be the antithesis of the radical Jihadi, but both are products of the political, social, economic, and religious context that is Saudi Arabia since the 1990s. While the Jihadi is believed to be the other, with whom we share nothing, the young Saudi woman novelist is sensationally exotic but she is like 'us'. The novelist is enchanted by her own aspirations and relationships, while the Jihadi is obsessed by the alleged suffering of the Islamic community, the *umma*. The woman novelist shatters secrets behind the veil, while the Jihadi strives to produce more veils. The first exposes myths about authenticity, virtue, and morality; the second asserts all of these qualities. With the pen, the novelist inscribes the beginning of the dismantling of old taboos; with the sword, the Jihadi engraves the taboo in ancient texts and utterances. The novelist launches war on hypocrisy and proclaimed virtue; the Jihadi launches war on those who threaten virtue. But they are both at war with their own society and with authority figures within it. Both are restless, searching for meaning and action in a society that has lost its balance as a result of its rapid immersion in the trappings of late modernity without being able to become truly modernist. Both find refuge in the new communication technology, from simple email to discussion boards, Twitter, and Facebook. Both draw on the pathways of globalisation and transnational links. Both are constrained by authoritarian religious, political, and social powers that deprive people of basic freedoms. Both resent the authority of religious morality-enforcing agencies, traditional religious scholars, and social elders.

As such, both young novelists and Jihadis divide opinions in Saudi society and stretch the limits of its tolerance. Both have strong support among certain circles within society. Young women novelists are celebrated by male literary critics, the Saudi media, and the international literary community, but are also condemned for their corrupting influence by religious scholars and Islamist activists. Jihadis are praised for their courage, piety, and commitment to the *umma* in some religious circles inside Saudi Arabia and beyond, but they too are despised and fiercely fought by others within their own society. Both Jihadis and young women novelists belong to the same generation, which aspires to change their world. The rise of the celebrity female novelists cannot be considered in isolation from the development of radicalisation and violence. In fact, a few

Arabian Peninsula and the Gulf', in Radwa Ashour, Ferial Ghazoul, and Hasna Reda-Mekadashi (eds.), *Arab Women Writers 1873–1999*, Cairo: American University Press, 2008, pp. 254–75.

young women novelists chose to focus on the personality of fictionalised
Jihadis in a soul-searching exercise to identify causes and cures.[13] While
there are no specific references to women novelists in Jihadi discourse,
novelists belong to a genre of women that Jihadis try to eliminate from
the public sphere. Their struggle is to purify this sphere from those who
imitate *ahirat al-rum* (Western prostitutes).[14] Badriyya al-Bishr, discussed
in the last chapter, in her novel *Hind wa al-askar* attributes the way her
heroine's brother, Ibrahim, becomes involved in violent *jihad* as a function of distorted motherly love that glorifies the firstborn son and ignores
the second. Sibling rivalry becomes the context in which the Jihadi is
born. Elsewhere I have pointed to the generation gap between brothers,
the product of men's serial marriages, as a mechanism to understand why
an old, privileged man may fail to understand the radicalisation of his
very young brother. The radicalism of the new young generation provides
an opportunity to overcome the limitations of youth, its subservience to
the authority of elders – including not only fathers but also older brothers, religious scholars, and princes in Saudi society.[15] Women novelists
offer an insight when they trace the origins of radicalisation to unequal
maternal love and affection.

Young women novelists are new voices, delving into desire, sexuality,
and passion, thus destroying the taboo that has always been associated
with these topics. While al-Khamis and the other novelists discussed in the
previous chapter write about lives constrained by history, geography, and
tradition and may make strong allusions to sexual themes, the new young
novelists choose explicit language. The body and its desire and passions
have become central in many novels published since 2000. Born in the
late 1970s, the new young novelists have indeed chosen to make war
against taboos. Their heroines are not mothers and grandmothers, they
are school and college students, struggling with restrictions on sexuality,
personal freedom, marriage choices, and relationships.

According to a study prepared by Nadi al-Baha al-Adabi, *Baha Literary Salon*, there has been a dramatic increase in the number of Saudi
novels that deal with sex. In 2007, fifty-five novels, written by both men
and women, had sexual themes. The number increased to sixty-four and

---

[13] Ala al-Hithlul, *al-Intihar al-majur* [Hired suicide], Beirut: Saqi, 2004.
[14] For detailed discussion of *jihad* and gender in Saudi Arabia, see Madawi Al-Rasheed,
    *Contesting the Saudi State: Islamic Voices from a New Generation*, Cambridge: Cam-
    bridge University Press, 2007, pp. 163–8.
[15] Al-Rasheed, *Contesting the Saudi State*, pp. 134–74.

seventy novels in 2008 and 2009 respectively.[16] These figures attest to the predominance of the economies of desire in which sexuality is central. As expected, novels with explicit sexual material have attracted criticism. In oral cultural settings, Saudi women, and Arab women in general, engage in informal and elaborate 'sexual' talk that may appear shocking to Western middle-class women. The latter are far more reserved in discussing their own sex lives in the company of female friends, but they have no qualms with exploring and exchanging information gathered from sources such as *Cosmopolitan* and *Elle* magazines and popular television series dealing with explicit sexuality. Saudi women's sexual conversations are neither condemned nor embarrassing for those who engage in them, provided that they take place among married women. These conversations often exclude young unmarried girls who are equally engaged in constant sex talk among themselves. What is shocking for Saudis is the entry of sex talk into the public sphere through novels written by unmarried girls. Religious sex manuals are accepted and widely circulated in Saudi Arabia, provided that they are supported by religious evidence and opinions. However, the novels discussed in this chapter are different. They are narratives of personal female desires, passions, and sexual encounters that are still not welcomed in the public sphere – hence the strong reactions of many Saudis when confronted with novels such as *Girls of Riyadh*. When informal, private, girls' sex talk moves from the oral context in which it usually takes place to become international literature, the majority in Saudi society are shocked – with the exception of a small cosmopolitan, government-employed intellectual and business elite. For example, the poet, diplomat, and civil servant Ghazi al-Gosaybi endorsed *Girls of Riyadh* and wrote the prologue.

In general, women's sex novels have been condemned by many literary critics and a large section of the public. Even Arab literary figures and observers have been astonished by the daring literary productions of this later generation of Saudi novelists. Layla al-Othman, a Kuwaiti novelist and essayist, who herself had written daring texts with explicit sexual references, accused Saudi novelists of overdoing the sexual theme.[17] Many Saudi women writers agreed. Sharifa al-Shamlan and Siham al-Qahtani

---

[16] See Yasir ba Amer, 'Jadal al-jins fi al-riwaya al-saudiyya' [The controversy of sex in Saudi novels], 8 May 2010, available at http://www/aljazeera.net/Portal/Templates/Postings/PocketPcDetail.

[17] For details of Layla al-Othman's long journey through the courts where she had to defend her novels, see Layla al-Othman, *al-Muhakama* [The trial], Beirut: Dar al-Adab, 2009.

accepted al-Othman's criticism. Al-Qahtani wrote that she is sometimes ashamed to read sections of these novels. While al-Othman's long writing experience allows her to deal with sexual themes in sophisticated ways, many new Saudi women novelists lack such skills, and hence their sex scenes tend to be vulgar without the benefit of dramatisation, according to some critics. But other Saudi women writers were surprised that al-Othman, who suffered ostracism and imprisonment in Kuwait as a result of her daring literary productions, should voice a criticism relating to explicit sexual material found in recently published Saudi novels.[18]

Many Saudi novelists explain the saturation of the new literature with sexual themes as a reflection of the obsession of Saudi society with this human instinct. Novelist and essayist Badriyya al-Bishr argues that sexual themes in the new literature do not equate to society's excessive obsession with sex. Contemporary Arab literature 'is saturated with sexual scenes but critics do not concern themselves with this. Only when Saudi women write about sex, they are singled out. This is because the country has been grounded in darkness and now things have changed. Women's voices, which were absent, are now heard around the world'.[19] Saudi society, in her opinion, is 'organised around sex, either to make it permissible or to prohibit it. Sex is everywhere. Obsession with sex permeates all institutions like marriage and education. Young girls encounter sex as children if they are sexually harassed, they then come face to face with it as adolescents, whose mothers groom them for marriage. Later in marriage, sex is the primary purpose'.[20] In general, many Saudi women criticise their reduction to sex objects, not only in novels but in society in general. Educationalist Mounira al-Jamjoum forcibly argued that 'we had enough of limiting our humanity as women to sex'.[21] This overwhelming presence of sex and representations of sex in popular fiction is not unique to Saudi Arabia. Iran, a country that shares many features with Saudi Arabia, has also engaged with promoting, regulating, or condemning sex in more recent years in an unprecedented manner at the level of both state and society. In Iran, sex has become both a source of freedom and an act of

---

[18] Huda al-Daghfaq, 'Saudiyat yuwajihna itihamat al-Othman hawl al-jins al-rowai' [Saudi women respond to al-Othman's accusations regarding sex in novels], *al-Watan*, 4 May 2010.
[19] Interview with the author, Dubai, 5 January 2011.
[20] Interview with the author, Dubai, 5 January 2011.
[21] Mounira Jamjoum, 'Kafana hasran li insaniyatana fi boutaqat al-jins' [We have had enough of limiting our humanity as women to sex], interview in *al-Hayat*, 8 March 2011.

political rebellion.[22] But since the 1980s, the regulation of the sex life of the citizens has been taken as a state policy, explained and propagated by religious scholars in the country.[23]

The overwhelming place of sex in contemporary Saudi society may not be simply a function of an innate and eternal 'Saudi' obsession, amounting to a pathologically compulsive condition, but rather a reflection of interrelated contemporary factors. First, the alleged obsession with sex is nothing but a reflection of the marriage between two forces: religious nationalism and its focus on the private sphere as a protected and heavily regulated arena, and the state's desire to gain religious legitimacy through controlling and regulating the private sex lives of its citizens. This regulation is manifested in the endless signs separating men and women in the public sphere, from the market to mosque, university, and school; the regulation of marriage to foreigners, subject to the requirement of obtaining permission from the Ministry of Interior; the guardianship system imposed on women; and many other legal restrictions, at the heart of which is the regulation of the body and its desires, in addition to family and marriage. The political and religious forces have combined to generate the obsession that baffles novelists such as Badriyya al-Bishr and many outside observers. In order to comply with the tenets of the old religious nationalism, the state must be seen as regulating, controlling, and managing all personal and private desires. The occasional raid on a mixed encounter between a man and a woman in a restaurant or cafe, the central theme in a novel discussed later in this chapter, is very important. It is a symbol signifying the state's commitment to protecting the public sphere from the excess of desires, initially stimulated by the state and its entrepreneurs under elaborate urban shopping development plans and private entrepreneurial initiatives to transform the landscape into one where the cosmopolitan fantasy flourishes for all to see but not consume or enjoy. To distinguish this newly created urban space from any other one in the world, control of sex and desire must become a priority for the state to remind its people occasionally of its commitment to religious nationalism.

Second, Saudi immersion in a capitalist economy that fetishises sex, promotes unlimited desires, and stretches the imagination in the service

---

[22] Pardis Mahdavi, *Passionate Uprisings: Iran's Sexual Revolution*, Stanford: Stanford University Press, 2009.

[23] For example, Iranian state and religious circles endorsed and popularised temporary marriage in the 1980s. See Shahla Haeri, *Law of Desire: Temporary Marriage in Iran*, London: I. B. Tauris, 1989.

of gratification must have turned a natural instinct into an obsession. The oil economy had a tremendous impact on gender relations, marriage, and sexual life. Sudden wealth opened new opportunities for sex while social mores and religion were not able to advance at the same speed. As discussed earlier, Saudi *ulama* have struggled to accommodate old desires that became more urgent under the new oil economy. The popularity of *misyar* and *urfi* marriages in the 1980s is an example of the constant quest for solutions to problems imposed by a changing economic, social, and demographic context. The solutions obviously remain grounded in the requirements of religious nationalism, that is, privileging procreation within the legitimate Islamic framework of the family. Saudi *ulama* justified these marriages, and from the 1990s invented more daring unions such as *misfar* (travel), *nahar* (daytime), and boyfriend marriages in order to respond to contemporary issues. A Saudi student at King Abdul Aziz University in Jeddah shocked a public student forum in which discussion of *misyar* was organised by students in higher education when she announced that 'like men, women too look for sexual pleasures'.[24] Other girls supported her in private. These new unions remain controversial, but they are increasing – especially among older unmarried women who live with their parents. *Misyar* marriages are now organised informally by female matchmakers who have good knowledge of the local marriage 'market' and arrange compatible unions.[25] Matchmakers are reported to say that they receive between seven and ten applications daily from men seeking *misyar* in Jeddah. Religious shaykhs who run offices attached to mosques for facilitating marriage in Jeddah conduct *misyar* marriages regardless of whether the shaykhs accept them or not. Many women still object to solutions seen as privileging male interest, without any consideration of the impact of such unions on women.

While the oil economy contributed to the consolidation of the obsession with sex and enforcement of sex segregation, the recent neo-liberal monetisation, privatisation, consumption, and excessive advertising since the late 1990s are all contributing factors that have pushed young Saudi women novelists to privilege sex stories in their recent literature. Saudi society is not essentially or naturally obsessed with sex; it is simply being drawn into global images and practices of old and new desires, sex being only one of them. It is therefore not a surprise that novelists have

---

[24] *Wakad* (electronic newspaper), http://waked.net, 4 March 2010.
[25] Mariam al-Hakeem, '*Misyar* Marriages Gaining Prominence among Saudis', gulfnews. com, 21 May 2005.

internalised the alleged obsession with sex and saturated their stories with a quest to enjoy it against the background of disappointing marriages, social, legal, and religious restrictions, punishment, and denial. The 'sex novel' appeared exactly at the time when the state decided under pressure to reverse previous restrictions and promote the cosmopolitan woman. The erotic theology discussed in Chapter 3 is no longer the only manual that determines sexual desires and regulates sexual acts. Today Saudi society is exposed to other sexual paradigms that are eroding previously taken-for-granted wisdom on sex and desire. The new novels reflect these new developments and articulate the tension between old and new.

This chapter explores the literature of some of the young women writers who represent and articulate the cosmopolitan fantasy of the state and sections of Saudi society, mainly the upper middle class that is part of the state apparatus through education, privilege, employment, entrepreneurial activities, and global business. This group includes both celebrities such as Raja al-Sani and other less well-known writers, for example journalist and novelist Samar al-Moqrin. More daring novelists use pseudonyms, for example Saba al-Hirz and Warda Abd al-Malik, both of whom focus on premarital sex and homosexuality. These two capture the surge in Saudi women novelists' focus on explicit sex scenes, both heterosexual and homosexual. They turn the body and its desires into instruments of war against social taboos and religious restrictions. The 'struggle of the body' may not be the only challenge facing contemporary Saudi women, as observed by Layla al-Othman,[26] but these novelists have chosen to highlight aspects of this struggle that touch not only relations between men and women but also homosexuality, which has become a public concern in recent years as a result of globalised international discourse on the subject. All four novelists published their books in Beirut. Al-Saqi, their publisher, promotes this literature in the Arab world and abroad. At the time of writing, only al-Sani and al-Hirz's novels have been translated into other languages.

RAJA AL-SANI: HIP-HOP SAUDI MUSLIM GIRLS

In 2005, Raja al-Sani's first novel, *Banat al-Riyadh*, enjoyed great success in both Saudi Arabia and the Arab world.[27] It was translated into more than twenty languages. The novel does not exploit explicitly sexual scenes

---

[26] *al-Watan*, 4 May 2010.
[27] Raja al-Sani, *Banat al-Riyadh* [The girls of Riyadh], London: Saqi, 2005.

but is focused on young women's seduction and desire. On her own web page, Raja wants to be known as 'a Muslim writer from Saudi who became famous through her bestselling novel...the author received death threats for bringing her nation's women into disrepute'.[28] To an English-speaking audience, this biographical statement encompasses all the attractive dimensions that fascinate and enchant those who seek the secrets of Arabia 'behind the veil'. Together with a photograph of the veiled novelist, the statement ensures interest and fascination. 'Muslim', 'Saudi', 'women', and 'death threats' are combined here to open realms of excitements and promises of scandals. The series of words responds to a set of images that have become dominant about Muslim women and their oppression, and confirm an old, well-entrenched stereotype about Saudi Arabia. But audiences must explore further to arrive at critical moments at which the stereotype begins to be challenged.

The daughter of two doctors, al-Sani lived in Kuwait before her parents returned to Saudi Arabia. She is a dentist who started her training at King Saud University, and after the publication of her first novel, she moved to Chicago – partly for graduate education and partly to remove herself from the storm that erupted after the novel's publication. Although al-Sani challenges many perceptions about her own society, on her web page she confirms her Muslim identity and commitment to her country. She informs her audiences that she has plans to return to Saudi Arabia and develop her own private dental practice. She is then a committed Muslim woman who does not wish to escape to the West permanently, as she wants to work in her country and cause change from within. Such a narrative is familiar in the context of Saudi Arabia. Working and changing the system from within is the ideal choice. Its advocates escape labels such as 'Westernised', 'traitors', and 'agents of foreign domination' and replace them with commitment to Islam – but with a new cosmopolitan outlook. It is a strategy that avoids condemnation and reinforces the high moral ground of its advocates. In many ways, this narrative remains grounded in religious nationalism, with a modern twist. This, however, did not spare Raja al-Sani the wrath of some of her compatriots. Two Saudi citizens went as far as to file a lawsuit against her because her novel 'is an outrage to the norms of Saudi society. It encourages vice and also portrays the Kingdom's female community as women who do not cover their faces and who appear publicly in an immodest way'.[29] The lawsuit was rejected by the Court of Grievances in Riyadh.

[28] See http:www.rajaa.net.
[29] Riad Qusti, 'Court Rejects Case Against Rajaa al-Sanea', *Arab News*, 9 October 2006.

The success of al-Sani's novel in Saudi Arabia and beyond[30] is attributed to the fact that many young women were able to see themselves in one of her four characters. More importantly, its success is a function of the cosmopolitan fantasy that the author promotes about sophisticated, mobile elite women and their families, who are competent in many cultures, languages, and dialects, and who are constantly searching for excitement and contrasts rather than conformity. No interview in the Western press would be complete without the interviewer commenting on the novelist's elegant appearance, which can be described as 'hip-hop Muslim'. In the words of a journalist, al-Sani 'erupts from the lift, a whirlwind of designer labels, perfect manicure and lip gloss, consulting her Gerald Genta watch, a white saucer, inset with diamonds. She looks fabulously glitzy, as you would expect from the writer of a novel widely hyped as "Saudi-style *Sex and the City*"'.[31] *Girls of Riyadh* is considered to be a Saudi version of British and North American 'Chick Lit', combining concern with identity, race, and class with a depiction of messy social realities facing young women.[32]

In the novel, the narrator, who remains unknown, promises to describe a series of local scandals and rave parties involving her four girl friends, using the liberating new medium of the Internet pages. The narrator, who calls herself *moi*, is a cybernaut who promises hot stories about scandals assembled through email messages on Yahoo. Every week, she replies to emails and proceeds to tell more stories about her characters. She warns readers and subscribers to her 'seerawenfadha7et' Yahoo group that any resemblance between the characters in these stories and reality is deliberate (*maqsud*), and thus from page one she merges fiction with reality. The lives of four young women are centred on education, entertainment, their aspirations for love and career, marriage, divorce, achievement, and disappointment. The university is the context in which the girls mix with others whom they would not have encountered in old Riyadh. Shia girls from the Eastern Province intermingle with local Najdi, Hijazi, and Qasimi girls. The intermingling serves as a context to highlight difference and diversity. The girls come face to face with religious and cultural differences that make the local a heterogeneous mix, contrasted with the

---

[30] Reviews of the novel in the English press highlighted its 'sex' dimension. All reviews focused on acts that were simply alluded to rather than described. See Alev Adil, '"Girls of Riyadh", by Rajaa Alsanea, trans. Marilyn Booth', *The Independent*, 3 August 2007; Sally Williams, 'Sex and the Saudi', *The Telegraph*, 30 June 2007; and Rachel Aspden, 'Sex and the Saudis', *The Observer*, 22 July 2007.

[31] Sally Williams, 'Sex and the Saudi', *The Telegraph*, 30 June 2007.

[32] Marilyn Booth, 'Translator v. Author', p. 197.

homogenised image peculiar to the religious nationalist ideology, with obvious stereotypical, predetermined, and prejudiced opinions about the other.

In addition to tragedy, the four girls share a fascination with the rituals of seduction experienced by marriageable girls of every culture. Their longing for a 'love match' is crushed by old men and women who resist losing control of their girls and cooperate to continue their surveillance. An arranged marriage ends up in divorce (Qamra), while another awaited marriage stumbles when Sadim allows its consummation prior to the wedding night. Michele, the 'halfie' whose Arabic is not so good, cannot achieve full acceptance in society, as her mother is American. Mixed parentage becomes an obstacle in the face of marrying her first love. Finally, the only success is Lamis's marriage to a colleague in medical school. The girls move between Riyadh, London, Chicago, and San Francisco, very much like upper-class cosmopolitan Saudi girls. The boredom of life in Riyadh is intercepted by liberating holidays, education, and work experience abroad. While all the girls aspire towards the fulfilment of their love and career aspirations, they struggle with restrictive norms, traditions, and social pressure. They find refuge in a Kuwaiti divorcee who opens her house to the girls and their lovers. Her house becomes *multaqa al-ushaq* (the lovers' meeting place). The girls are even ready to venture into forbidden territory to meet potential marriage candidates, thus exposing themselves to severe punishment and harassment. The theme of girls pursuing men is a reversal of traditional marriage arrangements in which men and their mothers would embark on a search that would culminate in finding a suitable wife. Al-Sani's girls are in many ways similar to others in the Arab world who have recently shocked their society through their daring narratives about finding a suitable husband.[33] Al-Sani's girls are all skilful in circumventing the endless limitations of their society. They seem to know what they want and pursue it despite restrictions. Some fail while others succeed. The novel moves seamlessly between

---

[33] In Egypt, the phenomenon is illustrated by a very successful blog turned into a book that was translated into several European languages: see Ghada Abd al-Al, *Ayza atgawiz* [I want to be married], Cairo: al-Shorouq, 2008. The current marriage crisis in Egypt is discussed in many scholarly works. For further details, see Hanan Kholoussy, *For Better, For Worse: The Marriage Crisis that Made Modern Egypt*, Stanford: Stanford University Press, 2010; Hanan Kholoussy, 'The Fiction and Non-Fiction of Egypt's Marriage Crisis', *Middle East Report*, December 2010, available at http://www.merip. org. For a comparison between Egypt and the United Arab Emirates, see Frances Hasso, *Consuming Desires: Family Crisis and the State in the Middle East*, Stanford: Stanford University Press, 2011.

tragedy, irony, laughter, and trivial occupations. It anticipates the stardom of its author, the newspaper controversies, and finally an interview on al-Arabiyya television hosted by Turki al-Dakhil, known for choosing controversial figures to interrogate. Al-Sani achieved the stardom depicted for her narrator. An endorsement by novelist, poet, and minister of labour, Ghazi al-Gosaybi, reflects local connectivity, encouragement, and support. Al-Sani may have enraged many religious scholars and Islamists, and offended the guardians of religious nationalism, but she was protected from above.

Each chapter opens with a couple of lines from a poem, a phrase from a famous writer, a verse from the Quran, or a saying from the *hadith*s. The text becomes anchored in a hybrid space that invokes multiple layers of meaning and experience. But in this pastiche, al-Sani exposes hypocrisy in Saudi society, which explains the strong negative reaction she received in the country. She tells familiar stories such as those associated with aeroplane toilets where women swap their Saudi attire for Western fashions and vice versa, depending on which direction the plane is flying. She highlights the lies that people fabricate and the risks they take to overcome the prohibited. She exposes the double lives of upper-class Saudis who move between languages and cultures assisted by substantial wealth and privilege. When things get 'too much', a recurrent theme in the novel, heroines can pack their suitcases and leave – either for short breaks or permanently – choices that remain beyond the reach of the majority of the population.

Islam and culture are not taken for granted, but their troubled relationship is explored with insight into how they collide at one level while reinforcing each other at another. For example, after the religious marriage formalities are completed, sexual relations between husband and wife are rendered licit in Islam. However, social tradition prohibits the sexual act until after the wedding night, and even then, a bride is supposed to resist it for several nights to show her shyness and purity. In the novel, a girl is divorced for the simple reason that she practised what is permissible in Islam but prohibited by society. In a society that practises severe sex segregation, a girl's dream to mix with the opposite sex may push her to choose to study medicine for the very limited educational contexts in which she will be exposed to boys. Segregation forces boys to accompany girls to shopping centres under the pretence that they are their brothers. The youth emerge in this novel as assertive and skilful in overcoming social and religious obstacles. But many tragedies are unavoidable. These are anchored in a world where the veneer of piety and tradition poses real

challenges for the privileged classes who by virtue of their wealth, education, and consumption patterns become intolerant of their own society
and alienated from its control agencies. While fathers struggle to hide
behind the facade of conformity, thus allowing themselves liberties they
deny their daughters, the girls live, at night and on the pages of the Internet, a life denied them during the day. The girls of Riyadh are both strong
and weak, resilient and vulnerable. They invoke sympathy, admiration,
and pity. The novel invites the reader to consider fictionalised Saudi girls
as real, hence the extraordinary success of the novel at a time when only
trashy fiction written about life behind the veil dominated the market for
fictional books about Saudi Arabia. Here we have a voice portrayed as
'authentic' and 'Muslim', speaking to Saudi, Arab, and (via translation)
Western audiences. While the assessment of the literary credentials of this
novel is beyond the scope of this author,[34] what is important from my
perspective is how the success of a specific genre of fiction authored by a
young Saudi woman is yet another step towards finding the cosmopolitan
woman who might be a fantasy or a reality. In both situations, she is a
desired outcome, a long-awaited gift to save the nation from previous
stereotypes, prejudices, violence, and misconceptions. While the cosmopolitan woman is already a fixture in real Saudi society, fiction depicts
her as a woman embarking on a long journey in search of individuality,
love, and desire. Although she engages in consumption made available
in an open market, and enjoys all the education and degrees made available as a result of high purchasing power, she is in search of romantic
love as advertised around the time of Valentine's Day. The traditional
socially legitimate love, intimacy, and even eroticism celebrated in traditional culture and ancient poetry and praised in old Islamic texts is simply
not the one that a consumer age makes young girls and boys desire or
seek. Today fictionalised Saudi women and many real ones seek 'dating',
that 'alien' and forbidden practice, whose paraphernalia are red roses,
chocolates, ribbons, and plastic balloon hearts. All are imported into the
heart of Saudi Arabia. In al-Sani's words, 'Yes, there are dates. But in
Saudi Arabia we eat them'.[35]

Dating, whether fictionalised or real, does not appear to be a solution,
as Saudi men who date are believed to be weak and under the authority of
their mothers and fathers. In fiction and reality, and in the privacy of their
homes, men parade their big bellies, wearing only their underwear and

---

[34] See Booth, '"The Muslim Woman" as Celebrity Author'.
[35] Raja al-Sani, 'My Saudi Valentine', *New York Times*, 13 February 2008.

reflecting the light on their bald skulls. In al-Sani's novel, Saudi men are a bleak and miserable group. The hypocrisy of fathers, the weakness of young men, and the treachery of passionate lovers paint a gloomy picture of those who assume control over women.

*Girls of Riyadh* is a challenge that celebrates the women who are denounced and despised by the guardians of religious nationalism, the feared, upper-class, Westernised hybrid women who confuse boundaries, and embrace multiple cultures, lifestyles, and languages. While the girls in the novel do not represent Saudi women, in reality their kind is becoming more common in urban Saudi Arabia.[36]

## SAMAR AL-MOQRIN: IMPRISONED COSMOPOLITAN FANTASIES

If al-Sani's novel avoided explicit sex scenes in favour of a focus on the quest for seduction and flirtation, with *Nisa al-munkar* (Women of vice) Samar al-Moqrin throws her heroine wholeheartedly into the forbidden act of adultery. While al-Sani's novel engages in aspects of self-orientalising, al-Moqrin delves into the heart of the orientalising project, namely sexualising Saudi women in an overt market economy of desire. In *Nisa al-munkar*, the heroine is described as selfish to begin with, thus anchoring her in a realm that challenges broad traditional expectations associated with motherhood, giving, and sacrifice. She occupies that twilight zone between marriage and divorce, a liminal, ambiguous, and dangerous phase experienced by women who are married but have not been granted a divorce. After eight years of marriage, Sara is *mu'alaqa*, hanging between marriage and divorce. Her appeals in the central Riyadh court for a divorce result in frustration until a new man, Raif, appears in her life, renewing her vitality and joy. She finally finds love on the streets of London, in particular in Queensway when she meets her lover. But meeting the lover whom she had previously encountered in the virtual world – through email, text messages, telephone conversations, and chat

---

[36] The study of youth culture in Saudi public space is captured in Lisa Wynn, 'The Romance of Tahliya Street: Youth Culture, Commodities, and the Use of Public Space in Jiddah', *Middle East Report*, 204, 1997, pp. 30–1. See also Amelie Le Renard's study of urban college girls in Riyadh and the ways they challenge restrictions in their daily shopping and consumption habits that centre around the shopping mall. They can be considered real versions of the fictionalised girls in al-Sani's novel: Amelie Le Renard, 'Engendering Saudi Consumerism: A Study of Young Women's Practices in Riyadh's Shopping Malls', paper presented at a conference on Saudi Arabia, Princeton, November 2009. For an alternative view regarding youth culture, see Yamani, *Changed Identities*; Yamani, 'Saudi Youth'.

rooms – proves to be daunting when their meetings become real. Nevertheless, in London the lovers satisfy their quest to encounter each other away from the policing agents of Riyadh who discipline every woman they encounter. Hyde Park becomes synonymous with freedom. It is enjoyed for its flowers and green grass, but most importantly for the sight of lovers exchanging kisses. While the rest of the world remains oblivious to such intimacy in public places, a Saudi mother shouts her insults: 'Infidels!'[37] In addition to love and courting, there is debate in 'speak corner' (Speakers' Corner, Hyde Park), allegedly where Saudi dissidents started their opposition to the government. She is reminded that 'this is Britain, the bastion of democracy'.[38] After days enjoying the company of her lover and London, the moment of return arrives. Back in Riyadh, she sends messages to her lover who resists her appeals and ignores her calls. Obviously, he is someone who practises the usual hypocrisy, enjoying a woman while condemning her for her lost morality. Finally a meeting in a Riyadh restaurant with Raif ends in members of the Committee for the Promotion of Commanding Right and Forbidding Wrong raiding the restaurant and arresting those who are together without being married or related. Raif serves a short prison sentence, while Sara is sentenced to four years in a women's prison and 700 lashes. She initially refuses to sign the documents that implicate her in more serious offences and continues to profess innocence. Love and meetings are crimes. The shaykh in charge of her case insults her, using strong language that refers to her intimate organs. Scandal follows, and the family abandons Sara, inevitable outcomes after being caught by the Committee, regardless of the offence. In prison, Sara encounters murderers, prostitutes, and adulteresses. They tell their stories while invoking both defiance and repentance. Four months after being released from prison, Sara gives up on finding Raif. With no future or career, she works as coffee server (*sababa*) at wedding parties, a job for the poor and old. Women are hired during wedding parties to perform this job for which they get a meagre income. Despite being worried that she may be recognised by her friends during a wedding, she continues to work. At one wedding, using the microphone, the singer calls upon women guests to cover themselves as she announces that the bridegroom will enter the women's hall to meet his bride. When the bridegroom arrives, it is Raif who enters the room only to leave Sara's soul forever.

[37] Samar al-Moqrin, *Nisa al-munkar* [Women of vice], Beirut: Saqi, 2008, p. 20.
[38] al-Moqrin, *Nisa*, p. 21. Al-Moqrin's essay are found at http://www.salmogren.net/Default.aspx.

The cosmopolitan fantasy that *Girls of Riyadh* entertains is repeated in *Nisa al-munkar*. Its characters move between Riyadh and London to experience pleasure and escape the limitations of society and religion. In this novel, the boundaries between inside and outside are more rigid. Transgression is only possible outside, while adventures involving the crossing of boundaries inside result in tragedy. This black-and-white depiction of place seeks the fantasy abroad, as it is denied freedom and engulfed with danger at home. While 'inside' is the antithesis of cosmopolitan free life, it turns into a prison, the ultimate confined space, where vice is pushed away from the virtuous society. Longing for the outside and the pleasures that are permissible there is punished by banishment from the hearts of men. Men seek women as objects of desire abroad, after which they condemn them for their 'immorality'. Women seek love and affection from such men, only to be disappointed by their neglect after a sexual encounter. Men do not want to marry a woman who succumbs to their desires, a well-rehearsed theme in many other literary productions. In al-Sani's novel, Sadim's marriage is annulled because she surrenders to her husband before the wedding night. Similarly, in *Nisa al-munkar*, Sara prematurely gives away too much and pays the price.

Al-Moqrin directs attacks at both Islamists and liberals: the first saturate the public sphere with their preaching; the second preach what they do not practise. The religious see vice everywhere and aspire to eradicate it, while *hadathi* (modern, secular) men are hypocrites when it comes to relations with women. Such blunt political messages and statements diminish the literary value of the novel and make it shallow, giving the impression of an immature literary style in which the novel is to be read as a statement about the plight of women rather than as a work of literature. It seems that the hasty publication of this short novel in 2008 was a response to a market that welcomed and celebrated al-Sani's novel. *Nisa al-munkar* seeks fame by repeating a formula that has already been successful. Its opening adulterous act is punished by a vindictive society, while the desire to seek a cosmopolitan life remains unfulfilled. As the novel moves between the bars of London and the bars of the Riyadh prison, it desperately seeks to appeal to an audience beyond Saudi Arabia. It remains a short statement with serious limitations, but it is symptomatic of the context in which it was written, published, and marketed. 'Breaking the taboo' has become a marketing tool promoted by publishers and authors at the expense of serious literary qualities, but it cannot always guarantee fame. The fact that the taboo is about Saudi women and their sexuality has become standard, and in some cases, it results in success for the author and the novel. However, many Saudi women novelists and their publishers underestimate the sophistication of Arab readers and the even more demanding tastes among an international audience, especially if they hope that their work will be translated – particularly into English. Novels such as the two discussed above represent a quest for the cosmopolitan fantasy on the part of both novelists and their heroines. Saudi women novelists are prepared to go as far as fetishising love and sexuality in the pursuit of breaking the taboo and appealing to Saudi, Arab, and international audiences. While some critics would applaud women novelists' 'courage', 'bravery', and determination to seek the individual freedoms that other women enjoy, others condemn them as agents of corruption and Westernisation. A small minority of critics offer nuanced assessment of the emerging genre of literary production and assess the recurrent themes of sexuality, prohibition, denial, indulgence, and punishment. There is nothing new about these reactions to literary works that aim to shock, defy, and undermine many automatic assumptions about Saudi women. The authors and their novels, together with reactions to them, offer, however, a great opportunity to map the context in which gender issues became central not only to Saudis but also to the international community with its policymakers, journalists, publishers, and book markets. Authors who use their real names are prepared to go far, but not as far as those women novelists who use pen-names.

## WARDA ABD AL-MALIK: BORN AGAIN FREE

Published under the pseudonym Warda Abd al-Malik, the novel *al-Awba* (The return) explores religion and sex, dismantling these taboos in London, Sharm al-Shaykh, and Riyadh. Sara, a young, bright girl, leaves school to marry pious Abdullah, the brother of her school's social worker, the spinster Filwa. Filwa introduces the young girl to preaching and religious study circles, where girls learn about the unlimited rights of husbands and the protocols of sexual intercourse. Sara becomes indoctrinated in interpretations that make the road to heaven pass through the marital bed: women who please their husbands and refrain from tormenting them by denying them sex are guaranteed a place in heaven. The religious cassette of the religious awakening becomes her companion. In the religious study circle, she learns about the hell awaiting the *hadathiyat*, the modern corrupted girls, who should be banished from society. But Sara does not hate Satan as respectable Muslim girls are expected to do.

Abdullah, a *mutawwa*, is a repulsive lover and a boring husband. With no alternatives and with burning desires, Sara succumbs to him in bed, only to be revolted by his 'out-of-proportion beard', smell of piety, and manners in bed. On the wedding night, the act of deflowering a virgin, which amounts to rape, turns into a nightmare: 'He started showering me with crazy kisses on my cheeks. He devoured my mouth, chewed my tongue, and ground my teeth against his. His fingers squeeze my apple. My pain reached my neck. He did not leave me until the caller of prayer announced the early morning ritual'.[39]

Abdullah falls ill as a result of being possessed by an infidel *jinn*. His pious sister subjects him to exorcist rituals run by shaykhs who spit on their patients, prepare amulets, and read Quranic verses to drive the *jinn* out. Abdullah is exhausted and demoralised. He loses his sexual potency, and Sara, driven by the power of Satan, jumps on him in bed while he lies half-conscious and subjects him to a violent sexual encounter while he remains passive.

After abandoning a pious life that centred on the trinity of kitchen, prayer mat, and marital bed, Sara drifts into a life of adultery, enjoying sexual encounters at home and abroad. From upper-class drinking parties in Riyadh to London's Hyde Park, Sara is 'born again, breathing the air of freedom'.[40] Tormented by her regression into a life of debauchery, she becomes ill and disturbed. Her eyes sink, and her skin turns pale. Like her husband before her, she is taken to a shaykh to find a cure for her melancholy. The healing turns into a molestation session in which the shaykh mixes spitting, chanting, and physically abusing his patient. Sara does not abandon hope: 'I want to live every minute of my life. I want to love. I want to be admired. I want to travel, read, go to the cinema, live every minute of life, sink in its *halal* and *haram* before it is over'.[41]

She feels that she needs to get rid of the remains of her narrow religious convictions. She swaps her religious cassettes for relaxation tapes, hoping to learn how to unwind and enjoy life. She swaps her high heels for comfortable, sporty trainers to cope with walking the streets of London from Bloomsbury to Edgware Road. Above all, she feels the need for a sophisticated short hairstyle, the ultimate cosmopolitan symbol of liberation, consumer culture, and sophistication. The haircut fits with the new lifestyle of consuming what Western modernity can offer – mainly parties, alcohol, and dancing. Her ignorance of real happiness ends with her 'finger discovering the strawberry . . . I used to exhaust myself so that

---

[39] Warda Abd al-Malik, *al-Awba*, p. 19.
[40] Warda Abd al-Malik, *al-Awba*, p. 65.
[41] Warda Abd al-Malik, *al-Awba*, pp. 65–6.

the sheikh is satisfied ... when he finishes with his dirt, I go to the bath to caress the strawberry. I cry with pleasure, that pleasure that I never experienced with Abdullah on top of me or under me'.[42]

This short novel focuses on the suffering of the body in a disappointing and frustrating marriage, the quest for real pleasures with other men, and opting out from the comfort of the prayer mat. The journey takes the heroine to forbidden territory and prohibited foreign men. But at the end she finds comfort and hope in returning to education after she was denied this opportunity after her early marriage. The novel challenges tradition, which suppresses the personal in the service of the common good. Here we have private pleasures explored in a cosmopolitan context where men and women feel free. The longing for a Western place and context, both seen as liberating, comes through clearly. A sense of liberation is attached to short visits abroad, although the novel also creates islands of freedom inside Saudi Arabia. The text falls into the trap of orientalising the self against deliberate glorification of the freedoms enjoyed by others. Stereotypical images of the other and the self are an inevitable consequence of seeing the world as divided between those who are free and those who are oppressed. Freedom in the West and denial in the East become meaningless polar conditions that the novel fails to explore in a more sophisticated style. However, the novel aims to shock, to convey a sense of sophistication, and to engage in an unfulfilled cosmopolitan fantasy.

### SABA AL-HIRZ: THE BODY AND THE HELL OF OTHERS

Drawing on Jean Paul Sartre's famous expression 'L'enfer c'est les autres', Saba al-Hirz's novel *al-Akharun* (The others)[43] stretches the limits even further when she captures the theme of minority women who are both lesbian and Shia. This blunt double engagement with 'perversion' prompted two Saudi critics to see the novel as expressing private dilemmas rather than Saudi social issues. According to Ahmad al-Wasil, the critics Abdullah al-Ghathami and Muhammad al-Ali both respond to and evaluate the novel from a purely masculinist, patriarchal position: 'They

---

[42] Warda Abd al-Malik, *al-Awba*, pp. 82–3.

[43] Saba al-Hirz, *al-Akharun* [The others], Beirut: Saqi, 2006. The novel was translated into English as *The Others*, New York: Seven Stories Press, 2009. Saudi writer Wajiha al-Howeider was suspected of writing this novel. In an interview, she declined to divulge whether she is the author. However, she admitted that she published a novel under a pen-name in 2006, the year *al-Akharun* appeared in Beirut.

are both unable to surpass their patriarchal cultural tradition, hence they were dismissive of the novel as an exploration of private issues that are not bounded by place or time'.[44] The back cover of the English version promises the reader a serious, sensational, taboo-breaking, and courageous novel. It deals with the ultimate prohibition: lesbian sex among Saudi women. In this endeavour, the taboo is no longer prohibited but represented in fiction, which as usual is taken to represent a window of opportunity to observe real lives, desires, and struggles within a restrictive society.

All we know about the woman using the name Saba al-Hirz is that she was born in the 1970s in Qatif. She initially posted her writings on Internet discussion boards. In 2006, she published her first novel in Beirut.[45] Like other novelists of her generation, she has used new communication technology to open up fresh avenues for exploration and expression. Al-Hirz's story focuses on reality with its truths and diversity. Pretending to be a male homosexual at times, and at others a lesbian, the narrator joins discussion groups, learning from members' private experiences and appropriating them as her own. The Google search engine offers an opportunity to find out more about 'bisexuals' and 'homosexuals'. Such a search gives the heroine headaches, as she encounters opinions that criminalise these sexual acts or make them religiously *haram* (forbidden).[46] She soon discovers that Google may not have the solutions that she seeks, but she continues to explore its pages in search of her real self. It offers her the unique opportunity of addressing a man as *azizi* (dear), a forbidden expression in the reality of her environment. 'Mr Net' is a golden opportunity for women to experience reality. Her constant return to the Internet leads her to the realisation that it breaks the isolation of women, and allows them to meet others and establish networks outside the usual family and kin.

The narrator finally learns how to listen to her own body in a society where young women listen to the preaching of their elders. This body is wrapped in shame and embarrassment; she used to refrain from observing it naked in the mirror. On one occasion, we are told that she comes back from school to find a woman waiting for her. She forces her to open her legs and extracts a piece of her flesh. No explanations are given,

---

44 Ahmad al-Wasil, 'Satair wa aqlam sarikha: takwin al-muthaqafa al-saudiyya wa tahawulataha' [Curtains and sharp pens: Saudi women intellectuals and their changes], *Idhafat*, 7 (2009), p. 102.

45 al-Wasil, 'Satair wa aqlam sarikha', p. 101.

46 Saba al-Hirz, *al-Akharun*, p. 17.

leaving the reader to resort to guesswork. Is this female circumcision? Or is it an act of violence and abuse? Saudi society is not known for the former. The novel's desire to shock leads to absurd incidents that have no meaning and are not put in context. The centrality of the body leads the author into obscure references. Characters are mentioned once and then dropped without any explanation, for example the narrator's father, and the brother who leaves home to go to university.

The narrator finally finds a lesbian lover called Dhay through whom she learns to find pleasure. In the confines of the bedroom, they explore their bodies and identify their pleasures, away from a society that condemns them as sinful. Each encounter is immediately followed by the longing for another. The bedroom scenes become repetitive, culminating in boredom for the narrator. The relationship between Dhay and the narrator ends. The search for an alternative partner yields some results, and the reader is introduced to other girls.

The novel moves between the Husayniyya, where Shia women meet and volunteer for social work, college lecture rooms, and the bedroom, where the forbidden body is explored. The narrator is a voluntary worker at the Husayniyya, where piety and propriety are expected. She initially conforms to the expected role, but in secrecy she ventures into forbidden thoughts and actions. She isolates herself in her bedroom, keeping the door locked, to the annoyance of the mother, who demands that her daughter join her for meals and leave her bedroom door open. When she ventures outside her private universe, she is an active Shia woman who contributes to magazines and distributes forbidden Shia religious literature. While her articles are regularly edited and cut to reflect conformity, the narrator rebels and objects. But in the end, the will of the female editor, who guards tradition and values, triumphs over that of the narrator. In college, distributing Shia literature is punished, especially after sectarian conflicts erupt between the students. Again the Internet allows an escape from the vigilant eyes of the security directors. Despite her engagement with the community, the generation gap is clear. She is not interested in the songs and struggles of a previous Qatifi generation. She finds her entertainment in American music, films, and sport on Aramco's Dhahran Channel. She asserts her individuality against the background of a community engaged in a struggle against its minority status in a country where its identity must remain subdued. The double struggle of the narrator as a lesbian Shia woman is expressed not only against mainstream society but also against her own Shia microcosm. Her battle against both does not leave many options. She is either *tahira* (pure) or *ahira* (a prostitute). Her single self becomes split between the two. The body has its own pleasures, but her self must remain pure. Hypocrisy means that she has to hide the second aspect of herself, the bodily pleasures. Eventually she abandons her charitable voluntary work and her regular contributions to the literary magazine of her community. She cannot be conformist because she is a destroyer of norms and tradition. She finds pleasures in her rebellion and her body. Adventure is sensational and pleasurable.

The novel ends with a sex scene with Omar who falls asleep immediately after the act. They converse in English to refer to 'dirty acts', escaping shame through a linguistic device. The move from homosexuality to bisexuality highlights personal freedom and choices. Surprised at how quickly Omar succumbs to sleep, the heroine muses on a less than satisfactory exploration of sex with men.

*Al-Akharun*'s literary qualities may be rather rudimentary, but the novel remains important for its engagement with religious discrimination and social and religious taboos. Both Shiism and lesbian relations bring out questions about not only minorities but also minorities within minorities in Saudi Arabia. The oppression and controls that are exercised within a minority community, coupled with discrimination from the majority, are important themes highlighted in this novel. Moreover, many liberal Saudi writers consider lesbian relations, which are now openly being discussed in the media, to be a product of religious and social rules that prohibit mixing between the sexes. Those who are in favour of *ikhtilat* in schools and fewer restrictions on male–female encounters in the public sphere consider the 'surge' in lesbian relations a function of strict segregation. In their opinion, this leads girls to gravitate towards other girls in schools and universities, in addition to falling in love with women authority figures such as teachers. On the other hand, Islamist and traditional commentators consider lesbian relations in Saudi Arabia a function of the invasion of 'Western' values that are corrupting Saudis. A new phenomenon known as *boyat* (boys), in which young girls dress in men's clothes, have short hair, and exhibit masculine behaviour, has become a recurrent theme touted as symptomatic of the corruption of the nation and the crisis of the youth under excessive consumption, media, and travel abroad. *Al-Akharun* deals with a number of themes that challenge society, its religious establishment, and political control at a time when many Saudis are searching for answers to the many new behavioural patterns they encounter among the young generation.

NEW WOMEN'S LITERATURE: SUBVERSION OR HEROIC
RESISTANCE?

Assessing the literature of the new generation of women novelists provides
an opportunity to explore the shifting practices and relations of power in
Saudi society.[47] These practices are generated by the state and theorised
by the guardians of religious nationalism. The appearance of this new
literature marks the changing balance of power between the state and the
guardians of religious nationalism in favour of the former. This affects
women in social and cultural contexts that are not always so different
from the traditional contexts of the rest of the Muslim and Arab world.
If there is anything unique about Saudi Arabia, it is the long historical
association between the state and religion to which women have been
central. Throughout the modern history of the nation state, women have
been highlighted as a matter of concern not only for the state but also its
religious guardians. The two worked together to enforce discrimination
that projects the required images and practices of piety and propriety.
While secular Arab nation states have, since the 1950s, espoused women
and their emancipation as legitimate causes under the rhetoric of national
development, the Saudi state declared women in need of protection, welfare, and paternalistic support under the umbrella of Islam. Protecting
women, enforcing their modesty, and guarding their honour were state
projects from 1932. In recent years, emancipating women, developing
them, and promoting them are themes that have replaced the old fixation with the protection, piety, and honour of women. This concern
over women was shared with other states in the region, but Saudi Arabia
remained within the fold of religious nationalism, unable to free itself
from its requirements.

However, it is in the political context after 9/11 that a weakening of
the principles of religious nationalism has been deemed necessary to save
the regime and improve its image. It is at this specific historical moment
that the state switched from its traditional vision to one that specifically highlights the cosmopolitan woman and her contribution to culture,

---

[47] Lila Abu-Lughod warns against romanticising women's resistance expressed in subversive acts, gossip, words, and songs. She argues that this resistance should be seen as
diagnostic of power: see Lila Abu-Lughod, 'The Romance of Resistance: Tracing Transformations of Power through Bedouin Women', *American Ethnologist*, 17, 1 (1990),
pp. 41–55. For an evaluation of scholarly work on resistance, see Sherry Ortner, 'Resistance and the Problem of Ethnographic Refusal', *Comparative Studies in Society and
History*, 37, 1 (1995), pp. 173–93.

society, and the economy. Together with a new generation of women entrepreneurs, the promotion of Saudi women novelists during the last decade is a product of this shift in state strategies. Moreover, serious economic measures such as restructuring, privatisation, and liberalisation, and pervasive consumption, advertising, and media expansion all led to the increased incorporation of Saudi women in global markets of commerce and publication. While Saudi Arabia's men had already been drawn into this global market since the discovery of oil in the 1930s, the new economic changes that were introduced in the late 1990s began to have a dramatic impact on society, urban space, gender relations, and many aspects of social and political life. Violent religious and political trends consolidated their efforts to thwart the Saudi *infitah* (openness), which brought about dramatic change at the level of the individual, family, and society. Highly educated and well-connected young novelists challenged the image of Saudi Arabia as a hotbed of religious radicalism. Their novels dismiss myths about piety and highlight the quest for the cosmopolitan fantasy that had been nourished by the state and the conditions of the new economy with its excessive consumption and media activities. Women's literature with its recurrent focus on sexual themes, the struggle of the body, and confrontation with the religious guardians of the Islamic tradition and society reflects the new restructuring of power relations in Saudi society. The state with its new modern development discourse, and society's immersion in the forces of the new consumption economy that fetishises desire, pleasure, and sexuality, are the new context.

If resistance is narrowly defined as actions that challenge or subvert unequal power relations, then the new literature is neither subversion nor heroic resistance. But if one adopts a wider definition of resistance to include subtle utterances, practices, silences, gestures, and rituals, then the new Saudi novel is without doubt a textual critique of society and religion, with the state remaining beyond criticism. Young women novelists promote individualism at the expense of communal and collective solidarities, identities, and restrictive norms. They celebrate choice rather than conformity. But they remain avid supporters of the regime and unable to see that their exclusion is partly a function of political decisions and partly a function of the political paying lip service to religion. One of the most daring novelists discussed in this chapter, Samar al-Moqrin, launched an attack on those 'Saudi liberals who criticised the King's decision to reward the religious establishment for prohibiting demonstrations on 11 March 2011. The religious establishment deserves to be strengthened and rewarded for its position in support of the ruling family and protecting the country from dissent'.[48] Her frustration with Saudi liberal men, described as hypocritical, pushes her towards endorsing some of the most conservative interpreters of Islam, who have deprived her of basic human rights.

The novels are literary discourses that reflect the new relations of power between state and market on the one hand, and state and religious circles on the other. They demonstrate the power of the state in dictating the new change in gender policy at the expense of that of the religious scholars. Women novelists are not engaged in heroic acts of rebellion, as claimed by the media advertising these novels, or even researchers who have dealt with similar issues in other Muslim countries.[49] The new Saudi novelists celebrate and endorse the powers that both the state and the new economy exert on them, rather than resisting them. Like the state, they consider the guardians of religious nationalism as obstacles to fully engaging with the opportunities that the new state/market offer in terms of cosmopolitan fantasies. This position, which many women have taken in the last decade, is easily reversed, as the position of Samar al-Moqrin in supporting the religious establishment demonstrates. This means that these women novelists are more likely to follow the state's agenda rather than their own. Moreover, their novels express a disappointment with men as fathers, brothers, husbands, and lovers who fail to live up to the expectation of the cosmopolitan fantasy. The disappointment leads some novelists to explore the true meaning of passion, love, and understanding with other women, thus undermining the myths about Saudi men and their potency, in addition to exposing their hypocrisy.

For a long time, the state, the market, and religious nationalism have privileged men over women. State bureaucracy, surveillance, and resources allow greater sex segregation, leading to strict divisions between men and women, controlling the marriage choices of both but empowering men over women. Men regulate women's entry into the public sphere and their access to government bureaucracy and new benefits. In addition to state bureaucracy, extreme wealth has led to differential access to traditional support networks. This exaggerates economic inequality between

---

[48] Samar al-Moqrin, 'al-Libiraliyun yakhlutun al-habil bi al-nabil' [Liberals are confused], al-Wiam electronic newspaper, 30 March 2011, available at http://alweeam.com/2011/03/30/%D8%B3...7%D8%A8%D9%84/.

[49] For example, Pardis Mahdavi argues that young Iranians use sex as freedom and rebellion. This approach fails to see the wider context in which both the state and the market make sex appear as an act of rebellion whereas in fact it is nothing but an endorsement of the economy of desires. See Mahdavi, *Passionate Uprisings*.

men and women of the same family. Women novelists capture the new power relations between the genders; their work reflects a quest to be at the centre of the new cosmopolitan fantasies. The newly established shopping centre becomes an arena where groups of young men assert their power through simply roaming, driving, and flirting with women. On the other hand, young Saudi women resort to a sexualised femininity to lure and control men.[50] Both the state and the religious police strive to control these new spaces.

Grounded in an analysis of the power of the state, market, and religion, this chapter has shown how this gender contest, which is above all played out under state control, unfolds in contemporary Saudi women's literature and society. The sexualised femininity that is fetishised in the new consumer economy has infiltrated literature, as this chapter has demonstrated. Resistance through either violent or non-violent action may be too narrow to explain the new phenomenon of Saudi 'Chick Lit'. It is perhaps better to imagine a continuum of resistance. Saudi women are stretching the boundaries with their words and deeds, partly in response to state and market forces and partly in response to their quest for freedom, individuality, and choice, all a product of the country's immersion in late modernity.

---

[50] In this respect, Saudi women share the obsession with sexualised femininity of their counterparts among Awlad Ali, studied by Lila Abu-Lughod. See Abu-Lughod, 'The Romance of Resistance'.

# 7

## Guarding Self and Nation

*Women Preachers and Activists*

The editor of the newspaper addressed me, 'Hello Nura "al-Zarqawi"'. I replied, 'Hello Turki "Bush"'.

Nura al-Saad, 12 October 2008

Mass education allowed women to develop their own voices even at times of economic marginality and low contribution to the labour force. The *muthaqafa* and later the celebrity novelist were products of rapid expansion in education that was not matched by greater participation in the labour force. This chapter explores another product of the same education system: the newly religiously educated *multazimat*, women who are committed to the Islamic tradition on the basis of which they offer Islamic solutions to everyday challenges and interpretations of current affairs. The institutionalisation of religious education and knowledge since the 1960s and later higher education in the 1970s, combined with training in the natural sciences, social sciences, and the humanities at universities and colleges, resulted in many women assuming the role of guardians of the religious nation and defenders of the Islamic tradition. In their writings and practices, they offer an alternative to the messages of the women discussed in the previous chapters. These religiously committed women work in the new educational institutions and media spaces made available to Saudi women since the 1980s. The religious literacy that dominates even the most secular subjects has led to women assuming new roles in defending the most important incubators of the religious nation, namely the family, genealogy, and domesticity. While education in general may lead to criticising and changing religious knowledge, in Saudi Arabia the ideological religious education was meant to preserve the status quo rather than challenge it. This education was an embodiment of the tenets of religious nationalism with its emphasis on purity, boundaries, authenticity, and the preservation of gender roles. This is reflected in the position that a number of women preachers and Islamic activists adopt vis-à-vis personal development, the new global discourse on gender equality, and the Islamic tradition. These women find new opportunities to assert themselves and their world view in the educational spaces of the country as subordinate voices to men. Many women defend male supremacy, seek men's protection, and support the discriminatory and exclusionary measures that their sisters mentioned in the previous chapters fight to abolish. Any social and gender change, especially that promoted by international and global forums, is seen as a Western conspiracy against Muslims. More importantly, change is considered a human intervention in a divine design for the universe. In exploring these views, this chapter shows that women are often motivated by their concern over their own personal interests rather than simply by a radical Islamic orientation. In a society where male supremacy flourishes unchallenged under a masculine state, some women may seem to have no option but to defend their Islamically guaranteed rights to be protected and supported by men. Whenever they gain access to the public sphere, they unexpectedly use it to assert and defend the institutions and values that contribute to maintaining the supremacy of men over women.

One new public arena is the lecture halls of Saudi universities, where a new generation of *multazimat* is produced. An example of this is a recent lecture given by a group of specialists in Commanding Right and Forbidding Wrong, commonly referred to as *hisba*, delivered to girls at King Saud University in Riyadh. Dr Sulayman al-Eid, holder of King Abdullah Academic Chair for *hisba* (at King Saud University), Dr Abd al-Mohsin al-Qafari, spokesman of the Directorate of the Committee for Commanding Right and Forbidding Wrong, and Shaykh Bandar al-Mutairi, director of the Riyadh branch of the Committee for the Promotion of Commanding Right and Forbidding Wrong (commonly known as *haiya*), beamed their presentations on the meaning of *hisba* to the two girls' campuses in Alysha and al-Malaz.[1] The audience, a combination of women academics and students, gathered to listen to the latest opinions on the 'science' of *hisba*.

---

[1] The girls' university campus was built in al-Malaz, a modern neighbourhood developed since the 1960s, with Mediterranean-style villas, away from the traditional quarters of Riyadh. For further details on the urban development of this area, see George Glasze, 'Gated Housing Estates in the Arab World: Case Studies in Lebanon and Riyadh, Saudi Arabia', *Environment and Planning: Planning and Design*, 29 (2002), pp. 321–36.

After the presentations, the audience was given a chance to ask questions and hear answers from the three specialists. The fact that such a forum took place within an academic institution rather than a centre for *dawa* conferred on the meeting an aura of 'scientific' and objective legitimacy. The *hisba* chair was established at an academic higher education institution to 'modernise' both perceptions and practices of *hisba*, following the criticism of this institution in the post-9/11 period. Those who lecture on the topic are known as *al-shaykh al-doctor* (doctor shaykh). Teaching, researching, and innovating *hisba* perceptions and practices were deemed important in the process of reaching the moderate Islam propagated by the king as part of his social and religious reform package. The science of *hisba* is researched and taught at a university dedicated to other academic subjects in addition to religious studies.

The topic proved to be extremely popular among both students and their lecturers, mostly from the faculty of religious studies, but the audience also attracted students from other academic departments in the university. Dr Shafaqa al-Utaibi, an academic in the religious education department who presided over the women's audience hall, counted more than 100 questions that the girls wanted to ask. She informed the press that most of the girls supported the work of *haiya* and its men. They endorsed the view that *haiya* protects society from negative impulses. She criticised those who undermine the good work of *haiya*. The girls, she said, demand that *haiya* expand its activities and surveillance in shopping centres and public places. Another academic, Dr Risha al-Assiri, demanded that *haiya* establish a strong presence at airports to protect women from harassment. More importantly, she requested that it open offices on the girls' university campus to control 'alien behaviour in our conservative society'. In order to ensure maximum control, social worker Badriyyah al-Fawzan strongly suggested that women should be employed as *muhtasibat* (vigilantes). Women graduates in religious studies and jurisprudence are in a better position to play the role. Both educationists and sociologists are well suited to advise girls and eliminate perversions such as the phenomenon of *boyat* (girls dressing and behaving like boys), *mustarjilat* (masculine women), and *mutaharishat* (women who sexually harass other women), and those who wear inappropriate clothes. Students enquired about why certain large shopping centres do not have *hisba* men, saying that these men should be granted access to control the illicit behaviour that has become so common in Riyadh's most prestigious shopping malls. Girls in the audience complained about why Shaykh Ghamdi, discussed in Chapter 4, was not sacked following his strange *fatwa* that depicted *ikhtilat* as licit, even after the *ulama* agreed that it is prohibited. The female audience criticised those who undermine the *haiya* and its brave men, a reference to 'liberal women and men' who are the enemies of religious scholars and *hisba*.

The three male speakers answered all questions while praising Saudi women for being *multazimat*, committed to religion and its teachings. They concluded that 'our women have defended *wali al-amr* [the ruler], the *ulama*, and the *hisba* men. They are aware of the floods of globalisation and prepared to resist them. Their input will no doubt improve the *haiya*'s performance and training'. They asked the girls to keep in touch with *haiya* officers to inform them about any deviations and perversions, as 'our society has its own exceptionalism'. They then passed on the telephone numbers of several *haiya* hotlines for future communication and reminded the audience of other means such as the Internet, and special *haiya* email addresses to reach the offices and report perversions.[2] Among the many women attending the lecture, a few aspire to become *nashitat islamiyat* (Islamic activists) and *muhtasibat* (vigilantes).

Within days of reports on the *hisba* lecture, Saudi liberal women, including several novelists discussed in the previous chapters, denounced those 'radical' women who not only enjoy their oppression but demand the expansion of the regime of control and surveillance to spaces currently outside the reach of the *hisba* men. Calling for restricting the work of the Committee, writing in the local press to highlight its excessive surveillance, dramatising in literature its intrusion in people's lives, and even demanding the termination of its role, many liberal Saudi women writers and activists could not understand how other women can be accomplices in promoting and supporting an institution whose main aim is to control men and women. What was more shocking, according to one woman, was the unexpected support for *hisba* coming from the floor of a university seen by many as an island of moderation in a sea of radicalism. One lamented that if this is the opinion of students at King Saud University and their teachers, what should we expect from women graduates of the religious university in Riyadh, known as the Imam University?

The King Saud University lecture on *hisba* is one example of new spaces of modernity that have emerged in contemporary Saudi Arabia whereby male religious studies lecturers and practitioners of *hisba* address women with the objective of enlisting them as Islamic activists. In the modern surrounding of the university, the lecture confirms the superiority of men over female audiences. Religious activist women can only hope to play

---

[2] The Saudi press reported on the lecture, but the most detailed account remains in the electronic newspaper *Sabaq*, 27 April 2010, available at http://sabaq.org.

an auxiliary role enforcing the rulings of religious men. Women aspire to extend men's control in areas where they cannot reach. Many new women seek this role, and volunteer to practise *hisba* over other women.

These new committed women cannot in any way become a religious authority over men, initiating public Islamic discourse or practising *hisba* over them. Gender dominance, articulated in the principle of *qawama*, the dominance of men over women, is upheld in the public sphere, official Internet religious websites, and in regular rituals such as prayers and pilgrimage, not to mention the private domain. Female Islamic activists and preachers are excluded as potential Islamic educators in contexts where both men and women are potential audiences. Female preachers enter the public sphere only as women preaching to other women, thus creating a parallel yet structurally inferior space for women in order to preserve overall male dominance. Women activists' texts, often articles and short essays, are grouped together under sections entitled 'for women' in many religious websites. Women active in defining and redefining women's piety, rituals, role, and place in society on the basis of their own reading and interpretation of the religious texts enter the field with complete acceptance of their own subordination. They complement the role of men as preachers but can never replace them. Their words are meant to be consumed by women only. Before exploring the messages of activist women, it is important to sketch the educational journey that has made their appearance possible in the last three decades.

## THE EDUCATION OF THE NEW RELIGIOUS WOMEN

The first women's higher education college (the Riyadh College of Education) opened in Riyadh in 1970, a decade after the first girls' school was established. The purpose was to produce Saudi women teachers in all subjects to replace other Arab teachers. Furthermore, the mission of the college was to 'train girls to be good Muslims, successful housekeepers, ideal wives, good mothers, and highly qualified scholars'.[3] Colleges of education appeared in Jeddah in 1974, Mecca in 1975, and Medina, Burayda, and Abha in 1981. There were also colleges of social work, arts, and sciences in Dammam and Riyadh.[4] Although these colleges succeeded in partially replacing Arab women teachers in girls' schools,

---

[3] Ibtisam al-Bassam, 'Institutions of Higher Education for Women in Saudi Arabia', *International Journal of Educational Development*, 4, 3 (1984), p. 256.

[4] al-Bassam, 'Institutions of Higher Education for Women', p. 256.

their performance and the quality of the training women received had mixed success. Assessing these colleges more than a decade after their opening, al-Bassam argued that the colleges should not be subject to further expansion as the needs of the existing colleges had not been met. The quality of education offered to girls tended to be of low quality. The colleges faced a shortage of qualified staff, and occupied buildings with insufficient space and facilities.[5]

For women college graduates, finding employment in the expanding education system became difficult. In the 1980s, many women with this training replaced the Arab teachers who had delivered the Saudi religious education curriculum for several decades. But it seems that the Saudi market for religious education has become saturated in recent years. Many graduates of the old women's colleges find themselves without jobs even fifteen years after graduation. Women's colleges became less prestigious after the expansion of female university education. College graduates remained on the margin of employment, and in 2008 a group of such graduates pressed for jobs with the Ministry of Education. Their case attracted attention and the king ordered that they should be immediately given jobs in schools. The private sector remains closed to female college graduates; a small minority among them may find work or volunteer in women's branches of religious charities.

The expansion of university education for girls began to supplement the opportunities offered by the colleges of education. Since the 1970s, the main universities in Riyadh and Jeddah opened new women's campuses. These offered limited subjects for girls, with the main focus on social sciences, humanities, and arts subjects. Religious universities in Riyadh, Mecca, and Medina followed suit and opened women's campuses.[6] By 2011, Saudi Arabia had several religious universities with women's campuses. The Imam Muhammad ibn Saud University in Riyadh with branches in Qasim, the Medina Islamic University, and the Omm al-Qura University in Mecca are the most well-known higher education centres that specialise in religious studies for both men and women. This expansion has meant that women have greater opportunities to acquire religious knowledge. While previously Saudi Arabia relied on Arab women to teach its religious curriculum at schools, it was expected that the new religious

---

[5] al-Bassam, 'Institutions of Higher Education for Women', p. 258.

[6] Princess Nura bint Abd al-Rahman University, established in 2008, does not have a faculty for religious studies, although religious lessons are part of the curriculum. See Ministry of Higher Education, *University Education for Saudi Women*, Riyadh, n.d. (leaflet).

universities would produce Saudi advanced religious studies specialists who can teach at both school and university levels.

Together with the colleges of education, the religious universities offered multiple educational and career opportunities for women from different social, economic, and tribal backgrounds. The settled populations of the cities where universities were established were the first to enrol their daughters. Later, with the increase in rural–urban migration, newly settled rural immigrants in Riyadh, Jeddah, Mecca, and Medina sent their girls to religious universities. Many women graduates became religious studies schoolteachers, university lecturers, counsellors, administrators, and social workers.

Although Islamic education is an integral part of education in schools and universities in general – it amounts to thirty per cent of teaching time in elementary schools and twenty-four per cent at intermediate level[7] – the entry of girls into the religious education departments in universities began to produce specialists in Quranic interpretation, jurisprudence, creed, *hadith*, and other religious subjects taught in greater depth among the new recruits. After relying mainly on Egyptian women teachers since the 1960s for teaching Islamic studies, from the 1980s onward Saudi Arabia had its own local women religious lecturers who could teach at university level. The religious teacher of the college and the lecturer at the university replaced the informal *faqiha* and *alima* and their study circle, mentioned earlier in this book.

College and university graduates of the religious faculties had different experiences as teachers. These women face many challenges in their daily lives, according to a recent study that explores their roles in a changing society.[8] Most women choose to become religious teachers because of fate, a desire to accumulate religious deeds, and making a difference to society, according to a sample of religious studies teachers. They try to establish discipline, which they describe as a struggle against unpredictable forces. They face the challenge of increasing Islamic knowledge, correcting misguided behaviour, persuading students about their own religion, and keeping up with student debates.[9] Those who choose to take their religious knowledge outside the classroom become preachers. While religious studies encompasses specialisation in many

[7] Michaela Prokop, 'The War of Ideas: Education in Saudi Arabia', in Aarts and Nonneman (eds.), *Saudi Arabia in the Balance*, pp. 57–81.

[8] Munira Jamjum, 'Female Islamic Studies Teachers in Saudi Arabia: A Phenomenological Study', *Teaching and Teacher Education*, 26 (2010), pp. 547–58.

[9] Jamjum, 'Female Islamic Studies Teachers', pp. 552–6.

sub-branches of religious education, it is important to emphasise that these teachers are the first source of knowledge that girls encounter to formally learn Islamic rituals, doctrine, Quranic and *hadith* recitations and interpretations. Around the age of eleven, pupils are introduced to Islamic knowledge about the body, puberty, fluids (urine, semen, blood, discharge), purity and pollution, ablution, the veil, Islamic sexuality, birth and breastfeeding, and many other topics that are often taught to girls within biology lessons or sex education in other countries. While this knowledge is acquired at school, many preachers propagate it to adult women who missed out on education or need to be reminded in old age. In social informal contexts, female preachers volunteer Islamic views on these matters and offer advice to less-informed women. My encounters with some religious studies graduates reveal that they maintain a religious world view in their daily lives, enforcing the Islamic awareness of their children, reminding them of the importance of religious rituals, and developing an Islamic identity among them.

NEW RELIGIOUS WOMEN

Since the 1990s, new terminology has begun to appear to refer to women whose education in religious studies and later work in related fields reflect a commitment to Islam and an awareness of this commitment. One can say that women in Saudi Arabia are religious in the sense that they adopt Islam as a religious, moral, and behavioural framework, but not all women articulate this commitment and express it in their work and personal lives. The new religious women are known by a generic name (*multazimat*) or specific labels such as *nashitat islamiyat*, a specific category that includes the performance of diverse but interrelated personal and communal activities. At the lower end of the religious ranking system, women preachers (*daiyat*) and defenders of the principle of commanding right and forbidding wrong (*muhtasibat*) are now common 'labels' given to women whose world view is defined by Islam and its teachings.[10] These women are transmitters of religious knowledge produced by male figures, but their activism is performed among other women. Women who are known by these labels are female equivalents of the male *daiya* (preacher), *nashit* (activist), and *mutawwa* (old-fashioned name for preacher or

---

[10] On the emergence of the new religiosity among Saudi women, see Amelie Le Renard, 'Droits de la femme et développement personnel: les appropriations du religieux par les femmes en Arabie Saoudite', *Critique Internationale*, 46 (2010), pp. 67–86.

religious scholar). They have in common with men the defence of Islamic principles, especially those relating to women, in addition to offering an Islamic perspective on aspects of private and public life.

After acquiring a doctorate in Islamic studies or other subjects, a woman may be elevated to a higher intellectual rank, one that allows her own Islamic opinions to reach men, albeit indirectly through the medium of publications or voice in forums and media spaces. More recently, and in the context of the National Dialogue Forums[11] that started in 2003, many women Islamist activists addressed men via microphones during the meetings, seated in a separate area of the conference hall. Together with liberal women, they offered their opinions on the topics of the conferences (radicalisation, youth and women's unemployment, and religious tolerance). Female lecturers and activists presented research papers on the various topics discussed in these forums. Outside the state-initiated forums it is, however, still unusual for female activists to be invited to address all-male audiences. Since 2000, with the proliferation of independent Islamist satellite television channels such as Iqra, al-Majd, and al-Dalil, Saudi Islamist women academics have been invited to call during discussion programmes and offer their views on matters related to women, for example driving and mixing between the sexes at school and work. In most cases, these women confront 'liberal' guests and denounce their points of view. They reject their opinions and criticise the Westernisation of women.[12] Women activists reprimand men for discussing issues relevant to women. The new Saudi religious media have so far not allowed women to lead religious programmes or appear on the screen. State television, however, hosts both women who are completely veiled and others who leave their faces exposed. They are shown on television with male presenters and discussants. Like the independent religious media, official television channels do not allow women to lead discussion in religious programmes such as the famous *fatwa* television series.

Female religious activists are concerned with society, its piety, and commitment to Islamic principles and practices. A reading of their many

---

[11] See Madawi Al-Rasheed, *Contesting the Saudi State: Islamic Voices from a New Generation*, Cambridge: Cambridge University Press, 2007, p. 54.

[12] The topic of the Westernisation of Saudi women is predominant among Islamists and their writings. Recently a Ph.D. thesis of 750 pages was submitted to al-Azhar on the subject. A summary of the findings of this research project was published. See Abd al-Aziz al-Badah, *Harakat al-taghrib fi al-saudiyya: taghrib al-mara'a inmuthajan* [Westernisation in Saudi Arabia: A case study of women], Riyadh: Silsilat Markaz al-Dirasat al-Insaniyya, 2010.

publications, web pages, and interviews in the press reveals that their main worry is the increasing Westernisation of Saudi society, excessive consumption, spinsterhood, high divorce rates, smoking, drug addiction, and perverse sexuality. In their Islamic discourse, propagated in *dawa* forums, lectures, the media, petitions, and personal web pages, they see themselves as central figures guarding against the loss of tradition, piety, and morality. Many men and women in Saudi society see the new religious women as an Islamic alternative to the liberal intellectuals and novelists.

Combining a degree in religious studies with training in secular subjects such as the sciences, arts, and humanities widens job opportunities while the person remains anchored in Islamic studies. A small minority of *nashitat* specialise in non-religious subjects, but they always have grounding in Islamic discourse and debates acquired through attending special religious seminars, courses, and informal religious gatherings. The women attending the *hisba* lecture at King Saudi University in Riyadh would seek new employment opportunities after graduation. *Haiya* institutions are but one such opportunity. A job in such an institution offers a salary, recognition, moral prestige, and good religious deeds. Students listening to the *hisba* lecturers clearly were demanding employment in its various branches. Unemployed women may become self-appointed preachers while aspiring to be attached to the many state religious institutions. Women with higher degrees and eminence become active members in the Saudi Society for Call Studies (*dawa*), the Saudi Scientific Society for the Tradition of the Prophet, the Saudi Society for Education and Psychology, and many other forums that have sprung up around the mushrooming state religious bureaucracy and welfare services.

While a few Saudi women respond to the subordination of women through literature condemning society's strict norms and radical religious opinions, it seems that other women carve a space for themselves through an assertion of religious tradition and their central role in upholding Islamic principles. Novelists criticise traditional society, celebrate a cosmopolitan fantasy, and represent women as sexual agents. In contrast, Islamist activists not only reiterate old religious treatises on women, propagated by both previous and contemporary *ulama*, but sometimes stretch the boundaries of Islamic teachings to respond to the challenges of modernity. Like novelists, they seek inclusion within modernity's expanding horizons as guardians of a noble past, advisers on social and psychological problems, and participants in religious forums that require women's input on specific issues relevant to their lives. The Islamic past remains a source of inspiration for developing new interpretations suitable for the conditions of modernity and its challenges. Women novelists appeal to a globalised discourse on gender discrimination, international treaties on gender equality, and more general human rights conventions. Islamic activists resort to Islamic discourse in which they find solutions to gender issues such as gender discrimination, inheritance, marriage, divorce, and employment. They denounce international conventions and treaties on gender equality, and dismiss them as a Western conspiracy against Muslim women. They conduct a war against Saudi women whom they consider agents of the West, for example those calling for driving and mixing between the sexes.

Female Islamist activists see themselves as pillars of religious nationalism, guarding the chastity of the nation and its children. Combining family obligations and work, they conform to Islamic piety and practice, and bring up the ideal Islamic *usra* (nuclear family). Psychologists among them offer counselling, and advise on child development, adolescent problems, marriage, and divorce, all anchored in Islamic solutions – although the inspiration may derive from Western psychology manuals and training. Educationists offer opinions on how to implant Islamic education and world view among the youth. Sociologists propose solutions to society's ills such as antisocial behaviour, perversions, divorce, suicide, alcoholism, drug addiction, and subversive media. In general, activists specialise in Islamising secular knowledge in education, psychology, and sociology. They offer Islamic interpretations and solutions to the many problems in Saudi society.

In an urban environment such as contemporary Saudi Arabia, the majority of women are atomised in small households away from the extended network of support and surveillance traditionally practised by large families, clans, and tribes. It is estimated that approximately eighty per cent of Saudis live in major cities such as Riyadh, Jeddah, Mecca, and Medina. In 2011, thirty-three per cent of Saudis lived in apartments, twenty-five per cent in villas, and twenty-eight per cent in traditional houses. The average family size was five or six in one unit.[13] This clearly indicates that nuclear families (*usra*) are now the dominant mode in contemporary urban Saudi society. Only extremely wealthy families live in gated compounds that consist of multiple villas for extended families.[14]

[13] John Sfakianakis, *Under Construction: Saudi Steps up Efforts to Meet Home Loan Demand*, Economics Report, Riyadh: Banque Saudi Faransi, 20 March 2011 (electronic publication).
[14] On wealthy Saudi gated compounds, see Glasze, 'Gated Housing Estates'.

Moreover, women now routinely move away from their native cities after marriage. Teachers are often posted to distant villages and towns, while husbands accept job offers away from their kin. Since the 1950s, the high level of rural–urban migration has created urban communities that are detached from the intimacy and surveillance of old traditional extended families and neighbourhoods.

Female Islamist activists provide an arena in which traditional values are maintained in this sprawling urban environment, which is slowly beginning to allow people to drift away from the close family networks and the supervision they had historically been able to exercise in small rural communities. The majority of women are now urban dwellers, and in addition to irregular visiting patterns, they socialise in new spaces such as the shopping centre, the cafe, work, and educational institutions. Young women regularly go to school, university, work, and shops in spaces that are no longer controlled by family members but by state agencies such as the police, *hisba* staff, and other men. In the public sphere, women mix with other women and men who are total strangers. The new Islamist activists are replacing the traditional system of knowledge, control, support, and surveillance in the new urban spaces of large Saudi cities. The shift to urban living led many women to seek instruction and monitoring of their own behaviour and that of men in the public sphere. Both low-ranking *daiyat* and *muhtasibat* are a new modern urban phenomenon, a product of the expansion of mass education, employment, and the increasing urbanisation of Saudi society.

The first generation of female Islamist activists are descendants of well-known religious families. Male members of these families have been active in the religious field as judges, lecturers in Islamic studies, administrators in state religious institutions (education, jurisprudence, pilgrimage, media, *dawa* [call]), school and university teachers, and low-ranking mosque *imams* and *mutawwas*. But with the expansion of religious education and mass schooling since the 1960s, women preachers and activists are now a large category that goes beyond the old religious families to include new urbanites. Hijazi, Najdi, and Assiri women preachers and activists are present in the major cities of Riyadh, Jeddah, Mecca, Medina, Dammam, Burayda, and Unayza. While some are still members of the old religious families (e.g. al-Sheikh, al-Jurays, al-Saad, and Nassif), there are newcomers to the field drawn from tribal groups such as the Otaybi, Harthi, Qahtani, Assiri, and Harbi.

While there are full-time female activists, many women combine their roles as religious teachers and lecturers with preaching in formal and informal centres and forums. They also combine these activities with membership in the religious societies mentioned earlier. Those who teach at universities are often essayists and columnists in the local press and active permanent members of religious bureaucracies. Religious activism and preaching can take place in adult literacy centres and charities where women learn basic literacy and other skills.

Since 2000, many preachers and activists have set up their own web pages, either attached to mainstream male-administered religious web-site pages or independent of such outlets. One official religious site dedicates one page to women preachers, listing their names, biographies, and articles.[15] Women's articles are also posted on the web pages of important shaykhs, usually under the subsection 'women's issues'. Many such women are active in signing petitions addressed to the leadership in which they express their concern over the prospect of abolishing the male guardianship system, lifting the ban on driving, or mixing between the sexes in education and at work. Several Islamist women's petitions circulated on special websites denouncing so-called liberal proposals calling for change in gender policy, the expansion of women's employment in mixed settings, the lifting of the ban on driving, and the abolition of the guardianship system.

Female activists consider change in gender relations and the role of women as a form of interference in God's plan for the universe and Saudi Arabia's special commitment to Islam. Change can only mean a threat to religious nationalism, the disintegration of the nation, and its defeat by its enemies. Enemies are believed to enter and thwart the religious nation through its weakest link, mainly women and young, impressionistic men. According to many female activists, women are particularly vulnerable to Western pressures, which provide so many temptations. Many women believe in this discourse, as they continue to consider themselves weak and dependent on men for their survival. However, the theme of a Western conspiracy against Muslim women that dominates essays, preaching, and everyday conversation cannot be the only reason behind women's endorsement of existing restrictions that affect them directly and prevent them from enjoying freedom of movement or work with men in mixed surroundings. Many women cherish the fact that they are not in charge of the economic maintenance of the family, a right protected in Islam. In return for men's financial support, they willingly provide a comfortable home and bring up children without challenging the traditional roles expected of them.

---

[15] Saaid al-Fawaid, 'Multaqa al-daiyat', available at http://saaid.net/daeyat/index.htm.

The debate on lifting the guardianship system whereby men remain in control of women's legal *persona* exemplifies the position of many Saudi women. Many Islamist activists signed a petition after liberal women started a campaign to lift the guardianship system, following an important Human Rights Watch report.[16] To highlight their opposition, a group of female Islamist activists established an Internet campaign with the slogan 'My Guardian Knows Better What Is Good for Me' to counter the campaign against the guardianship system. Rawdah al-Yusif, a social worker, initiated the campaign, which attracted hundreds of followers, who denounced the Westernised women behind the initial campaign to abolish the guardianship system. Many preachers and Islamist activists do not want to lose what they regard as the protection – rather than control – exercised by men over women. The fact that the system is anchored in an Islamic tradition makes its benefits to men and women self-explanatory. The view from the other side is obviously different. It is not only liberal women who object to the system: a small number of Islamist activists who are developing new religious interpretations to restrict the pervasiveness of the guardianship rules have expressed concern over its abuse by men, resulting in many women not enjoying their true Islamic rights. Suhayla Zayn al-Abdin, an Islamist who has published several books on women's rights in Islam and criticised official Wahhabi religious restrictions on women, lamented that 'even at age sixty, a Saudi woman is considered a minor'.[17] Among Islamist women, al-Abdin offers a modern interpretation of religious texts dealing with women and does not shy away from criticising the official religious views initiated by the religious establishment. She is, however, one Islamist voice among many others who do not share her convictions.

## DIVERSITY AMONG FEMALE ACTIVISTS

### Traditional Salafi *Daiyat*

Traditional female Salafi preachers are known as *daiyat*. These preachers focus on *ibadat* (the rituals of worship), purity, and pollution (under topics that are commonly known as *haydh wa nafas* [menstruation and birth]), marriage stability, women and media, veiling, non-mixing, and other

---

[16] Human Rights Watch, *Perpetual Minors*.
[17] Suhayla Zayn al-Abdin, 'al-Mara al-saudiyya qasir wa law balaghat situn aman' [A Saudi woman is a minor even at the age of sixty], al-Arabiyya, available at http://www.alarabiya.net/save_print.php?print=1&cont_id=1102632, June 2010.

deeds that bring women closer to God and in conformity with Islamic teachings. The majority of *daiyat* do not deal with the general human and civil rights of women. Rather, they focus on women's duties towards husbands, parents, children, and family, in addition to the Islamic tradition of worship. Good Islamic conduct and the performance of regular rituals and the duties of motherhood are main responsibilities. Accepting polygamy, male guardianship, and the ban on mixing and driving are but a few examples of what they endorse as reflecting Islamic principles. When these preachers are invited to preach at women's gatherings, they often tend to focus on the minute details of women's responsibilities towards their husbands, and the husbands' rights over their wives. According to an informant, a preacher was invited to a funeral in order to help the women gathering for *taziyya* (mourning) cope with grief and sorrow. Instead of fulfilling this function, she launched into a monologue about how to please husbands and fulfil their desires according to Islamic teachings. The mourners were extremely surprised and upset. Many *daiyat* promote polygamy as a remedy for spinsterhood, and encourage young girls to accept old married or divorced men as suitors. It is well known that some may act as *khataba*s (matchmakers), and use their access to the women's world and knowledge of families and their daughters to find suitable brides for male clients.

*Daiyat* endorse the official religious interpretations of the mufti and the Higher Council of Ulama. Unless the Council changes its *fatwa*s in areas relevant to women, these traditional Salafi preachers will continue to endorse male opinions on matters that touch their lives. They accept the official view, and never demand any rights other than those allowed by the religious establishment and the state.

While the majority of preachers lack the skills to contribute articles or essays to magazines and web-based sources, there is now a growing number of women who are capable of such tasks. Their opinions on women's issues are often part of the women's sections of official religious propaganda and websites.[18] Their articles are posted on the official Salafi web pages of important *ulama*, for example Saaid al-Fawaid, a directory of recognised official male scholars that propagate the views of traditional *ulama* such as Abd al-Aziz Ibn Baz, Muhammad al-Uthaymin, Abdullah al-Jibrin, and many others. Female preachers who are trusted to endorse official messages and never question rulings on women are listed under the *daiyat* forum. This includes the names of important, well-known celebrity

[18] See http://saaid.net/daeyat/index.htm.

preachers/writers such as Juwahir al-Sheikh,[19] Omayma al-Jalahima,[20] and Ruqayya al-Muharib.[21] In 2011, Saaid al-Fawaid listed more than thirty *daiyat*, with each one having her own web page accessible with a click on the name. These tend to be higher in status than the preachers who are called upon to preach at funerals, social gatherings, and other family-based contexts.

Women preachers urge the state to enforce and extend its control over the public sphere, and to expand female employment in all women-only spaces, while restricting women's entry into mixed surroundings (at work, schools, hospitals, banks, and shopping centres). They consider mixing between the sexes an obstacle to women's employment rather than an opportunity to increase women's participation in the workforce. Such preachers object to calls by women in the major chambers of commerce for mixing in the workplace. Furthermore, they see any economic forum bringing together Saudi women, international business, and Western policymakers as an opportunity for Westernising Saudi women that would lead to a loss of piety and morality. While employment in the state sector is still governed by the ban on mixing between the sexes, there are a few exceptions. Employment in state media and the medical profession offers occasions where the ban is relaxed. Saudi women journalists attend press conferences when foreign politicians visit Saudi Arabia, especially those given by the Foreign Minister, Saud al-Faisal, but women are unlikely to be present during press conferences held by the Minister of Interior, Prince Naif. Since 2010, the Minister of Higher Education, Prince Faisal, and his wife, Adilla, the king's daughter, have organised special forums where men and women coexist in a quasi-mixed setting. Several religious scholars, for example Nasir al-Omar, criticise these occasions and similar economic forums where men and women attend meetings and conferences.[22] Nasir al-Omar called for the resignation of the prince and accused him of corrupting Saudi women. Many female traditional activists agree with his opinion.

---

[19] Juwahir al-Sheikh's page is available at http://saaid.net/daeyat/jawaher/index.htm.

[20] Omayma al-Jalahima's page is available at http://saaid.net/daeyat/omima/index.htm.

[21] Ruqayya al-Muharib's page is available at http://saaid.net/daeyat/roqea/index.htm.

[22] In May 2011, forty *ulama* signed a letter to the king criticising the education policy of his son-in-law. They accused Prince Faisal of normalising mixing and corrupting Saudi girls. The *ulama* called for his resignation and reprimanded him for his Westernising projects. They aspire to a return to the situation in which they were in control of girls' education, before the king took the responsibility away from them following a school fire in Mecca that led to the death of several girls.

It is increasingly becoming possible for men and women to work together in the private business sector without strict segregation rules. Female employees in the offices and boardrooms of al-Walid bin Talal's Kingdom Holding Company are no longer a guarded secret. Women chair meetings and intermingle with male employees unveiled. This remains an exception that is not replicated in other Saudi private companies. Al-Walid's company does seem to be above the law. While the religious police know about the mixing, the company is never raided. It is, however, attacked in virtual forums for its corrupting influence. Opportunities for men and women to work together remain limited in the country, as many private companies prefer not to employ women given that this requires compliance with so many strict rules and regulations, not to mention providing separate spaces for meetings, work, and recreational activities. In general, women preachers do not usually seek employment in the private sector, and they object to linking plans for the expansion of female employment involving mixing. They see mixing as an obstacle to female employment and a violation of Islamic tradition.

Women preachers want to protect not only themselves but also other non-working women against what they see as multiple threats to their personal and family security. They struggle to prevent men from meeting female colleagues in the workplace for fear of intimacy with other women in a society that remains suspicious of such encounters. While mixing between the sexes is seen as a violation of Islam's teachings, there are more profound sociological and cultural reasons for resisting it. It is therefore important to go beyond Islam to explain these women's support for certain practices that may appear to entrench male dominance and female subordination. Women do not simply turn into accomplices in maintaining their exclusion. In fact, by resisting *ikhtilat*, women defend their own interests as women in a patriarchal society.

While many women preachers accept polygamy as an Islamic right under certain conditions, deep down they continue to fear it and prefer not to come face to face with it. They realise that men and women are exposed to alternative ideals relating to marriage and the choice of partner as a result of the country's immersion in the neo-liberal economy and advertising. These alternatives promote new meanings attached to marriage – such as love, educational compatibility, attraction, and other criteria associated with 'modern' perceptions of the conjugal bond. It is not surprising that many *daiyat* resist the idea that a man and a woman should spend time with each other prior to marriage, even in the presence of guardians. Many call for the adoption of the approach suggested by

the *ulama*, for example conducting telephone conversations with potential marriage candidates before marriage in order to 'get to know' the
person and discuss practicalities and preferences. They favour a fleeting introductory meeting attended by other members of the family. This
is referred to as *al-nathra al-shariyya*, a religiously sanctioned fleeting
glimpse whereby a man can see a woman's face before marriage provided
that the right familial context is prepared for the display. According to
the *daiyat*, a woman would feel threatened and undermined if a man
were allowed to see her before marriage for extended periods and on
several occasions, after which he might change his mind and no longer
wish to marry her. Such an encounter would allow malicious gossip that
might deter future potential suitors. Therefore, it seems that when *daiyat*
endorse the strictest position on male–female interaction by resorting to
religious opinions and *fatwas*, they defend their own interests as women
in a society that is still not ready to rise above its social and cultural
codes when it comes to gender relations. The nightmare scenario for a
woman is to be visited by several suitors without a subsequent marriage
announcement. There is a fear of losing one's reputation after exposure
to so many male candidates, which would result in a diminishing of the
prospect of future marriage proposals. Religious convictions thus become
a shield that protects women from both their own male-dominated society and the new social changes that are sweeping the country. The *daiyat*
remain as committed to sex segregation as many men, if not more so.
In this narrow example, Saudi women use religion to defend and protect
themselves from social and cultural norms. Islam provides a legitimate
solution in the practice of *al-nathra al-shariyya*, but society is still not
willing to accept multiple encounters that do not lead to marriage, thus
compromising a woman's reputation. Many women would prefer to see
the candidate rather than be seen by him. This is easily achieved in Saudi
society, as completely veiled women are in a good position to see men
who cannot see them. By a certain age, women will have amassed full
information about the physical appearance and financial background of
several potential candidates. In contrast, men have to rely on descriptions
offered by their own female relatives, mainly mothers and sisters. New
communication technologies have expanded the possibilities of exposure
to the other sex, but extremely religious men and women would limit their
use of technology to telephone conversations and messaging. Sending a
photo to a male candidate could leave a woman vulnerable to blackmail.
The case of Fatat al-Qatif, a woman who was gang raped in 2007 after
she tried to retrieve her photo from a man with whom she had had an

encounter, became notorious.[23] New technology has opened many avenues for interaction between men and women, but has also provided new opportunities to harm women and confirm their vulnerability in a male-dominated society. A woman's photo in the hands of a man or on his mobile phone screen can lead to serious unanticipated consequences. A YouTube video clip is even more dangerous.

The *daiyat* want the state to play a greater role in controlling the media, in which images of women and inappropriate scenes are often singled out as a threat to marital harmony, young men, and the nation in general. In this respect, they share with liberal women the quest for state intervention as a shield against violence and abuse from men, believed to result from their incessant exposure to sexual images. Religious women call upon the state to restrict and control virtual media, especially the rising consumption of pornographic material. Many women blame pornography for the high divorce rates among Saudi couples. A *fatwa* was issued in 2011 prohibiting men from forcing their wives to watch pornographic films with them. To protect marriages, *daiyat* denounce the standards of sexualised femininity that the new consumer culture and media promote. Although excessive consumerism remains beyond the reach of many Saudi women, they continue to spend vast sums on beauty products. Many women feel that there is too much pressure to look beautiful and conform to advertising images of seduction and sex appeal. While many preachers encourage women to indulge their husbands and reveal their charm and beauty in privacy, they worry about the changing and ever-increasing popular expectations brought about by exposure to consumer culture, advertising, and media. Many *ulama* have issued *fatwa*s against the excessively demanding wife who drains her husband's resources and demands more purchases, especially jewellery and clothes for weddings and parties. Such women are labelled *musrifat* (excessive consumers). Watching video clips of Egyptian and Lebanese singers on al-Walid bin Talal's Rotana multiple media empire is denounced as responsible for breaking up families and corrupting the youth of the nation. More objectionable is reality television, which borrows Western models of media performance using real Arabs performing together in normal and everyday situations.[24]

---

[23] For details of the victim and the sentence passed, see 'Saudi Gang Rape Sentence Unjust', at http://news.bbc.co.uk/1/hi/7098480.stm.

[24] For a full discussion of the debate about the contradictory messages of contemporary Arab satellite reality television and the Saudi Rotana connection, see Marwan Kraidy, *Reality Television and Arab Politics: Contention in Public Life*, Cambridge: Cambridge University Press, 2010, pp. 91–118.

Religious scholars criticise these channels, as does Prince Khalid, the brother of al-Walid. One scholar went as far as calling for the death of owners of such corrupting media. Many *daiyat* support such criticism of media that offer a fantasy world of beauty, charm, and seduction, not easily imitated even in the privacy of a marital relationship.

## Islamist Women and Current Affairs

If traditional conformist *daiyat* limit their preaching to women's issues and do not aspire to compete with men in the public sphere, a new type of activist has emerged who will venture into the public sphere with messages that touch the lives of both men and women. These women support the status quo and aspire to enforce greater restrictions on women to uphold the purity of the nation, its piety, and conformity. However, they do not write only for women, as the topics they raise and the causes they defend are local, regional, and global. They voice their own Islamist orientation and engage with wider national and global Islamic issues, but without challenging the Saudi status quo. In addition to women's issues, these new *multazimat* offer a feminine voice in support of official political and religious policies. Nobody exemplifies this position more than Juwahir al-Sheikh.

*Juwahir al-Sheikh: A Return to Women's Nature.* Juwahir al-Sheikh comes from the religious family that produced Muhammad ibn Abd al-Wahhab, the founder of the Wahhabi movement, and several religious scholars over the last 250 years. The current Saudi grand mufti, Abd al-Aziz, is a member of the family. However, it should not be assumed that belonging to the family automatically entails endorsement of its religious heritage. Another member of the family, Muhammad al-Sheikh, is a writer who moved away from his family's religious heritage to adopt a liberal position. He is an ardent supporter of what is often described as liberal thought – a fairly ambiguous description in the Saudi context. But his opponents criticise him for his deviation from the Wahhabi tradition of his ancestors. Juwahir al-Sheikh's discourse, however, remains faithful to that of the Wahhabi founder, invoked to reassert the tradition, which is reputedly being undermined by the forces of Westernisation. In addition to writing essays and columns in the local press, she is a teacher at the Women's College in Riyadh.

A selection of al-Sheikh's essays is posted on an official web page of prominent religious scholars, reflecting her membership in this growing religious field.[25] One of her most interesting articles is 'A call for women's voluntary work',[26] in which she encourages women to engage in informal and unofficial voluntary religious preaching and work. This involves working in orphanages, poverty-eradication programmes, prisoners' family help centres, and marital counselling welfare agencies. Women should also volunteer to facilitate marriage and arrange it for the increasing number of young bachelors and spinsters. Elsewhere she denounces all forms of marriage that undermine the stability of the family: for example, marriages that men conduct outside the country, temporary marriages, and other forms of contemporary cohabitation that have become legitimate. She sees all these marriages as a way to manipulate women emotionally and weaken them further.

Al-Sheikh sums up the importance of the 'new religious woman' in Saudi society and the role expected of her. She urges women to see themselves as part of the larger nation. Voluntary work is an Islamic exertion (juhd) that is required by God. She then moves on to explain why voluntary work is compatible with women's nature. God created women to give love, nourish children, and develop their motherhood skills. Voluntary work is therefore an extension of this nature. But there is also another important reason for engaging in voluntary work. Al-Sheikh encourages women to see life as a bank with a savings account. What one does in this world is saved up for the afterlife. Women volunteers add good deeds to their savings, which are then used in the afterlife to cancel out sins. The monetisation of Islamic voluntary work is a reflection of al-Sheikh's adoption of two discourses, one anchored in women's nature and obligations as defined in Islam, and one in the capitalist sphere. The state, in her opinion, cannot provide sufficient welfare and should not be expected to do so. In this respect, al-Sheikh calls for a minimalist state in which women step up to fill a vacuum in social services, based on their natural maternal instincts created by God. This argument combines the Islamic rhetoric on women and the neo-liberal philosophies of the minimalist state. The state's welfare obligation should be shared by the voluntary sector in which women are predisposed by their nature to provide major charitable contributions. They can then shine and assume an elevated status in their own society while accumulating good religious savings.

---

[25] All articles referred to here can be accessed at http://saaid.net/daeyat/jawaher/index.htm.
[26] Juwahir al-Sheikh, 'Dawa ila al-amal al-tatawui al-nisai' [A call for women's voluntary work], available at http://saaid.net/daeyat/jawaher/index.htm.

In another article, 'Life is a woman',[27] al-Sheikh addresses women's nature in greater detail. In her opinion, women are born with a predisposition towards modesty, purity, and softness.[28] Women are a 'container' that preserves genealogy (*nasab*) in addition to morality and authenticity. A woman's role in preserving the genealogical purity of the nation and the small family unit is paramount. In recent times, according to al-Sheikh, women have been encouraged to unveil in a literal and metaphorical sense. They are asked to remove the *burqa* of modesty. She laments that the noble Arab man, known for his jealousy and protection of his women, has become part of this conspiracy when he asks women to unveil. There is an obvious appreciation of overtly masculine qualities, embodied in men guarding their women and expressing jealousy in the process. Al-Sheikh values the jealous nature of men, and laments its disappearance among those men who call for or accept women's loss of *haya'* (modesty).

Modesty does not, however, mean passivity. One should emulate the example of the early women companions of the Prophet and *umahat al-muminin*, the mothers of the pious ancestors, who had a long history of contributing to the well-being of their communities. Contemporary women have become daring in ways that surpass men themselves. They have forgotten their religion and succumbed to the Western invasions and their deadly missiles, according to al-Sheikh.

Al-Sheikh warns against the increasing unveiling and consumption patterns in society and their negative impact on the nation. She criticises the media for promoting images of beautiful and seductive women under the guise of promoting women's issues and concerns. If the media are serious about supporting women, she asks, why do the same magazines and newspapers not highlight images of old poor women who beg in the streets? Images of unveiled women with full make-up on the front pages of the press do not promote women's causes. In fact, this visual representation of women violates women's modesty. Most importantly, these images precipitate dilemmas for men, rendering them incapable of practising an Islamic obligation encouraging them to lower their gaze. How can they do so when the public sphere is saturated with women exposing their beauty and dressed in clothes that reveal more than they cover? Al-Sheikh's logic centres on blaming women for diverting men's

---

[27] Juwahir al-Sheikh, 'al-Hayat imrara' [Life is a woman], available at http://saaid.net/daeyat/jawaher/index.htm.

[28] Women as soft and men as hard is fully explored in Pierre Bourdieu, *Masculine Domination*, trans. Richard Nice, Cambridge: Polity Press, 2001.

attention and distracting them in ways that violate their piety and integrity. This interpretation of men's dilemmas simply reiterates most religious scholars' view that women remain the source of *fitna* (seduction) for men and that they should be controlled in order to preserve men's chastity. Women's nature as motherly, soft creatures is expanded to include the power of seduction that many men find irresistible. Men's nature is currently affected as they lose their predisposition towards jealousy and resistance against temptation.

In addition to blaming women for the seduction of men and the degeneration of the nation, al-Sheikh argues that women have not been subjected to injustice by the *sharia*, the state, or society. In 'A new weapon called women',[29] she argues that *sharia* gives women all rights. In addition, the state provides employment and excludes women from professions that are demeaning or expose them to danger. She claims that she has encountered Western women who envy Saudi women for all the protection and opportunities they enjoy.[30] At the level of society, women have become respected. They voice their opinions, which are listened to. Fathers take time off to accompany their daughters and take them to work or school. This is interpreted as 'protection' and 'security' rather than control or loss of autonomy. Al-Sheikh values this protection and would not like it to diminish. Husbands also take care of their wives and are ready to sacrifice for them. Man as 'provider' is a mirror of the state. In this world, men protect women against the violence of other men. In return, women provide and raise the second generation of men. While the state has taken over many of the responsibilities of ordinary men towards women, mainly protection, al-Sheikh cherishes the private man, a jealous guardian against the hazards and violence of other men in society.

In this symbolic order, any discrimination against women becomes a product of individual errors of judgement and a perversion of the natural

---

[29] Juwahir al-Sheikh, 'Silah jadid ismuhu al-maraa' [A new weapon called women], available at http://saaid.net/daeyat/jawaher/index.htm.

[30] Soliciting Western women's praise for the seclusion and comfort of Saudi women has become common in many conferences and public relation forums in which the Saudi state often invites Western journalists, academics, and activists to praise its tradition and practices. One such forum resulted in the publication of many short articles by Western women who praised the Saudis for their sensible gender policies. See the report entitled *Women in Saudi Arabia: Cross-Cultural Views*, Riyadh: Ghainaa Publications, n.d. The report included the assessment of Tanya Hsu who offered a Western voice in support of Saudi women's exclusion.

conditions of society. Men who oppress women and violate their Islamic rights are sick and psychologically disturbed. They have a diminished understanding of Islam and their masculine role. While man the protector is the ideal type, man the violator of women is the antithesis, emphasising the importance of holding the first quality in esteem. One quality is meaningless without the other, for the protector and the violator are mirrors in which one image reinforces the other. Any focus on women with the intention of liberating her – that is, asserting her autonomy against the dual image of man the protector/violator – is a 'Western crusade that often comes before occupation', al-Sheikh warns her readers. Even in the West, she argues, women are not numerous in high positions in business and politics. Her advice to men and women is to stop being enchanted by Western civilisation and its alleged achievements in gender equality. The illusion of gender equality in the West is not substantiated by real empirical data. Women leaders remain an exception. Muslims' enchantment with the West would, if pursued, lead to a loss of Islamic identity and personal integrity.

Al-Sheikh glorifies Islam, the state, and society. She attributes the 'high status' of women to the Islamic teachings and rulings. In her discourse, Islam provides the guiding principles that dictate women's rights and obligations, both of which are protected by the state. The state is the provider of prosperity in this world whereby jobs become available to women in order to free them from poverty and need while respecting their 'nature' as women. The state will never make available jobs that interfere with motherhood, or endanger the lives of women. The state rightly restricts women's employment and excludes women from working in mixed environments or in professions that require physical effort and long hours. At another level, society – mainly men – seems to have accommodated women. Fathers and husbands facilitate and support women's education and employment. But the situation has not reached perfection. This is due to weak personal qualities, misjudgement, and other psychological defects. In this explanatory model of gender, positive gains are the products of religion, state, and society, while defects and shortcomings are reflections of individual failure either to understand or to apply good Islamic teachings. The individual can fail to achieve as a result of his weakness in the face of temptations, especially those offered by Saudi openness to Western influences in the form of consumption, illusory discourses on gender equality, and the prevalence of new behavioural models. These influences have given rise to a plethora of misconceptions about Saudi society, especially those that focus on its alleged intolerance of others and their ways of life.

Al-Sheikh deals with the theme of religious intolerance and racism as she moves away from gender-specific topics to wider concerns with the image of the nation and its reputation. This theme became a subject of debate particularly after 9/11 when international media and a few Saudis engaged in constructing the country as xenophobic, especially towards other religious traditions and ethnic groups. Many inside Saudi Arabia claimed that country's intolerance of others contributes to the growth of Jihadi violence. Scrutiny of Saudi religious teaching material revealed strong anti-Jewish and anti-Christian messages that were taken as an indication of hatred towards the others.[31] Moreover, several human rights reports highlighted Saudi racism towards foreign non-Arab workers, who are subjected to inhumane treatment by their employers.[32] In response to these claims, in 'Who said we don't like the other',[33] al-Sheikh focuses on the global aspects of Islam and its incorporation of multiple ethnicities, in addition to offering a commentary on contemporary Saudi Arabia and its openness. She lists several important personalities from Islamic history to demonstrate the openness of Islam and its tolerance of racial differences. The list is long. It includes personalities such as Bilal, the freed black slave who became the Prophet's first caller for prayer; Saybawayh, the first non-Arab authority on Arabic grammar; and the *hadith* collector Bukhari, in addition to Hijazi, Iraqi, and Levantine jurists of the medieval period.

In the contemporary period, al-Sheikh mentions that Saudi Arabia is host to thousands of foreign workers who are incorporated in the labour

---

[31] The first American think tank to highlight religious intolerance in the Saudi school curriculum was Freedom House, *Saudi Arabia's Curriculum of Intolerance*, Washington, DC: Freedom House, 2006. For an academic study of Saudi religious education, see Prokop, 'The War of Ideas'. The debate about the intolerance of Saudi religious education was extended to cover Saudi religious missions abroad, especially in Saudi-sponsored schools and cultural centres in the United States. Eleanor Doumato refutes the accusations. For an academic assessment of the alleged intolerance of the Saudi exported religious education, see Eleanor Abdella Doumato, 'Saudi Arabian Expansion in the United States: Half-Hearted Missionary Work Meets Rock Solid Resistance', in Madawi Al-Rasheed (ed.), *Kingdom without Borders: Saudi Arabia's Political, Religious and Media Frontiers*, London: Hurst & Co., 2008, pp. 301–21.

[32] Human Rights Watch, *Saudi Arabia: Country Summary*, New York: Human Rights Watch, January 2011.

[33] Juwahir al-Sheikh, 'Man qal anana la nuhib al-akhar' [Who said we don't like the other], available at http://saaid.net/daeyat/jawaher/index.htm.

force. She reminds her readers that in Saudi Arabia foreign workers 'enter our houses and live in the intimate domain of the private family'. She is not concerned with several highly publicised cases of foreign maids who were abused by their employers. She then moves to emphasise that 'our shopping centres are full of goods from all over the world so how could we be accused of not liking the other when we aspire to consume their products, and host them in our country?' She argues that we can openly love people who love us and shun those who despise us, as love from one side is bound to fail and is emotionally wrong. She saturates her essay with Quranic verses and prophetic sayings in order to anchor her thoughts in an authentic tradition. While loving the other is anchored in the authentic historical tradition, she invokes an Islamic cosmopolitanism that incorporates other cultures and ethnicities, exhibited in the urban spaces of Saudi Arabia. This Islamic diversity is contrasted with the cosmopolitanism promoted in the various novels discussed in the last chapter. The shopping centre with its urban sophistication and intermingling is appreciated not as a free space but as proof of Saudi tolerance and consumption of other nations' goods. Al-Sheikh's cosmopolitanism is embedded in a universal religion that incorporates rather than excludes others. The contemporary manifestations of this cosmopolitanism are the incorporation of foreign workers in Saudi Arabia and the consumption of goods imported from all over the world. However, she uses irony when she refers to this foreign penetration of Saudi Arabia, as she asks rhetorical questions reflecting her dissatisfaction with these intrusions. Yet she accepts them as proof of an Islamic openness and contemporary tolerance. While she does not criticise the new cosmopolitanism brought about by neo-liberal economies in this article, she takes its manifestations as indications of the level of contemporary acceptance of the other and its products.

Al-Sheikh engages with the debate about Jihadi violence in Saudi Arabia in a tone that reiterates the position of the official religious establishment, mainly gently reprimanding Jihadis for their misconceptions when they made the land of the two Holy Mosques the battlefield. In 'An amicable and urgent call',[34] she invokes the large *usra* consisting of mothers, fathers, and brothers, thus forging an intimate nucleus with Jihadis. A motherly message follows, calling upon Jihadis to reconsider

---

[34] Juwahir al-Sheikh, 'Nida wid ajil' [An amicable and urgent call], available at http://saaid.net/daeyat/jawaher/index.htm.

and eventually abandon the strategy of bringing *jihad* to the intimate confines of the Saudi homeland. The victims are the people closest to Jihadis, their families and friends, in addition to other Muslims. The result is anarchy, social chaos, and outside political pressures exerted on the government. Rebellion against the pious rulers and the slaughter of Muslims cannot be a legitimate *jihad*. These actions can only serve the interests of the enemies of Islam. She calls upon Jihadis to raise the flag of Islam in other ways, for example propagation of religion, fighting religious innovations and blasphemy, and calling for monotheism. She issues a final call to the righteous *ulama* asking them to advise the youth, described as faithful to religion, and loving of the people. Jihadis need to be brought back to the right path.

Juwahir al-Sheikh is a conformist state *multazima* who does not challenge any of the taken-for-granted official religious and political narratives on gender relations. She fears women's autonomy lest it deprive them of male protection and security. While her concern remains with defending official religious positions on women, she ventures into current affairs to articulate a religious narrative in line with state policies on political topics. Many women activists express a female interpretation of terrorism by drawing on the official *ulama*'s position. The causes were restricted to problems of misjudgement and misinterpretation, in addition to confusion about the legitimate location of *jihad*. Al-Sheikh mobilises her maternal language to invoke a return to the fold of warmth and love for those who abandon their misconceptions. Violence against the nation and its rulers becomes an abhorred act similar to the violation of the intimate confines of family and kin. Al-Sheikh's interpretation of Jihadi misconceptions is contrasted with that of Badriyya al-Bishr, discussed in Chapter 5. While al-Sheikh invites Jihadis back to the fold using the language of motherhood, al-Bishr situates their violence in a troubled relationship between mothers and sons. Overindulgent mothers may have contributed to violence in this interpretation of *jihad*. In al-Sheikh's discourse, if *jihad* is to be conducted inside Saudi Arabia, it must be directed against blasphemous and innovative practices, in addition to those who change the natural order between men and women, and ruler and ruled. Saudi Arabia is governed by a 'natural' religious logic that cannot be changed, altered, or modified, as this would lead to the break-up of the family, united thanks to religious nationalism. Women cannot play roles naturally associated with men and subjects cannot question their pious leaders and religious scholars. In this universe, gender roles are predetermined and divinely prescribed under the umbrella of one religious nation.

## Critical Islamist Voices

Other women activists have a wider project that encompasses the acquisition of rights within an Islamic framework. They engage with public debates on the guardianship system, women's employment, women driving, child marriage, mixing between the sexes, custody of children after divorce, polygamy, and other less formal marriage arrangements. They adopt current public causes, and give opinions on gender practices and policy, but also address wider political issues, mainly related to Westernisation, social liberalisation, and women and Islam. They are more concerned with contemporary current affairs and their impact on Muslim women than with performing specific Islamic rituals or reiterating official religious discourse. They can also take up and defend causes involving men rather than simply offer a woman's perspective on social and political issues.

Islamist activist women associated with the 1970s Sahwa movement began to be outspoken in the late 1980s and early 1990s. They tend to adopt a modern activist interpretation of gender and current affairs that encourages women to engage with society outside the home. They are active in formal religious centres, educational institutions (schools, universities, women's teacher-training colleges), and women's charitable centres. These activists compete for a public space among female audiences in contemporary urban Saudi Arabia. They try to offer interpretations that correspond to a modern 'feminist' agenda, although they do not regard their discourse as such. In fact, some of them denounce the feminist movement and its impact on the *usra* (the family). They would also object to the label 'Islamic feminists'. They regard their position on gender issues as purely Islamic – neither traditional, conformist, feminist, nor radical. They are occasionally called upon to participate in debates about women without physically mixing with men. The new independent religious media such as al-Dalil and al-Majd that flourished after 2000 invite such women to comment on current gender policies and issues by phone. They engage with *ulama*, Islamic intellectuals, and liberals in debates relating to early marriage, divorce, spinsterhood, driving, mixing, and other hot topics that dominate and saturate the public sphere. They also write about American hegemony, the Iraq war, the Palestine conflict, Zionism, economic liberalisation, and other issues that dominate the local Saudi press. They may appear on television, but most of them write books and short articles in which they express their Islamic opinions on gender as well as other current political affairs.

*Nura al-Saad: The Challenges of Western Liberalism.* Nura al-Saad is perhaps one of the most well-known Islamist activists to be engaged in public life. In addition to a master's degree in sociology from the United States, she was trained in Islamic studies at Muhammad Ibn Saud University where she wrote a thesis on Algerian thinker Malik Bennabi.[35] She worked as a lecturer at King Abdul Aziz University in Jeddah. While al-Saad has not published any books, her articles over the last thirty years in the local press constitute a good summary of her thinking on social and political issues. Her columns address two interrelated concerns: first, global Western pressures on Saudi Arabia that push the country to abandon its Islamic heritage;[36] and second, the injustices experienced by Saudis in general as a result of corruption, unemployment, and poverty.

Al-Saad is willing to take her religious interpretations so far as to be labelled 'Nura al-Zarqawi' by Turki al-Sudayri, a veteran of the Saudi local press and editor of *al-Riyadh* newspaper. She earned this nickname not because of her deeply religious interpretations but because of her profile as a hardline Islamist writer, too critical of the United States. She was a regular columnist in *al-Riyadh* until the editor, whom she nicknamed 'Turki Bush', suspended her. The change in the tone of the Saudi press from one that glorifies Islamic perspectives on current affairs to one that denounces radical Islamic interpretations led to al-Saad being dismissed from the newspaper after 9/11. After three decades, she stopped writing her column, *Rabi al-harf* (Letter's spring). She explains that, from 2001, the newspaper reduced the frequency of her articles as a prelude to terminating her contract. She found that her criticism of American atrocities in Afghanistan and Iraq was not accepted or tolerated by the editor. The deputy editor gave the excuse that he would like to allow other writers to contribute to the newspaper, but the main reason remains her radical tone, she claimed in an interview. She rejects the right of the editor to modify articles unless they violate Islam. *Al-Riyadh* is known for promoting alternatives to Islamist perspectives, and her dismissal after 2001 was a natural outcome of official policy to curb the spread of Islamist propaganda. She laments that 'freedom of speech' is used in

[35] Le Renard, *Femmes et espace*, p. 75.
[36] Al-Saad perpetuates an old tradition among some women writers who considered that the challenges of Western liberalism should be addressed by women in Muslim societies. The writings of Juahyr al-Musaid and Suhayla Zayn al-Abdin are good examples of responses to this challenge. For further details, see Sadeka Arebi, *Women and Words in Saudi Arabia: The Politics of Literary Discourse*, New York: Columbia University Press, 1994, pp. 184–245.

Saudi Arabia to attack religion in the press. She feels that the press must have a glorious role, to unite Muslims and show their superiority while at the same time exposing shortcomings in their lives and institutions so these can be corrected. But in the post-2001 period, the Saudi press allows authors 'to criticise Muslims like Ibn Taymiyya and glorify atheists like Abdullah al-Qasimi.[37] Those who criticise the *ulama* and religion and call for *ikhtilat*, and glorify United Nation charters on gender equality are rewarded'.

On the recent changes in Saudi society since 2001, al-Saad expresses appreciation of the move towards greater visibility for women in institutions that care for women and in participating in conferences and forums, but she has a serious warning. She sees in calls for gender equality a potential threat to family solidarity. Her main concerns remain 'the threat of Westernisation and adopting a Western model that contradicts our *sharia*'. In her opinion, it will take decades to return to the authentic tradition following its corruption by the international discourse on gender equality. Saudi Arabia is afraid of and paranoid about international criticism when it comes to women's issues, so it tries to please outsiders. Al-Saad writes:

How could a poor illiterate village woman benefit from the one who sits unveiled in the Chamber of Commerce? When women participate in parliaments, work in mixed surroundings, and follow the Western model, do we get rid of poverty, illiteracy, crime against women, divorce, spinsterhood, sexual abuse, unemployment, drugs and many other ills? Whatever change we have must remain faithful to religious and family tradition. Instead of adopting United Nations charters on equality, we must practise *sharia* law that insists on women's right in inheritance, custody of children, maintenance after divorce, and a *sharia* based understanding of *qawama*.[38]

Al-Saad does not want to see Saudi women adopting an individualistic approach to human rights or a Western definition of these rights. She wants women to remain anchored in the social family contexts while

---

37 Abdullah al-Qasimi was a Wahhabi scholar who went to al-Azhar in Egypt to continue his religious training. After he finished his studies, he became an atheist. He remained in exile and died in Egypt. The local Saudi press ignored him for several decades, but after 9/11 he began to be remembered in short essays and columns. For a biography of al-Qasimi, see Jurgen Wasella, *al-Qasimi: bayn al-usuliyya wa al-inshiqaq* [al-Qasimi: Between fundamentalism and atheism], trans. Muhammad Kibaybo, Beirut: Dar al-Kunuz al-Adabiyya, 2005.
38 Nura al-Saad, 'Dharutat himayat al-mara min badh bunud itifaqiyat al-sidaw' [The need to protect women from some of the clauses in CEDAW], *al-Riyadh*, 15 December 2005.

enjoying rights dictated by the *sharia*. She cherishes the family as protection for women rather than a constraining force in their lives. She praises women's participation in the National Dialogue Forums, but does not think that it led to the desired results. In fact, she explains that these forums trivialised women's problems by focusing on mixing between the sexes, driving, cinema, and theatre, as if these minor new freedoms would make women's lives better. Saudi Arabia cannot simply follow the global model of gender equality, as it should remain faithful to the *sharia*. Women have benefited from new educational and employment opportunities, but the real challenge is not to be engulfed by the global model of women's rights at the expense of the religious and social tradition. Al-Saad adopts the approach of Algerian thinker Bennabi. She argues that new practices and cultures cannot be simply implanted in the body of another nation. They are like a blood transfusion: if the wrong type of blood is pumped into someone's body by mistake, the reaction will be fatal and violent. Scientific and biological images are borrowed to explain the danger of introducing alien 'substances' into the body of the Muslim *umma*.

Among these 'foreign substances' are conferences such as the Jeddah Economic Forums, an international arena in which international politicians, economists, and business personalities make an appearance. They intermingle with selected Saudi officials and women – including princesses, entrepreneurial women, and professionals. The Saudi organisers claim that such meetings encourage economic entrepreneurial activities and promote the country as a liberal economic hub for investment and innovation. So far, the forums are part of the 'charm offensive' launched by the government after 9/11 as guarded spaces where Saudi cosmopolitanism, especially that related to women's recent increased appearance in the media and the public sphere, can be displayed. Al-Saad offers a critical ethnographic reading of a 2004 forum meeting in which she was invited to participate. Men and women mixed freely in the meeting, which was condemned by the grand mufti, Abd al-Aziz al-Sheikh. According to al-Saad, during the meeting women were unveiled, mixed with men, and used English as the language of the conference – all of which are, in her opinion, against the *sharia*, which is the basis of government in Saudi Arabia according to the Basic Law of Government.[39]

She claims that the meeting focused on a number of slogans without leading to concrete and tangible results. When she enquired about the forum's recommendations, she was told that the meeting was meant to

---

[39] On the 1991 Basic Law of Government, see Al-Rasheed, *A History*, pp. 166–71.

be for networking, listening to views, and expressing opinions. She sees the forum as a project to dissolve the Islamic and Arab identity of the region in favour of an ambiguous Middle East identity that will include the integration of Israel. After exploring critical Saudi businessmen's views on the forum, she concludes that it is a path towards Westernising Saudi society. Presentations at the conferences dealt with freedom for women, democracy, and women driving. She notes that presenters spoke in their own languages, thus showing their respect for their mother tongues, while Muslims do not show the same deference to the language of the Quran. While intermingling with other female participants, one of whom was an Israeli who holds an American passport, al-Saad comments on the triviality of the discussion that revolved around why Saudi women cannot drive and why the veil is black. Al-Saad exposed 'the hypocrisy of Western governments' when she mentioned the plight of Afghan women and children who were constantly bombed by American planes. She writes that the chair of the meeting told her to stop her comments in order not to create more embarrassment for the organisers. She criticises Saudi women participants for their enthusiasm for American projects and their denunciation of Saudi Arabia, and says that personalities such as Firyal al-Masri (an American Saudi woman living in the United States), Nadiya Bakharji, and others who call for the liberation of women are blinded by Western slogans about liberty. The objective of the regular annual meetings is to introduce mixing in the workplace and to allow women to work in any job, both rejected by al-Saad.

Al-Saad's critique of the Jeddah Economic Forums is an extension of her reservations on the Convention on the Elimination of All Forms of Discrimination against Women (CEDAW) adopted by the United Nations in 1979. Saudi Arabia ratified the treaty in 2000 but expressed reservations on certain clauses. Al-Saad objects to the treaty becoming *marjiyya*, a reference framework determining how societies deal with gender issues. She considers this treaty an imposition of a foreign system on Islamic societies that had no say in designing it. She is highly critical of Saudi women who supported ratifying the treaty, as their intention was to sideline religion as a main factor in determining and defining the position of women in society. According to al-Saad, the treaty encourages 'sexual freedom, the rights of perverts (homosexuals), abortion, and adultery'.[40] The treaty removes women from the family and turns them into lonely individuals pursuing projects other than the well-being of their children.

---

40 Nura al-Saad, 'Dharurat himayat al-mujtama min badh bunud itifaqiyat al-sidaw' [The need to protect society from some articles in CEDAW], *al-Riyadh*, 15 December 2005.

It calls for equality in inheritance and the end of the guardianship system. In personal matters, the treaty contradicts Islam, which should remain the reference point.

Al-Saad is dedicated to thwarting the so-called Saudi liberal project and its manifestations, which take many forms and platforms. In addition to criticising the orchestrated, government-sponsored conferences and economic forums, she defends Islamic institutions in the country. One such important government institution is the Committee for the Promotion of Commanding Right and Forbidding Wrong. Since 9/11, the Saudi press has devoted special attention to the excesses and mistakes – and occasionally fatal errors – of this committee. The lecture cited at the beginning of the chapter was an attempt to 'modernise' the committee and make it more acceptable to university students in an academic institution such as King Saud University. As part of the attempt at modernising the committee and making its approach more scientific, its directorate introduced training courses for its members to learn how 'to respect other religions' and to learn English so that they can communicate with non-Arabic speakers in Saudi Arabia. Al-Saad notes that the liberal print and visual media highlight individual mistakes committed by *haiya* men, without focusing on their positive contribution to guarding morality and protecting men and women. She is astonished that journalists have called for the committee to be abolished and replaced with morality police, as in other Arab countries. Citing several Quranic verses in support of the principle of commanding right and prohibiting wrong, al-Saad concludes that the committee is important for the well-being of society. Its history attests to great work, which was initially voluntary. When Ibn Saud established his rule in Riyadh, great religious men performed *hisba* without any financial reward. She refers to Shaykh Abd al-Aziz al-Sheikh, whose individual efforts meant that people were regularly reminded of prayers and young men prevented from creating chaos as a result of gathering in public spaces. When the Hijaz became part of the Saudi realm in 1925, the king established formal institutions and committees to cover the whole country. Those who attack the committee in the press are so superficial, according to al-Saad, that they would blame it for all the ills in Saudi society including poverty, unemployment, inflation, and health problems. While the *haya* may have made mistakes, they can be corrected without abolishing an important duty in a Muslim society.[41]

---

[41] Nura al-Saad, 'Dharurat himayat al-mujtama min badh bunud itifaqiyat al-sidaw' [The need to protect society from some articles in CEDAW], *al-Riyadh*, 15 December 2005.

In addition to engaging with wider global and political issues relating to gender, Islam, and the West, al-Saad is known for defending members of society who experience injustice. She took up the cause of a group of diploma students, whose degrees were not ratified by the relevant educational institutions, known as *qadiyat al-diplom*. These diplomas cost students and their families a lot of money without leading to employment. What was peculiar about these diplomas was the fact that they were issued by Imam Muhammad Ibn Saud University in Riyadh after students paid substantial fees. The diploma scandal erupted in 2004 when students were denied employment because their degrees had not been recognised. The university refused to reimburse the students for what was described as 'imaginary degrees'.

Al-Saad wrote more than thirty articles in the press helping to publicise the plight of those whose diplomas had not been ratified. In her words, she is 'a Muslim citizen who loves the oppressed and defends their rights. When they have a right, they will always get it. A Muslim is obliged to work hard and become a role model, following the steps of the Prophet'.[42] Al-Saad exposes corruption and dishonesty in government institutions and highlights the damage to students' careers as a result of educational officials and administrators abusing their positions. In this respect, she differs from Juwahir al-Sheikh, who absolves the state and its agencies from any shortcomings. For al-Saad, *dhulm* (injustice) cannot be tolerated and must be resisted. She defends widows who had to sell their land and jewellery to pay for their sons to train at the university so that they could find employment, saluting women's unlimited love that encourages sons to give to their nation. Their dreams, however, were shattered when they realised that their certificates were not recognised, and al-Saad condemns the corruption of those in the Ministry of Education who refused to sort out the problem. In her interpretation of the spread of corruption among officials, al-Saad points to the decay of contemporary Muslim identity, lack of the fear of God, and disrespect for others. Intellectuals have a role to play in highlighting the plight of the oppressed and creating a new consciousness among the masses. She laments the inadequacies of the Saudi justice system, which is gradually losing its authority and integrity as a result of not defending people's rights and punishing culprits.

From defending Islam and asserting its superiority over international discourse and global practices and norms, to taking up the causes of ordinary people, al-Saad has carved a space for herself as an Islamist writer

---

[42] Interview in *Islam Today*, 12 October 2008.

and activist. In her columns and interviews, she does not preach like the conformist *daiyat* whose main concern is to propagate the religious teachings and *fatwa*s of the official religious establishment. Al-Saad engages with contemporary issues and supports Islamic solutions to current challenges in Saudi society. While she is not openly critical of the government, she finds a space that allows her to undermine the new state cosmopolitan project indirectly. Along with male Islamists, she attributes the new project to the work of those Saudi liberal bureaucrats and advisers, commonly known as *al-batana* (court advisers) whose bad advice to the king and other ministers led to abandoning tradition and immersing the country in the Westernisation project. There is nothing new in her argument. She is simply a female voice that defends Islam but cannot in the current circumstances express overt criticism of the ruling group and its gender policies. She appeals to history and the commitment of the founder of Saudi Arabia in order to remind current officials of the historical pact on the basis of which Saudi Arabia was founded. Like her male counterparts, she sees the battle over gender as a confrontation between misguided Westernised bureaucrats and an Islamic society facing serious challenges. Women's issues remain a disputed arena in which liberals and Islamists fight fierce but inconclusive battles. The role of the state in determining gender policies is hardly explored, asserted, or criticised. The two camps cannot voice open criticism of high-ranking princes under whose patronage international forums are organised inside the country. Criticism of these officials remains vibrant in alternative media forums but cannot be expressed on the pages of the official press.

The new female religious activists are the other side of the education coin in Saudi Arabia. They differ from the women described in the previous chapters in their outlook and solutions to current social and economic problems facing women. While some are simply female voices that are an extension of the official religious establishment, others are more involved in responding to wider challenges that touch the lives of both men and women. However, all religious activists share one common feature with their liberal counterparts: both *muthaqafat* and *multazimat* call upon the authoritarian state to act in the field of gender. The *muthaqafat* want state intervention to limit the misogyny of men and religious institutions, and grant women rights in line with international standards. The *multazimat* call for state intervention to contain the corrupting influence of liberal men and women and to resist foreign pressure on Saudi Arabia. The *multazimat* devise strategies to 'bargain with patriarchy' trading rights for protection, as proposed by Deniz Kandiyoti, discussed in the introduction to this book. Both the *muthaqafat* and *multazimat* want the state to police men who either deny women their rights or contribute to their corruption and moral degeneration. In their efforts to enlist state support for their causes, both liberal and Islamist women contribute to the expansion of state power and its greater intervention in their lives. So far, Saudi women have not been able to act as autonomous agents, and have hesitated to identify the state publicly as a major contributor to their marginalisation and exclusion. Those who share this conviction have preferred to be silent for fear of persecution. As in Egypt and the United Arab Emirates, women 'need authoritarian states more than men do, not least for their ability to police men and extract resources from them within a corporatist family framework that requires men to provide for wives, children and parents'.[43] However, in extremely wealthy authoritarian states with great purchasing power and expanding welfare services, such as Saudi Arabia, the state has in many ways marginalised men by becoming not only a provider for women but also the guardian of their honour – at least, this is how the state is presented in its own official narratives. Women whose families and husbands have failed to provide for them consider the state as their last refuge. In return for protection and support, the Saudi state has turned women, both *multazimat* and *muthaqafat*, into loyal subjects. The battle in the twenty-first century is not between marginalised women and authoritarian misogynist policies but between two groups of women who struggle to make the state privilege their own vision of their role in society. As long as the two groups remain divided, the state can be sure that women are divided and consequently kept in their place. The state mobilises women only when political circumstances, or economic need, relevant to the state itself, require such mobilisation.

[43] Hasso, *Consuming Desires*, p. 14.

# Conclusion

## *Light at the End of the Tunnel*

My intention in this book was to go past the contradictory images of Saudi women and situate the 'woman question' in a wider context beyond religion and tribalism. The persistent marginalisation of Saudi women that is perhaps unmatched in the Muslim world needs to be understood within a historical and political context. While recognising the patriarchal inclination embedded in existing religious tradition, cultural, and social norms, shared in various degrees by all women in the Muslim world, Saudi women's marginalisation is a function of a historical process in which religion was turned into a state religious nationalist ideology. This makes other variables less convincing on their own in explaining the 'woman question'. Too much ink has been spilt over the restrictions imposed by the Saudi religious tradition and the essentially conservative society in which this tradition is upheld. There is no doubt that Saudi religious scholars and judges initiate the most restrictive religious opinions and sentences, perpetuate women's exclusion, and contribute to their confinement and marginalisation. But these religious opinions are neither new nor the sole prerogative of Saudi *ulama*. Many other Muslim scholars endorse them and propagate their origins in old treatises on women. Equally, tribal social organisation and ethos survive in other countries, not to mention the neighbouring Gulf states of Kuwait, Qatar, and Oman. In these countries, women have gained relatively more rights, and their inclusion in the labour force and public life has taken place at a time when Saudi women are still banned from driving cars. This is not to say that women in these societies have achieved real equality in social, economic, and political life, but compared to Saudi women they definitely enjoy greater recognition and economic participation. The struggle of Gulf women seems to have moved beyond driving and the male guardianship system. They share with Saudi women the experience of living under the umbrella of authoritarian states whose difference is only a matter of degree. But their states were founded without invoking a religious nationalist ideology.

The analysis here privileged the role of the state, consisting of multiple actors and institutions, and its quest for political legitimacy, initially situated in a religious nationalist narrative but later moving towards a modernity in which women become central. The role of the state and its intimate connection with a religious revival movement-turned-religious nationalist project seem to be crucial for understanding why Saudi women continue to lag behind their Arab and Gulf counterparts who have progressed to demanding more fundamental rights. Saudi religious nationalism provided a framework in which the marginalisation and exclusion of women became important for a political project. Unlike in other countries, including Gulf monarchies and emirates, the rationale behind Saudi state formation was to create a pious domain in which women became symbols. In this respect, Saudi Arabia differed from secular Arab nationalist states and Gulf monarchies in which women began to be perceived as signs of modernity, national pride, and empowerment. Non-oil Arab states needed women's labour to generate wealth, while oil wealth contributed to confining Saudi women to limited roles. Small, wealthy Qatar was able to increase women's participation in the labour force while Saudi Arabia lagged behind. For Saudi women, education became an ideological tool to instil the ethos of religious nationalism – mainly the preservation of the nation's boundaries, piety, and authenticity – rather than to prepare them for the labour market. Education was also used to enforce women's loyalty to the state as recipients of welfare. The exclusion of women became an affordable luxury, difficult to sustain without massive oil wealth and the import of cheap expatriate labour. As such, debating the 'woman question' remains entangled with discourses about how precious and protected they are.

Despite initial objections and restrictions, it must be recognised that Saudi women have benefited from education, both at home and abroad. But this education has allowed them only limited access to employment, with the majority finding jobs in educational institutions and the health sector. It has, however, enabled them to articulate their own grievances and aspirations: despite the traditional rationale behind education, Saudi women benefited from schooling and began to develop a feminist consciousness and an awareness of their subordination. Both Islamist and liberal women are today speakers whose voices have found a niche in the public sphere. They contribute regular commentaries on women's issues and general social, political, and economic problems specific to them as women. The explosion in women's literature in the second half of the twentieth century is a reflection of their ability to engage with their own experience and expose contradictions in their society. They have been active agents in imagining solutions, often consisting of bargains with the patriarchy of their state and society. Prevented from real mobilisation and greater economic participation, their literature became an arena to reflect on the 'woman question' without facing serious punishment. They may not have common visions or solutions, but they no doubt talk about their experiences as agents with an awareness of their marginalisation. They call upon the state to intervene and promote their interest as women. This is not surprising given that many women often see authoritarian states as a refuge from social exclusion and marginalisation. Saudi women invoke the state as an arbiter and provider that can give them access to more rights and protection. Above all, they demand that the state act on their behalf to restrict the social, religious, and familial patriarchy dominant in their own society. In this process, they willingly court state patriarchy, which in the short term might offer them more limited rights but in the long term may not work in their own interest.

This book has traced the projects of both women and the state as they come face to face with contemporary challenges, from education and employment to segregation and driving. The old religious nationalist narrative of the state, itself a modern development associated with its consolidation in the second half of the twentieth century, collided with other aspects of modernity, namely individualism, self-fulfilment, gender equality, and global human rights discourse. Saudi modernity is entangled with oil and the capitalist economy in which the state took the leading role. In order to assert this modernity and make it visible, women were ironically used to represent the opposite of modernity: communal piety, authenticity, and conformity to an imagined past. Schooling women, itself a product of modernity, was introduced with a pledge to remain faithful to the model of the ideal Muslim woman. Saudi Arabia struggled to create 'an alternative modernity', combining commitment to Islam with selective borrowing from what world modernity can offer, namely education, science, medicine, surveillance technology, and speedy transport and communication. The state and many sections of Saudi society aspired to appropriate the modern package without wholesale borrowing of its value system, especially those values that undermine commitment to religious nationalism, the perpetuation of which women had been visible signs.

Claims that there is an alternative modernity to be pursued are often mis-guided. According to Zubaida, modernity by its nature generates debates, controversies, clashes, and dissent, often mistaken for an alternative.[1] In reality, the chapters in this book document how the emergence of the state as an arbiter and provider, a modern development facilitated by the country's incorporation in oil-based capitalism, generated many debates and controversies, initially monopolised by men but in which women later became active participants. Today, with Saudi women actively par-ticipating in defining what it means to be a woman, what rights they seek, and how they imagine their future, these women challenge their society, religious tradition, and the state to allow them entry into the precincts of modernity on their own terms. Even religious scholars and preachers are compelled to deal with the modernity of Saudi women, often amount-ing to banal opinions on their hairstyles, the tightness of their veils, and physical fitness. Such opinions are often considered bizarre, outrageous, and trivial, but these scholars and their followers are simply being mod-ern. Mirroring the Western obsession with fashion and consumption, a symptomatic outcome of modern fetishism, consumption, and obsession with beauty and the body, Saudi scholars are simply joining the trend and asserting their own modernity by contributing to public debates on the female body. Women themselves are presented with unlimited choices. Some women fetishise their desires and bodies, and articulate this fetish-ism in short stories, like a previous generation of Western women, while others seek alternative lifestyles and attire. They are all immersed in mod-ernity, benefiting from the many choices that modernity itself offers. Yet another group of women challenge the religious narrative that asserts the purity of the nation, its conformity, and alleged piety. They deconstruct local tradition and highlight heterogeneity, hybridity, and bewilderment. They hide behind fictive voices to undermine taken-for-granted and cher-ished common wisdom about women and Saudi society.

As elsewhere in the world, Saudi modernity comes with heated debates about identity, the cosmopolitan person, the dislocated hybrid, and the wandering and uprooted world citizen. Against religious nationalist nar-ratives about homogeneity, certainty, and authenticity, women writers expose a reality that many Saudis would prefer not to see or acknow-ledge. The celebrity novelist emerges at the juncture where the state and global forces impinge on the lives of Saudis, thus shattering myths about

---

[1] Sami Zubaida, *Beyond Islam: A New Understanding of the Middle East*, London: I. B. Tauris, 2011.

their conservatism, conformity, and homogeneity. They shock their own society and surprise outside observers for a simple reason: they talk about sex and desire, long confined to the private domain or the preaching of religious scholars in what amounts to an 'erotic theology'. Their writing charts the new feminist consciousness emerging at a critical moment in Saudi history where the individual rather than the nation, the community, or the tribe is the basis for belonging. Their daring sexual novels challenge the authority of the religious scholar's 'erotic theology' in which desire and sex are both regulated according to the Islamic tradition. Women offer their own reflections on a topic the discussion of which in public has been so far dominated by male *ulama*. Other women protect their own interests by appealing to the state to increase surveillance, control the media, and honour pledges to uphold the Islamic tradition. Like Christian fundamentalist women elsewhere in the world, they aspire to reinsert their own narrative in the public sphere, thus making it a legitimate framework within which their rights, aspirations, and dreams can be fulfilled. Above all, they seek the protection of the state and its greater intervention in matters that affect their lives. Women religious activists are modern too, although their projects may not be entirely modernist.

In its quest to appear modern, the state provides a protective framework for some women's voices, shielding them from the wrath of their own society and the institutions it has created. This is taking place at a critical moment, in which the state faces global pressures, related to wider political issues around security and terrorism, and internal challenges focused on widespread unemployment among an educated youth bulge. The state carefully watches the gender battles that are going on in Saudi society, leaning towards one group at one time and switching its patronage to other groups as its political agenda dictates. Sometimes the state can simultaneously patronise both those who oppose women's emancipation and others who support it, as the multiplicity of state political actors allows diversification of patronage networks. We have seen how the state supports and enforces religious opinions when this is required to secure its control and legitimacy, but it can also undermine conservative elements in Saudi society when it wishes to project a new modern and reformist image.

While this book captures a plethora of women's voices and traces the historical engagement of the state in the gender question over several decades, events in the Arab world moved in a dramatic way in 2011. The so-called Arab Spring of 2011 succeeded in removing three Arab presidents: in Tunisia, Egypt, and Libya. In the first two cases, young, electronically connected men and women kept the crowds in large cities chanting *al-Sha'b yurid isqat al-nitham* (the people want the overthrow of the regime). This leaderless movement spread across the Arab world, from Egypt and Tunisia to Libya, Syria, Yemen, and Bahrain.[2] In the Arabian Peninsula, dormant Oman, volatile Yemen, and divided Bahrain witnessed similar protest in which women of all political and religious persuasions participated across the region. They joined crowds, chanted slogans, and composed inflammatory poetry in support of rebels and revolutionaries. They voiced no specific gender demands, but their participation reflected great engagement with national issues. Middle-class Western-educated women, heavily veiled activists, feminists, and working-class mothers assembled in squares and demanded the overthrow of dictatorships.

The Saudi regime felt nervous as a result of this tide of historical change sweeping neighbouring countries. It offered refuge to Tunisian president Zeine al-Abdin bin Ali and supported Egypt's Hosni Mubarak until the last minute. Within the Arabian Peninsula, it fearfully watched the Yemeni and Bahraini revolutions close to home. In Bahrain, 14 February 2011 marked the beginning of a mass protest movement calling for serious political change. With a Shia majority closely connected to the Saudi Eastern Province population, Bahrain was simply too close to be left to pursue its own destiny and aspirations for real democracy. The Saudi state immediately dispatched a military force under the umbrella of the Gulf Cooperation Council to suppress the protest movement and assist the Sunni Al-Khalifa ruling family retain power, sweeping protestors from Manama's Pearl Square. Saudi Arabia could not tolerate political change that may have led to the overthrow of a neighbouring monarchy with close kinship ties to the Saudi ruling family. Bahraini women were active in the protest, leading women's marches, addressing crowds denouncing the regime, providing logistical support, and caring for injured protestors in the streets and hospitals of Bahrain. As women were integral to the Bahrain protest movement, they too became victims. Ayat al-Qurmazi, a young teacher who composed inflammatory poetry denouncing the Bahraini king and delivered it to gathered protestors, was put in prison for violating a taboo and tarnishing the reputation of Bahrain's ruler.[3] The protestors were removed from the centre of Manama, and retreated

---

[2] While serious analysis of the Arab Spring is yet to be written, tentative commentaries have appeared. See Jean-Pierre Filiu, *The Arab Revolution: Ten Lessons from the Democratic Uprising*, London: Hurst & Co., 2011.

[3] 'Bahrain: From a New Awakening to a Divided Nation', *The Independent*, 3 August 2011.

to their own villages as they had done in the past. A veneer of calm was quickly established without either the ruling family or the protestors achieving a final victory. The saga of Bahrain is far from being resolved, with sporadic protests continuing to erupt daily. The Bahrain pro-democracy movement's denunciation of the Saudi intervention found echoes among the Saudi Shia population, only sixteen kilometres across King Fahd's causeway. In Oman, the Saudis kept their distance while offering financial support and solidarity to the Omani ruling dynasty. In Yemen, the uprising remains difficult to contain, with Saudi Arabia trying to push for a settlement but without great success. Heavily veiled young Yemeni women denounced Saudi interventions as meddling in their nation's affairs. Amidst clashes and bloodshed, the youth of the Arab world felt empowered and determined not to let a generation of older politicians or outside powers hijack their ongoing revolutions.

It is this sense of empowerment that led many Saudi women to mobilise, both in the virtual world and on the ground. By March 2011, the Saudi Shia were staging minor protests in Shia-dominated towns such as Qatif, Seyhat, and Awamiyya. Saudi Shia supported their co-religionists in Bahrain and denounced the violent suppression of the Bahraini pro-democracy movement.[4] Most importantly, they turned their attention to their own grievances against the Saudi regime. The minor demonstrations in March and April 2011 highlighted the plight of Shia political prisoners, some of whom had been in jail for several years. Saudi Shia women became active in night marches, referred to as Zaynabiyat processions, after Zaynab, the Prophet's granddaughter and the sister of Hasan and Hussein, in which heavily veiled women surrounded by their children marched in the streets at night carrying candles.[5] Activists publicised these regular night marches on YouTube, with local and international media channels allowed only limited access to the protestors. Heavy censorship and control over international media operating in Saudi Arabia ensured that such protests were not widely reported. At the time of writing in May 2012, eight Shia activists have been shot by security forces, and several bloggers, poets, and professionals put in prison. Shia women activists try to build bridges with other women in Jeddah and Riyadh, in order to overcome the sectarian dividing lines between the Shia minority and

---

[4] For more details on Shia mobilisation during the Arab Spring, see Madawi Al-Rasheed, 'Sectarianism as Counter-Revolution: Saudi Responses to the Arab Spring', *Studies in Ethnicity and Nationalism*, 11, 3 (2011), pp. 513–26.

[5] See al-Multaqa, http://www.moltaqaa.com/?p=7108.

the Sunni majority. One such woman is Fawziyya al-Hani whose Safwa-based Gherass Elkhair Centre, an independent civil society organisation, coordinates a network of like-minded women in order to press for citizenship, equality, and political participation among women. As it moves towards building national consensus with respect to gender reform and emancipation among a cross-section of educated and committed women from various regions and sects, she finds that her initiative is constantly circumvented by the state, which blocks social initiatives outside its control. The centre was, however, instrumental in mobilising Saudi women to press for participation in municipal elections, coordinating its activities with other professional women in Riyadh and Jeddah.

The problem of political prisoners proved to be a strong mobilising force, at least among relatives of prisoners. In Riyadh, women staged marches towards the Ministry of Interior asking for the release of their fathers, sons, and husbands who had been in jail for years without trial. Encouraged by the spectacle of protest across Arab capitals and the mobilisation of newly established independent but not officially recognised Saudi human rights organisations, women took the opportunity to draw attention to arbitrary detention, torture, and abuse of basic human rights. As the regime tightened its grip over activists, many men found themselves in prison, leaving women without guardians or breadwinners. It was not uncommon for several men from one family to be rounded up by the regime's security services for expressing political opinions or simply blogging. While official Saudi human rights organisations remained silent on the plight of political prisoners, the Committee for Civil and Political Rights, an unofficial activist organisation, took the lead in publicising individual cases and encouraged relatives of the prisoners to protest and sign petitions demanding the release of prisoners. Female relatives of prisoners lined the streets in front of the Ministry of Interior, carrying signs denouncing arbitrary detention. Several women protestors were held for questioning, after which they were released. Others remained in prison due to their continuous demonstrations, staged by HASM, an independent human rights organisation. Women protesters and their supporters posted video clips of these minor demonstrations on YouTube.

In response to the Arab Spring, the government announced that the delayed municipal elections, which had been due to take place in 2009, would instead be held in September 2011. To the disappointment of many women, the government insisted that once again women would be excluded from either voting or standing as candidates in this round of minor elections. Many women had hoped that fear of the domino effect of the Arab Spring would prompt the government to introduce more inclusive policies and allow them to participate fully in the elections. They resorted to electronic campaigns: several pages were set up on Facebook and YouTube calling on the government to allow women their right to participate in the elections. A small number of women gathered at the gates of municipal offices and engaged in heated arguments with civil servants who turned them back with apologetic statements. Women activists voiced their anger and reminded officials of King Abdullah's promises to empower women and increase their participation in Saudi society and economy.

Women's mobilisation for elections relied on individual initiatives carried out by a handful of outspoken women who staged minor, symbolic protests whose images found their way to the virtual world. Small groups of female activists met regularly in Jeddah, Dammam, and Riyadh to pressurise other women to join the protest over their exclusion from the September 20011 municipal elections. The small number of defiant women who took part in these protests was determined to register their anger and disappointment with a regime that is still far from responding to their demands. The municipal elections themselves were beginning to be increasingly seen as insignificant in the light of the revolutionary spirit that was sweeping the Arab world. The propaganda and enthusiasm that surrounded the 2005 municipal elections could not be reproduced in 2011. Many male bloggers and activists announced that they would not register to vote, and encouraged others to boycott these insignificant elections because they excluded half of the population. The government's announcement of the election date took place at a time when Arabs in other countries had gone a long way on the path of toppling their own authoritarian regimes. Many Saudi activists saw the limited municipal elections as window dressing that failed even to include women.

On 25 September 2011, the day of the second municipal elections, King Abdullah announced that women would be appointed to the Consultative Council, and would participate in the 2015 municipal elections. Notwithstanding the limitations of the appointed Consultative Council and the half-elected municipalities, many women across Saudi Arabia welcomed the decision as a first step towards increasing their future political participation. Other voices lamented the fact that this decision will only benefit a small minority of women, the majority of whom continue to lack civil and political rights. Those who doubted whether the appointment of women to the Consultative Council would improve women's participation cited judge Abd al-Majid al-Luhaidan's decision to subject Shaima Justaniya in Jeddah to ten lashes because she defied the ban on driving.[6] The king's decision to empower women by appointment and enfranchisement clashed with the reality on the ground. The judicial institutions, appointed by the king, were able to cast a shadow on the political leadership's vision of piecemeal reforms, while the institutions of the state remain patriarchal and dismissive of women's role in society. The contradiction between the king's alleged reforms and the conservatism of the judiciary can only enhance the progressive role of the former and the reactionary position of the latter, thus confirming the state as more enlightened than its many constituencies. The Saudi state is eager to highlight these images in the imagination of its subjects and the international community. The 'woman question', however, remains hostage to this duality and the grand political agenda of the state, itself increasingly fragmented by a plethora of princes and institutions that do not share a common vision and policy.

Unemployment among women teachers has become a hot issue since Abdullah became king in 2005. Teachers who had been working for years in adult education centres within programmes for the eradication of illiteracy among women demanded an end to their precarious employment contracts. Groups of women appeared at educational administrative centres in the main cities and provincial towns asking for official permanent contracts, as did new graduates seeking employment. Teachers raised signs on which they wrote slogans praising the king and asking officials to implement his policies regarding women's employment. They accused state employees of delaying the king's reforms. They paid homage to the king and put all the blame on minor officials in the civil service. What was initially planned as a mobilisation to demand the right to employment became an occasion to celebrate the king and his promises. Officials prevented women from entering government offices and calmed them down with more promises. Holding photos of the king while demonstrating has become a common strategy to avoid arrest and harassment. By pleading allegiance to the king, female protesters hope to avoid harassment by security services and the religious police who are depicted as not

---

[6] 'Ten Lashes for a Woman Driver in Jeddah and Arrest of Another in Riyadh', *al-Quds al-Arabi*, 28 September 2011, available at http://www.alquds.co.uk/index.asp?fname= today\27z492.htm&arc=data\2011\09\09-27\27z492.htm; 'Saudi Woman to be Lashed for Defying Ban on Driving', *The Guardian*, 28 September, available at http://www.guardian.co.uk/world/2011/sep/28/saudi-woman-lashed-defying-driving-ban.

complying with the monarch's policy on the ground. Authoritarian rule in Saudi Arabia has so far succeeded in creating a buffer zone between the constituency and the real power holders, often referred to as *al-batana* – a group of state employees, consultants, and advisers whose main job is to implement top-down initiatives. Failures and shortcomings are often attributed to the corruption of this group, thus shielding the more powerful actors from public anger and frustration.

These minor women's protests spread to universities, as school-leavers found that they were not offered places to study at local universities. Crowds of young girls attacked registration centres and destroyed locked doors. Security guards, often expatriate Asian workers, watched in amazement without being able to stop them. Others used protest to challenge their results in school and university tests. Echoing the slogans of the Arab Spring, they chanted *al-Sha'ab yurid isqat al-mudira* (the people demand the fall of the headmistress).

In March–April 2012, young women students' protests spread to the provincial and main universities, starting in Abha in Asir. Students staged spectacular protests against the administration and the university dean who was accused of not attending to his duties and neglecting the infrastructure. Young women raised slogans demanding his resignation and the dismissal of foreign lecturers who were accused of being unhelpful, unqualified, and dismissive of student initiatives. Foreign lecturers are said to have a vested interest in delaying Saudi students' emancipation and knowledge in order to perpetuate dependency on them, thus keeping their own jobs secure at a time when the Saudi graduate population has reached an unprecedented level. The huge protest movement on the women's campus immediately triggered a similar supporting event at the men's branch. Young men disrupted teaching and walked out in substantial crowds, thus expressing cross-gender solidarity. Within days, students in Riyadh and Qasim staged similar events, both in sympathy and to express distrust and dissatisfaction with the standard of education in their own institutions. The youth mobilisation proved to be so serious that the security services, accompanied by the religious police, moved into the campuses to disperse the protestors. Key female activists were arrested for interrogation. In the absence of civil society youth organisations and independent student unions, young men and women used the new media, especially social networking sites such as Facebook and Twitter, to gather support, publicise protest, and gain consensus over their demands, which cut across regions and gender.

While the Arab Spring seems for the moment to have bypassed Saudi Arabia,[7] it has no doubt left a strong impression, breaking decades of inertia among women who are no longer satisfied with electronic campaigns. In fact, some of them get together to march to places where they think solutions can be sought. In this atmosphere of frequent minor protest and peaceful assemblies, the old ban on women driving became the focus of yet another campaign. The first had taken place in 1990 when professional women staged a driving demonstration in Riyadh. It started again in April 2011 as a Facebook page, gathering both Saudi and non-Saudi supporters. Manal al-Sharif, a young mother and computer specialist working in the Saudi oil company in the Eastern Province, took the lead in the campaign and designated 17 June as the day when women in all Saudi cities should stage a driving demonstration. Together with Wajiha al-Howeider, a veteran feminist activist, Manal decided to test the ban and drive a car in Khobar before 17 June. She was accompanied by her brother and al-Howeider. After driving in Khobar for almost an hour, Manal returned safely to her house. She was later detained for questioning and remained in custody for more than a week. It transpired that her campaign had caused the authorities more offence than the act of driving. She was released after she pledged to stop the Internet campaign. She was banned from giving interviews to the media. On 17 June, the designated day for the driving demonstration, only thirty or forty women drove their cars in the streets of Riyadh and Jeddah. Security forces did not take the incidents seriously: many women escaped arrest, with only a handful ending up in police stations. The electronic campaign failed to encourage a large number of women to defy the ban and drive their cars. What was most interesting was the counter-campaign, also on Facebook, in which men threatened to harm women and beat up those seen behind the wheel on the designated day. Once again, the driving campaign split Saudi society, dominating discussion in the public sphere throughout May 2011 and masking more serious issues related to general political reform as well as specific demands to end arbitrary detention, corruption, and unemployment and to provide welfare benefits and housing. Those who opposed lifting the ban on driving assumed that they had won the battle against those who are determined to corrupt society, especially women. Officials reiterated that women are banned from driving according to

---

7  Madawi Al-Rasheed, 'So Saudi Spring: Anatomy of a Failed Revolution', *Boston Review*, March 2012, pp. 33–9.

Saudi law. An early generation of women activists who participated in the 1990 driving demonstration in Riyadh expressed their amazement that, twenty years later, driving remains a hot topic while the rest of the Arab world has moved swiftly into a higher level of political protest. At the time of writing, Saudi women remain banned from driving, but they are promised appointment to the Consultative Council and participation in future municipal elections.

Saudi women were inspired by the images of protest and mobilisation resulting from the Arab Spring. While the state needs the loyalty of women at this critical moment, women themselves hope to extract more rights under the patronage of the state and the pressures of the ongoing Arab Spring. However, gender issues will remain divisive in Saudi society, as they have always been. Women's real emancipation and equality may not be possible without serious movement towards participatory democracy in which both men and women gain the right to represent themselves and become active in formulating policy. In the short term, this limited democracy may in fact have negative consequences on women as more conservative forces assert their own visions. But in the long term, Saudi Arabia cannot continue to exclude women if the country needs their labour. In the past, oil wealth has contributed to excluding women, although it created some opportunities. The real change will come only when the economy cannot function without them. Today there are more than seven million foreign workers in Saudi Arabia. One day, the new generation of educated and skilled women will have to replace foreign labour. Only then are women likely to become a powerful pressure group that cannot simply remain a token of the authoritarian state's commitment to either religious nationalism or modernity. Their real empowerment will become a goal pursued for its own sake rather than for the sake of changing state political agendas.

AUTHORITARIAN STATES AND WOMEN: LOW COST, HIGH PROFIT

Weaving the story of Saudi women's exclusion together with religion and politics opens new avenues for contextualising and interpreting why authoritarian states such as Saudi Arabia champion women's causes. While in the past Saudi religious nationalism dictated the position of women and insisted on their seclusion, today the state promotes women's empowerment. The cost of this about-face remains low compared with the high cost of losing international legitimacy, internal political dissent, and, eventually, revolution. The Saudi regime adopts a policy of fragmenting its public along regional, tribal, sectarian, and gender lines. As long as women mobilise to pursue women's demands, they are not seen as a challenge to authoritarian rule. The real challenge will be when men and women mobilise together to demand rights such as political participation, equality, an end to corruption, and more representative government at a national level. This is when the 'woman question' will cease to be only a women's issue and gain consensus among the population as a struggle that cannot be separated from general political change.

Women's empowerment under King Abdullah coincided with the advent of many new challenges, both internal and external, to the Saudi state. Terrorism, strained relations with the United States – the guarantor of the security of the regime – rising unemployment, an agitated youth bulge, and more recently a changed Arab world where friendly dictators may appear a thing of the past are but a few of the real threats facing the ageing Saudi leadership. And, through both real and virtual mobilisation, women themselves are challenging the state to act on their many grievances. International human rights reports continue to embarrass Saudi Arabia in the global community, not to mention sensational stories about women flogged for driving or victims of rape stoned while their attackers go unpunished. The state can no longer hide behind the rhetoric of Islamic specificity, as many women themselves are aware that Islam alone does not explain their persistent marginalisation.

In this changed context, the king has shifted the legitimacy of the ruling family to a new level, seeking to feminise the masculine state. From the point of view of the state, women are needed as a group in order to fight political dissent (by men) and appease the West. The state is playing on women's aspirations and co-opting their mobilisation to achieve new local and external legitimacy. Faced with new mobilisation around several campaigns, from driving to employment rights, as discussed above, it has pre-empted the outcome by patronising women and channelling their activism towards state-controlled objectives. This culminated in promising women the right to vote in the future and to be appointed to state institutions, all announced during the Arab Spring.

Moreover, women's causes, which the regime would like to keep isolated from national demands for political reform, do not always directly challenge authoritarian rule. When the state decided that its religious nationalism had endangered state security and survival, it immediately championed women's causes as a means to defeat those Islamists who challenge it using both peaceful and violent means. It reached out to the new liberal and democratic political constituencies, consisting of both men and women, that have emerged in the country over the last decade. In this respect, the authoritarian state kills two birds with one woman. It contrasts itself with the radical backward and conservative elements in society while appealing to dissenting liberal voices. As such, the Saudi state has been compelled to champion women's causes to achieve its local and international objectives. Since 2005, King Abdullah has joined other rulers in the Arab and Muslim world to become a gender reformer, seeking new legitimacy through the 'woman question'. The king's old age and marginality within the royal circles of power also prompted him to seek new loyal subjects who had been marginalised in the past. Women have proved to be receptive.

If the authoritarian state benefits from championing women's causes, why do some women ally themselves with authoritarian patriarchal structures to achieve more rights and visibility while others invite the state to maintain the status quo? Saudi women have not been able to achieve consensus within their society with regard to their emancipation. In fact, some women resist the idea, and seek greater restrictions on what they consider to be threats to their interest as women. Given such a lack of unity, weak groups such as liberal women seek state intervention and protection to avoid reprisals from society. This is compounded by the fact that women are denied the right to organise themselves into an autonomous pressure group. In fact, Saudi Arabia remains one of the countries where civil society is curtailed by a legal system that leaves very little space for non-governmental organisations to operate outside state control. Even women's charities are heavily controlled by the state through extensive princely patronage networks. Saudi women of all persuasions look for the state to increase its policing of men, restrain their excesses, and force them to fulfil their obligations and responsibilities towards women. In such a political context, Saudi women are left with limited choices. An authoritarian state proved to be willing to endorse some of their demands, increase their visibility, and free them from the many restrictions to which they are subjected. The power of the state and its wealth have proved too good to resist.

This book has showed that *a most masculine state* is today, at critical moments of historical crisis, compelled to espouse its own feminisation. It is not possible to maintain a purely masculine state, continuing to ignore feminine voices. By championing women's causes, the authoritarian Saudi state may in the short term have succeeded in containing women's mobilisation. But in the long term, no doubt Saudi women, like other women in

*Conclusion*

the world, will try to move beyond state-sponsored feminism and their dream of becoming full citizens. The journey may be long an ous, but it has certainly started. The voices of the many Saudi discussed in this book represent light at the end of the tunnel. This book is an attempt to capture this.

# Glossary

| | |
|---|---|
| *abaya* | black veil |
| *abla* | teacher (Egyptian Arabic) |
| *abu al-harim* | ('father of women') a man who spends too much time with women |
| *adala* | justice |
| *adl* | justice |
| *ahira* | prostitute |
| *ahirat al-rum* | Western prostitutes |
| *alima* | female religious scholar |
| *alimat al-haramayn* | female religious scholars in Mecca and Medina |
| *amir* | prince, ruler |
| *amr bil maruf wa* | commanding right and forbidding |
| *Ansar* | the Prophet's helpers in Medina during his exile from Mecca |
| *aql* | reason |
| *ar* | dishonour |
| *araf ijtimaiyya* | social and cultural tradition and norms |
| *awra* | prohibited parts of the body |
| *ayb* | shame |
| *baya* | oath of allegiance |
| *al-bikr* | firstborn son |
| *boyat* | ('boys') girl dressed like a boy |
| *burqa* | veil covering the whole body |
| *daiya* (f. pl. *daiyat*) | preacher |

| | |
|---|---|
| *dallala* | pedlar |
| *dawa* | Islamic call |
| *dayrama* | traditional lipstick |
| *dharb yasir* | mild physical punishment |
| *dhulm* | injustice |
| *dima al-nisa* | women's blood |
| *diyana* | religiosity |
| *fahisha* | debauchery, sin |
| *faqiha* | woman knowledgeable in jurisprudence |
| *fatwa* | religious opinion, ruling |
| *fiqh* | Islamic jurisprudence |
| *fitna* | chaos, dissent; seduction |
| *hadari* | sedentary population |
| *hadathiyat* (adj. *hadathi*) | modern, corrupt women |
| *hadith* | traditions concerning the Prophet and his companions |
| *hajr* | ostracisation |
| *halal* | religiously permitted |
| *haram* | religiously prohibited |
| *al-harim* | a community of women |
| *haya* | committee |
| *haya'* | modesty |
| *haydh wa nafas* | menstruation and birth |
| *haywan* | animal |
| *hina* | traditional dye for hair and body |
| *hisba* | commanding right and forbidding wrong |
| *hudud* | Islamic punishment |
| *hujjar* | settlements |
| *hukm* | religious ruling in response to a question |
| *husayniyya* | Shia mourning ritual place |
| *ibadat* | worship, rituals |
| *iftar* | Ramadan meal |
| *ikhtilat* | mixing between the sexes in permitted circumstances |
| *ikhwan man ta' allah* | 'the brothers of those who obey God' |
| *imama* | leadership in prayer |
| *imara* | political leadership |
| *immo* girls | girls who adopt black Gothic garb |
| *infitah* | openness |

| | |
|---|---|
| *israf* | excessive spending, consumption |
| *istilab* | alienation |
| *jahiliyya* (adj. *jahili*) | pre-Islamic age of ignorance |
| *jihad* | holy war |
| *juhd* | exertion, effort |
| *jund al-tawhid* | soldiers of monotheism |
| *kafa'a bi al-nikah* | compatibility between spouses |
| *kafir* (f. pl. *kafirat*) | infidel |
| *khadiri* | non-tribal |
| *khal* | divorce initiated by the wife |
| *khataba* | matchmaker |
| *khatib* | preacher |
| *khikri* | effeminate man |
| *khilwa* | illicit mixing between men and women |
| *khurafat* | mythologies |
| *khususiyya* | exceptionalism |
| *kohl* | traditional eye make-up |
| *kuttab* | traditional religious study circle, school |
| *mahr* | bridewealth, dowry paid to women |
| *mahram* | male guardian |
| *majlis* | council |
| *maqsud* | deliberate |
| *marjiyya* | authority, reference point |
| *maslaha* | interest, public good |
| *mauakhira* | at the end, back seat |
| *mihan wathia* | degrading professions |
| *misfar* | marriage conducted for the purposes of travel |
| *misyar* | 'visiting' marriage, where the wife remains in her parental home |
| *muadhdhin* | person who gives the call to prayer |
| *muakhira* | seating in the back row |
| *mu'alaqa* | awaiting a divorce |
| *mudabira* | supervisor, manager |
| *muhaditha* | *hadith* reciter |
| *muharaba* | harassed |
| *muhtasibat* | women commanding right and forbidding wrong, vigilantes |
| *multazimat* | religiously committed women |
| *munaqaba* | a woman who wears a face veil |

| | |
|---|---|
| *munkar* | sinful act |
| *munkashif* | exposed |
| *murtad* | apostate |
| *musrifa* (pl. *musrifat*) | a woman who spends too much, excessive consumer |
| *mustarjilat* | masculine women |
| *mut'a* | Shia temporary marriage |
| *mutaharishat* | women who sexually harass other women |
| *mutawwa* | religious scholar, vigilante |
| *muthaqafa* (f. pl. *muthaqafat*) | intellectual, educated person |
| *nafas* | childbirth |
| *nahar* | day; daytime marriage |
| *al-nahy an al-munkar* | wrong |
| *nakhwa* | war cry |
| *nasab* | genealogy |
| *nashit* | activist |
| *nashitat islamiyat* | female Islamist activists |
| *nasiha* | advice |
| *al-nathra al-shariyya* | Islamic 'legitimate gaze'; a fleeting glimpse of one's fiancée |
| *nikah* | marriage |
| *niqab* | face veil |
| *nisa al-gharb* | Western women |
| *qabili* | tribal |
| *qada* | judiciary |
| *qawaid al-nisa* | old women |
| *qawama* | dominance of men over women, superiority |
| *al-raiya* | subjects, community |
| *rujula* | masculinity, manly qualities |
| *rukn* | pillar of Islam |
| *sababa* | coffee maker, server |
| *sad al-tharai* | pre-emptive prohibition to avoid sinful acts |
| *sadaq* | dowry |
| *sadaqa* | alms, charity |
| *sadara* | priority seating; the front row |
| *sahabiyat* | early women companions of the prophet |

| | |
|---|---|
| *sharia* | Islamic law |
| *shirk* | blasphemy, idolatry |
| *shrouq* | pejorative Hijazi term for Najdis |
| *sidr* | traditional soap |
| *sitr* | modesty |
| *sunna* | tradition of the Prophet |
| *ta'a* | obedience |
| *tabi'a* | nature |
| *tadarruj* | gradual evolution |
| *tafra* | boom, oil affluence |
| *tahira* | pure |
| *tajdid* | renewal |
| *takfir* | declaring someone an apostate |
| *takruni* | pejorative Saudi term referring to a black person |
| *talaslus* | spying on people |
| *tamayyuz* | distinction |
| *taqlid* | imitation |
| *tarawih* | evening prayer after breaking fast during Ramadan |
| *tarsh al-bahr* | ('rejects of the sea') a pejorative term to refer to Hijazis |
| *tawaf* | circumambulation of the Ka'ba during the *hajj* |
| *tawhid* | the oneness of God |
| *taziyya* | mourning ritual |
| *that* | self |
| *thawabit shariyya* | established principles of *sharia* |
| *thawb* | long white shirt |
| *thur* | bull |
| *ulama* | religious scholars |
| *umahat al-muminin* | the mothers of the pious ancestors |
| *umma* | Muslim community |
| *urf* | traditional, unregistered marriage |
| *usra* | family |
| *wadh* | advice, preaching |
| *waitha* | preacher |
| *wali al-amr* | male guardian, also term used to refer to Saudi rulers |
| *wara* | piety |

| | |
|---|---|
| *wasta* | nepotism |
| *wazir* | minister |
| *zakat* | alms-tax |
| *zaniya* | adulteress |
| *zawaj misfar* | 'travel marriage': temporary marriage while abroad |

# Bibliography

Short Arabic and English media articles are fully referenced in the notes.

## Books and Articles

Abd al-Al, Ghada, *Ayza atgawaz* [I want to be married], Cairo: al-Shorouq, 2008.

Abd-al-Malik, Warda, *al-Awba* [The return], Beirut: Saqi, 2006.

Abdullah, Anwar, *Khasais wa sifat al-mujtama al-wahhabi al-Saudi* [Characteristics of Saudi Wahhabi society], Paris: al-Sharq, 2005.

Abou El-Fadl, Khaled, *Speaking in God's Name: Islamic Law, Authority, and Women*, Oxford: Oneworld, 2001.

Abu-Lughod, Lila, 'Do Muslim Women Really Need Saving? Anthropological Reflections on Cultural Relativism and its Others', *American Anthropologist*, 104 (2002), pp. 783–90.

Abu-Lughod, Lila, 'The Romance of Resistance: Tracing Transformations of Power Through Bedouin Women', *American Ethnologist*, 17, 1 (1999), pp. 41–55.

Abu-Lughod, Lila, *Veiled Sentiments: Honour and Poetry in a Bedouin Society*, Berkeley: University of California Press, 1988.

Adams, Melinda, '"National Machineries" and Authoritarian Politics', *International Feminist Journal of Politics*, 9, 2 (2007), pp. 176–97.

Adorno, Theodor, *Minima Moralia: Reflections on a Damaged Life*, London: Verso, 2005.

Almunajjed, Mona, *Women in Saudi Arabia Today*, New York: Palgrave, 1997.

Alsharekh, Alanoud (ed.), *The Gulf Family: Kinship, Politics, and Modernity*, London: Saqi, 2007.

Altorki, Soraya, 'The Concept and Practice of Citizenship in Saudi Arabia', in Suad Joseph (ed.), *Gender and Citizenship in the Middle East*, Syracuse: Syracuse University Press, 2000, pp. 215–36.

Altorki, Soraya, *Women in Saudi Arabia: Ideology and Behavior among the Elite*, New York: Columbia University Press, 1986.

Altorki, Soraya, and Abu Bakr Bagader, *Jeddah: umm al-rakha wa al-shidda* [Jeddah: A city of affluence and hardship], Cairo: Dar al-Shorouq, 2006.

Altorki, Soraya, and Donald Cole, *Arabian Oasis City: The Transformation of Unayzah*, Austin: University of Texas Press, 1989.

Anderson, Benedict, *Imagined Communities: Reflections on the Origins and Spread of Nationalism*, London: Verso, 1991.

Arebi, Sadeka, *Women and Words in Saudi Arabia: The Politics of Literary Discourse*, New York: Columbia University Press, 1994.

Awad, Muhammad, 'Kayfa anti' [How you are], *Huqul*, 2007.

al-Azeri, Khalid, 'Change and Conflict in Contemporary Omani Society: The Case of Kafa'a in Marriage', *British Journal of Middle Eastern Studies*, 37, 2 (2010), pp. 121–37.

al-Azeri, Khalid, *Social and Gender Inequality in Oman*, London: Routledge, forthcoming.

al-Badah, Abd al-Aziz, *Harakat al-taghrib fi al-saudiyya: taghrib al-mara'a inmuthajan* [Westernisation in Saudi Arabia: A case study of women], Riyadh: Silsilat Markaz al-Dirasat al-Insaniyya, 2010.

Badran, Margot, *Feminists, Islam and the Nation: Gender and the Making of Modern Egypt*, Princeton: Princeton University Press, 1995.

Bagader, Abu Bakr, Ava Heinrichsdorff, and Deborah Akers (eds.), *Voices of Change: Short Stories by Saudi Women Writers*, Boulder: Lynne Rienner Publishers, 1998.

Baki, Roula, 'Gender-Segregated Education in Saudi Arabia: Its Impact on Social Norms and the Saudi Labour Market', *Education Policy Analysis Archives*, 12, 28 (2004) (electronic journal).

Baron, Beth, 'Women, Honour and the State: Evidence from Egypt', *Middle Eastern Studies*, 42, 1 (2006), pp. 1–20.

Basrawi, Fadia, *Brownies and Kalashinkovs: A Saudi Woman's Memoir of American Arabia and Wartime Beirut*, Reading: South Street Press, 2009.

al-Bassam, Ibtisam, 'Institutions of Higher Education for Women in Saudi Arabia', *International Journal of Educational Development*, 4, 3 (1984), pp. 255–8.

Baudrillard, Jean, *The Consumer Society: Myths and Structures*, London: Sage, 1998.

al-Baz, Rania, *al-Mushawaha* [Disfigured], Beirut: Dar Owaydat, 2006.

Bell, Gertrude, 'A Journey in North Arabia', *Geographical Journal*, 44 (1914), pp. 76–7.

al-Bishr, Badriyya, *Hind wa al-askar* [Hind and the soldiers], 3rd edn, Beirut: Saqi, 2011 [2006].

al-Bishr, Badriyya, *Maarik Tash ma Tash* [Battles over *Tash ma Tash*], Beirut: al-Markaz al-Thaqafi al-Arabi, 2007.

al-Bishr, Badriyya, *al-Urjuha* [The swing], Beirut: Saqi, 2010.

al-Bishr, Badriyya, *Waq' al-awlama fi mujtama al-khalij al-arabi Dubai wa al-Riyadh* [The impact of globalisation in Gulf societies: Dubai and Riyadh], Beirut: Markaz al-Dirasat al-Wihda al-Arabiyya, 2008.

Blunt, Lady Ann, *A Pilgrimage to Nejd, the Cradle of the Arab Race: A Visit to the Court of the Arab Emir and 'Our Persian Campaign'*, 2 vols., London: John Murray, 1881; repr. 1968.

Booth, Marilyn, '"The Muslim Woman" as Celebrity Author and the Politics of Translating Arabic: Girls of Riyadh Goes on the Road', *Journal of Middle East Women's Studies*, 6, 3 (2010), pp. 149–82.

Booth, Marilyn, 'Translator v. Author (2007): Girls of Riyadh go to New York', *Translation Studies*, 1, 2 (2008), pp. 197–211.

Bourdieu, Pierre, *Masculine Domination*, trans. Richard Nice, Cambridge: Polity Press, 2001.

Bristol-Rhys, Jane, *Emirati Women: Generations of Change*, London: Hurst & Co., 2010.

bu Humaid, Sarah, 'La tamnau al-ilm an fatayatikum' [Do not deprive your girls of education], *Huqul*, 2007.

Charrad, Mounira, *States and Women's Rights: The Making of Postcolonial Tunisia, Algeria and Morocco*, Berkeley: University of California Press, 2001.

Chatterjee, Partha, *Nationalist Thought and the Colonial World: A Derivative Discourse*, Minneapolis: University of Minnesota Press, 1986.

Chatterjee, Partha, *The Nation and its Fragments: Colonial and Postcolonial Histories*, Princeton: Princeton University Press, 1993.

Cook, Michael, *Commanding Right and Forbidding Wrong in Islamic Thought*, Cambridge: Cambridge University Press, 2000.

Delong-Bas, Natana, *Wahhabi Islam: From Revival and Reform to Global Jihad*, London: I. B. Tauris, 2004.

al-Dhamin, Samaher, *Nisa bila umahat* [Women without mothers], Beirut: al-Intishar al-Arabi, 2010.

Dickson, H. R. P., *The Arab of the Desert: A Glimpse into Bedouin Life in Kuwait and Saudi Arabia*, London: George Allen & Unwin, 1951.

Dickson, H. R. P., *Kuwait and her Neighbours*, London: George Allen & Unwin, 1986.

Doumato, Eleanor Abdella, 'Education in Saudi Arabia: Gender, Jobs and the Price of Religion', in Eleanor Abdella Doumato and Marsha Pripstein Posusney (eds.), *Women and Globalisation in the Arab Middle East: Gender, Economy and Society*, Boulder: Lynne Rienner Publishers, 2003, pp. 239–57.

Doumato, Eleanor Abdella, 'Gender, Monarchy and National Identity in Saudi Arabia', *British Journal of Middle Eastern Studies*, 19, 1 (1992), pp. 31–47.

Doumato, Eleanor Abdella, *Getting God's Ear: Women, Islam and Healing in Saudi Arabia and the Gulf*, New York: Columbia University Press, 2000.

Doumato, Eleanor Abdella, 'Saudi Arabia', in Sameera Nazir and Leigh Tomppert (eds.), *Women's Rights in the Middle East and North Africa: Citizenship and Justice*, Freedom House, New York: Rowman & Littlefield, 2005, pp. 257–74.

Doumato, Eleanor Abdella, 'Saudi Arabian Expansion in the United States: Half-Hearted Missionary Work Meets Rock Solid Resistance', in Madawi Al-Rasheed (ed.), *Kingdom Without Borders: Saudi Arabia's Political, Religious, and Media Frontiers*, London: Hurst & Co., 2008, pp. 301–21.

Doumato, Eleanor Abdella, 'Women in Saudi Arabia: Between Breadwinner and Domestic Icon?', in Suad Joseph and Susan Slyomovics (eds.), *Women and Power in the Middle East*, Philadelphia: University of Pennsylvania Press, 2001, pp. 166–75.

El-Or, Tamar, *Educated but Ignorant: Ultraorthodox Jewish Women and their World*, Boulder: Lynne Rienner Publishers, 1994.

Facey, William, *Saudi Arabia by the First Photographers*, London: Stacey International, 1996.

Filiu, Jean-Pierre, *The Arab Revolution: Ten Lessons from the Democratic Uprising*, London: Hurst & Co., 2011.

Flynn, Patrice, 'The Saudi Labour Force: A Comprehensive Statistical Portrait', *Middle East Institute*, 65, 4 (2011), pp. 575–86.

Foley, Sean, *The Gulf Arab States Beyond Oil and Islam*, Boulder: Lynne Rienner Publishers, 2010.

Freedom House, *Saudi Arabia's Curriculum of Intolerance*, Washington, DC: Freedom House, 2006.

Friedland, Roger, 'Religious Nationalism and the Problem of Collective Representation', *Annual Review of Sociology*, 27 (2001), pp. 125–52.

Gellner, Ernest, *Nations and Nationalism*, London and New York: Cornell University Press, 1983.

al-Ghathami, Abdullah, *Hikayat al-hadatha fi al-mamlaka al-arabiyya al-saudiyya* [The story of modernity in Saudi Arabia], Casablanca: al-Markaz al-Thaqafi al-Arabi, 2004.

al-Ghathami, Abdullah, *al-Mara wa al-lugha* [Women and language], 4th edn, Beirut: al-Markaz al-Thaqafi al-Arabi, 2008.

Glasze, George, 'Gated Housing Estates in the Arab World: Case Studies in Lebanon and Riyadh, Saudi Arabia', *Environment and Planning: Planning and Design*, 29 (2002), pp. 321–36.

Haeri, Shahla, *Law of Desire: Temporary Marriage in Iran*, London: I. B. Tauris, 1989.

Hafez, Sherine, *An Islam of Her Own: Reconsidering Religion and Secularism in Women's Islamic Movements*, New York: New York University Press, 2011.

Hamdan, Amani, 'Women and Education in Saudi Arabia: Challenges and Achievements', *International Education Journal*, 6, 1 (2005), pp. 42–64.

Hamza, Fuad, *al-Bilad al-arabiyya al-saudiyya* [Saudi Arabia], Riyadh: Maktabat al-Nasr al-Haditha, 1936.

al-Hanafi, Abdullah, *Ifadat al-anaf fi akhbar bilad al-haram (1290–1365 AH)* [News of the Holy Land], vol. 4, 2005.

al-Harbi, Dalal, *Nisa shahirat min najd* [Famous Najdi women], Riyadh: Darat al-Malik Abd al-Aziz, 1999.

al-Hashemi, Sharifa Nur, 'Imraa saudiyya min jil umahat al-awail' [A Saudi woman from the mothers' generation], *Huqul*, 2007.

Hasso, Frances, *Consuming Desires: Family Crisis and the State in the Middle East*, Stanford: Stanford University Press, 2011.

Hatem, Mervat, 'The Pitfalls of the Nationalist Discourse on Citizenship in Egypt', in Suad Joseph and Susan Slyomovics (eds.), *Women and Power in the Middle East*, Philadelphia: University of Pennsylvania Press, 2001, pp. 185–211.

Hausmann, Ricardo, Laura Tyson, and Saadia Zahidi, *The Global Gender Gap Report*, Geneva: World Economic Forum, 2010.

Hegghammer, Thomas, *Jihad in Saudi Arabia: Violence and Pan-Islamism since 1979*, Cambridge: Cambridge University Press, 2010.

Hegghammer, Thomas, and Stephane Lacroix, 'Rejectionist Islamism in Saudi Arabia: The Story of Juhayman al-Utaibi Revisited', *International Journal of Middle East Studies*, 39, 1 (2007), pp. 103–22.

al-Hirz, Saba, *al-Akharun* [The others], Beirut: Saqi, 2006; trans. as *The Others*, New York: Seven Stories Press, 2009.

al-Hithlul, Ala, *al-Intihar al-majur* [Hired suicide], Beirut: Saqi, 2004.

Hobsbawm, Eric, and Terence Ranger (eds.), *The Invention of Tradition*, Cambridge: Cambridge University Press, 1992.

Human Rights Watch, *Perpetual Minors: Human Rights Abuses Stemming from Male Guardianship and Sex Segregation in Saudi Arabia*, New York: Human Rights Watch, 2008.

Human Rights Watch, *Saudi Arabia: Country Summary*, New York: Human Rights Watch, 2011.

Human Rights Watch, *Saudi Arabia: Looser Reign, Uncertain Gain*, New York: Human Rights Watch, 2010.

Ibn Bishr, Othman, *Unwan al-majd fi tarikh najd* [Glory in the history of Najd], 2 vols., Mecca: n.p., 1930.

Ibn Ghannam, Hussein, *Tarikh Najd* [History of Najd], Cairo: Dar al-Shurouq, 1994.

Ismael, Shereen, 'Gender and State in Iraq', in Suad Joseph (ed.), *Gender and Citizenship in the Middle East*, Syracuse: Syracuse University Press, 2000, pp. 33–57.

al-Jahni, Layla, *Jahiliyya* [Ignorance], Beirut: Dar al-Adab, 2007.

Jamjum, Munira, 'Female Islamic Studies Teachers in Saudi Arabia: A Phenomenological Study', *Teaching and Teacher Education*, 26 (2010), pp. 547–58.

Joseph, Suad (ed.), *Gender and Citizenship in the Middle East*, Syracuse: Syracuse University Press, 2000.

Joseph, Suad, and Susan Slyomovics (eds.), *Women and Power in the Middle East*, Philadelphia: University of Pennsylvania Press, 2001.

Juergensmeyer, Mark, *Global Rebellion: Religious Challenges to the Secular State from Christian Militants to Al Qaeda*, Berkeley: University of California Press, 2008.

al-Juhaiman, Abd al-Karim, 'Nisfuna al-akhar' [Our other half], *Huqul*, 2007.

al-Juhany, Awaidah, *Najd before the Salafi Reform Movement: Social, Political, and Religious Conditions During the Three Centuries Preceding the Rise of the Saudi State*, Reading: Ithaca Press, 2002.

al-Jurayssi, Khalid, *Fatawi ulama al-bilad al-haram* [*Fatwa*s of the *ulama* of the land of the Two Holy Mosques], Riyadh: Maktabat al-Malik Fahd al-Wataniyya, 2007.

Kabbani, Rana, *Imperial Fictions: Europe's Myth of Orient*, London: Pandora, 1986.

Kandiyoti, Deniz, 'Bargaining with Patriarchy', *Gender and Society*, 2, 3 (1988), pp. 274–90.

Kandiyoti, Deniz, 'The Politics of Gender and the Conundrums of Citizenship', in Suad Joseph and Susan Slyomovics (eds.), *Women and Power in the Middle East*, Philadelphia: University of Pennsylvania Press, 2001, pp. 52–8.

Kandiyoti, Deniz (ed.), *Women, Islam and the State*, London: Macmillan, 1991.

Kechichian, Joseph, *Faisal: Saudi Arabia's King for All Seasons*, Gainesville: University of Florida Press, 2008.

al-Khamis, Umayma, *al-Bahriyat* [Women from foreign shores], 1st edn, Damascus: al-Mada, 2006.

al-Khamis, Umayma, *Madhi, mufrad, muthakar* [Past, singular, masculine], Beirut: Dar al-Intishar, 2011.

al-Khamis, Umayma, *al-Warifa* [Lush tree], Damascus: al-Mada, 2008.

Khannous, Touria, 'Virtual Gender: Moroccan and Saudi Women's Cyberspace', *HAWWA*, 8 (2011), pp. 358–87.

Khashoggi, Samira, 'al-Mara wa al-talim' [Women and education], *Huqul*, 2007.

al-Khatib, Salwa, 'The Oil Boom and its Impact on Women and Families in Saudi Arabia', in Alanoud al-Sharekh (ed.), *The Gulf Family: Kinship Policies and Modernity*, London: Saqi, 2007, pp. 83–108.

Kholoussy, Hanan, 'The Fiction and Non-Fiction of Egypt's Modern Marriage Crisis', *Middle East Report*, 2010.

Kholoussy, Hanan, *For Better, For Worse: The Marriage Crisis that Made Modern Egypt*, Stanford: Stanford University Press, 2010.

al-Khuthaila, Hind, 'The Meaning of Saudi Elections', *American Behavioral Scientist*, 49, 4 (2005), pp. 605–9.

Kostiner, Joseph, *The Making of Saudi Arabia 1916–1936*, Oxford: Oxford University Press, 1993.

Kraidy, Marwan, *Reality Television and Arab Politics: Contention in Public Life*, Cambridge: Cambridge University Press, 2010.

Lacroix, Stephane, *Awakening Islam: Religious Dissent in Contemporary Saudi Arabia*, Cambridge, MA: Harvard University Press, 2011.

Lancaster, William, *The Rwala Bedouin Today*, Cambridge: Cambridge University Press, 1981.

Lawrence, Bruce, *Shattering the Myth: Islam Beyond Violence*, Princeton: Princeton University Press, 1998.

Le Renard, Amelie, 'Droits de la femme et développement personnel: les appropriations du religieux par les femmes en Arabie Saoudite', *Critique Internationale*, 46 (2010), pp. 67–86.

Le Renard, Amelie, 'Engendering Saudi Consumerism: A Study of Young Women's Practices in Riyadh's Shopping Malls', paper presented at a conference on Saudi Arabia, Princeton, November 2009.

Le Renard, Amelie, *Femmes et espaces publics en Arabie Saoudite*, Paris: Dalloz, 2011.

Le Renard, Amelie, '"Only for Women": Women, State, and Reform in Saudi Arabia', *Middle East Journal*, 62, 4 (2008), pp. 610–29.

Limbert, Mandana, *In the Time of Oil: Piety, Memory and Social life in an Omani Town*, Stanford: Stanford University Press, 2010.

Mahdavi, Pardis, *Passionate Uprisings: Iran's Sexual Revolution*, Stanford: Stanford University Press, 2009.

al-Mana, Suad, 'The Arabian Peninsula and the Gulf', in Radwa Ashour, Ferial Ghazoul, and Hasna Reda-Mekdashi (eds.), *Arab Women Writers 1873–1999*, Cairo: American University Press, 2008, pp. 254–75.

Massad, Joseph, *Colonial Effects: The Making of National Identity in Jordan*, New York: Columbia University Press, 2001.

Massad, Joseph, *Desiring Arabs*, Chicago: University of Chicago Press, 2007.

Meeker, Michael, *Literature and Violence in North Arabia*, Cambridge: Cambridge University Press, 1979.

Minkus-McKenna, Dorothy, 'Women Entrepreneurs in Riyadh, Saudi Arabia', UMUC Working Papers Series, no. 2009. University of Maryland University College.

al-Moqrin, Samar, *Nisa al-munkar* [Women of vice], Beirut: Saqi, 2008.

Mouline, Nabil, *Les Clercs de l'islam: autorité religieuse et pouvoir politique en Arabie Saoudite, XVIII–XXI siècles*, Paris: Presses Universitaires de France, Proche Orient, 2011.

al-Mughni, Haya, *Women in Kuwait: The Politics of Gender*, London: Saqi, 2001.

al-Mughni, Haya, and Mary Ann Tetreault, 'Citizenship, Gender and the Politics of Quasi States', in Suad Joseph (ed.), *Gender and Citizenship in the Middle East*, Syracuse: Syracuse University Press, 2000, pp. 237–60.

Musil, Alois, *Manners and Customs of the Rwala Bedouins*, New York: American Geographical Society, 1927.

al-Nabulsi, Shakir, *al-Libiraliyya al-saudiyya bayn al-wahm wa al-haqiqa* [Saudi liberalism between myth and reality], Beirut: al-Mouassasa al-Arabiyya li al-Dirasat wa al-Nashr, 2010.

Nafi, Basheer, *The Rise and Decline of the Arab Reform Movement*, London: Institute for Contemporary Arab Thought, 2000.

al-Najjar, Baqir, *al-Mara fi al-khalij al-arabi wa al-tahawulatal-hadatha al-asira* [Women in the Gulf and difficult challenges of modernity], Casablanca: al-Markaz al-Thaqafi al-Arabi, 2000.

Ortner, Sherry, 'Resistance and the Problem of Ethnographic Refusal', *Comparative Studies in Society and History*, 37, 1 (1995), pp. 173–93.

al-Othaymin, Abdullah, *Tarikh al-mamalaka al-arabiyya al-saudiyya* [History of Saudi Arabia], vol. II, Riyadh: Maktabat al-Malik Fahd al-Wataniyya, 1995.

al-Othman, Layla, *al-Muhakama* [The trial], Beirut: Dar al-Adab, 2009.

Prokop, Michaela, 'Saudi Arabia: The Politics of Education', *International Affairs*, 79, 1 (2003), p. 77–89.

Prokop, Michaela, 'The War of Ideas: Education in Saudi Arabia', in Paul Aarts and Gerd Nonneman (eds.), *Saudi Arabia in the Balance: Political Economy, Society, and Foreign Affairs*, London: Hurst & Co., 2005, pp. 57–81.

al-Qasimi, Abdullah, 'al-Insan hiya am sil'a' [Is she a human being or a commodity?], *Huqul*, 2007, pp. 70–5.

al-Qasimi, Abdullah, *al-Kawn yuhakim al-illah* [The universe judges God], Tunis: n.p., 1981.

Ranchod-Nilsson, Sita, and Mary Ann Tetreault (eds.), *Women, State and Nationalism*, London: Routledge, 2000.

Al-Rasheed, Madawi, 'Arabie saoudite: demain, la tempete?', *Politique Internationale*, 132 (2011), pp. 199–222.

Al-Rasheed, Madawi, 'The Capture of Riyadh Revisited: Shaping Historical Imagination in Saudi Arabia', in Madawi Al-Rasheed and Robert Vitalis (eds.),

*Counter Narratives: History, Contemporary Society and Politics in Saudi Arabia and Yemen*, New York: Palgrave, 2004, pp. 183–200.

Al-Rasheed, Madawi, 'Caught between Religion and State: Women in Saudi Arabia', in Bernard Heykal, Thomas Hegghammer, and Stephane Lacroix (eds.), *Complexity and Change in Saudi Arabia: Insights on Social, Political, Economic and Religious Transformation*, Cambridge: Cambridge University Press, forthcoming.

Al-Rasheed, Madawi, 'Circles of Power: Royals and Society in Saudi Arabia', in Paul Aarts and Gerd Nonneman (eds.), *Saudi Arabia in the Balance: Political Economy, Society, Foreign Affairs*, London: Hurst & Co., 2005.

Al-Rasheed, Madawi, *Contesting the Saudi State: Islamic Voices from a New Generation*, Cambridge: Cambridge University Press, 2007.

Al-Rasheed, Madawi, 'Economies of Desire, Fictive Sexual uprisings', *Le Monde Diplomatique*, May 2011.

Al-Rasheed, Madawi, *A History of Saudi Arabia*, Cambridge: Cambridge University Press, 2001; 2nd edn, 2010.

Al-Rasheed, Madawi, 'Political Legitimacy and the Production of History: The Case of Saudi Arabia', in Lenore Martin (ed.), *New Frontiers in Middle East Security*, New York: St Martin's Press, 1999, pp. 25–46.

Al-Rasheed, Madawi, *Politics in an Arabian Oasis: The Rashidis of Saudi Arabia*, London: I. B. Tauris, 1991.

Al-Rasheed, Madawi, 'Sectarianism as Counter-Revolution: Saudi Responses to the Arab Spring', *Studies in Ethnicity and Nationalism*, 11, 3 (2011), pp. 513–26.

Al-Rasheed, Madawi, 'So Saudi Spring: Anatomy of a Failed Revolution', *Boston Review*, March 2012, pp. 33–9.

Al-Rasheed, Madawi, 'Yes it Could Happen Here', *Foreign Policy*, February 2011.

Redissi, Hamadi, 'The Refutation of Wahhabism in Arabic Sources, 1945–1932', in Madawi Al-Rasheed (ed.), *Kingdom without Borders: Saudi Arabia's Political, Religious and Media Frontiers*, London: Hurst & Co. 2008, pp. 157–81.

Ross, Michael, 'Oil, Islam and Women', *American Political Science Review*, 102, 1 (2008), pp. 107–23.

Rugh, William, 'Education in Saudi Arabia: Choices and Constraints', *Middle East Policy*, 9, 2 (2002), pp. 40–55.

Ryan, Sally, 'The Woman Question', transcribed for Marxist.org, 2000 at http://www.marxists.org/archive/eleanor-marx/works/womanq.htm.

al-Saif, Muhammad, *Abdullah al-Tariqi*, Beirut: Riad al-Rayyes Books, 2007.

Sakr, Naomi, 'Women and Media in Saudi Arabia: Rhetoric, Reductionism and Realities', *British Journal of Middle Eastern Studies*, 35, 1 (2008), pp. 385–404.

al-Sani, Raja, *Banat al-Riyadh* [The girls of Riyadh], London: Saqi, 2005.

Schlaffer, Edith, Ulrich Kropiunigg, and Fawziah al-Bakr, *Bridging the Gap – But How? Young Voices from Saudi Arabia*, Vienna: Women Without Borders, 2010.

Sfakianakis, John, *Employment Quandary: Saudi Arabia Economics*, Riyadh: Banque Saudi Fransi, 16 February 2011 (electronic publication).

Sfakianakis, John, *Under Construction: Saudi Steps up Efforts to Meet Home Loan Demand*, Economics Report, Riyadh: Banque Saudi Faransi, 20 March 2011 (electronic publication).

Shafi'i, Lamiya, *Makanat al-mara al-ilmiyya fi al-saha al-makiyya* [Women's status in the intellectual arena of Mecca], Mecca: Umm al-Qura University, n.d.

Shryock, Andrew, *Nationalism and the Genealogical Imagination: Oral History and Textual Authority in Tribal Jordan*, Berkeley: University of California Press, 1997.

Sibai, Ahmad, 'Hajatna ila talim al-banatshai yuquruhu al-mantiq' [We need to educate girls), *Huqul*, 2007.

Smith, Anthony, D., *Nationalism and Modernism: A Critical Survey of Recent Theories of Nations and Nationalism*, London: Routledge, 1998.

al-Tamimi, Dalal, 'Saudi Women in Academic Medicine: Are They Succeeding?', Department of Pathology, College of Medicine, King Faisal University, 2004 (electronic publication).

Teitelbaum, Joshua, *The Rise and Fall of the Hashemite Kingdom of Arabia*, London: Hurst & Co., 2001.

Teitelbaum, Joshua, 'Sharyf Husayn ibn Ali and the Hashemite Vision of the Post-Ottoman Order: From Chieftaincy to Suzerainty', *Middle Eastern Studies*, 34, 1 (1998), pp. 103–22.

Tillion, Germaine, *The Republic of Cousins: Women's Oppression in Mediterranean Society*, London: Saqi, 1983.

al-Utaibi, Tariq, *Shabab al-Riyadh* [Boys of Riyadh], Beirut: Dar al-Shafaq, n.d.

Vitalis, Robert, *America's Kingdom: Mythmaking on the Saudi Oil Frontier*, Stanford: Stanford University Press, 2007.

Walby, Sylvia, *Theorizing Patriarchy*, Oxford: Blackwell, 1990.

*Women in Saudi Arabia: Cross-Cultural Views*, Riyadh: Ghainaa Publications, n.d.

Wasella, Jurgen, *Min usuli ila mulhid qisat inshiqaq Abdullah al-Qasimi 1907–1996* [From fundamentalism to atheism: The story of Abdullah al-Qasimi (1907–1986)], trans. Muhammad Kibaybo, Beirut: Dar al-Kunuz al-Adabiyya, 2001.

Wasella, Jurgen, *al-Qasimi: bayn al-usuliyya wa al-inshiqaq* [al-Qasimi: Between fundamentalism and atheism], trans. Muhammad Kibaybo, Beirut: Dar al-Kunuz al-Adabiyya, 2005.

al-Washmi, Abdullah, *Fitnat al-qawl bi talim al-banat fi al-mamlaka al-arabiyya al-saudiyya* [Discord over girls' education in Saudi Arabia], Casablanca: al-Markaz al-Thaqafi al-Arabi, 2009.

al-Wasil, Ahmad, 'Satair wa aqlam sarikha: takwin al-muthaqafa al-saudiyya wa tahawulataha' [Curtains and sharp pens: Saudi women intellectuals and their changes], *Idhafat*, 7 (2009), pp. 82–105.

Wynn, Lisa, 'The Romance of Tahliya Street: Youth Culture, Commodities and the Use of Public Space in Jiddah', *Middle East Report*, 204 (1997), pp. 30–1.

Yamani, Maha, *Polygamy and Law in Contemporary Saudi Arabia*, Reading: Ithaca Press, 2008.

Yamani, Mai, *Changed Identities: The Challenge of New Identities in Saudi Arabia*, London: Royal Institute of International Affairs, 2000.

Yamani, Mai, *Cradle of Islam: The Hijaz and the Quest for an Arabian Identity*, London: I. B. Tauris, 2004.
Yamani, Mai, 'Saudi Youth: The Illusion of Transnational Freedom', *Contemporary Arab Affairs*, 3, 1 (2010), pp. 7–20.
Zaman, Muhammad Qasim, *The Ulama in Contemporary Islam: Custodians of Change*, Princeton: Princeton University Press, 2007.
Zubaida, Sami, *Beyond Islam: A New Understanding of the Middle East*, London: I. B. Tauris, 2011.

## Newspapers and Magazines

*Arab News*
*The Economist*
*Le Figaro*
*The Guardian*
*Gulf News*
*al-Hayat*
*The Independent*
*Japan Times*
*al-Jazeera*
*Khabar*
*Laha*
*Los Angeles Times*
*al-Madina*
*al-Majalla*
*al-Masri al-Yawm*
*al-Masry*
*Nahar*
*New York Times*
*The Observer*
*Okaz*
*The Peninsula*
*al-Quds al-Arabi*
*al-Rai*
*al-Riyadh*
*Sabaq*
*Saudi Gazette*
*al-Sharq al-Awsat*
*The Telegraph*
*Time*
*al-Watan*
*Wiam*
*al-Yawm*

## Online sources

AKBK
Akhawat Tariq al-Islam
al-Arabiyya

Bawabat Asia
BBC
Bin Baz
CNN
Dalil
Fox News
Gulf 1 Bank
Harf News
al-Ifta
Ihtisab
Islam Today
Islamway
Al-Jazeera
Jeddah Chamber of Commerce and Industry
Jihadica
Laha on Line
Madawi Al-Rasheed
Minbar al-Hiwar wa al-Ibda
Middle East on Line
Middle East Transparent
Ministry of Education, Saudi Arabia
Ministry of Labour, Saudi Arabia
al-Multaqa
Multaqa al-Daiyat
al-Nahda
Olayan
PBS
Raja al-Sani
Reuters
Riyadh Chamber of Commerce and Industry
Saaid al-Fawaid
Samar al-Moqrin
Saudi Women Voices
*Wakad*

# Index

## List of Books in the Series

CPSIA information can be obtained at www.ICGtesting.com
Printed in the USA
LVOW06s0349070214

372614LV00003B/3/P